Physics Begins with Another M . . .
Mysteries, Magic, Myth, and Modern Physics

Physics Begins with Another

M...

Mysteries, Magic, Myth, and Modern Physics

John W. Jewett, Jr.

California State Polytechnic University, Pomona

Allyn and Bacon

Boston · London · Toronto · Sydney · Tokyo · Singapore

Series Editor: Nancy Forsyth
Editorial Assistant: Kate Wagstaffe
Manufacturing Buyer: Megan Cochran
Cover Designer: Suzanne Harbison

Copyright © 1996 by Allyn and Bacon
A Division of Simon and Schuster, Inc.
160 Gould Street
Needham Heights, Massachusetts 02194

QC 30 .J49 1996
34640857

Printed in the United States of America

10 9 8 7 6 5 4 3 2   00 99 98 97

To Lisa Jewett, my wife and best friend, who lovingly kept her mouth closed while her mind was screaming, "whaddya mean 'another book'?"

Contents

Preface

This book is a follow-up to *Physics Begins with an M...Mysteries, Magic, and Myth,* which contained over 400 items related to the teaching and learning of classical physics. This previous book will be referred to often in what follows, and will be noted as *PBWM* for brevity. The first 16 chapters of this second book offer additional items related to classical physics. The remaining seven chapters introduce the "M's" treatment to the concepts of *modern physics*—relativity and quantum physics. Together, the two books offer over 800 items for classroom use in teaching classical and modern physics.

The chapters on modern physics have an inevitably different flavor than those in classical physics. The material is necessarily more sophisticated and requires more familiarity with physics concepts. Some of the "M's" in these chapters are related to everyday life and/or experiences of the layperson (e.g.,"Why does your electric stove burner glow red?", Mystery #1, Chapter 17). Others require previous knowledge that is obtained through coursework or experience in the physical sciences (e.g., "Why do emission spectra have more lines than absorption spectra?", Mystery #7, Chapter 19).

Most of the material that follows in the Preface appeared in *PBWM* and is paraphrased here for those not familiar with the first book or the "M's" strategy.

This is a book for *teachers* and *students*—teachers in formalized classrooms at the pre-college and university levels and students in formalized classrooms as well as those who are forever students and are always striving for more understanding of the world around us. The information in this book is intended to allow for exploration into the applications of physics in everyday life and to provoke the reader to examine his or her own understanding of physical concepts and his or her strategies for transferring knowledge to others.

The chapter organization is similar to the standard order in many introductory physics textbooks. This is not intended to represent advocacy for this particular schedule of teaching or learning but is followed more for the ease of the reader in finding information about a particular topic. The material is presented in three formats within each chapter: *Mysteries*, *Magic* and *Myth*. These "M's" are described below, followed by suggested uses for various readers.

Mysteries

These are questions about everyday life and simple physical concepts that can be understood by means of applications of the principles of physics. Some refer to common observations (e.g., "Why does hot water clean clothes better than cold water?", Mystery #5, Chapter 8) while others represent questions that may not have crossed the reader's mind (e.g., "If you have ever been snorkeling, you may recall that snorkels are only a fraction of a meter in length. Why isn't it possible to buy a longer snorkel, so that you can dive deeper?", Mystery #15, Chapter 8). Each of the Mysteries can be "solved" with an appropriate understanding and application of physical principles.

Magic

The Magic "tricks" in this book are demonstrations and activities that can be performed in and out of the classroom. In general, they belong to the classification of *discrepant events*, in that the outcome is different from that which one might expect. Most of the demonstrations can be performed with simple apparatus available from the hardware store or supermarket. A small number require simple laboratory equipment such as a laser or an oscillator, but none requires sophisticated equipment. Some require a trek to an appropriate location, such as near a particular type of apartment building, and others require waiting for appropriate phenomena, such as a bright sunny day, to occur.

Myth

The Myths in this book are presented as statements of fact, but the reader needs to be aware that *the statements are generally untrue*. The Myths are common misunderstandings, misconceptions and mistakes from our everyday culture. Some are well-established, but errant, beliefs such as the "incompressibility" of water (Myth #1, Chapter 8) or the visibility of steam (Myth #6, Chapter 9). Others are misuses of physics in the print, broadcast and movie media, such as the ability of a perfectly invisible human to see (Myth #4, Chapter 14). Others fall into a variety of other categories.

Each of the modern physics chapters (Chapters 17 – 23) also contains a brief outline of the concepts that will assist in focusing the reader's thoughts on some of the principles to be used in addressing the Mysteries, Magic and Myth in the chapter. (The concepts for Chapters 1 – 16 have already been provided in *PBWM*.) This is not a traditional physics textbook, so these sections are by no means complete expositions of the topic of the chapter. The author refers the reader to physics textbooks for more complete descriptions of the physical principles. At the end of each chapter is a discussion section, in which comments on each "M" are available. Note that this is not called an "Answer" section. The important goal in this book, as should be the case in all science endeavors, is the motivation to perform effective *thinking*, not to obtain the right "answer". The discussion section contains scientific explanations of phenomena that are well understood, but there are also examples of cases where science has not been able to establish the definitive "answer". Please refrain from the temptation to jump immediately to the back of the chapter after reading an "M". Important learning (and enjoyment) will take place by pondering these items for a while and developing and testing various hypotheses.

The discussion sections also contain many references to other printed material related to the phenomenon being discussed. Most of the references are to physics teaching journals (e.g., *The Physics Teacher, American Journal of Physics, Physics Education*) or to popular science journals (e.g., *Scientific American*). Some more advanced articles are referenced for the more mathematically adventuresome. Many books are also referenced, both textbooks and popular treatments of scientific ideas.

Suggested Uses

For teachers in formalized classrooms

The Mysteries can be used in a variety of ways. They can simply be presented to the class for classwide discussion. They can be presented as assignments to small groups of students for cooperative work in formulating a hypothesis. They can be given as homework assignments for creative and critical thinking. They can be assigned as research projects for library work. They can be presented on overhead transparencies for student thought while roll is taken at the beginning of class.

The Magic demonstrations can be performed before the appropriate material is covered, as a "teaser" or a motivator, or can be performed along with the material as visual applications of the concepts. Those that can be done, or need to be done, outside of the classroom can be given as special assignments or can even form the basis of a field trip.

Each of the Myths can be "debunked" by an appropriate application of the physical principles. These can be used in the classroom in a variety of ways. They can be grouped with other, true statements for students to determine which is the incorrect statement. Small groups can work on creating clear descriptions of why the Myth is untrue. The debunking of new Myths can be given as a homework assignment to help students develop critical thinking skills and communication skills.

Although the material is aimed at a high school or introductory university level, many of the activities and concepts are adaptable to the middle school and elementary level. The mathematics used in the book is primarily aimed at the algebra level, although there are a small number of uses of simple calculus in some of the modern physics chapters.

For students in formalized classrooms

Physics is an endeavor that requires clear and logical thinking. It is also an endeavor in which many misconceptions abound and there are many dead ends in logical thinking awaiting the unwary student. The items in this book allow an opportunity for the student to apply the knowledge from the classroom to real-world situations. Many of the items will be familiar from everyday life, helping you to keep in mind that physics is a relevant science. Thinking about these "M's" will test your understanding of the concepts and your sense of logical process. The Myths will help you to avoid some of the common misconceptions that occur in the physics classroom. The references in the bibliography will allow you to extend your knowledge beyond the necessarily compact discussions of the "M's" that appear in this book.

For those students who use this book in association with a science methods class, in preparation for becoming teachers, there is a wealth of teaching ideas contained in these pages. Challenge your future students with these, and help them to become the critical thinkers that we will need to solve global problems.

For the informed layperson

Physics is a fascinating science and is all around you all the time. This book contains a treasure of examples of how physics interacts with you in your everyday life. It will help you to appreciate the physics that surrounds you. There are some references here to social issues, such as nuclear energy, and these will help make you a better informed citizen. But the primary goal is ___*fun*___. Thinking is fun and these pages will give you plenty of opportunity to challenge your thinking skills. Share these "M's" with your spouse and children and help them to develop enhanced critical thinking. But, most importantly, for <u>all readers</u>—enjoy!

JWJ

Acknowledgements

A project such as this is not possible without the assistance of a great many people. First of all, let me make it perfectly clear that I am not claiming to have generated all of the ideas in this book on my own. This publication is the result of my own ideas combined with those of my previous teachers, previous and present colleagues, the writings of other scientists and the input of many members of the non-scientific public.

I would like to express specific thanks to some individuals who have been especially helpful in bringing this volume into existence. Special thanks go to John Mallinckrodt of California State Polytechnic University, Pomona and Roger Nanes of California State University, Fullerton for their efforts in reading the entire draft of this work and providing important suggestions for improvement. In addition, grateful acknowledgement is given to the following physics faculty at California State Polytechnic University, Pomona, who read portions of the draft and provided valuable feedback: Antonio Aurilia, Soumya Chakravarti, John Fang, Kai-Shue Lam, Harvey Leff and George Rainey. The high school physics teachers of SCAMPI (Southern California Area Modern Physics Institute) receive warm appreciation for their encouragement to prepare the "M's" in book form after being bombarded with them during several summer institutes. Special thanks go to California State Polytechnic University, Pomona, for awarding me summer research support to assist in the development of the original draft of this project.

I have benefited greatly from the external reviewers of the draft manuscript who provided me with numerous suggestions for improvement. Special thanks go to the following reviewers who provided in-depth analysis of the book: David Lamp, Texas Tech University (Lubbock, Texas) and Jerry D. Wilson, Lander College (Greenwood, South Carolina).

Deep gratitude is extended to Judy Fiske of the staff at Allyn & Bacon, for her help in the book production phase of the project, and to Nancy Forsyth for her many contributions to making this book as valuable as possible.

Finally, I am deeply indebted to my wife, Lisa Jewett, who endured many lonely evenings while I pounded on the keyboard, as well as many distracted conversations during which I responded to her discussions with my voice but was frantically searching in my mind for a clearer way to explain an "M".

Chapter 1
Vectors, Measurement and Other Mathematical Preliminaries

Mysteries:

1.) What is mass? What is time? What is space? What is electric charge?

2.) Here are some data on fundamental constants from a table published in a recent physics textbook:

Constant	Value		Uncertainty (parts per million)
G	6.67260	$\times 10^{-11}$ N·m²·kg⁻²	100
c	2.99792458	$\times 10^{8}$ m·s⁻¹	Exact
e	1.60217733	$\times 10^{-19}$ C	0.3

Now, wait a minute. Every measurement involves some uncertainty. How can it be claimed that c, the speed of light, is measured *exactly*?

Mysteries:

3.) In the Bible (Genesis 6:15), the length of Noah's Ark was commanded to be 300 *cubits*. What *is* a cubit?

4.) The height of a horse is measured in *hands*. But everyone's hand is different. Is there a "standard hand"?

5.) Which of these is a measurement unit related to the system of units known as SI (Le Système International d'Unités)?
> a.) carrot
> b.) carat
> c.) karat
> d.) caret

𝔐𝔶𝔰𝔱𝔢𝔯𝔦𝔢𝔰:

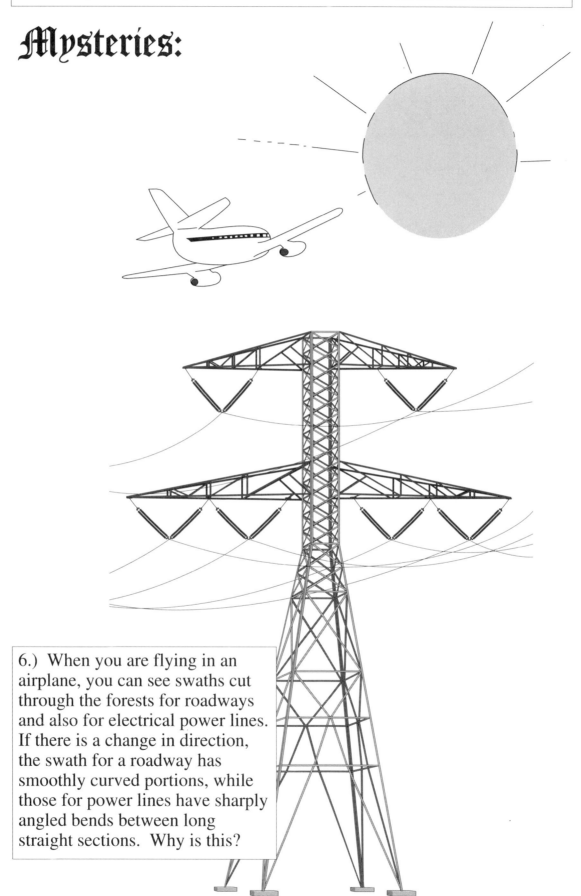

6.) When you are flying in an airplane, you can see swaths cut through the forests for roadways and also for electrical power lines. If there is a change in direction, the swath for a roadway has smoothly curved portions, while those for power lines have sharply angled bends between long straight sections. Why is this?

𝕸𝖆𝖌𝖎𝖈:

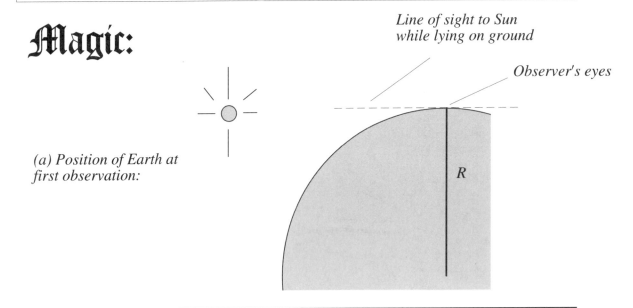

(a) Position of Earth at first observation:

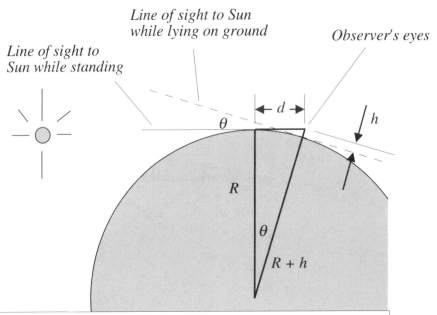

(b) Position of Earth at second observation, after having rotated clockwise from position in (a):

The Double Sunset

In a location where you have an unobstructed view of the sunset on the horizon, watch the Sun go down while you are lying on the ground. Just as the top of the Sun disappears below the horizon, start a stop watch. This situation is shown in diagram (*a*) above. Then stand up and watch the sunset again. When the top of the Sun disappears while you are standing, stop the stop watch, so that you have recorded a time interval Δt. The Earth has now rotated into the position shown in diagram (*b*) above. Now, measure the vertical distance (*h*) between the location of your eyes while standing and the location of your eyes when you were lying down. From these two measurements and the geometry indicated in the diagram above, the radius of the Earth can be determined.

𝕸𝖆𝖌𝖎𝖈:

(a)

Strong and Weak Thread

Hang a 1 kg mass from a *vertical* sewing thread, as in diagram (*a*); the mass is supported by the thread. Now, tightly tie the thread *horizontally* between two rigid supports and hang the same mass at the middle of the thread as shown in diagram (*b*). What happens?

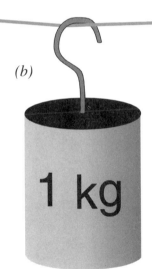

(b)

𝕸𝖞𝖙𝖍:

$$\frac{N \cdot m^{-2} \cdot Pa \cdot \Omega \cdot s \cdot \left\{\dfrac{m}{s^3}\right\}^4}{\sqrt{\dfrac{(C)(weber) \cdot kg \cdot A^2}{\dfrac{J \cdot s}{kg \cdot m^2 \cdot s^5}}} \cdot \left\{\dfrac{m}{s^2}\right\} \cdot (volt)} \cdot K \cdot (watt) \cdot \left(\frac{kg \cdot m}{s^2}\right)$$

1.) Dimensional analysis can verify that you've performed a problem correctly.

𝔐𝔶𝔱𝔥:

2.) There is mass at the center of mass of an object.

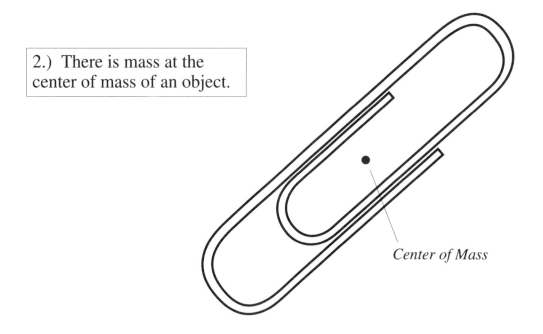

Center of Mass

3.) Noon is when the Sun is highest in the sky.

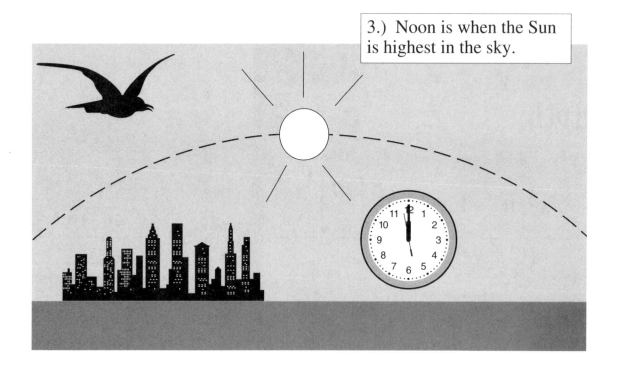

𝔐𝔶𝔱𝔥:

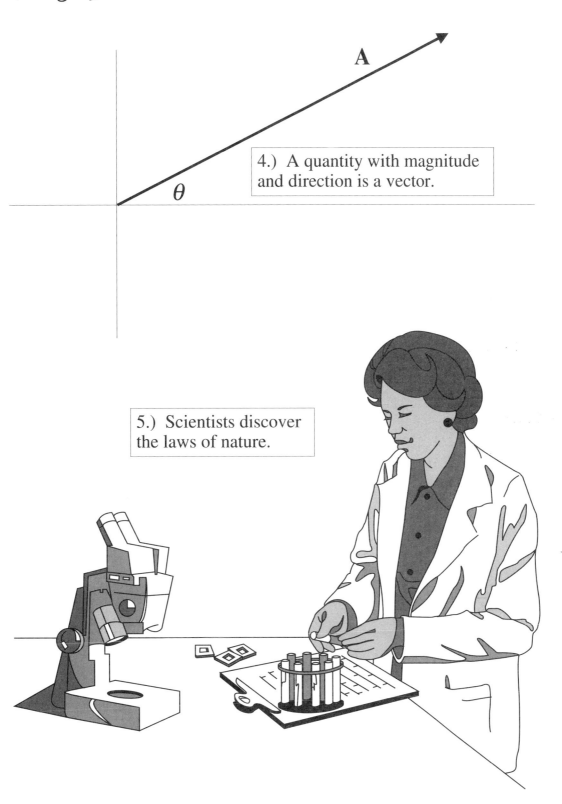

4.) A quantity with magnitude and direction is a vector.

5.) Scientists discover the laws of nature.

Discussions; Chapter 1—Vectors, Measurement and Other Mathematical Preliminaries

𝔐𝔶𝔰𝔱𝔢𝔯𝔦𝔢𝔰:

1.) What is mass? What is time? What is space? What is electric charge?

The answer to all four of these questions is: "We don't know". These are fundamental concepts that cannot be understood in terms of more basic ideas. We feel quite familiar and comfortable with these concepts, since we use them often in talking about physical processes and we understand how the behavior of the world is based upon these concepts. For example, we have many times experienced the difficulty associated with changing the motion of a *mass*, and we live in a frenzied world of not having enough *time* every day. We don't think twice about moving through *space*, and have experienced the effects of *electric charge* on our bodies that we accumulate by rubbing our feet over a carpet on a dry day. But these are demonstrations of the <u>behavior</u> associated with these concepts, not their fundamental <u>nature</u>.

In our quest to understand the universe, we start with basic ideas such as those listed in this Mystery, accept those as "givens", without questioning their nature, and build our model of the universe from there. That does not mean that there are not attempts to explore the nature of these concepts. The work of Einstein (see Chapter 22—Relativity) led to new understanding about space and time and their unification into the concept of *spacetime*. These investigations are conceptually difficult, however, and are not necessary for us to understand the world that we experience in everyday life.

2.) Here are some data on fundamental constants from a table published in a recent physics textbook:

Constant	Value		Uncertainty (parts per million)
G	6.67260	x 10^{-11} N·m^2·kg^{-2}	100
c	2.99792458	x 10^8 m·s^{-1}	Exact
e	1.60217733	x 10^{-19} C	0.3

Now, wait a minute. Every measurement involves some uncertainty. How can it be claimed that c, the speed of light, is measured *exactly*?

The exact value for the speed of light was adopted in 1983 and is related to the story of the definition of the meter as a length standard. Before 1960, the meter was defined as one ten millionth of the distance from the North Pole to the equator along a meridian through Paris. From 1960 to 1983, the meter was defined according to an atomic standard—1,650,763.73 wavelengths of a particular spectral line emitted from the atom ^{86}Kr (see Chapter 21, Concepts section, for information on this notation). In 1983, a new definition of the meter was internationally accepted: the distance traveled by light in a vacuum in 1/299,792,458 of a second (which is defined as the time period during which occur 9,192,631,770 oscillations of the radiation corresponding to a transition between two hyperfine levels of the ^{133}Cs atom). In essence, then, this *establishes* the speed of light as an exact value, as given in the table above, and the meter is defined in terms of this value. Of course, with better measurements in the future, the value of the speed of light may change slightly, resulting in a small change in the meter.

3.) In the Bible (Genesis 6:15), the length of Noah's Ark was commanded to be 300 *cubits*. What *is* a cubit?

The cubit is a length unit used by several early cultures and is based on the distance from the tip of the middle finger to the elbow. Since people come in various sizes, each individual's personal cubit is different from that of others. The "standard" Hebrew cubit is equivalent to 17.58 inches. Since the Bible indicates that the length of the Ark was commanded to be 300 cubits, this corresponds to a length of about 440 feet or 134 meters.

4.) The height of a horse is measured in *hands*. But everyone's hand is different. Is there a "standard hand"?

The hand is a unit used to measure the height of a horse, from the ground to the *withers* (the highest point over the shoulders when the head is down to graze). There *is* a standard hand and it is equal to a length of *four inches*, which is close to 10 cm in the metric system. This unit is based on a typical width of a male hand. As we discussed in Mystery #3, the cubit is also a unit based on an anatomical measurement. We can even identify a conversion factor for these two units: 1 cubit = 17.58 inches = 4.395 hands.

Horses can be categorized according to their height, measured in hands. A *pony* has a height of 10 to 14.5 hands (approximately 100-145 cm) and weighs 300 to 850 lb (equivalent to a mass of 135-380 kg). A *light horse* has a height of 14.5 to 17 hands (145-170 cm) and weighs 800 to 1,300 lb (equivalent to a mass of 360-590 kg). A *draft horse* has a height of 15.5 to 19 hands (160-190 cm) and weighs 1,500 to 2,600 lb (equivalent to a mass of 700-1200 kg). Notice that the categorizations in terms of height are not well-defined; there is an overlap in height between light horses and draft horses. The decision between these two types must be made on the basis of the weight of the horse; there is no overlap in this parameter.

Within these categorizations by size, there are a number of breeds of horses. The division is not clear-cut, however. There are some breeds, such as the *Hackneys*, that have members in two of the above categorizations.

5.) Which of these is a measurement unit related to the system of units known as SI (Le Système International d'Unités)?
        a.) carrot   **b.) carat**   **c.) karat**   **d.) caret**

While all four of these words sound the same, they represent completely different concepts. The answer to the question is b.) *carat*, which is a measure of mass equal to 200 milligrams, used to measure gems. A *carrot* (a.) is shown in the diagram accompanying the Mystery, and is recognized as an orange-colored vegetable. A *karat* (c.) is used to describe the purity of gold alloys and represents a fraction of one twenty-fourth. Thus, twenty-four karat (24K) gold is pure gold. On the other hand, 14K gold is $^{14}/_{24}$ gold and $^{10}/_{24}$ other metal. Finally, a *caret* (d.) is a small mark ($\wedge$) used in proofreading to indicate the location in written text at which something is to be inserted.

6.) When you are flying in an airplane, you can see swaths cut through the forests for roadways and also for electrical power lines. If there is a change in direction, the swath for a roadway has smoothly curved portions, while those for power lines have sharply angled bends between long straight sections. Why is this?

Power lines are under tension, since they are hanging under the effect of gravity. For towers at which there is no change in direction, the horizontal components of the forces on the towers, due to this tension, are perpendicular to the towers. This is shown in diagram (*a*) below, in which we imagine looking down on the towers from above.

If there is a change in direction of the power lines, then there exists a force pulling sideways on the tower, as indicated in diagram (*b*) below.

This results in a net horizontal force, which is the sum of all of the horizontal components, to the right, of the forces in diagram (*b*). This requires a *stronger tower* to counter the resulting torque around the base of the tower, which results in a higher cost for this tower. Now, if a change in direction for power lines were taken in steps over several towers, there would be a number of towers with lateral forces. This would require *several* stronger towers and even more construction costs. If the change in direction occurs at a single tower, then only one stronger tower must be built.

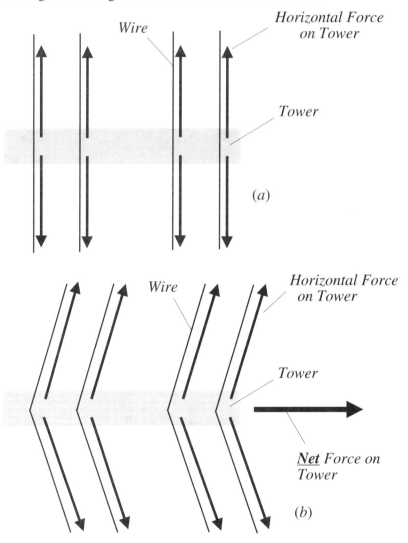

Even though this one tower would be required to withstand all of the lateral force, building one *very* strong tower is a much less expensive proposition than constructing several *somewhat* stronger towers. Thus, for financial reasons, we see the change in direction of power lines occur at a single tower rather than over a series of towers.

Roadways, on the other hand, are not under tension and we do not need to address the considerations discussed above. Thus, roadways can exhibit gentle curves which are safer for the automobiles.

Magic:

The Double Sunset

The diagrams accompanying the description indicate the appropriate geometry for the calculation of the radius of the Earth. The dashed line in diagram (*a*) represents the line of sight to the Sun while the observer is lying down. Between the times of the first observation and the second, the Earth rotates through a small angle *θ*. In diagram (*b*), the rotated Earth is shown at the time the second observation is made. The amount of rotation during this short interval is exaggerated for clarity. In (*b*), the tilted dashed line is the original line of sight to the Sun made when the observer was lying down. The horizontal line of sight in (*b*) is that of the observer when standing up, so that the eyes are a distance *h* above the original position. The bold lines in the diagram indicate a right triangle formed by the radius *R* of the Earth, another radius plus the height *h*, and a distance *d* along the standing line of sight. We now use this geometry to calculate the radius of the Earth.

Let us first apply the Pythagorean Theorem to the dark triangle in diagram (*b*):

$$d^2 + R^2 = (R+h)^2 = R^2 + 2Rh + h^2 \qquad \rightarrow \qquad d^2 = 2Rh + h^2$$

Now, since the height *h* is so small compared to *R*, we can ignore the h^2 term on the right hand side and we have the approximate relationship,

$$d^2 = 2Rh$$

The dark right triangle also allows us to relate *d* and *R* through the angle *θ*, as follows,

$$d = R \tan \theta$$

We can eliminate *d* between these two equations:

$$R^2 \tan^2 \theta = 2Rh \qquad \rightarrow \qquad R = \frac{2h}{\tan^2 \theta}$$

Now, the angle *θ* through which the Earth rotates in the time interval between the observations can be determined by relating the rotation to a full rotation of the Earth of 360°, which takes place in one *sidereal* day of 23 h, 56 min, 4 s = 86,164 s. A sidereal day is the time required for the Earth to rotate once (through 2π radians) relative to the <u>stars</u>. During the period from noon to the next noon (a *solar* day of 24 hours), the rotation is through slightly more than 2π, since the Earth has moved to a new position in its orbit around the Sun. Thus, the angle θ can be related to the time interval Δt by,

$$\frac{\theta}{2\pi} = \frac{\Delta t}{86,164\,\mathrm{s}} \quad \rightarrow \quad \theta = \frac{2\pi}{86,164\,\mathrm{s}}\Delta t = \left(7.3\times10^{-5}\,\mathrm{s}^{-1}\right)\Delta t$$

so, finally, we obtain an expression for the radius of the Earth in terms of our two measurements, h and Δt:

$$R = \frac{2h}{\tan^2\left[\left(7.3\times10^{-5}\,\mathrm{s}^{-1}\right)\Delta t\right]}$$

For a typical value of h of 1.6 to 1.8 m, the typical time interval Δt between observations will be about 10 seconds.

For a different expression for the radius using a similar technique, see Z. H. Levine, "How to Measure the Radius of the Earth on Your Beach Vacation", *The Physics Teacher*, **31**, 440, 1993. For other similar types of measurements, see R. O'Keefe and B. Ghavimi-Alagha, "The World Trade Center and the Distance to the World's Center", *American Journal of Physics*, **60**, 183, 1992; D. H. Bruning, "Determining the Earth-Moon Distance", *American Journal of Physics*, **59**, 850, 1991; and F. O. Goodman, "Measuring the Earth's Radius While Boating on One of its Lakes", *American Journal of Physics*, **61**, 378, 1993.

Strong and Weak Thread

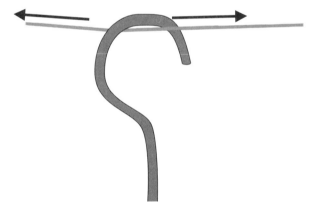

In the case with the weight hanging from the vertical thread, there will be no problem. The tension in the thread will balance the gravitational force on the hanging weight, and the thread is strong enough (for typical household thread) to withstand this tension.

For the weight hanging from the horizontal thread, the thread is likely to break. If this did not happen, increase the weight or tighten the thread. When the weight is hung on the horizontal thread, the thread will bend by a small amount, as shown in the diagram. The force holding the weight up is the sum of the two *upward* components of tension in the pieces of string on either side of the weight. Since the thread only deviates from the horizontal by a small amount, the tension in the string must increase by a <u>very large</u> amount, in order to provide enough upward force to balance the weight. This can exceed the breaking strength of the thread, causing it to fail.

A simple calculation will give us a feel for the magnitude of the force required in the horizontal thread. Suppose that the thread makes an angle of 2° with the horizontal on either side of the hook. Then, the upward component of the tension in the thread is:

$$T_{upward} = T\sin 2° = 0.0349T$$

The weight W hanging from the thread must be balanced by two of the forces given above, one for the string on each side of the hook:

$$F_{net} = 0 \quad \rightarrow \quad 2T_{upward} - W = 0$$

Thus, we can solve for the required tension, remembering that we have hung a mass of 1 kg on the thread.

$$2T_{upward} = W \quad \rightarrow \quad 2(0.0349T) = mg \quad \rightarrow \quad T = \frac{(1\,\text{kg})(9.8\,\text{m}\cdot\text{s}^{-2})}{2(0.0349)} = 140\,\text{N}$$

This value is to be compared to the 9.8 N of force required in the vertical string to support the weight. In the limit as the angle goes to zero, that is, the string becomes *perfectly* horizontal, the required force becomes *infinite*.

𝕸𝔶𝔱𝔥:

1.) Dimensional analysis can verify that you've performed a problem correctly.

Dimensional analysis can often be a useful method of checking a calculation, but it can only indicate that you have performed the problem *incorrectly*; it cannot guarantee that your work was correct. As an extreme example, suppose we attempt to calculate a speed by dividing the diagonal measure of a television screen by the time on the video-cassette recorder sitting next to it. We will obtain the correct dimensions of speed—$\text{m}\cdot\text{s}^{-1}$—but the calculation has no meaning at all. Dimensional analysis is not able to verify that we have performed this calculation correctly. But if we calculate a speed and arrive at units of, for example, $\text{m}\cdot\text{kg}^{-1}$, dimensional analysis will most definitely indicate that we have performed this calculation incorrectly!

2.) There is mass at the center of mass of an object.

The center of mass is a spatial average of the mass contained in an object. There is no requirement that there be mass at the center of mass. Consider a doughnut; the center of mass is at the center, which is in the hole! Other examples of objects with no mass located at the center of mass include coat hangers, top hats, horseshoes, drinking glasses, etc. See Mystery #6 in Chapter 7 for a calculation of the center of mass of the Solar System.

3.) Noon is when the Sun is highest in the sky.

In Mystery #6 of Chapter 1 in *PBWM* (for those who don't read prefaces, this is a reference to *Physics Begins with an M...Mysteries, Magic, and Myth* that will be employed in this book for brevity; those who don't read prefaces *or* first chapters are on their own!), we explored the inaccuracy of the belief that the Sun is directly overhead at noon. Here we investigate another inaccuracy about noon. The inaccuracy of the statement in the Myth can be understood if we realize that, when the clock strikes 12:00 in a certain time zone, there will be only *one longitudinal position* along which the Sun will have just reached its highest point. At points to the west of this position in the same time zone, it is also 12 noon, but the Sun has not yet reached the highest point for observers located at these points. Similarly, at points to the east of this position in the same time zone, the Sun will have already passed its highest point in the sky.

For an activity which leads to an angular position of the Sun at noon in your location, see H. Kruglak, "An Exercise on the Altitude of the Noon Sun", *The Physics Teacher*, **30**, 236, 1992.

4.) A quantity with magnitude and direction is a vector.

This statement leads to no problems in most of classical physics, but it is not a sufficient definition of a vector, if we wish to be strict in our thinking. The definition of a vector actually involves sets of numbers representing coefficients of members of a suitable basis (of unit vectors, of functions, etc.), but this definition is likely to be dangerous to present in an introductory physics course. Let us just show how the statement made in this Myth fails in two cases.

The first failure is in trying to represent <u>angular rotations</u> as vectors. Although we can identify a magnitude (say, 90°) and a direction (of a rotation axis) for these rotations, they do not obey the commutative rule for addition, as explored in the Magic demonstration, Adding Up Rotations, in Chapter 10 of *PBWM*. This same idea is explored again in the Magic demonstration, Arm Rotations, in Chapter 7 of this book. These demonstrations show that angular rotations do not obey the rules of vector algebra and fail as vectors.

Another property of vectors is that the "length" of the vector (sum of the squares of the components) must be invariant under a transformation of the coordinate system. For example, the distance between two points on a piece of paper, determined as the length of a displacement vector drawn between the two points, does not depend on the particular directions we choose for an *x*- and a *y*-axis against which we determine the components of the displacement vector. However, imagine a three-dimensional displacement vector and a transformation of the coordinate system performed by making a Lorentz transformation, as we do in Special Relativity (see Myth #10 in Chapter 22 for more discussion of this example). We find that the "length" of this vector is not invariant under this transformation! Thus, one of the simplest vectors we can think of—a length—fails as a vector in this situation!

In general, then, while it is convenient to think of quantities with magnitude and direction as vectors, strictly speaking, this is not a sufficient definition.

5.) Scientists discover the laws of nature.

While Nature proceeds in its endless processes, *descriptions* of the behavior of the universe, such as the common form of Newton's Second Law, $\mathbf{F} = m\mathbf{a}$, *are not lying in wait for us to discover*. These and many other laws, along with the fundamental concepts (such as those listed in Mystery #1 in this Chapter), are *creations of the human mind*, developed to explain our understanding of the processes of the universe. As we have seen often, these creations of the mind must be modified occasionally to enable a better description of the universe (such as the developments of Relativity, Chapter 22 and Quantum Physics, Chapters 17 and 18). This does not represent a change in Nature; it will always behave in the same way. These changes represent alterations in our created method of describing Nature for ourselves.

Chapter 2
Translational Kinematics

Mysteries:

Drinking fountain?
Where???
Did somebody say
drinking fountain?

1.) What is the shape of the water stream from a drinking fountain?

2.) As a tennis player serves the ball, at what point in the ball's trajectory is it struck?

Mysteries:

3.) A baseball hit deep to the outfield follows a parabolic trajectory (ignoring air resistance). What is the shape of the path of the daytime *shadow* of the baseball?

4.) Why do basketball players seem to "hang" in the air when they jump?

Mysteries:

5.) If you are caught in a rainstorm with no umbrella, should you: a.) run through the rain, thus reducing the time interval, but running into more drops per unit time; or b.) walk, thereby increasing the time interval, but running into fewer drops per unit time? What's the better strategy?

Magic:

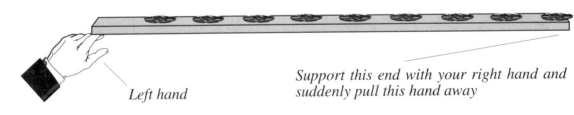

Left hand

Support this end with your right hand and suddenly pull this hand away

Falling Pennies

Lay out a series of pennies on a horizontal meter stick, with one penny every 10 cm. Now, support the meter stick with one finger of a hand at each end, keeping the meter stick level. Suddenly, pull one of the fingers away, so that situation is as appears above, with the meter stick supported at one end. The unsupported end of the meter stick will begin to fall. Which pennies lose contact with the meter stick *first* as the meter stick begins to fall?

Myth:

1.) The acceleration of a projectile at the top of its flight is zero.

2.) Ignoring air resistance for a projectile causes only a small error.

3.) If an unscrupulous football team were to fill the footballs they used with helium, they would have an advantage in punts and passes, because the more buoyant ball would be able to travel further through the air.

Myth:

4.) In a cathode ray tube, we do not need to worry about the gravitational deflection of the electron beam. This is because of the small mass of the electrons.

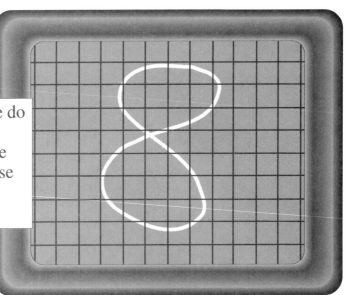

5.) Galileo has been universally accepted as a great scientist for centuries.

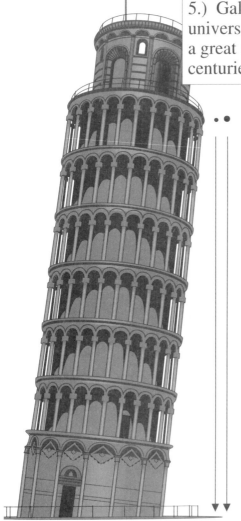

6.) The maximum range of a projectile is realized when it is launched at 45°. Thus, long jumpers leave the ground at 45°.

45°

Discussions; Chapter 2—Translational Kinematics

𝔐𝔶𝔰𝔱𝔢𝔯𝔦𝔢𝔰:

1.) What is the shape of the water stream from a drinking fountain?

Once water has been ejected from the opening of the fountain, it becomes a projectile. Thus, each portion of the water stream follows a *parabolic* trajectory, just like a rock or a ball does when thrown through the air. The whole collection of portions of water, then, forms a parabolic *arc*.

A nice example of this is available at the EPCOT Center at Walt Disney World, Orlando, Florida. One of the park's fountains issues "pulses" of water at an angle to the vertical, which fly through the air, forming distinct parabolic shaped segments until they land in an adjacent fountain.

A homemade version of the parabolic arc can be seen by projecting water from a garden hose into the air.

2.) As a tennis player serves the ball, at what point in the ball's trajectory is it struck?

The ball is struck when it is in the *top part of its trajectory*. There are two primary reasons for this. First, the ball is moving relatively slowly in this region. This provides a large time interval in which the server can observe the ball, plan the serve, send messages to the muscles and bring the racket to the right position.

The second reason concerns the angle subtended by the opposing team player's service court at the position of the ball. The diagram below shows the ranges of successful serves from two locations, one from a low position (dotted lines) and one from a higher point (solid lines). We have introduced two non-realistic features in the diagram in the interest of keeping the discussion simple: 1.) the length of the court is compressed and the height of the serve exaggerated to keep the diagram of reasonable size; and, 2.) the trajectories are drawn as straight lines rather than portions of parabolas. From the higher serving point, there is a larger angle (than in the case of the lower serve) between

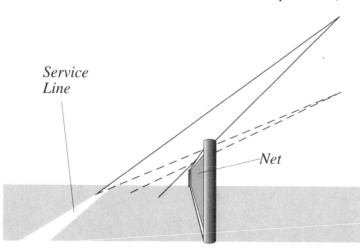

Service Line

Net

the serve which just strikes the service line at the back of the service court and that which just clears the net. Since any serve suffers from an uncertainty in the angle of the velocity of the ball, the higher serve results in a larger probability that the ball will land in the appropriate area of the opposing player's court.

For experimental techniques on determining the velocity of a tennis serve, see J. Eng and T. Lietman, "Measuring the Velocity of a Tennis Serve", *The Physics Teacher*, **32**, 168, 1994.

3.) A baseball hit deep to the outfield follows a parabolic trajectory (ignoring air resistance). What is the shape of the path of the daytime *shadow* of the baseball?

The light from the Sun will cast a shadow of the ball on the ground. The shape of the path of the shadow will depend on where the Sun is relative to the path of the ball.

Let us assume first that the Sun is in the plane defined by the parabolic path of the baseball. This would be true in two cases—the Sun is directly overhead *or* the ball has been hit in the direction toward, or away from the Sun. In this case, the movement of the shadow will represent the *projection of the ball's motion on the horizontal plane*. In the special case of the Sun <u>directly</u> overhead (see Myth #6 in Chapter 1 of *PBWM* for the conditions under which this can occur), the shadow motion will be a demonstration of the ball's horizontal component of velocity. Since there is no acceleration in the horizontal direction, the shadow of the ball will move with uniform velocity (but, as a reminder, only in the unlikely case in which the Sun is *directly overhead*).

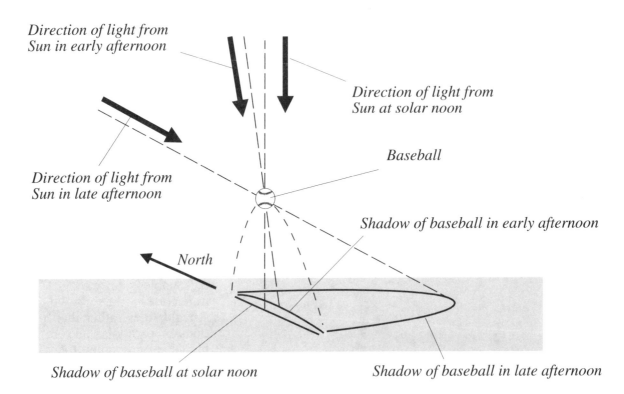

Direction of light from Sun in early afternoon

Direction of light from Sun at solar noon

Baseball

Direction of light from Sun in late afternoon

Shadow of baseball in early afternoon

North

Shadow of baseball at solar noon

Shadow of baseball in late afternoon

Now, let us look at the more likely case that the Sun is not in the plane of the trajectory of the baseball. If the Sun is to either side of the plane defined by the path of the ball, then the shadow will execute a *curved* path along the ground. The extent of the curve will depend on the angle of the Sun relative to the horizon. Let us suppose that the ball is hit due north, as shown in the diagram on the previous page. If it is solar noon, then the Sun is in the plane of the trajectory and we have a straight line for the path of the shadow, as discussed previously. If it is early afternoon, so that the Sun is slightly to the west of its highest point, the shadow will execute a gentle curve which might be hard to distinguish from a straight line, if it is only slightly past noon. If it is late afternoon, so that the Sun is low in the west, the shadow of the northward hit ball will follow a very exaggerated curve, as suggested in the diagram.

4.) Why do basketball players seem to "hang" in the air when they jump?

This question is related to that of Mystery #2, in which we discussed the serve of a tennis ball. When the basketball player jumps and becomes a projectile subject to the force of gravity, he or she follows a parabolic trajectory. In terms of the vertical motion, the slowest vertical velocities occur near the top of the flight, just as for the tennis ball. Thus, much more time is spent in the top, say, 25 cm of the flight than in the bottom 25 cm. This contributes to the "hanging in the air" effect.

In addition, it is important to remember that the *center of mass* is the only point which follows the simple parabolic trajectory. By changing the relationship among various parts of the body while in flight, the center of mass may follow the proper trajectory, while another part of the body may appear to behave in a strange way. Thus, if the arms and legs are brought upward during the jump, the center of mass of the basketball player may follow a parabolic trajectory while the torso moves almost horizontally. This further contributes to the hanging effect.

This phenomenon is used in ballet, in which dancers leap across the stage in a *grand jeté*, with their bodies seeming to move horizontally, in apparent violation of the laws of physics. In reality, during the rising part of the flight, the dancer raises his or her arms and legs. This causes the center of mass to rise within the body, as in the previous case of the basketball player. In turn, the center of mass can rise, following the normal parabolic trajectory, while, with excellent training, the head and torso will move almost horizontally for much of the jump. On the downward part of the flight, the arms and legs are lowered, so that the center of mass moves downward in the body, in concert with its normal downward trend due to gravity. Again, the center of mass falls naturally, but the head and torso continue to move almost horizontally. For more information on the physics behind dancing, see K. Laws, *The Physics of Dance*, Schirmer Books, New York, 1984, and K. Laws, "The Physics of Dance", *Physics Today*, **38**(2), 24, 1985.

5.) If you are caught in a rainstorm with no umbrella, should you: a.) run through the rain, thus reducing the time interval, but running into more drops per unit time; or b.) walk, thereby increasing the time interval, but running into fewer drops per unit time? What's the better strategy?

The answer to this question depends on which direction the rain is falling. If the rain is falling straight down or at an angle so that it has a component of velocity toward you, you should run as fast as possible. In this case, the minimization of the time is the primary objective.

If the rain is falling at an angle so that it has a component of velocity away from you, then you should run at a speed equal to the horizontal component of the rain. In the ideal situation, this means that only your head and shoulders will become wet, as you will collide with no raindrops with your front or back surfaces. We can also look at this from the point of view that, if you are running at the indicated speed, the velocity of rain, relative to you, is straight down.

For more information, including calculations and graphs, see H. E. Evans, "Raindrops Keep Falling on My Head", *The Physics Teacher*, **29**, 120, 1991 and S. A. Stern, "An Optimal Speed for Traversing a Constant Rain", *American Journal of Physics*, **51**, 815, 1983.

𝔐𝔞𝔤𝔦𝔠:

Falling Pennies

As the meter stick undergoes an *angular* acceleration (α) around one of its ends, each point on the meter stick undergoes a *tangential* acceleration (a), which is downward at the moment the stick starts to fall. The relationship between these two accelerations is $a = r\alpha$, where r is the distance of a point on the meter stick from the rotation point. By using Newton's Second Law (for rotation), it can be shown that for points farther from the end of the meter stick than about 67 cm (if the stationary finger is at the end of the meter stick), the tangential acceleration of the stick is greater than that due to the gravitational field on a freely falling object (compare this to the falling chimneys in *PBWM*, Chapter 9, Mystery #2). Thus, points on the stick farther out than 67 cm will accelerate faster than the pennies will and *pennies at these points will lose contact with the meter stick immediately*. Pennies closer than 67 cm will remain in contact with the meter stick (until the angle of the rotating meter stick is such that these pennies begin to slide!).

This demonstration is a good candidate for videotaping and playing back in slow motion for careful analysis.

𝔐𝔶𝔱𝔥:

1.) The acceleration of a projectile at the top of its flight is zero.

This is a common student misconception, in which the momentary vanishing of the (vertical component of) *velocity* is interpreted as a zero value of the *acceleration*. The misconception should be pointed out directly to students and they should be challenged with arguments such as the following. The acceleration is provided by the interaction of the mass of the projectile and the gravitational field of the Earth. If the acceleration is zero at the top, has gravity suddenly been <u>turned off</u> momentarily? Another argument goes as follows: If the projectile momentarily comes to rest <u>and</u> its acceleration is zero, there is no *change* in the vertical velocity component from zero—it will never come down!

2.) Ignoring air resistance for a projectile causes only a small error.

For relatively low velocities, such as those imparted to passed footballs, for example, the effects of air resistance are small (assuming the spiraling motion discussed in *PBWM*, Chapter 11, Mystery #2), so that the assumption of travel through a vacuum gives adequate results. As the velocity increases, however, the effects of air friction become significant. For example, for a baseball projected at 100 mi·h^{-1} at $60°$, the range calculated by assuming a vacuum is <u>80% larger</u> than that predicted by a computer model which includes the effects of air resistance.

The effects of air resistance are especially important for motor vehicles, since they move on a regular basis through the air at speeds on the order of 50-60 mi·h^{-1}. As a result, there is a great deal of research into the *streamlining* of automobile bodies. Similarly, it is common to see *airfoils* on top of truck cabs (see the diagram accompanying Mystery #7 in Chapter 9) to help reduce the effects of air friction. The main objective with these efforts is to improve the fuel economy of the vehicles.

For more details on the effect of air resistance on projectiles, see P. J. Brancazio, "Trajectory of a Fly Ball", *The Physics Teacher*, **23**, 20, 1985. M. A. Day and M. H. Walker, in "Experimenting with the National Guard: Field Artillery Gunnery", *The Physics Teacher*, **31**, 136, 1993, discuss a number of aspects of the flights of artillery projectiles through the air, with quite a bit of discussion on the effects of air resistance.

For discussions of the range of a projectile thrown from a cliff, see C. S. Inouye and E. W. T. Chong, "Maximum Range of a Projectile", *The Physics Teacher*, **30**, 168, 1992 and R. A. Brown, "Maximizing the Range of a Projectile", *The Physics Teacher*, **30**, 344, 1992.

3.) If an unscrupulous football team were to fill the footballs they used with helium, they would have an advantage in punts and passes, because the more buoyant ball would be able to travel further through the air.

If you were fooled by this statement, think again. Both an air-filled ball and a helium-filled ball, inflated to the same pressure, will occupy the *same volume*. Thus, there will be the *same* buoyant force due to the air on each ball.

Since the density of helium is significantly less than that of air, the helium-filled ball should be lighter than the one filled with air. How does this affect the punting distance? This question was researched and tested and the results were published in the prestigious scientific journal *Sports Illustrated* (J. Walters, "Football Physics", *Sports Illustrated*, **79(19)**, 143, 1993). Using an Auburn University physicist and an Auburn punt-er, punting tests were performed on both balls. The results were as follows:

Gas in Ball	Average punt distance (yds)	Average time in air (s)
Air	59.8	4.93
Helium	57.7	4.66

Notice that the helium-filled ball exhibited a *shorter* average punt distance and a *shorter* "hang time" in the air!

The difference appears to be related to the different masses of the two balls. The mass measurements showed 408.4 grams for the helium-filled ball and 416.3 grams for the air-filled ball. These masses are close to each other, since most of the mass is associated with the material of the ball, not with the gas inside. The research team theorized that the lighter ball was more susceptible to the effects of air resistance than the heavier ball, resulting in the shorter times in the air and, as a result, the shorter punt lengths.

4.) In a cathode ray tube, we do not need to worry about the gravitational deflection of the electron beam. This is because of the small mass of the electrons.

The absence of a need to consider gravitational deflection of an electron beam is <u>not</u> related to the mass of the electron; remember, all objects fall with the same acceleration in a given gravitational field (and in a vacuum, such as the evacuated interior of the cathode ray tube), regardless of mass! In a cathode ray tube, the electrons are accelerated by a high voltage and, as a result, move very quickly from the electron gun to the fluorescent screen. The absence of a measurable gravitational deflection is due simply to the fact that there is *so little time of flight* during which a deflection could occur.

A. B. Arons (*A Guide to Introductory Physics Teaching*, John Wiley & Sons, New York, 1990) points out that *more than 40% of candidates on a Ph.D. qualifying examination in physics* claimed that the smallness of the electron mass was the reason for the absence of a gravitational deflection!

5.) Galileo has been universally accepted as a great scientist for centuries.

This statement is true in the realm of science and scientists. Galileo had brilliant insights and is to be admired for his creativity. If one looks outside the scientific arena, however, one notices that the Roman Catholic Church has not accepted the philosophy of Galileo for centuries. It was this Church that summoned Galileo to Rome in 1633 to answer to the charges that he had committed heresy.

Galileo's crime was in holding to the Copernican system of the solar system, in violation of the decree issued in March of 1616, by the *Congregation of the Index**. All publications supporting the Copernican system were included in the *Index*. Galileo

---

*The *Index* is the *Index of Forbidden Books*, which, until 1571, was organized by the Pope of the Roman Catholic Church. The task eventually became too much work for one individual, especially one with so many other duties, so Pope Pius V founded the *Congregation of the Index* in 1571 to take on the task of identifying forbidden publications.

was sentenced to life imprisonment for this violation.

It was not until *1822* that the prohibition against works supporting the Copernican concept was removed from the *Index*. It was only relatively recently, *in 1979*, that Pope John Paul II established a commission to study the possibility that the Roman Catholic Church may have been mistaken in condemning Galileo. That process took thirteen years, with an admission by Pope John Paul II in October of *1992* that the Church had indeed erred in condemning Galileo for holding that the Earth moved around the Sun. Thus, the Roman Catholic Church has not accepted Galileo as a great scientist for centuries, as others have.

For more information, see H. F. Zandy, "Galileo, Einstein, and the Church", *American Journal of Physics*, **61**, 202, 1993 and J. J. Langford, *Galileo, Science and the Church*, 3rd ed., The University of Michigan Press, Ann Arbor, Michigan, 1992.

6.) The maximum range of a projectile is realized when it is launched at 45°. Thus, long jumpers leave the ground at 45°.

The first statement in this Myth is true, assuming that we are ignoring air resistance, and that the initial and final altitudes of the projectile are the same. The second statement is not true; a typical angle of launch for a long jumper is about 20°. Why would a long jumper not take advantage of the 45° benefit? There are two contributions to the answer to this question that can be addressed. There is a small effect causing a deviation from 45° as the desired angle, in that the jumper leaves the ground in a *standing* position and lands in a *crouching* position. Thus, the center of mass of the jumper does not return to the same height at the end of the trajectory as it was at the beginning. Under these conditions, the maximum range is achieved by projecting at an angle different from 45°. The change in height of the center of mass is relatively small in this case, however, so the deviation from 45° will be a few degrees at most.

There is a significantly larger effect, which can be understood more easily if we break the launch velocity into vertical and horizontal components. The vertical component of the launch velocity arises due to the push upward by the jumper's legs as he or she begins the jump. This vertical component is limited by the strength of the jumper. The horizontal component of the velocity arises due to the initial running toward the takeoff point. *A higher velocity can be achieved by running than by jumping.* Thus, the horizontal component of velocity is significantly larger than the vertical component, resulting in a relatively small angle of projection. The only way that the angle could be *increased* to 45° is for the jumper to *decrease* the running speed. While this may take the jumper closer to the 45° ideal, there is a net decrease in the range of the jump due to the smaller value of the initial velocity.

Thus, the best technique is to run as fast as possible to achieve a large horizontal velocity and then push upward as hard as possible to achieve the largest possible vertical component.

See Myth #3 in Chapter 6 for another technique (currently forbidden!) for increasing the length of a long jump by considering the physics involved.

Chapter 3
Force

𝕸ysteries:

1.) Why are football *linemen* usually heavier than *running backs*?

It was a dark and dreary night. The sounds of wolves howling at the Moon could be heard off in the distance. A thick fog hugged closely to the ground. A gentle wind rustled through the trees and occasionally gusted, sending cold shivers up my spine. Suddenly, from nowhere, appeared a tremendously ... with huge, frightening ...

2.) Before the days of computers, typewriters were used for writing. When erasures were made on a typewritten page, periods were much harder to erase than letters. Why?

3.) Why does jerking a paper towel from a roll cause it to tear better than pulling it smoothly?

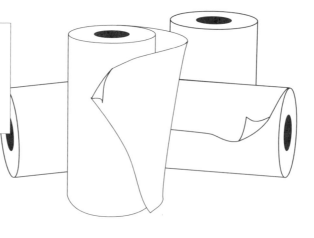

𝕸ysteries:

4.) The spokes on a bicycle wheel are made of relatively thin metal wires. How can these thin wires support the weight of the bicycle and the rider? Wouldn't they just *bend* due to this force?

5.) Why do you move your hands back when you catch a ball?

Oops!

Uh-oh!

6.) Why is whiplash so prevalent in rear-end collisions?

Mysteries:

??? Uh-oh!!??

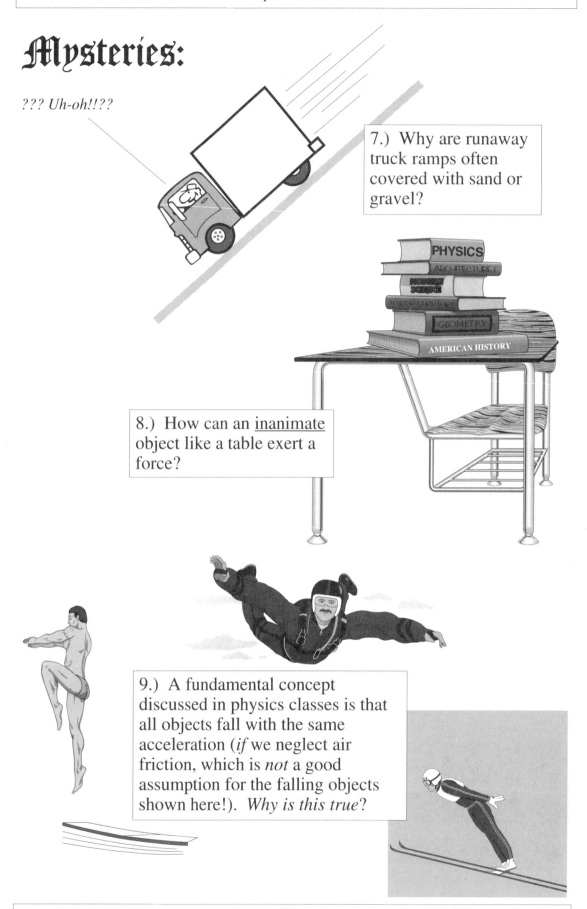

7.) Why are runaway truck ramps often covered with sand or gravel?

8.) How can an <u>inanimate</u> object like a table exert a force?

9.) A fundamental concept discussed in physics classes is that all objects fall with the same acceleration (*if* we neglect air friction, which is *not* a good assumption for the falling objects shown here!). *Why is this true*?

Mysteries:

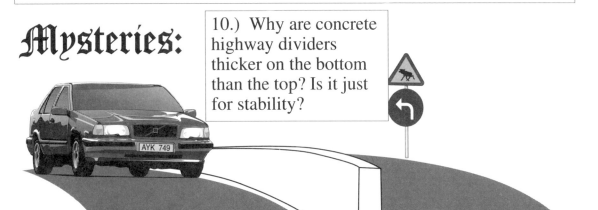

10.) Why are concrete highway dividers thicker on the bottom than the top? Is it just for stability?

11.) How does shaking or snapping a piece of clothing help to release the dirt and dust that may have accumulated on it?

12.) Where does the saying, "flying by the seat of your pants" come from?

𝕸𝖆𝖌𝖎𝖈:

Phone Book Friction

Interleave, page by page, the pages of two large retail catalogs or phone books. The pages should overlap by several centimeters. When the interleaving is complete, have two volunteers grab the spines of the books and try to pull them apart.

Surprising Scales

Hang one spring scale from the bottom of another. Now hang a 5 kg mass from the bottom scale. (This mass and others discussed below may need to be modified, depending on the spring scales available.) Both scales should read 5 kg (as shown on the left in the diagram below, and neglecting the mass of the lower scale). Now, hang an additional 2 kg mass from the bottom scale—both scales read 7 kg. Remove the 2 kg mass and hang it from the top scale (Place it on the hook of the top scale, along with the upper hook of the bottom scale.) The top scale now reads 7 kg and the bottom reads 5 kg (center diagram below). No surprise yet, right? Now, remove the 2 kg and 5 kg masses and *tie a string* from the hook of the bottom scale down to a rigid support, tightening the string until both scales read 5 kg, just like when the 5 kg mass was hanging on the bottom scale. Now, hang the 2 kg mass from the bottom and top scales in turn (diagram on the right below). Are the results the same as before?

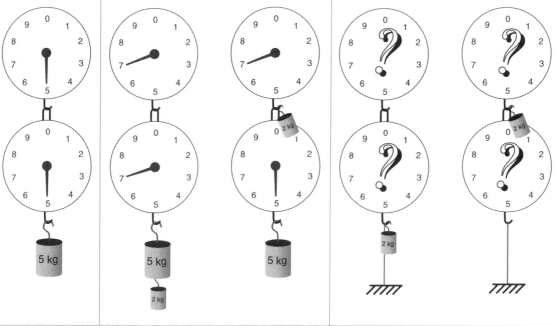

𝕸𝖞𝖙𝖍:

1.) An automobile moves because of forces applied on the car by the engine.

2.) If you are stuck in a non-functioning automobile, you cannot cause it to move without leaving the car.

3.) The mass of the Earth is 6.0×10^{24} kg. Therefore its weight is,
$$W = mg = (6.0 \times 10^{24} \text{ kg})(9.8 \text{ m}\cdot\text{s}^{-2})$$
$$= 5.9 \times 10^{25} \text{ N}$$

𝕸𝖞𝖙𝖍:

4.) Force is the cause of motion.

"Motion"

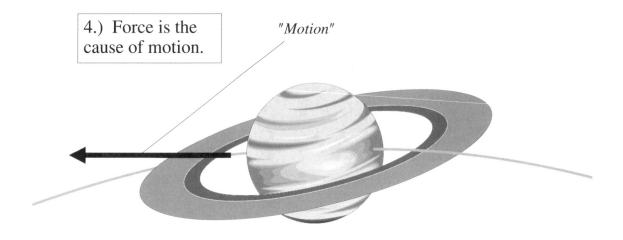

Inertia

5.) Newton's First Law originated with Newton.

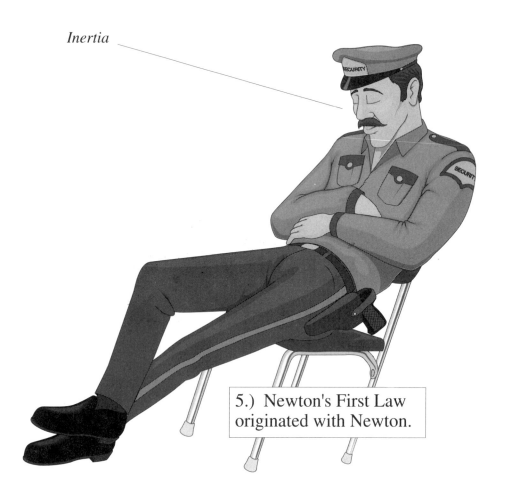

𝕸𝖞𝖙𝖍:

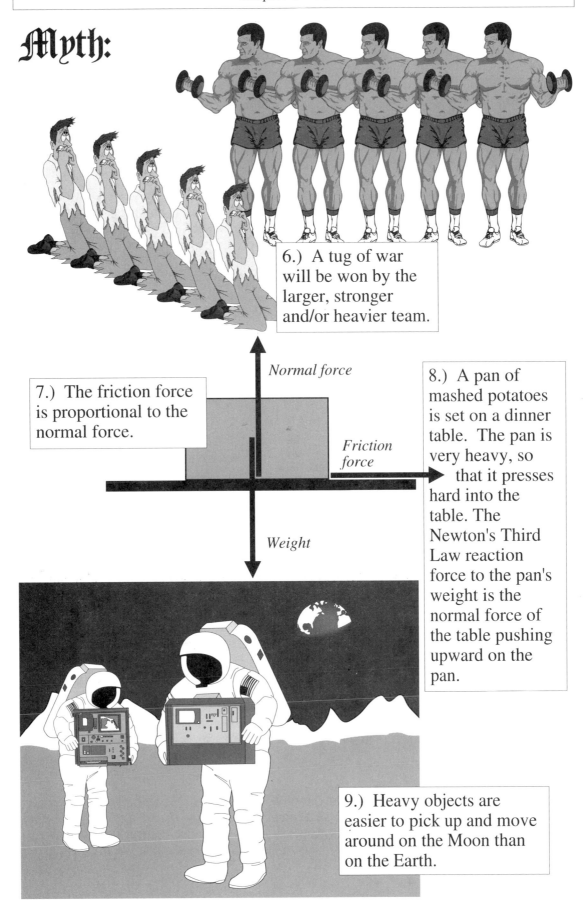

6.) A tug of war will be won by the larger, stronger and/or heavier team.

7.) The friction force is proportional to the normal force.

Normal force

Friction force

Weight

8.) A pan of mashed potatoes is set on a dinner table. The pan is very heavy, so that it presses hard into the table. The Newton's Third Law reaction force to the pan's weight is the normal force of the table pushing upward on the pan.

9.) Heavy objects are easier to pick up and move around on the Moon than on the Earth.

Discussions; Chapter 3—Force

𝔐𝔶𝔰𝔱𝔢𝔯𝔦𝔢𝔰:

1.) Why are football _linemen_ usually heavier than _running backs_?

The objective of a football _lineman_ is to protect the quarterback by preventing the opposing players from reaching him. An effective way to do this is to provide a large amount of resistance to changes in motion when there is a collision between the lineman and the onrushing opposing players. Resistance to changes in motion is another name for _mass_. Thus, a massive (and, therefore, heavy) lineman will be more effective at stopping the onrushing player than a less massive lineman.

Now, _running backs_ are the players who go out for passes or carry the ball from behind the line of scrimmage, which often requires following a complicated motion in the open spaces among the colliding linemen of the two teams. These tasks require bursts of speed to cover the distance down the field rapidly and/or the ability to make sudden and sharp turns to wind one's way through the other players on the field. These actions, which represent large accelerations, are easier if the player has a relatively small resistance to changes in motion. Once again, this translates to mass, so that less massive (and, therefore, lighter) running backs tend to be more successful than their more massive counterparts in these tasks.

2.) Before the days of computers, typewriters were used for writing. When erasures were made on a typewritten page, periods were much harder to erase than letters. Why?

When typewriter keys strike the paper, the force of the blow is spread out over the area of the character. Thus, we can approximate the <u>pressure</u> of the blow on the paper as the average force of the strike divided by the area of the character. The period represents the smallest area of all of the normal characters. Thus, the pressure on the paper is the largest for the period. This results in a deep depression formed by the typed period, or even a small hole through the paper. As a result, ink deposited in a typed period is driven deeper below the flat surface of the paper than it is for other characters. Thus, when an eraser is dragged across the paper surface, it cannot reach the deep ink of the period, and the period continues to appear on the page.

3.) Why does jerking a paper towel from a roll cause it to tear better than pulling it smoothly?

This is an example of Newton's Second Law. When the paper towel is pulled smoothly, you are demanding a relatively small acceleration of the towel and a correspondingly small angular acceleration of the roll of towels. This small acceleration can be provided by a small force, smaller than that necessary to tear the towel. When the towel is given a sudden jerk, however, you impose a relatively large acceleration on the towel in your hand as well as *attempt* to create a large angular acceleration of the towel roll. This large angular acceleration requires a large torque, which, if it is to occur, must be provided by a large force along the surface of the towels between your hand and the roll. This large force may be greater than that necessary to tear the towel, which is the result.

It is easier to tear the towels if the roll is full than if it is empty or near empty. A full roll possesses a larger *moment of inertia* than a partially full or empty roll. Thus, the full roll offers more resistance to having its rotational motion change, requiring a larger force from the unrolled towels to set it into rotation.

4.) The spokes on a bicycle wheel are made of relatively thin metal wires. How can these thin wires support the weight of the bicycle and the rider? Wouldn't they just *bend* due to this force?

If a spoke *below the hub* of the wheel were required to support this weight, the spoke would be in compression and it would be likely to bend and collapse. But the force holding the bicycle and rider up comes from the spokes *above the hub*, not below. The weight of the bicycle and rider tends to force the hub of the wheel downward, resulting in the upper spokes being in *tension*. Thus, the bicycle is not supported by the lower spokes, it *hangs* from the upper part of the wheel by means of the upper spokes.

Of course, *all* of the spokes are important, because they maintain the circular shape of the rim, which provides the rigid structure from which the upper spokes hang.

5.) Why do you move your hands back when you catch a ball?

If you caught a hard-thrown baseball with your arms held stiffly, it could be quite painful. In this case, the velocity of the ball is brought to zero over a very short displacement. As a result, there is a very large magnitude of acceleration of the ball. According to Newton's Second Law, this large acceleration must be provided by a very large force that you apply on the ball. According to Newton's Third Law, this large force is equal in magnitude to the force that the ball exerts on your hand. This is the origin of the pain.

This situation can be avoided by moving the hands backwards (in the direction of the ball's velocity). Thus, the velocity is brought to zero over a larger displacement, resulting in much lower acceleration and a much gentler force on your hands. This technique is very evident in egg-throwing contests at picnics. If an egg were caught with stiff arms, the shell would be extremely likely to break. This is also the basis of the Magic demonstration, Throwing an Egg with Confidence, in Chapter 3 of *PBWM*, in which an egg is thrown into a sheet. In this case, the flexibility of the sheet allows the egg to be brought to rest over a large displacement, reducing the force on the shell.

Another related example occurs in jumping and landing. If you were to hold your legs stiff when jumping from just a meter or two onto the ground, you could receive a painful injury to your legs, hips or back. This is due to the fact that the body is brought to rest over a short distance, resulting in a large acceleration and very large forces from the legs. To avoid this, you bend your knees upon landing. Thus, the body is brought to rest over a larger distance, requiring much smaller forces in the legs.

Another approach to all of these situations is from the point of view of the *Impulse-Momentum Theorem*:

$$\overline{F}\Delta t = \Delta(mv)$$

Whether the hands are moved or not in catching a ball, the change in momentum of the ball, on the right side of the equation above, is the same. If the hands are moved backwards, then the time interval, on the left side of the equation, during which the momentum changes, is lengthened over the case where the hands are held stationary. Thus, with a longer time interval on the left side of the equation, the average force must be smaller.

6.) Why is whiplash so prevalent in rear-end collisions?

The injury of whiplash is commonly argued from Newton's First Law. When an automobile is hit from the rear, the seat back pushes the body of the driver and passengers forward suddenly. The head, however, is not in contact with part of the seat. Thus, according to Newton's First Law, it tends to remain at rest. Relative to the car and the body, then, it moves backward suddenly, which is the cause of the whiplash. The seriousness of the injury can be reduced by providing head rests or high seat backs so that the head will strike a cushioned part of the seat after only a small displacement relative to the car. The head rest or top of the high seat back then accelerates the head forward along with the body.

Although we have invoked Newton's First Law in the above argument, there is a more correct, but less common, description based on Newton's Second Law. Newton's First Law is a statement about the behavior of an object if *no* net force acts on it. In reality, there *is* a net force on the head in a rear-end collision. The head is connected to the rest of the body via the neck. When the car is hit, the seat back can provide the very large force needed to accelerate the body. A large force is also needed to provide this same acceleration for the head, but the seat back cannot do this. Thus, the large force is provided by the <u>neck</u>, which causes the injury.

The more correct explanation in terms of Newton's Second Law is reminiscent of the Magic demonstration, The Slippery Tablecloth, in Chapter 3 of *PBWM*. When a tablecloth is pulled from underneath a collection of dishes, Newton's First Law is often given as the explanation. Once again, this is not a situation in which no force is acting. There *is* a frictional force between the tablecloth and the dishes. Due to the fact that the force is small and acts for only a short time, the dishes do not move appreciably. Turning to the whiplash accident for comparison, the time is also short in this case, but the force is large, since the head and body are <u>connected</u>. If the dishes were glued to the tablecloth, we would have an analogy to the head-body situation. When the tablecloth is pulled, we would have a large force in this case, also, possibly enough to overcome the adhesive strength and rip the dishes from the tablecloth!

7.) Why are runaway truck ramps often covered with sand or gravel?

Runaway truck ramps are often uphill roadways built as off-ramps to a downhill highway in the mountains. If a truck loses the function of its brakes, it can turn onto the runaway truck ramp and start moving uphill, reducing the speed of the truck. If the runaway ramp were paved with normal asphalt or concrete, a relatively large change in vertical position would be necessary for gravity to reduce the speed of the truck (or, in the language of Chapter 5 (Energy), a large change in vertical position would be necessary to transform the kinetic energy of the truck into gravitational potential energy). This has two possible disadvantages: the long roadway would be expensive to build, and there may not be enough vertical displacement available in the particular location of the ramp—the hill might not be high enough!

The sand or gravel provides much more rolling <u>friction</u> than a normal roadway. Thus, the truck is brought to rest in a much shorter distance, as the friction force assists gravity in causing an acceleration of the truck opposite to its velocity direction. In the language of Chapter 5, the additional friction will perform work which transforms part of the kinetic energy of the truck into internal energy in the tires and the roadway.

8.) How can an <u>inanimate</u> object like a table exert a force?

Many students of physics have difficulty understanding how inanimate objects can exert forces. It is useful here to first consider the action of a spring or a rubber band, which exerts a force upon a change in length, which is a <u>deformation</u>. Then we imagine that we place a heavy object on a table. As the Earth pulls on the object with a gravitational force, the table *deforms* in response to this force (see the *spring model* of solids in the Concepts section of Chapter 20). If we imagine that the table consists of a huge number of atoms connected by springs, then the upward force of the table can be understood as resulting from the deformation of these springs. It is also useful in this regard to model the table as similar to a mattress. When someone lays on a mattress, the springs deform and apply an upward force to support the person. A table is similar in this regard to a mattress, with many, many more (and/or much stiffer) springs!

A technique for using an overhead projector (or a laser) to demonstrate the bending of a table under a load can be found in J. Minstrell, "Explaining the 'At Rest' Condition of an Object", *The Physics Teacher*, **20**, 10, 1982.

9.) A fundamental concept discussed in physics classes is that all objects fall with the same acceleration (*if* we neglect air friction, which is *not* a good assumption for the falling objects shown here!). *Why is this true*?

This is a result of the equivalent values of inertial and gravitational mass for an object. In the model of gravitational forces espoused by Newton (which works well in many situations), mass plays two roles (this dual role is not necessary in Einstein's General Theory of Relativity). *Inertial mass* refers to the role of mass in *resisting changes in motion*. This is the mass m in Newton's Second Law, in the form $\mathbf{F} = m\mathbf{a}$. *Gravitational mass* refers to the role of mass in *determining the strength of the gravitational force*. This is either (or both!) of the masses m_1 or m_2 in Newton's Law of Universal Gravitation:

$$F = G\frac{m_1 m_2}{r^2}$$

It is an artifact of Newtonian mechanics that these two types of masses, which represent *completely different physical behaviors*, are directly proportional. We define the proportionality constant to be 1, so that the two masses are numerically equal. This can be better appreciated if we compare this with an electrical situation. Suppose we have a charged particle in an electric field, as an analogy to an object with mass in a gravitational field. The resistance to motion of the particle is represented by the value of its *mass*. The strength of the force on the particle is related to its *charge*. Charge and mass are completely separate concepts (as are inertial and gravitational mass!). The charge on the particle is analogous to gravitational mass. In fact, some have even taken to calling gravitational mass gravitational *charge*!

Now, consider a falling object, in the absence of air resistance (the "falling objects" shown in the diagrams accompanying this Mystery will be *significantly* affected by air resistance; let us assume that they are doing their activities in a vacuum!). Applying Newton's Second Law to the falling object, we realize that the net force is just the weight. Thus,

$$F = m_I a \quad \rightarrow \quad W = m_I a$$

where the symbol m_I indicates that the mass is *inertial* mass. We now replace the weight with its equivalent of *gravitational* mass, m_G, times some constant, as required by Newton's Law of Universal Gravitation. We will call the constant g (it's called the *gravitational field*), and it is a combination of G, the mass of the planet m_p, and the radius of the planet r, as can be seen from the equation for the Law of Universal Gravitation above (we let $m_1 = m_G$ and $m_2 = m_p$.). Thus, we have,

$$F = m_I a \quad \rightarrow \quad W = m_I a \quad \rightarrow \quad G\frac{m_G m_p}{r^2} = m_G\left(G\frac{m_p}{r^2}\right) = m_I a \quad \rightarrow \quad m_G g = m_I a$$

Now, in our model, *the inertial and gravitational masses have the same value*, so we can cancel them out on either side of the equation, resulting in,

$$a = g$$

Thus, *the acceleration of the object turns out to be independent of the mass and equal to the value of the gravitational field*. The mass and radius of our planet, the Earth, results in a value for g which is 9.8 m·s^{-2}, and we also call it the *acceleration of gravity*.

Compare this to an electrical situation again—Newton's Second Law for an electric charge in an electric field would become $qE = m_I a$; it is clear here that the mass and charge do not cancel—they are different physical quantities. Similarly, inertial and gravitational mass are different physical quantities; they happen to have the same numerical *value*, however, in the traditional version of Newtonian mechanics.

10.) Why are concrete highway dividers thicker on the bottom than the top? Is it just for stability?

Older style "guard rails" have the cross section shown on the left below, while the concrete barriers have a wider portion at the bottom, as indicated on the right.

If a vehicle were to strike the older style guard rail along a path at a small angle to the rail, the *metal rail* would make contact with the *metal side* of the vehicle. This results in relatively low friction and the velocity of the vehicle will change relatively slowly during the contact between the vehicle and the rail. If the same vehicle were to follow the same motion in making contact with the concrete barrier, the contact would be made between the concrete at the bottom of the barrier and the rubber *tires* of the vehicle. This results in much larger friction than in the previous case, and the velocity of the vehicle is reduced much more rapidly.

11.) How does shaking or snapping a piece of clothing help to release the dirt and dust that may have accumulated on it?

This technique can be explained (approximately) by making use of Newton's First Law. If a piece of cloth (along with the dirt) is in a uniform state of motion, a sudden change in the motion of the cloth, caused by shaking or snapping, will result in the dirt continuing in its state of motion. As long as the forces holding the dirt to the clothing are very small, this continuation of motion of the dirt will result in its leaving the cloth.

As we discussed in a similar situation in Mystery #6, we need to invoke Newton's Second Law for a more correct explanation. The sudden snapping of the cloth represents a large acceleration of the cloth and the dirt. If the force holding the dirt to the cloth is not strong enough to be able to cause this acceleration of the dirt, then the force will be overcome and the dirt and cloth will separate.

12.) Where does the saying, "flying by the seat of your pants" come from?

This is a phrase which originated in the early days of flying, before the introduction of instruments to help the pilots. While the pilot's eyes are certainly usable for making judgments about the current flying status of the airplane, another portion of the anatomy can be used to help. While the plane taxis down the runway for takeoff, the acceleration is horizontal and the pilot feels pushed back into his seat just as the driver of an accelerating automobile does. As the plane lifts upward off the runway, there is an additional acceleration in the upward direction. This will cause the pilot to feel as if he or she is pushed with a little more force *downward into the seat*. This assists the pilot in his or her determination that the airplane has left the runway. Additional "measurements" can be made in this way during the attainment of the desired flying height and during the landing process. Due to the location of this apparent force, the phrase "flying by the seat of your pants" arose.

𝔐𝔞𝔤𝔦𝔠:

Phone Book Friction

The books will be virtually impossible to pull apart, due to the friction force between the large number of pages. Let us see why the friction force is so large. First, imagine one book simply sitting on a table, with the assumption that the static coefficient of friction μ_s between the book and the table is the same as that between pages of the two books. Then, the maximum static friction force between the book and table is equal to the product of the static coefficient of friction and the weight of the book, since the normal force will be numerically equal to the weight:

$$F_{friction} = \mu_s N = \mu_s W$$

This would be the minimum horizontal force necessary to push the book so that it would break free and begin to slide across the table.

Now, let us think about the two books with the pages interleaved. We will assume that each book has 500 pages. Let us first estimate the normal force between pages. The pages at the tops of the books are pressed together with almost zero force, since the weight of a single page is so small. The pages on the bottom of the book are pressed together with a force equal to the weight of the portions of the pages from both books that overlap. Let us assume that the pages are overlapped by half of their width, so that each book provides approximately half its weight to the force on the bottom pages. Then, the weight on the bottom pages (in the region of overlap) is,

$$W_{on\,bottom\,pages} = \left(\frac{1}{2}W\right)(2\,\text{books}) = W$$

Since the book is in equilibrium, the normal force between a given pair of page surfaces is equal to the weight of the pages above. The normal force between pages varies from zero at the top to W at the bottom, so the *average* normal force between pages is one half of W. Thus, the maximum static friction force between a pair of page surfaces is, on the average,

$$\overline{F}_{friction} = \mu_s \overline{N} = \frac{1}{2}\mu_s W$$

Now, how many page surfaces are in contact? For each book, there are 500 pages, representing 999 surfaces in contact with pages from the other book (the thousandth surface will be open to the air). Thus, the total maximum static friction force between the pages is approximately,

$$F_{friction,TOTAL} = 999\left(\frac{1}{2}\mu_s W\right) \approx 5 \times 10^2 \mu_s W$$

Thus, the friction force between the books is *500 times as large* as the friction between one book and the table. This is why it is so difficult to pull the books apart.

Surprising Scales

The first two parts of this demonstration are designed to seduce the observer into believing that he or she understands the actions of the spring scales perfectly. The results of the third component, with the scale extension resulting from the tied string, may come as a surprise. Within the limits of the accuracy of the spring scales (and assuming that the scales themselves are massless!), when the 2 kg mass is hung from the bottom scale, *there is no change in the readings*. When it is hung from the top scale, *the top scale reads 6 kg* and *the bottom one reads 4 kg*. What's going on here?

We can answer this question by asking another question: do spring scales really measure weight (in normal use, they can be interpreted as measuring *weight*, even though they may be calibrated in *mass* units!) or do they measure something else? The answer is that spring scales do not directly measure the weight of an object—*they measure the extension of a spring*. In the normal situation, such as in the first two components of the demonstration, the weights hung on the spring scales cause them to stretch so that the extension of the spring is calibrated accurately so as to represent the mass (as long as the scale is used on the Earth!).

But in the third component, tying the string between the bottom hook and the rigid support destroys the capability of the scales to accurately measure weight. This is so because we have imposed a condition on the system: since the string is inextensible, as long as the string remains taut, then *the sum of the lengths of the two springs in the scales must be constant*. When the 2 kg mass is hung from the bottom hook, it does not cause the string to slacken. It does reduce the tension in the string, but the string remains taut. Thus, the sum of the lengths of the springs remains the same and both scales continue to read 5 kg.

When the 2 kg weight is hung from the top scale, we need to be a little more careful. Since the sums of the lengths of the springs must remain the same, the sum of the "force" readings must remain at 5 kg + 5 kg = 10 kg. Since the 2 kg weight pulls on the top scale, but not the bottom, the readings must differ by 2 kg. Thus, if the readings *differ* by 2 kg but *must add* to 10 kg, the readings must be 6 kg and 4 kg.

𝔐𝔶𝔱𝔥:

1.) An automobile moves because of forces applied on the car by the engine.

The engine of a car is certainly important for causing the car to move, but the statement implies that the engine applies forces on the car. If we think about this for a moment, we realize that it is impossible for the center of mass of a system (the car and the engine) to change its motion through space due to forces between members of the system (although see Myth #2). This can only happen if there is an external force on the system. This external force is provided by the road. The force of the engine results in a torque on the driving wheels. If the wheels are in contact with the road, this results in a force applied by the wheels on the road in the direction toward the rear of the car. By Newton's Third Law, then, the road exerts a force on the driving wheels in the forward direction and the car accelerates!

2.) If you are stuck in a non-functioning automobile, you cannot cause it to move without leaving the car.

There are actually a couple of tricks that you could use to cause the car to move. You could appeal to Newton's Third Law by throwing a heavy object out the window, in the direction toward the rear of the car. This would cause the car to move in the forward direction.

What's that.....you think that's cheating? It is certainly true that a lot of mass would have to be jettisoned to impart any significant velocity to the car. How about this? You break the front windshield, remove the hood of the car, take off the valve covers and upper part of the engine and push downward on a piston with the car in a forward gear. This will cause the tire to exert a force backwards on the road and the car will move forward. What's that.....this is unrealistic? Okay, you lean out the side window and grab the top of a tire and push forward. This will cause the tire to exert a force backwards on the road and the car will move forward. What's that......?

3.) The mass of the Earth is 6.0 x 10^{24} kg. Therefore its weight is
$$W = mg = (6.0 \times 10^{24} \text{ kg})(9.8 \text{ m·s}^{-2})$$
$$= 5.9 \times 10^{25} \text{ N.}$$

The technique indicated in this Myth is indeed that which would be used to find the weight of an object on the Earth, where the magnitude of the gravitational field is 9.8 m·s^{-2}. But the use of the word *weight* to represent the gravitational force is restricted to that situation in which a relatively small object is close to the surface of a planet. We describe this force as the *weight of the object*, but it is not a characteristic only of the object—it is really the gravitational force of attraction *between the planet and the object*. Now, the Earth is clearly not a small object on the surface of a planet. Thus, the concept of weight has no meaning for the Earth.

4.) Force is the cause of motion.

It is very important to state clearly the relationship between force and motion. The statement given in the Myth is one that could have been given by Aristotle. It implies that if an object is moving, a force is acting on it. But this is clearly in disagreement with Newton's First Law, which states that, in the absence of a net force, an object in uniform motion will continue in that state of motion. The correct statement is that a net force is the cause of a *change* in motion. The change in motion is described by the acceleration of the object and the relationship between this change and the applied force(s) is expressed as Newton's Second Law.

5.) Newton's First Law originated with Newton.

The mythical aspect of the phrase *Newton's First Law* is that the First Law is <u>Newton's</u>. The concept of continuing motion in the absence of forces was part of Galileo's thinking, although the full comprehension of the concept was not stated by him. This concept was also well understood by Descartes, who justified the law by appealing to the immutability of God. By the time Newton's *Principia* was published, the First Law was well accepted by clearly thinking philosophers. Thus, Newton included the First Law in his set of three laws of motion, but it did not originate with him.

6.) A tug of war will be won by the larger, stronger and/or heavier team.

All other factors being equal, tugs-of-war will generally be won by the larger, stronger and/or heavier team. But the crucial consideration is the *friction force* between the feet of the tuggers and the ground. This force will depend upon the types of shoes worn by members of the team and the condition of the ground. If one team is on grass and the other on mud, for example, the difference in the friction force will have a greater effect on the outcome than the strength of the team. This effect can be demonstrated convincingly in the classroom by setting up a tug of war between a small student standing on the ground and a large student *on a skateboard*!

7.) The friction force is proportional to the normal force.

Students are used to seeing and freely using the following two equations:

$$F_{static\ friction} = \mu_s N$$

$$F_{kinetic\ friction} = \mu_k N$$

While the use of the second equation generally leads to few difficulties, the first equation is used far too freely and is invariably applied to a situation for which it is inappropriate. Let us imagine that we have two surfaces in contact and we are applying a force parallel to the surfaces in an attempt to cause the surfaces to slide with respect to each other. The first equation only describes the situation in which the frictional force has reached its *maximum value* and the two surfaces involved are *just ready to break free if the applied force is increased slightly*. If the static situation is anything other than this, then the frictional force has no relation at all to the normal force, but is simply equal in magnitude and opposite in direction to the force applied parallel to the surfaces.

Another common student error in these types of problems is to, as a matter of course, set the normal force on an object equal to the weight of the object. While this may be true for an object on a horizontal surface that is not accelerating vertically, there are many situations in which this is not the case. It is instructive, for example, to imagine the normal force on an object sitting on the floor of an accelerating elevator. Another useful example to analyze is the amusement park ride called the *Spinout* or *Rotor*. This is a circular room with vertical walls against which the riders stand. As the room rotates, the riders feel "pressed" into the wall and the floor drops out from under them. The diagram below shows a rider in a Spinout, along with the relevant forces on the rider.

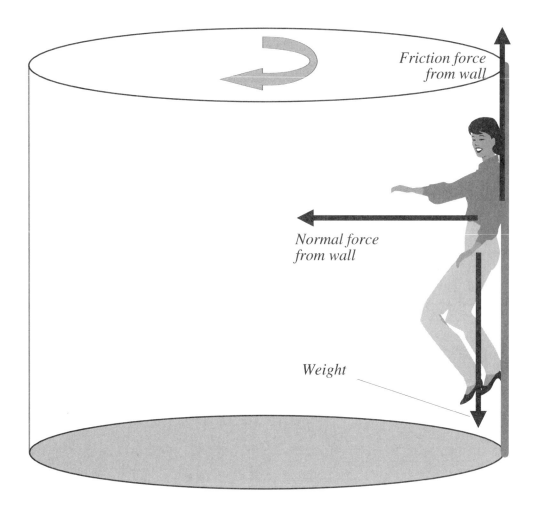

Friction force from wall

Normal force from wall

Weight

The riders do not slide down the wall due to the supporting friction force between them and the wall. In this case, the normal force has <u>no</u> relation to the weight at all, since the two forces are perpendicular. The normal force depends only on the radius and rotational speed of the cylindrical room—the normal force provides the centripetal acceleration in this situation.

8.) A pan of mashed potatoes is set on a dinner table. The pan is very heavy, so that it presses hard into the table. The Newton's Third Law reaction force to the pan's weight is the normal force of the table pushing upward on the pan.

This is a common misconception and can be seen to be incorrect because both of the forces mentioned act on the same object, the pan of potatoes, which is inconsistent with the correct understanding of Newton's Third Law. In this case, the reaction force to the pan's weight is the force upward on the Earth due to the gravitational attraction between the Earth and the pan. Because the table is between the pan and the Earth, the pan does press down on the table as it is attracted toward the Earth. The normal force of the table on the pan is the reaction to this force. Note again that these forces act on different objects—the *pan* presses on the *table*, and the reaction force is the force of the *table* on the *pan*.

9.) Heavy objects are easier to pick up and move around on the Moon than on the Earth.

The statement refers to two operations on a heavy object on the surface of the Moon— 1.) picking the object up; and 2.) moving the object around. Picking the object up would clearly be easier than on the Earth, since a force slightly larger than the weight of the object must be applied in the vertical direction to pick it up (*slowly*; a larger force would be needed to pick it up quickly, since this would involve a large acceleration). Since the gravitational field on the surface of the Moon is significantly smaller than that on the surface of the Earth, the required force would be much less. But now, what about moving the object around? This implies applying a force in the horizontal direction in order to accelerate the object to some velocity in the desired direction and then bring it to a stop in the new location. This acceleration is resisted by the *mass* of the object, which has not changed in taking it to the Moon. Thus, once the object is lifted, the operation of moving it horizontally requires the same force as it would on the surface of the Earth.

Chapter 4
Gravity

𝔐𝔶𝔰𝔱𝔢𝔯𝔦𝔢𝔰:

1.) The Sun's mass is 1.99 x 10^{30} kg. *How do we know this*? How do we "weigh" the Sun?

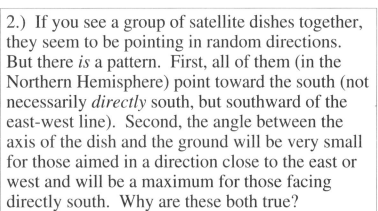

2.) If you see a group of satellite dishes together, they seem to be pointing in random directions. But there *is* a pattern. First, all of them (in the Northern Hemisphere) point toward the south (not necessarily *directly* south, but southward of the east-west line). Second, the angle between the axis of the dish and the ground will be very small for those aimed in a direction close to the east or west and will be a maximum for those facing directly south. Why are these both true?

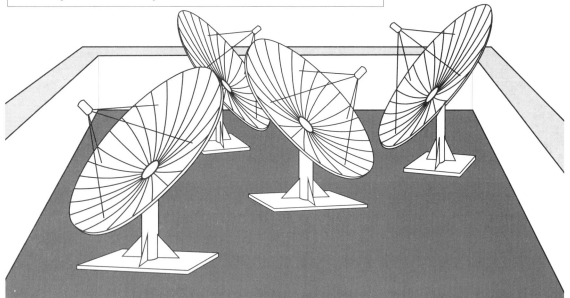

𝕸ysteries:

3.) It takes *more energy* to put up a geosynchronous satellite (2.2 x 10^4 miles above the Earth's surface) than a near Earth satellite (say, 200 miles above the surface). Yet the geosynchronous satellite moves *more slowly* in its orbit. What's going on here?

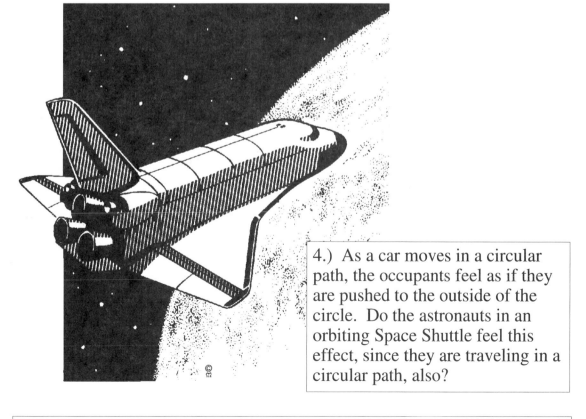

4.) As a car moves in a circular path, the occupants feel as if they are pushed to the outside of the circle. Do the astronauts in an orbiting Space Shuttle feel this effect, since they are traveling in a circular path, also?

Mysteries:

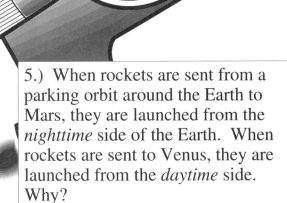

5.) When rockets are sent from a parking orbit around the Earth to Mars, they are launched from the *nighttime* side of the Earth. When rockets are sent to Venus, they are launched from the *daytime* side. Why?

6.) In the movie, *2001: A Space Odyssey* (MGM, 1968), gravity is artificially simulated in a spacecraft by rotating the craft around its central axis. An astronaut is shown running around the perimeter of the inside of the spacecraft as a means of exercise. If the rotation of such a craft is assumed to create the same effective gravitational field as on the surface of the Earth, would the astronaut feel *exactly* the same as if he or she were running on Earth?

𝕸agic:

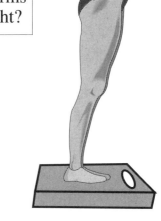

The Short-Lived Weight Gain

Stand on a mechanical (not digital) bathroom scale and note your weight as you stand quietly. Now, raise your arms quickly. What happens to your weight?

The Slowly Falling Weight

Fasten a circular piece of cardboard to the end coil of a Slinky. Now, hold the Slinky from the top coil, so that the rest of the coils hang below your hand. Place a 100 gram weight on the piece of cardboard. Let go of the Slinky. Does the weight fall along with the Slinky?

Cardboard

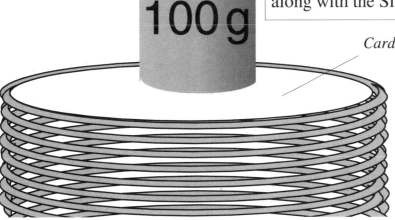

𝔐𝔶𝔱𝔥:

1.) The gravitational force of the Sun on the Earth is stronger than that of the Moon. Thus, tides due to the Sun are stronger than those due to the Moon.

2.) Spring tides occur in the Spring.

𝕸𝖞𝖙𝖍:

3.) A weight-conscious astronaut watches his or her weight during long space travel.

4.) Mass is independent of what planet you are standing on. Thus, if you take a bathroom scale calibrated in kilograms to Mars, it will read correctly.

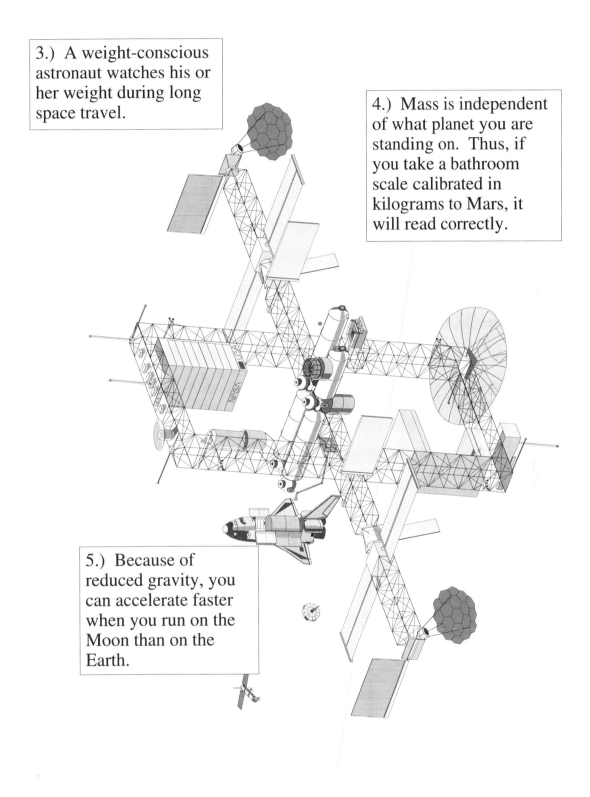

5.) Because of reduced gravity, you can accelerate faster when you run on the Moon than on the Earth.

𝔐𝔶𝔱𝔥:

6.) The reading on a bathroom scale is less at the equator than at the North Pole. This is due to the difference in the gravitational field between the two locations that is due to the bulge at the equator.

$$T^2 = \frac{4\pi^2}{GM_S} r^3$$

7.) Kepler's Laws are fundamental principles.

𝕸𝖞𝖙𝖍:

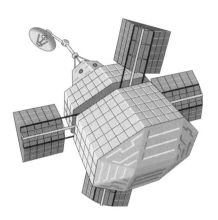

8.) You are in an orbiting spacecraft, trying to catch up with a satellite far ahead of you. You fire your rockets in a direction away from the satellite in order to catch up to it.

9.) An advertisement for the Steel Recycling Institute (Pittsburgh, Pennsylvania) appeared in a science teachers' journal (*The Science Teacher*, **61(3)**, 1, 1994). It asked the following question: "Did you know that over the last ten years, the amount of steel recycled weighs about the same as six billion science teachers stacked vertically?"

Discussions; Chapter 4—Gravity

𝔐𝔶𝔰𝔱𝔢𝔯𝔦𝔢𝔰:

1.) The Sun's mass is 1.99 x 10^30 kg. *How do we know this?* How do we "weigh" the Sun?

The mass of the Sun can not be measured directly, of course, but it can be *inferred* from the motions of the planets. Kepler's Third Law (See Myth #7) states that the semimajor axis of the orbit, a, and period, T, of a planet are related as follows:

$$T^2 = \left(\frac{4\pi^2}{GM}\right)a^3$$

where M is the mass of the object around which the planet revolves. There are a large number of objects in orbit around the Sun, the data (semimajor axis and period) for each of which can be substituted into this equation to calculate the mass of the Sun. It is instructive to calculate the ratio of the square of the orbital period to the cube of the semimajor axis for the Earth and other planets. This ratio should be equal to the expression in the parentheses in the equation above. The results of such a calculation are shown in the spreadsheet below, including data for Comet Halley.

Planet	Semimajor Axis		Period		Period Squared Divided by Semimajor Axis Cubed
	AU	10^6 km	Years	10^8 s	$s^2 \cdot m^{-3}$
Mercury	0.387	57.9	0.241	0.076	2.98 x 10^{-19}
Venus	0.723	108.2	0.615	0.194	2.97 x 10^{-19}
Earth	1.000	149.6	1.000	0.316	2.98 x 10^{-19}
Mars	1.523	227.9	1.881	0.594	2.98 x 10^{-19}
Jupiter	5.203	778.3	11.862	3.75	2.98 x 10^{-19}
Saturn	9.54	1427	29.46	9.31	2.98 x 10^{-19}
Uranus	19.18	2869	84.02	26.6	3.00 x 10^{-19}
Neptune	30.07	4498	164.77	52.1	2.98 x 10^{-19}
Pluto	39.44	5900	248	78.4	2.99 x 10^{-19}
Comet Halley	17.9	2685	74 - 79*	23.3 - 24.9	3.00 x 10^{-19}
				Average:	**2.98 x 10^{-19}**

Using the average value, we can calculate the mass of the Sun from the expression for Kepler's Third Law:

$$T^2 = \left(\frac{4\pi^2}{GM_S}\right)a^3 \rightarrow M_S = \frac{\left(\dfrac{4\pi^2}{G}\right)}{\left(\dfrac{T^2}{a^3}\right)_{avg}} = \frac{\left(\dfrac{4\pi^2}{6.67 \times 10^{-11} \mathrm{N} \cdot \mathrm{m}^2 \cdot \mathrm{kg}^{-2}}\right)}{\left(2.98 \times 10^{-19} \mathrm{s}^2 \cdot \mathrm{m}^{-3}\right)} = 1.99 \times 10^{30} \mathrm{kg}$$

*Variations in the period of Comet Halley are due to perturbations from Jupiter and Saturn.

which agrees with the tabulated value for the mass of the Sun.

This type of calculation can be done for any central object around which other objects revolve. Thus, the mass of the Earth can be calculated by using data for the Moon and the mass of other planets can be calculated from the data for their moons.

2.) If you see a group of satellite dishes together, they seem to be pointing in random directions. But there *is* a pattern. First, all of them (in the Northern Hemisphere) point toward the south (not necessarily *directly* south, but southward of the east-west line). Second, the angle between the axis of the dish and the ground will be very small for those aimed in a direction close to the east or west and will be a maximum for those facing directly south. Why are these both true?

Satellite dishes are aimed at *geosynchronous* satellites. These are located 4.2×10^4 km from the Earth's center, so that their period is 24 hours, the same as the Earth's. Thus, the satellite at this altitude will apparently stay fixed above a given longitude line on the Earth. But there is a second requirement. *The satellite must be in orbit directly above the equator.* If this were not true, the satellite would appear to undergo a North-South vibration along the longitude line during the day. If the satellite orbit is directly over the equator (and at the required height), then both the East-West and the North-South location of the satellite (relative to the observer on the Earth) will remain fixed.

In this way, according to an observer, the geosynchronous satellite will appear to stay fixed in a given location in the sky above the equator. For observers (and satellite dishes!) in the Northern Hemisphere, the equator is toward the South, which is why all of the dishes point in the southerly direction. The angle between the axis of the dish and the ground is determined by the direction to the satellite from the dish, relative to the south direction. For a dish aimed *due south*, the angle can be determined from the diagram below.

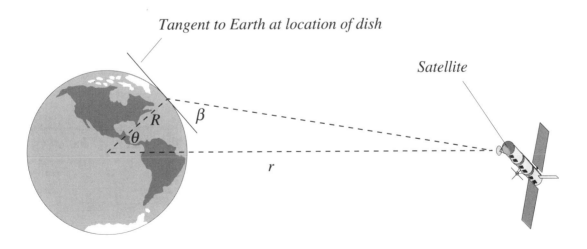

In the diagram, R is the radius of the Earth, r is the distance of the satellite from the center of the Earth, θ is the latitude angle of the satellite dish and β is the angle between the satellite dish and the ground. From the law of sines, it can be shown that,

$$\tan \beta = \frac{\cos\theta - \dfrac{R}{r}}{\sin\theta}$$

This provides the angle β between the aiming direction of the satellite dish and the ground (for a dish aimed due south), and, of course, depends on the latitude angle θ of the dish.

For a satellite dish which is not aimed due south, but must be rotated to the east or west of south, the angle will decrease from the value given by the expression above. For a group of dishes that do not include any aimed close to the east or west directions, the angles between the ground and the dish will visually be very similar.

3.) It takes *more energy* to put up a geosynchronous satellite (2.2 x 10^4 miles above the Earth's surface) than a near Earth satellite (say, 200 miles above the surface). Yet the geosynchronous satellite moves *more slowly* in its orbit. What's going on here?

It seems counterintuitive that providing more energy to something results in its moving more slowly. This is because it is sometimes a natural tendency to think of *kinetic energy* when the word *energy* is used. But, we must be careful to also include *gravitational potential energy* in this situation. We can argue this phenomenon from a conceptual basis as follows. If we raise a satellite to a higher position above the Earth's surface, its gravitational potential energy clearly increases. But, since the gravitational field strength has decreased, the satellite's centripetal acceleration is smaller than at the lower position. Since the centripetal acceleration is proportional to the square of the velocity, then the velocity is smaller than at the lower position.

We can also provide a more mathematical analysis as follows. We assume that the satellite, of mass m, is in a perfectly circular orbit. Starting from Newton's Second Law, letting the force be gravitational and the acceleration be centripetal,

$$F = ma \quad \rightarrow \quad G\frac{M_E m}{r^2} = m\frac{v^2}{r}$$

Now, if we multiply both sides of the equation by the radius of the orbit r, we have:

$$G\frac{M_E m}{r} = mv^2$$

We recognize the left side of the equation as the negative of the gravitational potential energy and the right side as twice the kinetic energy:

$$-PE_G = 2KE$$

Now, we can write this equation for two different satellite heights:

Height 1: $-PE_{G,1} = 2 KE_1$ *Height 2:* $-PE_{G,2} = 2 KE_2$

And, if we subtract the two equations,

$$-(PE_{G,1} - PE_{G,2}) = 2(KE_1 - KE_2)$$

$$\rightarrow \quad -\Delta PE_G = 2 \Delta KE$$

$$\rightarrow \quad \Delta KE = -\frac{1}{2}\Delta PE_G$$

Thus, we see that if there is an *increase* in gravitational potential energy (so that ΔPE_G is positive), there is a corresponding *decrease* in kinetic energy (ΔKE is negative)—the satellite moves more slowly!

4.) As a car moves in a circular path, the occupants feel as if they are pushed to the outside of the circle. Do the astronauts in an orbiting Space Shuttle feel this effect, since they are traveling in a circular path, also?

Let us first compare the typical accelerations experienced by the riders in the automobile and the Shuttle. Imagine an automobile traveling at 10 m·s⁻¹ (36 km·h⁻¹), while negotiating a circular curve of radius 50 m. This would lead to a centripetal acceleration of 2 m·s⁻². In comparison, the astronauts in the orbiting Shuttle will experience a centripetal acceleration that is slightly reduced from the acceleration of gravity at the surface of the Earth, 9.8 m·s⁻². Thus, the acceleration of the astronauts is about 5 times as great as that of the automobile riders. This might lead one to believe that the astronauts would feel the effect of the circular motion more strongly than the automobile riders, but let's analyze this more carefully.

In a turning car, the inertia of the occupants causes them to feel as if they are pushed to the outside of the circular path. An observer hovering above the turning car, however, would simply see the tendency for them to travel in a straight line, as described by Newton's First Law. The force turning the car is the friction force between the tires and the roadway. The occupant does not feel this force, so he or she tends to continue in a straight line motion. The occupant does turn, however; the force turning the occupant is primarily the friction between the occupant and the seat, and the normal force from the door, if contact is made with the door. Thus, the forces turning the car and the occupant are *different*.

The Space Shuttle astronauts *do not feel this effect*. Indeed, they are in a circular path, also, but the result is different. The force causing the Space Shuttle to move in a circular path is gravity. The force causing the Space Shuttle astronauts to move in a circular path *is also gravity*. Thus, the astronaut will not tend to travel in a straight line, since he or she is subject to the same gravitational field as the Shuttle. The Space Shuttle and the astronaut's body are both accelerating toward the Earth at the same rate. Thus, both the Shuttle and the astronaut follow the same circular path around the Earth without the need for any additional contact forces.

5.) When rockets are sent from a parking orbit around the Earth to Mars, they are launched from the *nighttime* side of the Earth. When rockets are sent to Venus, they are launched from the *daytime* side. Why?

Sending spacecraft to other planets is a tricky business. The craft is often placed in a parking orbit around the Earth. Then, when the conditions are correct, the craft is removed from this orbit by a rocket thrust. The intent of this rocket thrust is to place the spacecraft in an elliptical orbit around the Sun that will intersect tangentially with the orbit of the destination planet at just the time when the planet is at the same position as the spacecraft. Thus, these launches can only take place at the correct date (every few months, normally) so that the planet will be in the correct location when the spacecraft arrives. But why does the hour of day of the rocket thrust matter?

In sending a craft to Mars (or any outer planet), the intent is to place the craft in an elliptical orbit that has a major axis *larger* than the major axis of the Earth's orbit (it has to move <u>away from</u> the Sun). This is an orbit of more energy (considering orbits around the *Sun*) than when the craft is orbiting the Sun at the position of the Earth. Thus, the craft must be <u>speeded up</u> in its orbit around the Sun. We can save fuel by firing when the rocket is already moving as quickly as possible, relative to the Sun. The craft is in this position when it is on the *nighttime* side of the Earth, as shown below. In this position, the velocity of the spacecraft relative to the Earth adds to the velocity of the Earth relative to the Sun.

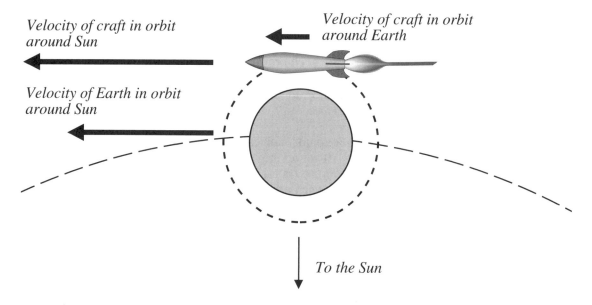

Velocity of craft in orbit around Sun

Velocity of craft in orbit around Earth

Velocity of Earth in orbit around Sun

To the Sun

In sending a craft to Venus (or Mercury), the intent is to place it in an elliptical orbit that has a major axis *smaller* than the major axis of the Earth's orbit (it has to move <u>toward</u> the Sun). This is an orbit of less energy (considering orbits around the *Sun*) than when the craft is orbiting the Sun at the position of the Earth. Thus, the craft must be <u>slowed</u> in its orbit around the Sun. We can save fuel if we fire when the spacecraft is already moving as slowly as possible. This occurs on the *daytime* side of the Earth, as indicated in the diagram on the next page. In this case, the velocity of the spacecraft relative to the Earth *subtracts from* the velocity of the Earth relative to the Sun.

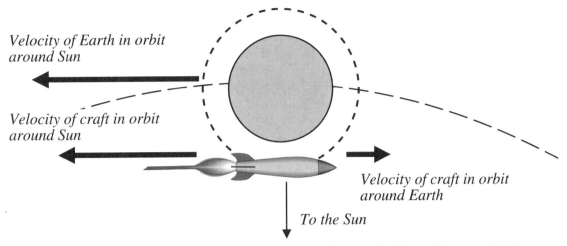

Velocity of Earth in orbit around Sun

Velocity of craft in orbit around Sun

Velocity of craft in orbit around Earth

To the Sun

Thus, we will fire the rockets on different sides of the Earth, depending on whether we want to move *toward* or *away* from the Sun.

6.) In the movie, *2001: A Space Odyssey* (MGM, 1968), gravity is artificially simulated in a spacecraft by rotating the craft around its central axis. An astronaut is shown running around the perimeter of the inside of the spacecraft as a means of exercise. If the rotation of such a craft is assumed to create the same effective gravitational field as on the surface of the Earth, would the astronaut feel *exactly* the same as if he or she were running on Earth?

It is certainly true that artificial gravity can be created by rotating the spacecraft. This effective gravity can be made to be equal to that on Earth, for an astronaut who is stationary with respect to the spacecraft, by adjusting the angular velocity so that the centripetal acceleration is equal to $g_{Earth} = 9.8$ m·s^{-2}. But now imagine that the astronaut is running around the inner circumference of the rotating spacecraft. Let us adjust the situation so that the velocity of the astronaut is equal in magnitude to the tangential velocity of the floor "beneath" him or her and opposite in direction. Thus, relative to the stars, *the astronaut is not in motion* (except for the forward motion of the spacecraft). Thus, the astronaut is at rest while the floor rotates beneath his or her feet. In this case, the artificially induced gravity vanishes and the astronaut runs as if he or she is *weightless*. This will feel quite different than the same running experience on Earth.

We can also imagine what happens as the astronaut turns and runs the other way. In this case, the centripetal acceleration of the astronaut *increases* over that of the spacecraft, and he or she feels heavier and heavier as the running speed increases.

𝕸𝖆𝖌𝖎𝖈:

The Short-Lived Weight Gain

The important point to keep in mind here is that *a bathroom scale does not measure your weight*. In normal use, with the person in equilibrium, it measures how much upward force is necessary to counteract the downward forces imposed by the person standing on the scale. If you are standing perfectly still, then the reading on the scale (the normal force upward from the scale on your body) is equal to your weight. But many of us are familiar with the old hand-on-the-sink technique. If you place your hand on the sink (or any other bathroom fixture) and push downward while weighing yourself, the reading is less, since the scale does not need to push so hard in the upward direction. Thus, the reading on the scale represents the normal force (of the scale on the person) necessary to maintain the equilibrium of the person (in cooperation with the sink or other fixture).

Now, suppose you raise your arms while standing on the scale. This represents an acceleration of your arms in the upward direction. In order for this acceleration to occur, a force must be applied on the arms in the upward direction. The muscles in your body exert this force. By Newton's Third Law, then, your arms exert a downward force on your body. Since your body does not accelerate downward, an additional force in the upward direction must be applied to balance out the downward force of the arms on the body. This force is provided by the increased normal force from the scale. But the reading on the scale is an indication of the normal force, so the reading on the scale goes up. This increase only exists while the arms are accelerating and the reading rapidly returns to the normal weight value after the acceleration vanishes.

The Slowly Falling Weight

The weight and the Slinky will *separate* as they fall. Before release, the Slinky is extended by the force of its own weight. When the system is released, the spring goes into free fall and the effective gravitational field is zero (see Chapter 22 for more discussion of this effect). As a result, the spring force in the Slinky causes the ends to pull in relative to the center of mass. Thus, as the center of mass of the Slinky falls at the acceleration *g*, the upper end is pulled down at a faster rate by the additional spring force. The end of the spring thus falls at a faster acceleration than the weight and the separation occurs.

For more information on falling Slinkies, see M. G. Calkin, "Motion of a Falling Spring", *American Journal of Physics*, **61**, 261, 1993.

Myth:

1.) The gravitational force of the Sun on the Earth is stronger than that of the Moon. Thus, tides due to the Sun are stronger than those due to the Moon.

The gravitational force of the Sun on the Earth is indeed stronger than the gravitational force of the Moon, as can be demonstrated with calculations using Newton's Universal Law of Gravitation. The strength of tides, however, depends on the *gradient* in the gravitational field, not the absolute strength. The variation in the gravitational field strength across the diameter of the Earth is the determining factor. The diameter of the

Earth is a smaller fraction of the Earth-Sun distance than it is of the Earth-Moon distance and this more than compensates for the different magnitudes of the gravitational forces. Thus, despite its weaker force, the Moon has a stronger effect on the tides than the Sun.

It can be shown with a simple calculation (e.g., on page 252 of H. V. Thurman, *Introduction to Oceanography*, 7th ed., Macmillan Publishing Company, New York, 1994) that the tidal effect of the Sun is about 46% of that of the Moon.

2.) Spring tides occur in the Spring.

Spring tides refer to the result of a situation in which the Earth, Moon and the Sun are aligned. Under these conditions, the tidal effects of the Sun and the Moon combine and cause stronger tides than normal. This does not occur only in the Spring, but occurs about twice every month, at the time of the full and new Moons. Conversely, at first quarter and third quarter phases of the Moon, the lines of sight from the Earth to the Moon and Sun are approximately 90° apart, and the effects of the tides are weaker, with lower high tides than normal and higher low tides. These are referred to as *neap tides*.

3.) A weight-conscious astronaut watches his or her weight during long space travel.

If you are on a rocket ship traveling in empty space, then you have no weight, since the gravitational field in your vicinity is essentially zero. Thus, you don't want to watch your *weight*, you want to watch your *mass*!

4.) Mass is independent of what planet you are standing on. Thus, if you take a bathroom scale calibrated in kilograms to Mars, it will read correctly.

Even if a bathroom scale is calibrated in kilograms, it is still a *spring scale*. Spring scales depend on the gravitational attraction of the Earth to provide a reading, by stretching or compressing a spring. As a result, scales measure a force related to the weight, they do not measure mass. Thus, the bathroom scale calibrated in kilograms will give an incorrect reading on Mars. Mass is measured by a *balance*, in which gravitational forces on objects located on either side of a pivot are in equilibrium. Thus, a balance taken to Mars will still provide correct readings of mass.

5.) Because of reduced gravity, you can accelerate faster when you run on the Moon than on the Earth.

This Myth is intimately related to Myth #9 in Chapter 3. In the discussion of that Myth, the point was made that the acceleration of objects in the horizontal direction on a planet is resisted by the mass of the object. Since the mass is unchanged, objects are just as hard to accelerate horizontally as on the Earth. In starting to run from a resting position, the body must be accelerated horizontally. Thus, your mass provides just as much resistance as on the Earth.

In fact, you may actually be able to accelerate only more *slowly*. Since your weight is reduced, the normal force of the ground on your feet will also be reduced. This, in turn, causes the friction force between your feet and the ground to be smaller. With less friction with the ground, you may not be able to accelerate horizontally as rapidly as on the Earth, despite the reduced gravity. You have the same mass to accelerate as you do on the Earth, and *less* force! In fact, your feet may just *slip* on the ground as you try to apply large horizontal forces on the ground in an attempt to accelerate quickly.

6.) The reading on a bathroom scale is less at the equator than at the North Pole. This is due to the difference in the gravitational field between the two locations that is due to the bulge at the equator.

There are actually *two* primary contributions to the difference in scale reading between the pole and the equator. One does indeed involve the difference in distance from the center of the Earth between the two positions due to the equatorial bulge, which leads to a variation in the gravitational field strength. A calculation using Newton's Universal Law of Gravitation shows a difference in gravitational field strength between the two locations of about 0.05 m·s^{-2}, with the field being weaker at the equator.

The second difference occurs because of the rotation of the Earth. This rotation results in a centripetal acceleration of the person standing on the scale. If we analyze this situation with Newton's Second Law applied to the person on the scale, we find,

$$F_{net} = ma \quad \rightarrow \quad N - W = m(-a_c) \quad \rightarrow \quad N = W - ma_c = m(g - a_c)$$

where W is the person's weight, m the person's mass and a_c is the centripetal acceleration of the person due to the rotation of the Earth. We have solved for the normal force N on the person, since that is what the scale actually measures, as discussed in The Short-Lived Weight Gain. The analysis above shows that the normal force is reduced from the actual weight, just as if the gravitational field were reduced, by the centripetal acceleration of the point on the Earth's surface at which the scale is located. There is no centripetal acceleration at the poles, so no correction is necessary there. At the equator, we can calculate the centripetal acceleration by means of the Earth's radius and the length of the day and find that the effective decrease in the gravitational field is about 0.03 m·s^{-2}, which is smaller than, but on the same order as, the size of the variation due to the equatorial bulge.

In total, then, the bathroom scale readings at the North Pole and the equator should reflect a combined actual and apparent variation in the gravitational field of about 0.08 m·s^{-2}, which should result in a difference of a little less than 1% in the readings.

7.) Kepler's Laws are fundamental principles.

A fundamental principle is a statement that cannot be derived from another, more basic statement. This idea was explored in Myth #4 in Chapter 7 of *PBWM*, in which it was shown that the work-energy theorem is not a fundamental principle. Rather, it is a special case of the more basic statement, the *energy continuity equation*. The energy continuity equation is explored further in Chapter 5 of this book. With regard to fundamental principles and the present Myth, let us look at Kepler's Three Laws:

1.) *The planets move in ellipses with the Sun at one focus.*

This can be shown, with Newtonian mechanics, to be a necessary result of the fact that the gravitational force varies as the inverse square of the distance (see an undergraduate mechanics text for a discussion of this). Thus, it is a result of *Newton's Universal Law of Gravitation* and *Newton's Second Law*, and is not a fundamental principle.

2.) *A line from the Sun to a planet sweeps out equal areas in equal times.*

Let us consider the sector defined by this line during a short time interval, as in the diagram below:

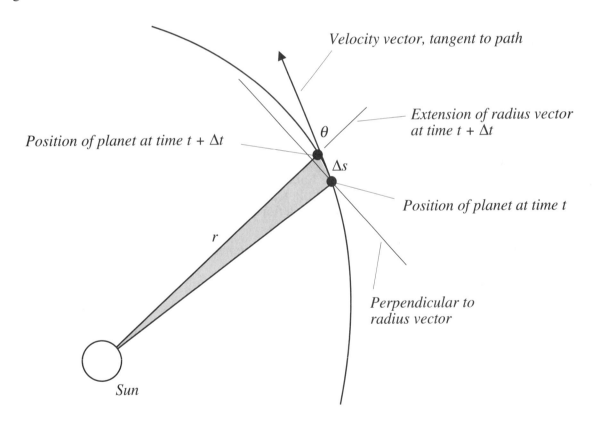

We will imagine a time interval that is very short. In this case, the distances of the planet from the Sun at the beginning and end of the time interval can be approximated as identical and are indicated by *r* in the diagram. In addition, since the movement along the path, Δ*s*, is very short, the sector shaded in the diagram above is almost indistinguishable from a long, skinny triangle. Thus, we can approximate the area of the sector as the area of a triangle with height equal to r and base equal to $\Delta s \sin \theta$:

$$\Delta A = \frac{1}{2}(\text{base})(\text{height}) = \frac{1}{2}(\Delta s \sin \theta)(r) = \frac{1}{2}r\Delta s \sin \theta$$

Now, we divide the equation by the time interval during which the motion occurred:

$$\frac{\Delta A}{\Delta t} = \frac{1}{2}\frac{r\Delta s \sin \theta}{\Delta t} = \frac{1}{2}r\frac{\Delta s}{\Delta t}\sin \theta = \frac{1}{2}rv\sin \theta$$

where we have recognized that the distance Δs divided by the time interval Δt is simply the tangential velocity of the planet in its orbit, v. Now we remember a relation from our studies of angular momentum for a central force. For a particle moving in a circular path, or for a particle moving in any path during a very short time interval in which the distance from a reference point, r, doesn't change, the angular momentum, **L**, can be expressed as a cross product:

$$|\mathbf{L}| = |\mathbf{r} \times \mathbf{p}| \quad \rightarrow \quad L = mrv \sin \theta$$

where θ is the angle between **r** and **p**, and is the angle indicated as θ in the diagram. Comparing the two expressions above, we can see that the rate at which area is swept out by the line from the Sun to the planet can be written,

$$\frac{\Delta A}{\Delta t} = \frac{L}{2m}$$

On the right hand side of this equation, we have the mass of the planet, which is certainly constant, and the angular momentum, which must be constant since there are no torques acting on the planet around the Sun. Thus, the fact that the rate at which area is swept out by a line from the Sun to the planet is constant is simply a statement of *conservation of angular momentum*, and is not a fundamental principle.

3.) *The square of the period of a planet is proportional to the cube of its semimajor axis.*

We will derive this for a circular orbit. With more work, it can also be shown to be true for an elliptical orbit. For a circular orbit, we can write Newton's Second Law, with the force being gravitational and the acceleration being centripetal:

$$F = ma \quad \rightarrow \quad G\frac{M_s m_p}{r^2} = m_p \frac{v^2}{r} = m_p \frac{1}{r}\left(\frac{2\pi r}{T}\right)^2$$

where M_S is the mass of the Sun, m_p is the mass of the planet, and T is the period of the planet in its orbit about the Sun. If we clean this up, we find,

$$T^2 = \frac{4\pi^2}{GM_S}r^3$$

which is the relation indicated in the Third Law. Thus, Kepler's Third Law is a result of *Newton's Universal Law of Gravitation* and *Newton's Second Law* and is not a fundamental principle!

8.) You are in an orbiting spacecraft, trying to catch up with a satellite far ahead of you. You fire your rockets in a direction away from the satellite in order to catch up to it.

Let's see what happens in this case. If you fire your rockets as indicated, you will *increase* your orbital mechanical energy (the exhaust gases will do positive work on the rocket). As a result, you will rise into a higher orbit (relative to the surface of the Earth). But, in this higher orbit, you actually travel more *slowly* (See Mystery #3). Thus, the satellite will move even farther ahead of you, even though you fired your rockets in what was intuitively the correct direction! In order to catch up to the satellite, you need to do the non-intuitive action. You fire rockets *in the direction of the satellite*, which will reduce your orbital mechanical energy (the exhaust gases will do negative work on the rocket). You will then drop into a lower orbit, with higher speed, which will allow you to catch up to the satellite.

One further correction is necessary in this process. You will catch up to the satellite in an *angular* sense by firing in the non-intuitive direction, but you will be in a lower orbit *radially*. Thus, you will have to wait until you are a bit ahead of the satellite in your orbit, and then fire your rockets in the opposite direction to your velocity in order to move back up into the higher orbit and a rendezvous with the satellite.

For very short distances, such as that between an orbiting Shuttle and astronauts performing a spacewalk, these considerations are not large enough to be of consequence.

9.) An advertisement for the Steel Recycling Institute (Pittsburgh, Pennsylvania) appeared in a science teachers' journal (*The Science Teacher*, 61(3), 1, 1994). It asked the following question: "Did you know that over the last ten years, the amount of steel recycled weighs about the same as six billion science teachers stacked vertically?"

The first question which comes to mind after reading this question might be, "Why does the Institute want to *stack* the science teachers?" Does this make the comparison any clearer? The next question might be, "Does the Institute realize that six billion stacked science teachers will reach far out into space, so that *the gravitational field will decrease* as one goes higher in the stack?"

Let us first estimate the height of the stack of science teachers. We assume that science teachers are of the same average height as the rest of the population. Let us estimate the height of a male science teacher as 1.8 m and that of a female science teacher as 1.6 m. We will also make the assumption that the science teachers in the stack are half male and half female. Thus, the height of the stack will be,

h = (3 x 10^9 male teachers)(1.8 m) + (3 x 10^9 female teachers)(1.6 m)
     = 1.0 x 10^{10} m

This is close to 7% of the distance from the Earth to the Sun and is almost 1600 times the radius of the Earth. At this distance from the Earth, the gravitational field, as can be calculated from Newton's Universal Law of Gravitation, is only about 0.00004% as strong as on the surface of the Earth. Thus, the six billionth science teacher, at the top of the stack, will only weigh about 0.00004% as much as he or she would on the surface.

We assume an average mass of 80 kg for the male teachers and 50 kg for the female teachers. For simplicity, we will also assume that the science teachers are stacked in a male-female alternating pattern. The total mass of the stack is,

$$m = (3 \times 10^9 \text{ male teachers})(80 \text{ kg}) + (3 \times 10^9 \text{ female teachers})(50 \text{ kg})$$
$$= 3.9 \times 10^{11} \text{ kg}$$

The weight of these science teachers, *if all were simply standing on the surface of the Earth*, would be,

$$W_{surface} = mg = (3.9 \times 10^{11} \text{ kg})(9.8 \text{ m·s}^{-2}) = 3.8 \times 10^{12} \text{ N}$$

We could now estimate, using calculus*, the total weight of the *stacked* science teachers, taking the variation in the gravitational field into account. This calculation gives us,

$$W_{stacked} = 2.4 \times 10^9 \text{ N}$$

which differs from the weight on the surface *by a factor of over 1500*. It is interesting to note that adding more teachers does not significantly alter the weight calculated above—each new teacher has virtually no weight, due to the very low value of *g* at the top of the stack!

Now, the final calculation is to compare this to the actual amount of steel recycled in the ten year period indicated in the advertisement. Consultation with the Steel Recycling Institute resulted in a steel recycling figure of *55 million tons per year* for the ten year period. Thus, the total weight of steel recycled in the ten year period is,

$$W_{steel} = (55 \times 10^6 \text{ ton·y}^{-1})(10 \text{ y})(2000 \text{ lb·ton}^{-1})(4.448 \text{ N·lb}^{-1}) = 4.9 \times 10^{12} \text{ N}$$

This number is on the order of the weight of the teachers *standing on the surface of the Earth* calculated above, and is over *2000 times as large* as our estimated weight of the stacked teachers. This would indicate that the Institute *did not* take into account the variation of the gravitational field over the height of the stack of science teachers. It is not clear why the concept of stacking is used in this advertisement.

---

*The stacked weight can be shown to be equal to

$$W_{stacked} = g_{surface} \lambda \left(R_E - \frac{R_E^2}{R_{top}} \right)$$

where $g_{surface}$ is the gravitational field at the surface of the Earth, R_E is the radius of the Earth, λ is the linear mass density (130 kg for each 3.4 m of height) and R_{top} is the distance between the center of the Earth and the top of the stack.

Chapter 5
Energy

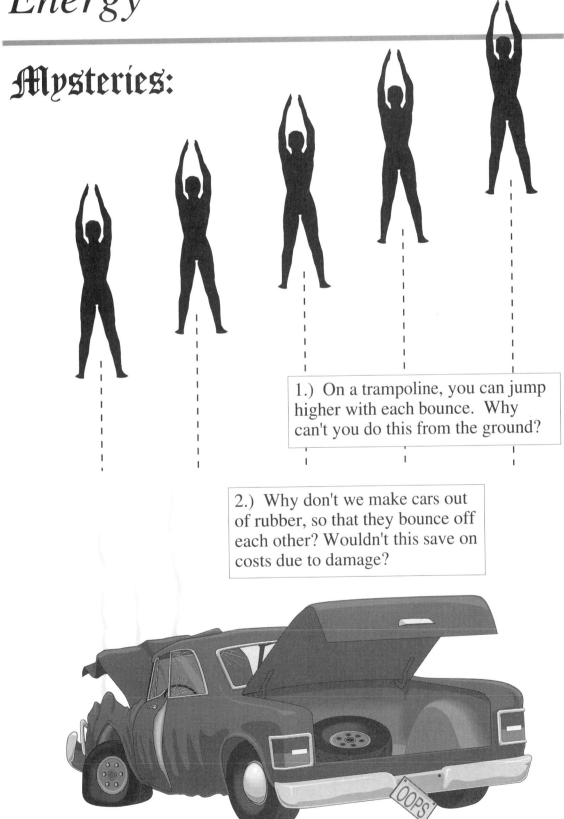

Mysteries:

1.) On a trampoline, you can jump higher with each bounce. Why can't you do this from the ground?

2.) Why don't we make cars out of rubber, so that they bounce off each other? Wouldn't this save on costs due to damage?

OOPS

𝕸𝖞𝖘𝖙𝖊𝖗𝖎𝖊𝖘:

3.) Crouch down and jump up off the ground. The force of the ground on your feet moves through no distance, so no work is done. Yet your body has kinetic energy as it leaves the ground. Is the work-energy theorem violated here?

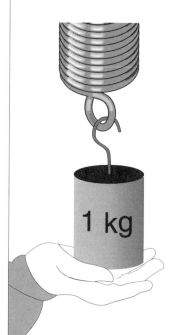

4.) Attach a mass to a vertical spring. Slowly lower the mass a distance x, to the point at which the mass hangs at rest on the spring. The change in gravitational potential energy (of the Earth-mass-spring system) during the process is,

$$\Delta PE_{grav} = -mgx$$

The change in spring potential energy is,

$$\Delta PE_{spring} = \frac{1}{2}kx^2$$

But, since the mass is now hanging in equilibrium, Hooke's Law tells us,

$$F \text{ (on spring)} = mg = kx$$

Therefore, substituting mg for kx in the previous expression,

$$\Delta PE_{spring} = \frac{1}{2}mgx$$

Thus, the overall change in energy for the system is,

$$\Delta E = \Delta PE_{grav} + \Delta PE_{spring} = -\frac{1}{2}mgx$$

which is *not zero*. Where did the energy go?

𝕸𝖆𝖌𝖎𝖈:

The Nutty Way to Boil Water

Hold a nut (walnut or pecan) on a needle, tweezers, tongs, or other means of support. Mount the needle or tweezers in a fixed support such as a clamp. Light the nut with a match. Hold a metal container with a small amount of water over the burning nut. You can boil the water with energy from the nut!

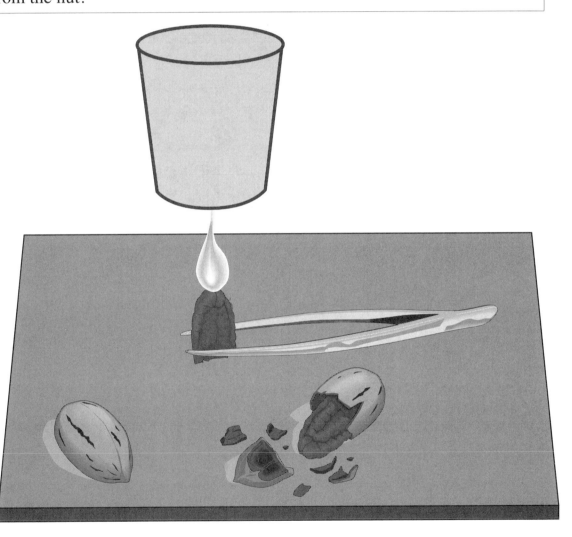

Myth:

1.) Energy is the capacity to do work.

50   **100**

MMM 817

2.) If you double your driving speed, it will take twice the distance to stop.

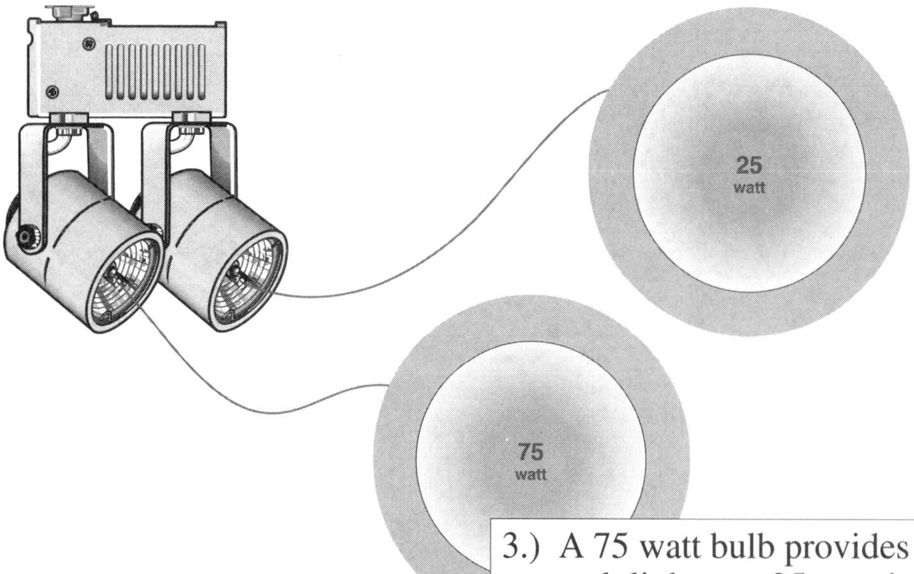

25 watt

75 watt

3.) A 75 watt bulb provides three times as much light as a 25 watt bulb.

𝕸𝖞𝖙𝖍:

4.) In *Bicycling Science* (F. R. Whitt and D. G. Wilson, The MIT Press, Cambridge, Massachusetts, 1974), there is a discussion of a bicycle riding over a rough road so that the wheel loses contact periodically with the road. When the wheel regains contact with the road, "the kinetic energy perpendicular to the surface at the point of contact can be considered to be lost".

5.) The information shown appeared in a Southern California newspaper three days after the Northridge earthquake.

Earthquakes release energy that scientists measure in metric units called ergs. One erg is the amount of energy it takes to move one gram of mass one centimeter in one second. Some examples of an earthquake's energy force:

Magnitude	Energy released (in millions of ergs)
9	20,000,000,000,000,000,000
8	600,000,000,000,000,000
7	20,000,000,000,000,000
6	600,000,000,000,000
5	20,000,000,000,000
4	600,000,000,000
3	20,000,000,000

Discussions; Chapter 5—Energy

𝕸𝖞𝖘𝖙𝖊𝖗𝖎𝖊𝖘:

1.) On a trampoline, you can jump higher with each bounce. Why can't you do this from the ground?

Let us consider the situation of jumping from the ground first. In this process, chemical potential energy in the body is transformed into kinetic energy and gravitational potential energy during the jump (see Mystery #3 for a deeper discussion of this). Now, what happens when the jumper hits the ground? Upon impact, some energy is carried away by sound through the air and through the ground, and a large amount is transformed into internal energy due to the "braking" action of the leg muscles (so that the body doesn't just collapse into a pile!). By the time that the jumper is ready for the next "bounce", he or she is right back at the initial condition—crouched on the ground with no "mechanical" energy (kinetic or potential). Thus, over a series of bounces, most of the chemical potential energy from the body is simply transformed into internal energy in the body (with some carried away by sound or convection/conduction transfers to the environment). The height of the bouncing remains constant since there is no means of storing the energy between bounces in a way that it can be returned as gravitational potential energy.

Now, consider the trampoline. When the body lands back on the trampoline mat after the first bounce, it does not have to stop as it does when jumping on the ground. The body can continue to move through the original height to a lower height. While this represents some decrease in gravitational potential energy, there is potential energy being stored in the springs of the trampoline. This stored energy can be released from the springs as the jumper begins to move upward, and *added to further energy* transformed from chemical potential energy as the jumper pushes off again. Thus, the height of the bounce will continue to increase. There is a limit to the maximum height, which will depend on several factors. These include the elastic limit of the springs and frictional transfers in the structure of the trampoline. The height is also limited by the fact that chemical potential energy is being transformed to internal energy in the body, since the feet are initially moving faster than the trampoline mat when the jumper lands, but the velocities must match after a short time. This requires bending of the legs and transformation of energy to internal energy by the "braking" action of the legs mentioned above, although not as severely as in the case of jumping onto the ground.

2.) Why don't we make cars out of rubber, so that they bounce off each other? Wouldn't this save on costs due to damage?

It probably *would* save money on insurance coverage for damage to automobiles if they were constructed of rubber. But there is a higher consideration than the damage to the automobile—the damage to the *driver*. Let us imagine that the rubber out of which an automobile is constructed is perfectly elastic—no kinetic energy is transformed during a collision. Let us also assume that the two cars are heading toward each other with the same speed and have the same mass. Then, during the time of contact (which would be very short for perfectly elastic rubber) between the two cars, the velocity of each car simply reverses direction. If we imagine that the driver is unsecured in the car, then, by Newton's First Law (ignoring the small friction force between the driver and the seat), he or she will continue forward with the original velocity, while the car is now moving backwards with the same magnitude of velocity. The resulting collision between the driver and dashboard will be disastrous. If the driver were wearing a seat belt, the very large force from the belt necessary to rapidly reverse the velocity of the driver would cause severe injury.

We can address this mathematically by considering the general form of Newton's Second Law:

$$\overline{\mathbf{F}} = \frac{\Delta \mathbf{p}}{\Delta t}$$

Considering the average force on the left of this equation to be that on the driver due to the seat belt, we see that the driver suffers a large change in momentum $\Delta \mathbf{p}$ in the rubber car collision. In addition, the change occurs in a very short time Δt. The large numerator and the small denominator both contribute to a very large force on the driver from the equation above.

Let us compare this to the actual situation of cars manufactured from metal. When the identical metal cars with identical speeds make a head-on collision, the metal construction of the cars is designed to crumple in an *inelastic* way. This has two major benefits to the drivers:

1.) The final velocity of the car is *zero*, rather than the backward velocity of the rubber car. Thus, the change in momentum is only half as much.

2.) The crumpling takes place over a rather long distance—a significant fraction of the length of the hood of the car. This transforms the kinetic energy of the car relatively slowly into internal energy, with some being transferred by sound and mass transfer (flying bits of metal and glass). Thus, the seat belt, with possibly some assistance from an air bag, can bring the driver to rest in a time interval that is non-fatal and, hopefully, non-injurious.

Thus, for the metal car, the change in momentum $\Delta \mathbf{p}$ is smaller and the time Δt for the momentum to change is longer than for the rubber car. As can be seen from the general form of Newton's Second Law above, both of these effects act to reduce the forces on the driver and decrease the probability of injury.

3.) Crouch down and jump up off the ground. The force of the ground on your feet moves through no distance, so no work is done. Yet your body has kinetic energy as it leaves the ground. Is the work-energy theorem violated here?

This is a point which is rarely addressed in physics textbooks, and it does seem to cut deeply into the common interpretation of the work-energy theorem. It is certainly true that no work is done by the normal force of the ground, since the point of application of the force remains fixed in space. What's even worse, consider this—the only external work done on the body is that done by the gravitational force. But since this force is opposite to the direction of motion as you spring upward, this force does *negative* work! How can negative work result in an increase in kinetic energy?

The reason that the work-energy theorem is in trouble here is that we are dealing with a *deformable* system—the jumper changes shape. The normal situation studied in introductory physics is that of work done on a particle or a rigid object, such as a box being pushed across a floor. In this situation, the source of a force causing an object to move must necessarily move along with the object, in order to maintain the force. Thus, the force moves with the object and the work can be calculated. The jumper problem is one in which, due to the change of shape of the system, the center of mass of the system moves while the point of application of the force remains stationary.

Let us address this in terms of the *energy continuity equation*, as developed in Chapter 7 of *PBWM*. This equation is reproduced below, with a list of the interpretation of each of the terms in the equation:

$$\Delta KE + \Delta PE + \Delta U = W + Q + E_{MT} + E_S + E_{ER} + E_{ET}$$

where

ΔKE = change in kinetic energy (of or around the center of mass of the system)
ΔPE = change in potential energy within the system (gravitational, spring, electromagnetic, nuclear)
ΔU = change in internal energy within the system

and

W = work (done across the boundary of the system)
Q = heat (passed across the boundary of the system)
E_{MT} = energy transferred by mass transfer (across the boundary of the system)
E_S = energy transferred by sound (across the boundary of the system)
E_{ER} = energy transferred by electromagnetic radiation (across the boundary of the system)
E_{ET} = energy transferred by electrical transmission (across the boundary of the system)

The first task in applying this equation is to define the system. Since we will be dealing with gravitational potential energy, we need to include both the earth and the jumping person as our system. Now, with this system, we realize that there will be no transfers of energy across the boundary—all transfers and transformations are internal to the system. If the system starts from rest and ends up with the person's center of mass moving at v_{cm} and at a height h_{cm} above its initial position, then we have three energy storage changes: an increase in kinetic energy of the center of mass of the jumper, an increase in gravitational potential energy of the system and a decrease in chemical (electromagnetic) potential energy in the body of the jumper (we will ignore any rotational kinetic energy of moving arms or legs, increase in temperature of the body of the jumper and any heat transfers to the environment). Thus, we have:

$$\Delta KE + \Delta PE + \Delta U = W + Q + E_{MT} + E_S + E_{ER} + E_{ET}$$

where we have used the same technique as that used in *PBWM*—dimmed terms in the equation are those that do not participate in the particular situation being investigated. Identifying the two types of potential energy in this situation gives us,

$$\Delta KE + \Delta PE_{grav} + \Delta PE_{chem} = 0$$

$$\rightarrow \quad \left(\frac{1}{2}mv_{cm}^2 - 0\right) + \left(mgh_{cm} - 0\right) + \Delta PE_{chem} = 0$$

$$\rightarrow \quad \Delta PE_{chem} = -\left(\frac{1}{2}mv_{cm}^2 + mgh_{cm}\right)$$

and the result tells us that the decrease in chemical potential energy in the body numerically equals the increase in kinetic and gravitational potential energies of the system.

Thus, we have analyzed this process from the continuity equation and have run into no trouble like that which we run into if we try to apply the work-energy theorem. There are other examples which can be used to solidify this idea. A person standing on a skateboard and pushing off a wall is very similar—the force from the wall moves through no distance, but there is a change in kinetic energy.

For more information on approaches to work and energy, see A. J. Mallinckrodt and H. S. Leff, "All About Work", *American Journal of Physics*, **60**, 356, 1992.

4.) Attach a mass to a vertical spring. Slowly lower the mass a distance x, to the point at which the mass hangs at rest on the spring. The change in gravitational potential energy (of the Earth-mass-spring system) during the process is,

$$\Delta PE_{grav} = -mgx$$

The change in spring potential energy is,

$$\Delta PE_{spring} = \frac{1}{2}kx^2$$

But, since the mass is now hanging in equilibrium, Hooke's Law tells us,

$$F \text{ (on spring)} = mg = kx$$

Therefore, substituting mg for kx in the previous expression,

$$\Delta PE_{spring} = \frac{1}{2}mgx$$

Thus, the overall change in energy for the system is,

$$\Delta E = \Delta PE_{grav} + \Delta PE_{spring} = -\frac{1}{2}mgx$$

which is *not zero*. Where did the energy go?

Although it appears that some energy is "lost" here, that is not the case. The apparent violation of conservation of energy is due to the fact that we *lowered* the mass with our hand. Imagine if we had simply *released* the mass once it was attached to the spring. In this case, when the mass has fallen through a vertical height x, it will have a non-zero velocity, which is very different than in the case where it was simply lowered to this position.

In the case in which the mass is lowered, the person's hand is an influence from outside the system of the Earth, mass and spring. Thus, *we have a transfer across the boundary of the system*. The transfer mechanism is work done by the hand. Let us write the energy continuity equation (see Mystery #3) for this situation:

$$\Delta KE + \Delta PE + \Delta U = W + Q + E_{MT} + E_S + E_{ER} + E_{ET}$$

leading to,

$$\Delta PE_{grav} + \Delta PE_{spring} = W$$

$$\rightarrow \quad -mgx + \frac{1}{2}kx^2 = W \quad \rightarrow \quad W = -mgx + \frac{1}{2}(mg)x = -\frac{1}{2}mgx$$

This is equal to the supposed "loss" of energy indicated in the Mystery. Thus, the "missing" energy in this situation is represented by a transfer of energy out of the system by work!

We can understand this transfer by considering the work as defined by the product of force and displacement. The hand lowering the mass has to apply an upward force on the mass in order to let it descend slowly. This force varies linearly from just a little less than the weight of the object at the highest point in the motion to zero at the lowest point, since the spring will exert a linearly increasing upward force on the mass as it descends. Since the force varies linearly, the average force over the displacement will be,

$$\overline{F} = \frac{1}{2}mg$$

Now, in general, work done can be expressed as,

$$W = \overline{F}\Delta x \cos\theta$$

where θ is the angle between the force and the displacement. Thus, the work done by the hand in this situation is,

$$W_{hand} = \overline{F}_{hand}\Delta x \cos\theta = \left(\frac{1}{2}mg\right)(x)(-1) = -\frac{1}{2}mgx$$

which, again, is just the "missing" energy that we calculated in the more naive approach.

For some energy considerations in another kind of spring, see P. G. Menz, "The Physics of Bungee Jumping", *The Physics Teacher*, **31**, 483, 1993.

𝔐𝔞𝔤𝔦𝔠:

The Nutty Way to Boil Water

This demonstration exhibits the potential energy transfer from food in a dramatic way. Burning is a combustion process which results in chemical reactions, converting chemical (electromagnetic) potential energy into internal energy. The energy is carried away from the system of the nut by mass transfer (convection) and passes through the metal cup by heat (conduction). The energy is then stored in the water as internal energy, resulting in a temperature increase in the water.

The spirit of another Magic demonstration, from *PBWM*, Boiling Water in a Paper Cup, can be incorporated into this activity by replacing the metal cup with a paper cup.

𝔐𝔶𝔱𝔥:

1.) Energy is the capacity to do work.

This statement is often given as a "definition" of energy. It is a little misleading, however, especially if we consider *internal energy*. The Second Law of Thermodynamics states that it is impossible for a heat engine to completely convert internal energy to "useful" energy by doing work on, for example, a rotating shaft attached to the engine. Thus, *not all of the internal energy has the capacity to do work.* Does that mean that not all of the internal energy is energy? Of course not. This "definition" of energy suffers from the misdirected efforts to define energy in the first place. If we can accept that we cannot define energy any more than we can define mass, time, space, electric charge (Mystery #1, Chapter 1) or money (Chapter 7, *PBWM*), then we will not be tempted to make up definitions like this that cause us to run into inconsistencies.

2.) If you double your driving speed, it will take twice the distance to stop.

This is incorrect due to the fact that the kinetic energy varies as the *square* of the velocity. Thus, doubling the velocity will increase the kinetic energy by a factor of four and will result in the requirement of four times as much work to be done in stopping the car. When the brakes are applied lightly, kinetic energy is transformed to internal energy by means of the work done by the friction force between the brake pads and the brake drum or disk. If the car skids, the transformation occurs due to the work done by the friction between the tires and the road. Let us consider the case of a panic stop, in which the car skids. If we assume that the friction force is constant and has the same value regardless of the velocity, then the friction force must be applied over 4 times the distance to bring the car to rest from the doubled velocity.

We can test this behavior by using data provided by the Department of Motor Vehicles. The velocities (in miles per hour) and stopping distances (in feet) for a typical automobile were listed in Myth #2, Chapter 2, in *PBWM* and are reproduced in the first two columns in the table below. The right hand column shows the result of dividing the stopping distance by the square of the velocity (in feet divided by $mi^2 \cdot h^{-2}$; this ratio has little meaning except for our interest in seeing if it changes with velocity!). The constancy of these values indicates the dependence of the stopping distance on the *square* of the velocity for the DMV data.

Speed, v $(mi \cdot h^{-1})$	Stopping Distance, d (ft)	Ratio, d/v^2 $(ft \cdot mi^{-2} \cdot h^2)$
25	34.7	0.056
35	68	0.056
45	112.5	0.056
55	168	0.056
65	234.7	0.056

3.) A 75 watt bulb provides three times as much light as a 25 watt bulb.

The "wattage" rating on a light bulb indicates the approximate value of the *electrical input power*, not the *output power of electromagnetic radiation*. The light bulb package often contains another power rating beside the "wattage". This rating is an approximation of the output power for light and is measured in *lumens*. The lumen is a unit of *luminous flux*, which represents the power radiated in the visible part of the spectrum, with adjustments made for the efficiency of the eye. A typical set of data, available on the bulb package, for two light bulbs is as follows: 25 watt, 190 lumens; 75 watts, 1170 lumens. Thus, notice that the input (electrical) powers are related by a factor of 3, while the output (light) powers are related by a factor of *6.2*.

An attempt to reproduce this result theoretically can quickly become complicated, since it involves a difference in temperature between the filaments of the two bulbs, which leads to changes in both the total power output and the wavelength distribution for a nonideal radiator (see Chapter 17). For more information and further discussion, see H. S. Leff, "Illuminating Physics with Light Bulbs", *The Physics Teacher*, **28**, 30, 1990. For an activity in which the power output of the Sun is measured by comparing the Sun to a light bulb, see K. J. Adney, "If the Sun Were a Light Bulb", *The Physics Teacher*, **29**, 96, 1991. For a confusing light bulb package, see J. Hall, *The Physics Teacher*, **30**, 367, 1992.

4.) In *Bicycling Science* (F. R. Whitt and D. G. Wilson, The MIT Press, Cambridge, Massachusetts, 1974), there is a discussion of a bicycle riding over a rough road so that the wheel loses contact periodically with the road. When the wheel regains contact with the road, "the kinetic energy perpendicular to the surface at the point of contact can be considered to be lost".

The phrase "kinetic energy perpendicular to the surface" suggests that kinetic energy is considered to be a *vector*, which is incorrect. All forms of energy storage and transfer are scalars. The phrase in the Mystery is exacerbated by an accompanying drawing in the cited reference, showing the trajectory of a bicycle wheel as it bounces off a bump in the road and moves through the air. At several points on the trajectory are drawn "kinetic energy vectors", complete with components parallel and perpendicular to the road surface!

5.) The information shown appeared in a Southern California newspaper three days after the Northridge earthquake.

Earthquakes release energy that scientists measure in metric units called ergs. One erg is the amount of energy it takes to move one gram of mass one centimeter in one second. Some examples of an earthquake's energy force:

Magnitude	Energy released
	(in millions of ergs)
9	20,000,000,000,000,000,000
8	600,000,000,000,000,000
7	20,000,000,000,000,000
6	600,000,000,000,000
5	20,000,000,000,000
4	600,000,000,000
3	20,000,000,000

There are a number of problems within this information. Some are relatively minor, such as the very large number of significant zeroes indicated, which are not supported by the calculations performed using the expressions given in Myth #4 of Chapter 17 in *PBWM*. The phrase "energy force" at the end of the text at the top is meaningless, and the unit *erg* is falling into disuse as more scientists communicate solely in SI units. The major problem, however, is in trying to assign some meaning to the definition of the erg given: *the amount of energy it takes to move one gram of mass one centimeter in one second.* It is not clear what this means. We can make some assumptions as to what might be going on with this one gram object:

- *The object is moving with constant speed (1 cm·s^{-1}) through empty space*; in this case, according to Newton's First Law, it would continue to do so with no required transfer of energy. This can't be it.

- *The object is moved vertically upward through one centimeter in one second in the gravitational field of the Earth*; in this case, the time of one second has no bearing on the energy calculation. Calculating the change in potential energy, this assumption results in an energy change of 980 ergs, not 1 erg. This can't be it.

- *The object is accelerated in empty space from rest to a speed of 1 cm·s^{-1}*; in this case, the calculation of the kinetic energy at the time of 1 second gives us 0.5 ergs, not 1 erg. This can't be it.

- *The object is accelerated in empty space from rest for one second so that it moves a distance of 1 centimeter in that time*; let us assume that the acceleration is constant. The average velocity must be 1 cm·s^{-1}, and, if the acceleration is constant, then the final velocity after 1 second is 2 cm·s^{-1}. Then, the kinetic energy of the particle at the 1 second time is 2 ergs, not 1 erg. This can't be it.

- *The object is accelerated in empty space from rest to a speed of 1.414 cm·s^{-1} in one second*; this is a forced effort to demand that the kinetic energy be 1 erg at the end of one second, which it would be with the indicated motion. It suffers from two defects, however, in attempting to match the given definition: 1.) The number 1.414 (the square root of 2) doesn't appear in the definition; and 2.) The one second time interval is not unique; for example, the acceleration could be increased so that the speed of 1.414 cm·s^{-1} is attained at the one half second mark and then the force could be removed, so that the object simply coasts during the last half second. At one second, the velocity is still 1.414 cm·s^{-1} and the energy is once again 1 erg, but the motion was very different than that in the first assumption.

There does not seem to be a reasonable way to make this definition correct. It is unfortunate that this kind of misguided information is published in a large circulation newspaper, but it does provide a potentially useful exercise for those studying physics. The search for a possible motion that would match this definition, such as that above, can lead to further enhanced understanding of the physics of motion.

A more reasonable definition of an erg is the work done by a force of one dyne moving through a parallel displacement of one centimeter (or the kinetic energy gained by an object on which the one dyne force is the *only* force). Notice that this definition is *independent* of the mass of any object on which the force acts, or the time during which it acts. Both the mass and the time were included in the incorrect definition in the Myth.

Chapter 6
Momentum

Mysteries:

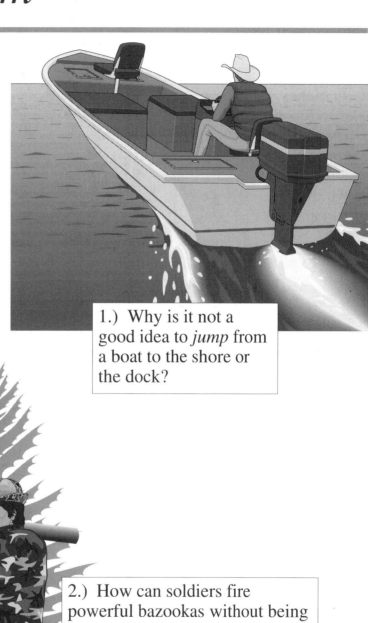

1.) Why is it not a good idea to *jump* from a boat to the shore or the dock?

2.) How can soldiers fire powerful bazookas without being knocked over by the recoil?

Mysteries:

3.) During the California Gold Rush, a man named Lester Pelton made more money than the prospectors by designing a new water wheel that had *scoop-shaped* paddles. Why was this new design so advantageous?

4.) When a jet airplane lands, you hear the roar of the engine increase. Why would the pilot <u>rev up</u> the engine if he/she wants to <u>stop</u>?

𝔐𝔞𝔤𝔦𝔠:

The Happy and Sad Block-Knockers

A common piece of demonstration apparatus for a physics teacher these days is a set of *happy and sad balls*. These are seemingly identical black balls which have very different bouncing characteristics. One ball (the happy ball) bounces nicely when dropped, while the sad ball hits the table and makes little, if any, bounce. Tie one of each of the balls to a string to make two pendula and let them swing down from the horizontal and hit identical short pieces of 2x4 building stud standing on end. Which ball is more effective at knocking the block over?

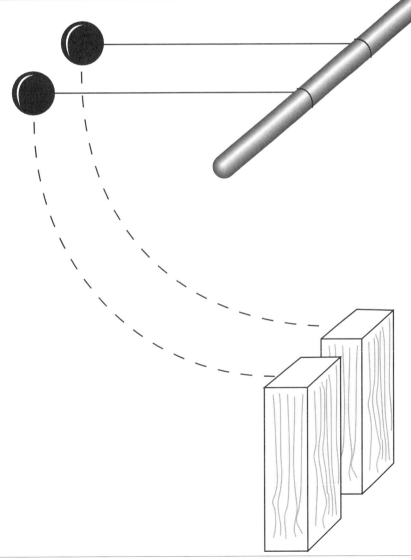

𝔐𝔞𝔤𝔦𝔠:

The Falling Pencil

Place a sharpened pencil so that it is standing on its tip on a piece of glass. Let the pencil go and watch the tip carefully as the pencil falls. As the pencil nears the table, the tip will slide in the direction *opposite* to that in which the body of the pencil is moving. Now, repeat the activity with the pencil standing on a piece of paper or sandpaper. As the pencil falls, the tip will stay fixed. As the pencil nears the table, the tip will not slip in the opposite direction and may even jump in the *same direction* as that in which the body of the pencil is moving. Why does this happen?

Stabbing the Eggshell

Place half an eggshell over the tip of a vertically held, pointed knife. Hold the handle firmly and tap it on the table. The knife should not pierce the eggshell. Now, with the eggshell still on the tip, hold the handle loosely and let the handle *fall* to the table. The knife should pierce the eggshell. Why is the result different in these two cases?

𝔐𝔶𝔱𝔥:

1.) A startling headline in the *Los Angeles Times* reads:

Momentum Only Lasts Three Minutes

2.) In a firing squad, only one gun has a real bullet. Thus, none of the firers knows who shoots the actual bullet.

3.) A human being first performed a long jump over 29 feet in 1968.

Discussions; Chapter 6—Momentum

𝕸𝖞𝖘𝖙𝖊𝖗𝖎𝖊𝖘:

1.) Why is it not a good idea to *jump* from a boat to the shore or the dock?

This is not a good idea for a combination of two reasons—lack of friction and conservation of momentum. When the occupant of a boat leaps forward off the boat, he or she estimates the landing point, based on years of experience in jumping from one point on solid ground to another point. This common experience, based on the enormous mass of the Earth and the large friction force between the shoe and the ground, teaches us that jumping is an activity in which we are propelled forward with nothing moving backward measurably. Of course, the force of the foot pushing off has a Third Law reaction force—the foot pushes backward on the Earth. When jumping from the ground, this has no *measurable* effect on the Earth due to its large mass. When jumping from the boat, however, the relatively small mass of the boat and the low friction between the boat and the water results in the boat moving backward in response. This is simply the law of conservation of momentum—if the jumper moves forward, the boat moves backward. Since the boat moves backward during the process of pushing off, the forward velocity of the jumper is significantly less than when jumping from solid ground, so that the jumper falls short of the intended target, often resulting in falling into the water!

2.) How can soldiers fire powerful bazookas without being knocked over by the recoil?

A bazooka differs from a common rifle in that the back end of the tube is *open*. The firing of an ordinary rifle depends on the pressure of gases enclosed in a barrel applying a force on the bullet. The bazooka, however, is a *rocket launcher*. The acceleration of the shell is due to gases being expelled from the back of the rocket. Thus, the rocket is accelerated by conservation of momentum, just like a rocket used for space travel. When the bazooka is fired, the expelled gases can simply escape out of the back. There is very little recoil of the tube of the bazooka, since the gases do not apply a significant force (parallel to the tube) on the tube.

3.) During the California Gold Rush, a man named Lester Pelton made more money than the prospectors by designing a new water wheel that had *scoop-shaped* paddles. Why was this new design so advantageous?

Before the new design, water wheels used in gold mining had flat paddles, so that water hit the paddle and (approximately) stopped, transferring the momentum of the water to the paddle. Pelton's contribution was to design a scoop-shaped paddle, such that the water would enter one side of the paddle and be forced in the opposite direction by the curvature of the paddle. Since the final momentum of the water is in the opposite direction from its original momentum, the net transfer of momentum is more than with the flat paddle. In effect, the water "bounces" off the Pelton paddle, resulting in a larger transfer of momentum. The diagram below shows this effect. On the left, water strikes a flat

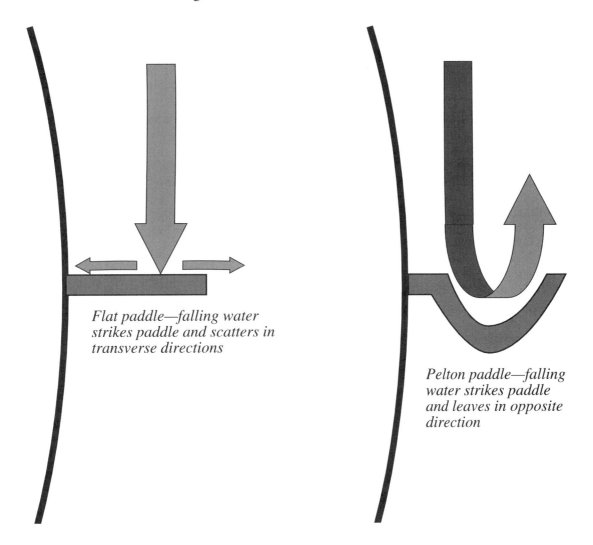

Flat paddle—falling water strikes paddle and scatters in transverse directions

Pelton paddle—falling water strikes paddle and leaves in opposite direction

paddle attached to a water wheel. After striking the paddle, the water scatters in *transverse* directions. Thus, the change in momentum of the water in the vertical direction, due to the striking of the paddle, is approximately equal to the original momentum of the water (it will be less than this, due to the downward motion of the paddle related to the rotation of the wheel). On the right, the water enters a scoop-shaped paddle attached to a water wheel. After striking the paddle, the final velocity of the water is in the *upward* direction. As a result, the change in momentum of the water in the vertical direction, due to the striking of the paddle, is more than the original momentum of the water (it won't be *twice* as much, though, since the paddle is already moving downward due to the rotation of the wheel). This has the effect of exerting a larger force on the scoop-shaped paddle than was the case for the flat paddle.

This concept is explored further in the Magic demonstration, "The Happy and Sad Block-Knockers" in this Chapter.

4.) When a jet airplane lands, you hear the roar of the engine increase. Why would the pilot <u>rev up</u> the engine if he/she wants to <u>stop</u>?

Today's commercial jetliners are massive and require very large forces to bring them to rest after they land on the runway. The brakes within the wheels are used, but it would be advantageous to provide the brakes with some assistance. To provide additional braking capability, the engines are equipped with deflector doors. When these doors are open, the exhaust gases simply leave the rear of the engine; this is the normal operating position for take-off and flight. After the airplane lands, the deflector doors are closed. This closes off the rear exit for the exhaust gases and has the result of deflecting the exhaust gases from the engine through openings in the side of the engine in the *forward* direction. Thus, the engine provides a forward momentum to the exhaust gases. By conservation of momentum, then, if the gases are given momentum in the forward direction, the airplane must *lose* momentum in the forward direction. This has the effect of additional braking. If you are in the right location in an airplane, you can see the deflectors doors opening and closing from your seat as the airplane brakes after landing.

𝔐𝔞𝔤𝔦𝔠:

The Happy and Sad Block-Knockers

This demonstration should be set up and practiced in advance so that the lengths of the strings can be adjusted to match the particular blocks of wood used. When properly adjusted, one of the balls will knock the block over and the other will not.

The result of this activity is often surprising to the observer who has not thought carefully through the physics. After observing the bouncing characteristics (when dropped) of the two balls, it is tempting to think that the sad ball "gives up all that it's got" and, thus, would be more effective at knocking over the block. The demonstration, however, shows that the *happy* ball will knock the block over and not the *sad* ball. If we think in terms of momentum, the sad ball will hit the block and (let us assume) stop completely. The impulse applied to the block is equal to the change in momentum of the ball, which is just the value of its momentum before hitting the block. On the other hand, the happy ball bounces back with almost as much momentum (in magnitude) as it had just before hitting the block. Thus, the impulse applied to the block is the ball's change in momentum, which is almost *twice* the momentum that it had before hitting the block. Thus, the happy ball applies much more impulse and knocks the block over.

This is a nice demonstration of the fact that, although the sad ball gives up all of its kinetic energy, it is the more effective *transfer of momentum* of the happy ball that results in the falling block. For further discussion, see F. Bucheit ("A Momentum Transfer Demonstration with 'Happy/Unhappy' Balls", *The Physics Teacher*, **32**, 28, 1994), who suggests doing the demonstration *before* showing the class the different bouncing characteristics. The author of this book has found it to be more effective to show the class the bouncing characteristics first and then ask about which ball will knock the block over. It often occurs that the class readily responds in unison, "Sad Ball", falling prey to the notion that the sad ball "gives up everything it's got".

The Falling Pencil

The behavior of the tip of the pencil depends on the friction force between the tip and the surface on which it rests. Let us imagine first a perfectly *frictionless* interaction between the pencil tip and the surface. Then, the only forces acting on the pencil are its weight and the normal force, both of which are vertical. There are no horizontal forces on the pencil. Thus, the horizontal component of momentum of the center of mass of the pencil, which is zero to begin with, must continue to have the value zero. In this case, as the eraser end of the pencil leans one way, the tip will slide the other way, so that the center of mass of pencil can fall straight down, as suggested in diagram (*a*) to the right.

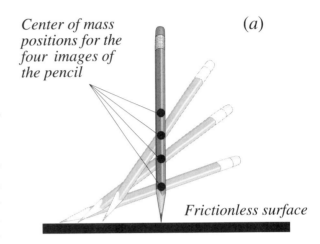

Center of mass positions for the four images of the pencil

(a)

Frictionless surface

When the pencil tip is on a glass surface, the friction force is relatively small, and we see an approximation to the behavior described above, as the tip starts to slide in the opposite direction, at least toward the end of the fall. As the pencil starts to fall in one direction, the tip has a tendency to slide in the other direction, which results in a friction force on the glass surface by the pencil tip. By Newton's Third Law, the surface applies a force on the pencil tip in the same direction as the fall. Thus, there is an external force on the pencil in the horizontal direction and the horizontal momentum of the pencil is not conserved. The center of mass of the pencil moves horizontally. As the pencil nears the surface, the normal force decreases, causing the friction force to decrease, and the tip breaks free and slips in the last part of the fall, as shown in diagram (*b*) to the right.

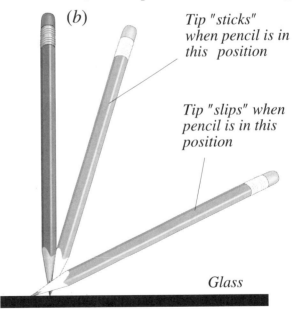

(b)

Tip "sticks" when pencil is in this position

Tip "slips" when pencil is in this position

Glass

When the pencil is on the paper, the friction force between the tip and the surface is larger than in the case of the glass. Thus, as the pencil falls, the tip does not slip. As the pencil falls, the horizontal friction force causes a horizontal momentum, which increases with time, since there is a horizontal force at all times during the fall. If we imagine the pencil rotating around its tip, however, and think of the tangential velocity vector of the center of mass of the pencil, this vector is approaching a *vertical orientation* as the pencil nears the table, as shown in the final diagram (*c*) to the right. Since the velocity of the center of mass is increasing in the horizontal direction (due to the horizontal force), but the tangential velocity is becoming more vertical, something must happen to maintain the horizontal momentum. Thus, as a result, the pencil does not continue to simply rotate about its tip, but takes on a horizontal translational velocity in the direction of the fall. This is the jump that the pencil makes toward the end of its fall.

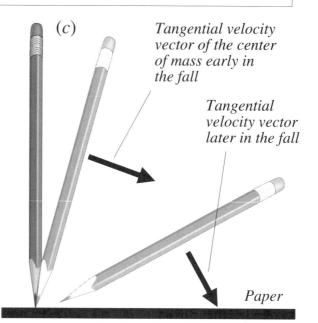

(*c*)

Tangential velocity vector of the center of mass early in the fall

Tangential velocity vector later in the fall

Paper

Stabbing the Eggshell

When the knife is held tightly and tapped on the table, it loses the momentum that it had before the tap. The eggshell and the knife tend to descend together and the eggshell is stopped by the force of the knife. The strength of the tap can be adjusted so that the eggshell does not break. When the knife is dropped, the knife and eggshell tend to separate slightly, due to the parachute shape of the eggshell. The knife *bounces* from the table with a change in momentum that is much larger than in the tapping situation. As the knife moves up and hits the still-descending eggshell, it will pierce it.

𝔐𝔶𝔱𝔥:

1.) A startling headline in the *Los Angeles Times* reads:

Momentum Only Lasts Three Minutes

This is not a new and amazing discovery in physics. The headline appeared in the *sports section* of the newspaper and referred to a short-lived lead that one football team achieved, only to have the opposing team pull ahead three minutes later. Is this a cheap Myth or what?

2.) In a firing squad, only one gun has a real bullet. Thus, none of the firers knows who shoots the actual bullet.

The firing of a real bullet has a much different result on the recoil of the gun than the firing of a blank (See the Mysteries section of Chapter 8 in *PBWM*). Thus, the firer who feels the strong recoil upon firing, due to conservation of momentum, will know that he or she fired the actual bullet.

3.) A human being first performed a long jump over 29 feet in 1968.

The date referred to in the Myth is that of the Mexico City Summer Olympics, at which the record for the long jump surpassed 29 feet.

A jump of 29 feet, 7 inches, however, was recorded *over 100 years before this date*, in 1854, by J. Howard, an Englishman. It is not listed as a valid record because there was some slight help from physics in this jump. Howard held two 5-pound weights over his head while he ran down the track and threw them downward as he left the ground. As a consequence, momentum conservation helped him to attain the very long result. He imparted a momentum *downward* on the weights to throw them down, resulting in an *upward* momentum on him. This momentum added to that achieved by his jumping into the air. The result was a larger vertical velocity than was possible without the weights, more time in the air, and, since he also had a horizontal velocity, a longer range than normal.

Chapter 7
Rotation

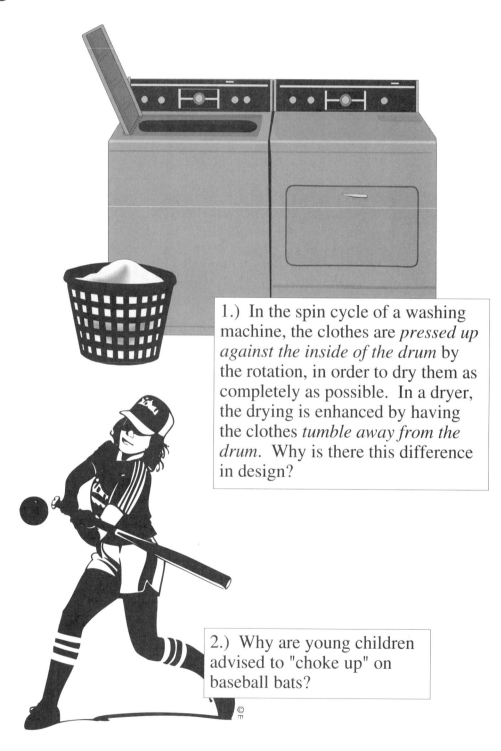

1.) In the spin cycle of a washing machine, the clothes are *pressed up against the inside of the drum* by the rotation, in order to dry them as completely as possible. In a dryer, the drying is enhanced by having the clothes *tumble away from the drum*. Why is there this difference in design?

2.) Why are young children advised to "choke up" on baseball bats?

Mysteries:

3.) Why do you hold your arms out when walking on a railroad track?

WARNING - walking on railroad tracks is dangerous!

4.) If you turn off your workshop grinder and your electric drill at the same time, the grinder takes longer to come to a stop. Why?

5.) Why do the front brakes on an automobile usually wear out before the rear brakes?

Mysteries:

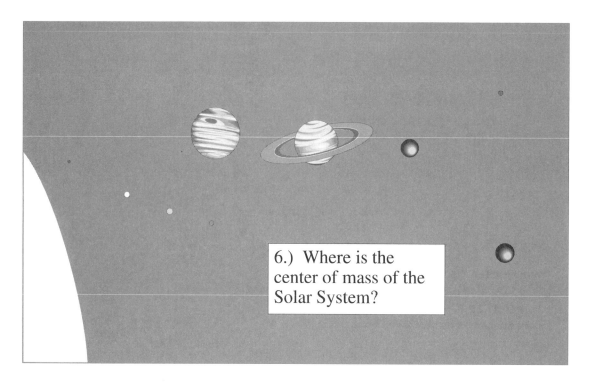

6.) Where is the center of mass of the Solar System?

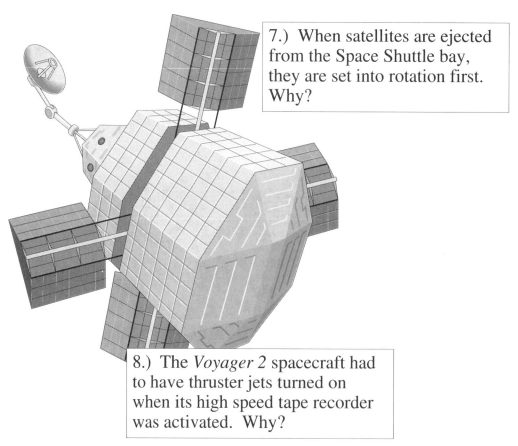

7.) When satellites are ejected from the Space Shuttle bay, they are set into rotation first. Why?

8.) The *Voyager 2* spacecraft had to have thruster jets turned on when its high speed tape recorder was activated. Why?

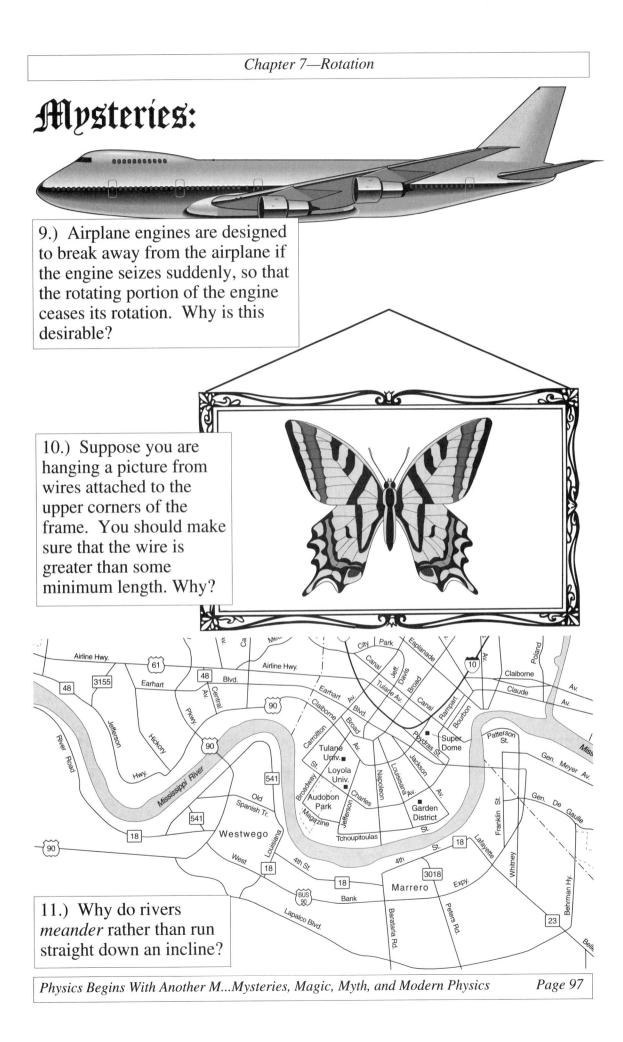

𝕸𝖞𝖘𝖙𝖊𝖗𝖎𝖊𝖘:

9.) Airplane engines are designed to break away from the airplane if the engine seizes suddenly, so that the rotating portion of the engine ceases its rotation. Why is this desirable?

10.) Suppose you are hanging a picture from wires attached to the upper corners of the frame. You should make sure that the wire is greater than some minimum length. Why?

11.) Why do rivers *meander* rather than run straight down an incline?

Mysteries:

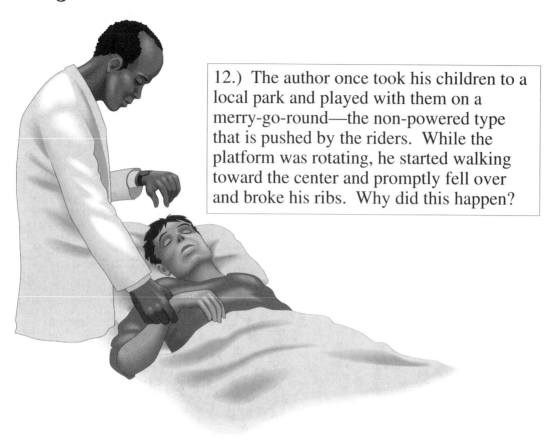

12.) The author once took his children to a local park and played with them on a merry-go-round—the non-powered type that is pushed by the riders. While the platform was rotating, he started walking toward the center and promptly fell over and broke his ribs. Why did this happen?

13.) Suppose you are coasting down a hill on your bicycle and one of the brakes fails. Which one would you rather have fail, front or back, and why?

𝕸agic:

The Sports Ball Race

Race a racketball and a golf ball down an inclined plane. Which one wins?

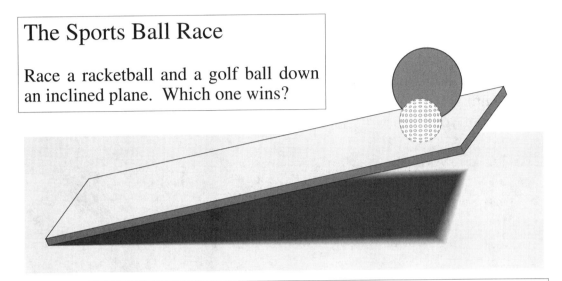

The Well-Behaved Yo-yo

The following demonstration can be performed with a normal yo-yo, but is more dramatic for presentation to a group if one uses a demonstration-sized yo-yo. Construct such a yo-yo by fastening together two large disks (records, plates, etc.) and one smaller disc (leftover cardboard masking tape center ring, coaster, etc.). Wrap a string around the smaller disk. With the yo-yo upright on a table, pull the yo-yo with the string at various angles. Which way does the yo-yo roll?

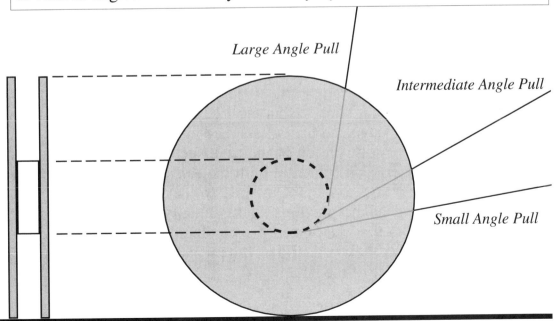

Large Angle Pull

Intermediate Angle Pull

Small Angle Pull

Magic:

Arm Rotations

Stand with your right arm hanging at your side and your palm facing to the left. Perform the following motions of your arm, without twisting your wrist:

1.) Lift your arm forward.

2.) Swing your arm to the right.

3.) Bring your arm back down to your side.

Your palm should now be facing forward. Now, start from the same beginning position, but do the above three steps (actually, the *opposite* of each step) in reverse order. Which way does your palm face now?

Meter Sticks Off the Table

Place a meter stick on a table so that the 12.5 cm mark of the stick coincides with the table edge and the end marked zero is off the table. Now, place another meter stick on top of the first, such that the 16.6 cm mark on the second meter stick coincides with the end of the first meter stick. Place a third meter stick on top of the pile so that the 25 cm mark coincides with the end of the previous stick. Finally, place another meter stick on the pile so that the 50 cm mark coincides with the end of the previous stick. Now, look at the pile from the side—the final meter stick is entirely off the edge of the table!

𝕸𝖆𝖌𝖎𝖈:

The Spinning Book

Wrap a large rubber band around a book so as to assure that it does not open. Now, toss the book up into the air so that it rotates. Do this so that the rotation is around three axes in succession—an axis perpendicular to the front of the book, an axis parallel to the spine, and an axis parallel to the bottom of the book. What do you notice about the *stability of rotation* for these various orientations?

Axis perpendicular to the front

Axis parallel to the bottom

Axis parallel to the spine

Myth:

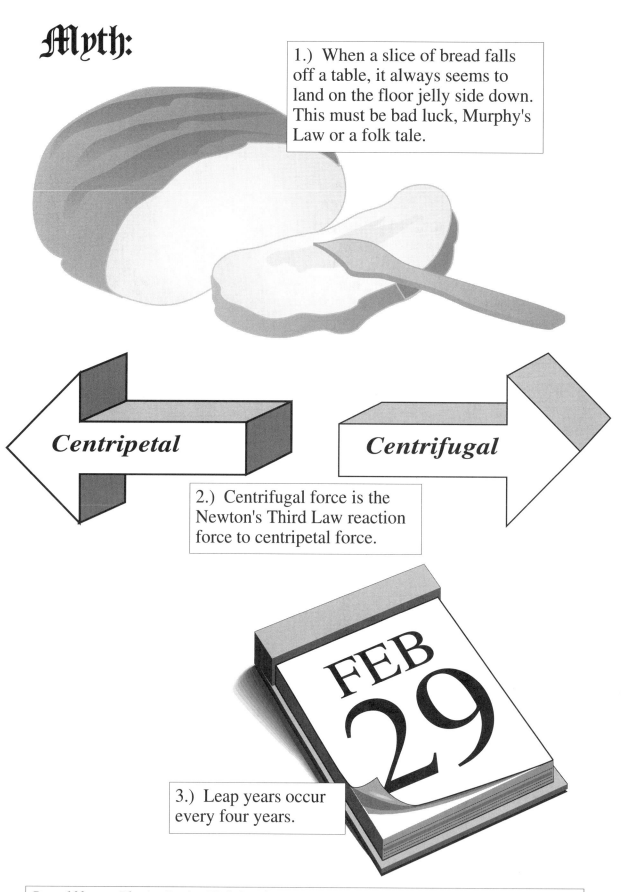

1.) When a slice of bread falls off a table, it always seems to land on the floor jelly side down. This must be bad luck, Murphy's Law or a folk tale.

Centripetal

Centrifugal

2.) Centrifugal force is the Newton's Third Law reaction force to centripetal force.

FEB 29

3.) Leap years occur every four years.

𝔐𝔶𝔱𝔥:

4.) Two identical cars are traveling toward each other at identical speeds, relative to the Earth, along a narrow roadway, one moving toward the east and one toward the west. They hit their brakes and start skidding at identical times and the coefficients of friction between the tires and the road are identical for each of the two cars. They crash at the midpoint of their initial positions. (Hint: The Earth is rotating.)

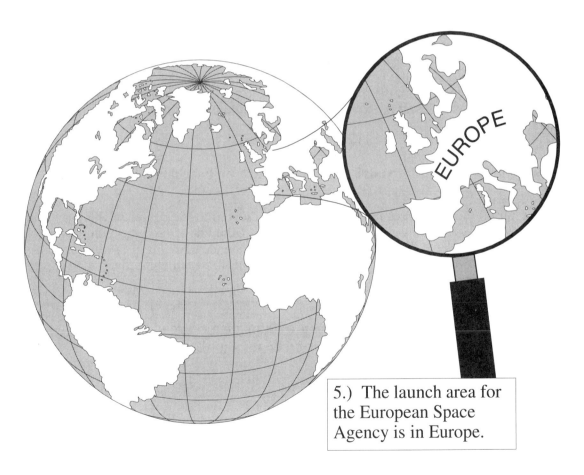

5.) The launch area for the European Space Agency is in Europe.

Discussions; Chapter 7—Rotation

𝔐𝔶𝔰𝔱𝔢𝔯𝔦𝔢𝔰:

1.) In the spin cycle of a washing machine, the clothes are *pressed up against the inside of the drum* by the rotation, in order to dry them as completely as possible. In a dryer, the drying is enhanced by having the clothes *tumble away from the drum*. Why is there this difference in design?

The spin cycle in a washer is designed to extract as much water as possible from the clothing by the application of *pressure*. Most of us are familiar with *wringing* a sponge or wash cloth to extract water. This has the effect of pushing the threads of the material closer together so as to squeeze out the water that is trapped between them. A similar phenomenon happens in the spin cycle. The clothes are pressed against the side of the drum by the rotation, pushing the threads closer together and squeezing out the water. The water thus released from the clothing moves outward (due to Newton's First Law), away from the center of the drum and through the holes in the side of the drum.

This process is effective at removing most of the water that is trapped *between* the threads of the clothing, but is not useful for extracting the water which is absorbed *in* the threads. For this, we must use an *evaporative technique*. The water is evaporated from the clothing by passing hot air through the threads. In order to pass the hot air through so as to contact as many threads as possible, we do not want the clothing to be compressed, as in the spin cycle. We want it to be "fluffed up" so as to present a large amount of surface area to the hot air. Thus, the dryer rotation speed is designed so that the clothing falls away from the drum (due to gravity) as it moves upward in the drum's rotation. This has the result of exposing a large amount of the clothing's surface area to the hot air.

2.) Why are young children advised to "choke up" on baseball bats?

Choking up on the bat moves the hands closer to the geometric center of the bat. This has the result of decreasing the *moment of inertia* of the bat around the point at which the hands make contact. Thus, the bat offers less resistance to changes in rotational motion and can be swung easier by the weaker muscles of the small child than when the bat is held at the end.

3.) Why do you hold your arms out when walking on a railroad track?
   WARNING - walking on railroad tracks is dangerous!

It is easier to keep your balance on a railroad track or other thin support with your arms *outstretched* from your side than if your arms are *hanging* by your side. This is due primarily to a combination of effects involving moment of inertia and Newton's Third Law. Let us first imagine a different situation—you are standing on *frictionless ice* and your body starts to lean to one side, say to the left. Your instinctive reaction is to lean the upper half of your body *to the left*. While this may sound like you are defeating the purpose, this has the desired effect. By leaning the top part of the body to the left, the middle of the body moves to the right. Since you are standing on frictionless ice, your feet will also slide to the left, so that your feet can stay under your center of mass.

Now, let's imagine that you perform the same feat while standing on a railroad track. When your body is folded, with the upper part moving to the left, the feet cannot move to the left, because of the friction force between the feet and the track. The feet <u>attempt</u> to move to the left, applying a force to the left on the track. By Newton's Third Law, the track exerts a force to the *right* on the feet. This is just the external force that you need to push the body to the right, counteracting the tipping of the body to the left. This is similar to the body-folding described in Mystery #2 in Chapter 3 of *PBWM*, in which you attempt to avoid being pushed off a cliff.

Now, we have said nothing about the outstretched arms. The process described above is only effective for very small tilts to either side. For a larger tilt, the center of mass of the body moves too far away from a point above the track to be able to be returned by the body-folding technique. In this case, some additional help is needed—the help provided by the outstretched arms. Imagine once again that the body begins to lean to the left. As viewed from behind, this is a *counterclockwise* rotation of the body. If the arms are rotated counterclockwise by forces from the body, by Newton's Third Law, the result is a torque on the body that tends to rotate the body in a *clockwise* direction. Thus, the body is rotated back to the vertical position. With the arms outstretched, *the moment of inertia of the arms about a point between the shoulders is maximized*. Thus, the arms then offer the largest possible resistance to rotational motion, requiring the largest torque to rotate them. This, in turn, provides the largest possible torque on the body back to equilibrium.

The same principles are involved with the very long poles carried by tightrope walkers. The poles are simply extensions of their arms to increase the moment of inertia!

4.) If you turn off your workshop grinder and your electric drill at the same time, the grinder takes longer to come to a stop. Why?

If we look at the rotating parts of the two tools, we see a major difference. Both tools have a rotating armature of the motor; let's ignore that. We will focus on the working part of each tool. The working part of the drill is a *bit* of very small radius—on the order of millimeters. On the other hand, the working part of the grinder is a circular *grinding stone*, several centimeters in diameter. The grinding stone has a much larger *moment of inertia* than the bit for two reasons: it is more massive, and the mass is distributed at larger distances from the rotation axis.

This larger moment of inertia is the primary reason why the grinder takes longer to stop than the drill. The torque which brings either device to a stop after the power is turned off is primarily that from the friction in the bearings of the device. The larger moment of inertia of the grinder results in more resistance to having its rotational motion changed; thus, it takes longer to come to rest than does the drill.

5.) Why do the front brakes on an automobile usually wear out before the rear brakes?

Let us consider the forces on an automobile when it brakes. These are shown in the diagram below.

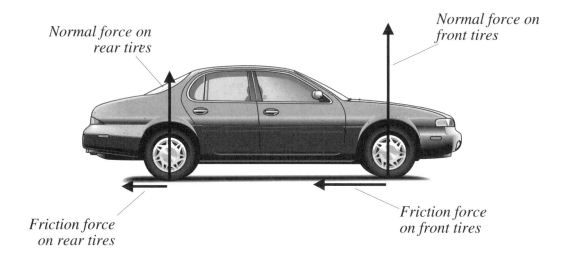

On each tire, there are the usual forces due to contact with a surface—friction parallel to the surface and the normal force perpendicular to the surface. When the car begins to brake, the friction forces apply a torque on the car, causing it to rotate in the clockwise direction in the diagram above. Drivers are familiar with the "nosing down" of a car under hard braking. In order to counter this rotation, the normal force on the front tires is larger than that on the back, as indicated in the diagram. Since the friction force is proportional to the normal force in this sliding situation, the friction force on the front wheels is larger than on the back, also indicated in the diagram. Finally, this larger friction in the front wheels results in a larger force from the brake mechanism to prevent the wheel from turning. Thus, the front brakes tend to wear out sooner than the back. See Mystery #13 in this Chapter for a similar discussion applied to the bicycle.

6.) Where is the center of mass of the Solar System?

There is no single answer to this question. The Solar System is not a rigid body. Thus, as various parts of the Solar System move, the center of mass shifts position. We can guess, due to the very large mass of the Sun, that the center of mass will not stray very far from the center of the Sun.

The largest deviation of the center of mass from the center of the Sun will occur in the rare instance in which all of the planets have lined up on one side of the Sun. Then, we can use the one-dimensional equation for center of mass, given on the next page, to calculate the location of the center of mass, x_{cm}, for N objects:

$$x_{cm} = \frac{\displaystyle\sum_{i=1}^{N} m_i x_i}{\displaystyle\sum_{i=1}^{N} m_i}$$

where m_i is the mass of the ith object and x_i is its distance from the center of the Sun.

If we calculate this using the data for the nine planets and the Sun (we will ignore the asteroids in the interest of achieving the result in a reasonable amount of time!), we find that the center of mass in this configuration is at a distance from the center of the Sun of about 1.5×10^6 km. This is about twice the radius of the Sun. Thus, the center of mass of the Solar system does take an *occasional* excursion outside the Sun. This is a very rare lineup of the planets, however. During most of the time, the planets are distributed around the Sun, so that the center of mass will lie very close to the center of the Sun.

The planet which has the greatest influence on the calculation of the center of mass is Jupiter, due to its large mass. If we repeat the calculation above, with all of the planets lined up on one side of the Sun, *except for Jupiter*, which we imagine to be on the *other* side of the Sun, but still in a straight line, we find the center of mass to be located 2.4×10^4 km from the center of the Sun, in the direction toward the other eight planets. This distance is only 3% of the radius of the Sun, so shifting Jupiter to the other side of the Sun makes a significant difference in the location of the center of mass.

7.) When satellites are ejected from the Space Shuttle bay, they are set into rotation first. Why?

This technique makes use of *conservation of angular momentum* to stabilize the satellite. A non-spinning satellite could have its orientation altered by a small torque, due to a variety of sources in space (interaction with the thin upper atmosphere, meteorites, unbalanced forces during release, even light pressure from the Sun). By setting the satellite into rotation, the large angular momentum is insignificantly altered by these small torques, resulting in a stable satellite. This is similar to the spiraling football discussed in Mystery #2, in Chapter 11 of *PBWM*.

8.) The *Voyager 2* spacecraft had to have thruster jets turned on when its high speed tape recorder was activated. Why?

When the tape recorder was turned on, part of the spacecraft (the tape recording mechanism) was set into a rotational motion. By Newton's Third Law, if the spacecraft exerts a torque to start the tape mechanism rotating, the mechanism will exert an equal and opposite torque on the spacecraft. Thus, the spacecraft will start rotating in the opposite direction. This is similar to the requirement for helicopters to have two sets of blades, as described in Mystery #1 of Chapter 3 in *PBWM*. A helicopter with only one blade would suffer a rotation of the body as a torque was applied to rotate the blades.

The *Voyager 2* question can also be understood from conservation of angular momentum. If we assume the initial angular momentum is zero, then, when the tape mechanism starts rotating, we have introduced an angular momentum to the system. In order to maintain the angular momentum at zero, the spacecraft must start rotating in the opposite direction to cancel out the angular momentum of the tape mechanism. To counteract this rotation of the spacecraft, thruster jets were fired briefly when the tape recorder was turned on and off.

9.) Airplane engines are designed to break away from the airplane if the engine seizes suddenly, so that the rotating portion of the engine ceases its rotation. Why is this desirable?

The engines of an airplane are mounted with "structural fuses", which are designed to break if subjected to a large, sudden force. These are for the protection of the airplane. The rapidly rotating parts of the engine, when operating normally, represent a very large amount of angular momentum, *which must be conserved*. If the engine encounters an operational problem so that the rotation suddenly stops, the angular momentum must be maintained by some other part of the airplane. If the engine is mounted on a wing, the angular momentum will be suddenly transferred to the wing. The wing will undergo a sudden rotation, which could rip it from the fuselage. If the engine is attached to the fuselage, the sudden transfer of angular momentum to the fuselage could cause a tear in the skin and loss of control of the airplane. These disastrous effects are counteracted by allowing the suddenly stopped engine to tear away from the wing or fuselage by means of the fuses.

10.) Suppose you are hanging a picture from wires attached to the upper corners of the frame. You should make sure that the wire is greater than some minimum length. Why?

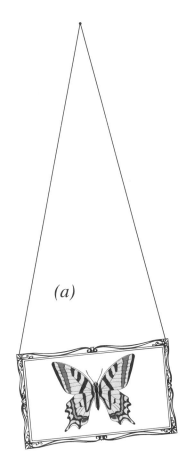

(a)

Let us compare two situations in a technique that could be called "taking the limit to the ridiculous". Suppose we hang a picture with a ludicrously long wire, as suggested in diagram (*a*) to the right (we will ignore any friction with the wall—imagine the picture to be hanging from a frictionless hook from the ceiling). If the picture tilts slightly, so that a short piece of wire passes over the nail from which the picture is hung, the center of mass will just move slightly so that it remains under the nail and the system remains in equilibrium.

Compare this to the situation in which the picture is hung from a wire tightly stretched between the two upper corners of the frame, as suggested in the second diagram, (*b*), on the next page. The distance between *(b)*  the support nail and the center of mass of the picture is very close to *half the height of the picture* in this situation. Suppose that there is a slight disturbance that causes the picture to tilt. If the wire slides across the nail until the nail is very close to the right corner of the frame, then the picture hangs as shown in the third diagram, *(c)*, below. In this configuration, the distance between the support nail and the center of mass of the picture is approximately *one half of the* <u>*diagonal*</u> *of the picture*. By the Pythagorean Theorem, this can be shown to be larger than half the height of the frame in the previous configuration. Thus, the last diagram represents a lower (gravitational potential) energy configuration than the second diagram. If we start off with the configuration shown in diagram *(b)*, and the wire-nail surface is frictionless, any small disturbance will send the picture into the configuration shown in diagram *(c)*—*the system is unstable*. In the configuration shown in diagram *(a)*, with the very long wire, the system is stable—a disturbance will simply move the system slightly into a new stable configuration.

(c)

Now, between these two situations, *there must be a boundary*, representing a certain length of the support wire that represents the limit between stable and unstable configurations. Thus, to be sure that our picture is not continuously straying from equilibrium, we should make sure that the support wire is longer than the minimum length defined by this boundary condition.

11.) Why do rivers *meander* rather than run straight down an incline?

It would seem natural for a river to run straight down an incline, but this is actually an unstable situation. Let us suppose that a river does run straight, but due to some asymmetry or obstruction in the river bed, one side of the river has water running a little faster or more turbulently than the other side. This more vigorous water will be more effective at eroding the bank of the river over a long period of time. This will result in the river taking on a small curve at that point as material from the banks is washed away. Once the curve has been established, the water on the "outside" of the curve must travel faster than that on the "inside". Thus, the outside of the curve becomes even more eroded. We have a runaway situation, although it is an extremely slow process. The riverbed will curve more and more until the curves are so sharp that the river can cut through a curve and re-establish the straight path, leaving the possibility of an *oxbow lake* next to the river, as shown in the diagram.

Before formation of oxbow lake:

After formation of oxbow lake:

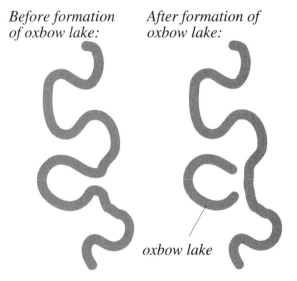

oxbow lake

It is useful to look at a road atlas of the United States, and consult maps of states along the Mississippi River. This river exhibits a large amount of meandering, as well as many oxbow lakes along its length. In fact, in the extreme southwest corner of the state of Mississippi, just across the river from Louisiana, there is an oxbow lake named Old River Lake, which suggests the original heritage of this lake!

12.) The author once took his children to a local park and played with them on a merry-go-round—the non-powered type that is pushed by the riders. While the platform was rotating, he started walking toward the center and promptly fell over and broke his ribs. Why did this happen?

This is a result of the *Coriolis force* (see *PBWM*, Chapter 9, Concepts, Mystery #4 and Myth #3). One way to understand this effect is as follows. When the author took one step closer to the center of the circle, he maintained his tangential velocity (according to Newton's First Law). But the platform under his new position was moving with a smaller velocity than that at his original position, since the radial position was closer to the center of rotation. Thus, there was a non-zero relative (tangential) velocity between the foot and the platform. When the foot was planted on the more slowly moving portion of the platform, there was a sudden difference between the velocity of his foot after contacting the platform and that before contact. In order to cause this acceleration of his foot, a force (applied by friction) was exerted in a lateral direction on his foot. This resulted in a torque on the body which caused it to rotate around an axis projecting forward from the body. As a result, the body rotated and the upper part of the body suffered (literally!) a strong retarding force when it hit the structure of the merry-go-round. The doctor at the emergency room had a difficult time appreciating the author's vivid description of the physics involved in this incident!

13.) Suppose you are coasting down a hill on your bicycle and one of the brakes fails. Which one would you rather have fail, front or back, and why?

In general, it is safer to have the front brake fail than the rear, but there is a disadvantage with only the rear brake working also. Let us begin by considering the forces on a bicycle as it rolls along level ground. These forces are shown in diagram (*a*) below.

The weight of the rider-bicycle system is supported by the normal forces on the two wheels. In this situation, the normal force on the rear wheel is larger than that on the front wheel. This is due to the fact that the center of gravity of the system is closer to the rear wheel, and follows from the requirements for rotational equilibrium.

Now, let's apply the brakes. There will be an acceleration in the direction opposite to that of the velocity of the bi-

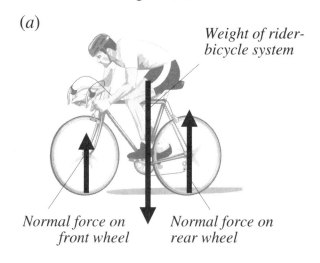

(*a*)

Weight of rider-bicycle system

Normal force on front wheel

Normal force on rear wheel

cycle. The force causing this acceleration will be the friction between the wheels and the road. The new force diagram (*b*) is shown to the right.

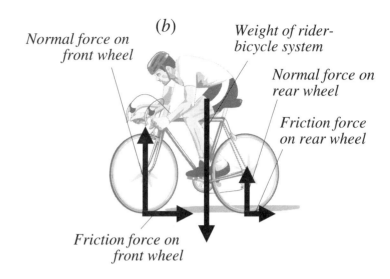

(b)

Normal force on front wheel

Weight of rider-bicycle system

Normal force on rear wheel

Friction force on rear wheel

Friction force on front wheel

There are two major changes in this new diagram. The first change is that we have added the friction forces responsible for the braking. This new pair of forces, however, results in a torque around the center of mass of the system, which would result in a counterclockwise rotation. To counteract this new torque, the normal forces on the wheels change, so that the normal force on the front wheel is now larger than that on the back wheel (This was discussed in Mystery #5 for an automobile.). This is the second change made in the diagram above. This difference between the normal forces is also reflected in a difference in the friction forces, as indicated in the diagram.

It is possible, if we apply the brakes even harder, that the normal force on the rear wheel will go to zero. According to Whitt and Wilson (F. R. Whitt and D. G. Wilson, *Bicycling Science*, The MIT Press, Cambridge, Massachusetts, 1974), this occurs for a braking acceleration of about 0.56*g* or 5.5 m·s^{-2}. In this case, two possibilities occur. One possibility is that the rider will be thrown over the handlebars. If we consider torques around the hub of the front wheel, we see the very dangerous situation here. The only two forces with non-zero torques around this point are the weight and the friction force on the front wheel. The friction force stays at a fixed distance from the hub, the radius of the wheel. As the rider starts to move up over the handlebars, however, *the weight vector moves closer to the hub of the front wheel*, reducing the torque of this force. This situation is indicated in diagram (*c*) to the right. Thus, we have an unstable situation—the ini-

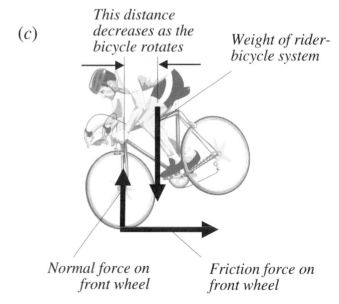

(c)

This distance decreases as the bicycle rotates

Weight of rider-bicycle system

Normal force on front wheel

Friction force on front wheel

tial rotation of the rider over the front wheel results in even more torque enhancing this motion and the rider is thrown over the handlebars violently.

The second possibility can be imagined if we view the bicycle from the top. Since the rear wheel has lost contact with the ground, it could drift to the side. Then, we have a torque, due to the friction force on the front wheel, causing a rotation of the bicycle around a *vertical* axis. Thus, according to the rider, the bicycle is suddenly thrown to one side and goes out of control.

Now, we are ready to address the question of the desirability of failing brakes. Let us suppose that the rear brake fails. Upon application of the brakes with a strength that his or her experience indicates is appropriate, the rider will notice that the acceleration is not what is expected, since there will be no friction force from the rear wheel. As a result, the rider will squeeze the brakes harder. This could result in the disappearance of the normal force on the rear wheel and the dire results discussed above.

This would seem to indicate that it is desirable for the front brake to fail. Before we make this conclusion, however, let us imagine that the front brake fails. As the rear brake is applied, the friction force on the rear wheel will result in a torque on the bicycle, as discussed above. As a result, the normal force on the front wheel will increase and the normal force on the rear wheel will decrease. Thus, the friction force on the rear wheel, which depends on the normal force, will not be as large as expected, due to the smaller normal force. We conclude, then, that the rear brake is not very effective at stopping the bicycle, due to the small friction force. Thus, although the violent events described above for the front wheel braking will not occur, the distance over which the bicycle stops with only the rear brake will be much longer than that with both brakes operational. If an emergency situation arises, requiring a quick stop, and only the rear brake is functional, then serious results could ensue.

Finally, let us address the fact that the Mystery indicated that we are coasting *down a hill* on the bicycle. How does this alter the situation? Diagram (*d*) to the right shows the forces.

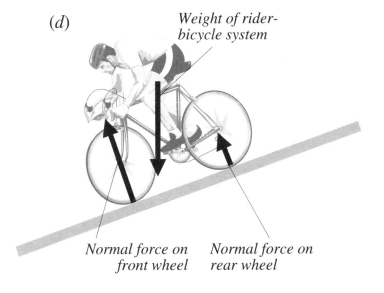

(*d*)   *Weight of rider-bicycle system*

Normal force on front wheel   *Normal force on rear wheel*

Due to the tilt of the bicycle, the torque of the weight around the front hub is smaller than on a level surface, since the line of action of the force is closer to the hub. As a consequence, considering rotational equilibrium, the normal force on the rear wheel is smaller than in the horizontal situation. Now, let us imagine that the rear brake has failed and the front brake is applied. Since the rear normal force is smaller than in the horizontal case, it will vanish at a lower braking acceleration than on a level surface. In addition, since the torque of the weight around the front hub is smaller than in the horizontal situation, it is less effective at counteracting the rotation of the bicycle around the front hub when the rider goes over the handlebars. Thus, the dangers of the rear brake failure are made worse by the fact that the rider is going down a hill.

𝔐agic:

The Sports Ball Race

The variation in rolling times depends on the moments of inertia of the different balls. The racketball is hollow and rolls very much like a spherical shell. The golf ball is not hollow, and, although the density is not constant, rolls very much like a solid sphere. Thus, the moment of inertia of the racketball is relatively larger (if we were to assume that the two balls have the same mass and radius), than that for the golf ball. Thus, the racketball should offer more resistance to changes in rotational motion and should roll more slowly.

But wait a minute. Do racketballs and golf balls have the same mass? They certainly do not have the same radius! Isn't this a more complicated problem than it appears?

Let us approach this from an energy point of view. We can use the special case of the energy continuity equation (see Mystery #3 in Chapter 5) that is called the *work-energy theorem*. We let the rolling object be the system and imagine that the gravitational force does work across the boundary of this system, resulting in an increase in kinetic energy. The kinetic energy is of two types—translational and rotational. The rotational kinetic energy will depend on the moment of inertia of the object, which, for objects with circular symmetry, can be written as,

$$I = CmR^2$$

where m is the mass of the object, R is its outer radius and C is a constant that depends on the shape and mass distribution of the particular object. For example, for a disk (or a cylinder) of mass m and radius R,

$$I = \frac{1}{2}mR^2 \qquad (C = \frac{1}{2})$$

Using the general expression above for the moment of inertia, we can write the work-energy theorem, assuming pure rolling (no slipping), as,

$$W = \Delta KE \quad \rightarrow \quad (mg)(h) = \frac{1}{2}mv^2 + \frac{1}{2}I\omega^2 = \frac{1}{2}mv^2 + \frac{1}{2}(CmR^2)\left(\frac{v}{R}\right)^2$$

$$\rightarrow \quad mgh = \frac{1}{2}mv^2 + \frac{1}{2}Cmv^2$$

where h is the vertical height from which the object rolls and v is the velocity upon reaching the bottom. For example, using models of the racketball and golf ball as hollow and solid spheres, we can find the moments of inertia from tables in physics texts:

$$Hollow\,Sphere: \quad I = \frac{2}{3}mR^2 \qquad (C = \frac{2}{3})$$

$$Solid\,Sphere: \quad I = \frac{2}{5}mR^2 \qquad (C = \frac{2}{5})$$

Now, if we solve the energy equation above for the velocity of the rolling object as it reaches the bottom of the inclined plane, we find,

$$v = \sqrt{\frac{2gh}{1+C}}$$

Thus, the velocity of rolling at the bottom of an incline depends only on the height of the incline, the gravitational field, and the type of object (through the parameter C). Notice that the mass m and the radius R are conspicuously missing from the expression. Thus, *the velocity does not depend on the mass or the radius of rolling objects*!

The Well Behaved Yo-yo

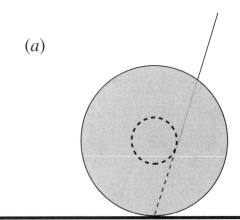

(a)

You will find that the behavior of the yo-yo is different for different angles of pull. If the angle that the string makes with the horizontal is small, the yo-yo will roll *in the (horizontal) direction of the pull*. If the angle is large, the yo-yo will roll *in the (horizontal) direction opposite to the pull*. Surely, there must be a boundary between these behaviors and we find that there is one angle at which we can pull such that the yo-yo simply slides along the horizontal surface without rolling. If you observe carefully while pulling at this critical angle, you will notice that the string is pointed directly at the contact point between the yo-yo and the table, as indicated in diagram (*a*) above.

Why should this be the case? Let us consider the *torques* on the yo-yo. These torques will arise from the four forces which act on the yo-yo—the weight, the normal force, the friction force and the tension in the string. These forces are shown for an arbitrary angle in diagram (*b*) below.

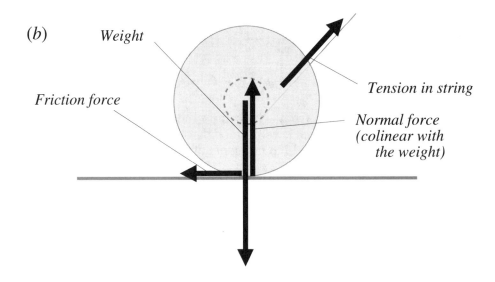

(b)   *Weight*   *Tension in string*   *Friction force*   *Normal force (colinear with the weight)*

Due to the circular symmetry of the yo-yo, the normal force and the weight are colinear—the center of the yo-yo is directly above the support point. The friction force acts at the contact point. Thus, if we choose the contact point as the reference point for our torques, we see that the lines of action of all three of these forces (weight, normal, friction) pass through the contact point. Thus, these forces exert no torque around this point. The only torque around the contact point is provided by the tension in the string. If the angle of pull is small, the line of action of the tension is above the contact point and the wheel rolls in the same direction as the pull (the rotation is clockwise in diagram (*b*) on the previous page). If the angle is large, the line of action of the tension is to the right of the contact point in diagram (*b*), resulting in a counterclockwise rotation—the yo-yo rolls away from the pull. Now, for a certain angle of pull, the line of action of the tension will pass through the contact point. In this situation, the lines of action of *all four forces* pass through the contact point, so there is no net torque. As a result, the yo-yo does not rotate—it simply slides along the surface.

A nice extension of this demonstration is to set the system up so that the string passes over a pulley and the tension in the string is supplied by hanging a weight from the end of the string, as shown in diagram (*c*) to the right. If the yo-yo is placed so that the string is at the critical angle, the system will be in equilibrium. If the yo-yo is pulled away from the pulley, the angle becomes smaller and the yo-yo is pulled back toward the pulley. If the yo-yo is moved toward the pulley, the angle becomes larger and the yo-yo moves away from the pulley. Thus, we have a situation with a *restoring force*. If the yo-yo is moved away from equilibrium and released, it will *oscillate* back and forth around the equilibrium position.

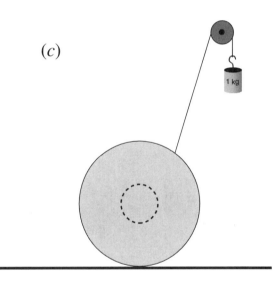

(*c*)

Arm Rotations

This is a demonstration, requiring no equipment (except arms!), of the fact that finite rotations do not act as vectors. This was discussed in the Magic demonstration, Adding up Rotations, in Chapter 10 of *PBWM*. Quantities which act as vectors must obey a number of mathematical rules, one of which is the commutative property—if we add vectors, it must not make any difference in what order we add them. The operations in the demonstration represent the addition of three rotations of the arm around the shoulder. It is clear from the results, however, that the order of addition makes a significant difference.

Meter Sticks Off the Table

In order for the meter stick combination to stay on the table, the center of gravity of the combination must be to the left of the edge of the table in the diagram accompanying the Magic demonstration. As a result, the torque due to the weight of the combination will tend to rotate the system counterclockwise about the end of the table, keeping it safely on the table. If the center of gravity were to be to the right of the edge of the table, the torque resulting from the weight would cause a rotation of the system off the table.

Let us find the center of gravity of this combination by realizing that the centers of mass and gravity will coincide to our desired degree of accuracy and by using the traditional expression for the center of mass, as we saw in Mystery #6:

$$x_{cm} = \frac{\sum\limits_{i=1}^{N} m_i x_i}{\sum\limits_{i=1}^{N} m_i}$$

We will choose our origin at the edge of the table. Then, given the data in the description of the Magic demonstration, we have the following positions of the centers of mass of the *individual* meter sticks, relative to the edge of the table:

Stick 1: $x_{cm,\,1}$ = −50 cm + 12.5 cm = −37.5 cm
Stick 2: $x_{cm,\,2}$ = −50 cm + 12.5 cm + 16.6 cm = −21.9 cm
Stick 3: $x_{cm,\,3}$ = −50 cm + 12.5 cm + 16.6 cm + 25 cm = 4.1 cm
Stick 4: $x_{cm,\,4}$ = −50 cm + 12.5 cm + 16.6 cm + 25 cm + 50 cm = 54.1 cm

Now, we find the center of mass of the combination, assuming that all meter sticks are identical and have mass m_{stick}:

$$x_{cm,\,combination} = \frac{\left[(m_{stick})(-37.5\,cm) + (m_{stick})(-21.9\,cm) + (m_{stick})(4.1\,cm) + (m_{stick})(54.1\,cm)\right]}{4m_{stick}}$$

$$= -0.3\,cm$$

Thus, the center of mass of the combination is just to the left of the table edge and the pile of meter sticks is in equilibrium!

An extension of this demonstration is to turn the last meter stick by 90° so that it is perpendicular to the others, as described by the view from above in the following diagram.

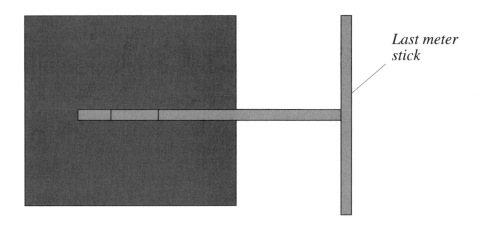

Last meter stick

This extension clearly shows that the weight of the meter stick can be considered to be concentrated at the center of mass. Many students will believe that the pile of meter sticks will fall when the last stick is rotated, since now, "*all* the weight is at the end of the third stick, whereas only *part* of it was applied there before". This extension of the demonstration makes believers out of these students.

The Spinning Book

You should have noticed that rotations around two of the axes are stable—the book simply continues to rotate nicely around the axes as it rises and falls back into your hands. These axes, for a normally shaped book, are those perpendicular to the front and parallel to the spine. If the book is tossed with the rotation about the axis parallel to the bottom, it tends to *tumble* as it spins—the axis of rotation does not stay fixed in space.

It is difficult to explain this phenomenon without appealing to *Euler's equations* for rotation, which are differential equations found in texts on classical mechanics. One such text, D. Kleppner and R. J. Kolenkow, *An Introduction to Mechanics*, McGraw-Hill Book Co., New York, 1973, discusses the spinning book problem as an example. For our purposes, let us just claim that the solutions to Euler's equations in the case of small perturbations from the original rotation show *trigonometric* solutions for rotations about the axes perpendicular to the front and parallel to the spine of the book. Thus, if there is a small perturbation due, for example, to air resistance, the book will simply *oscillate* around the original rotation. Thus, the rotational motion is *stable*.

For rotation about the axis parallel to the bottom, however, we find that the solutions to Euler's equations for small perturbations have an *exponential* solution, indicating a rotationally *unstable* situation. Thus, as soon as a small perturbation occurs, the book deviates quickly and extensively away from the equilibrium rotation—it tumbles.

𝔐𝔶𝔱𝔥:

1.) When a slice of bread falls off a table, it always seems to land on the floor jelly side down. This must be bad luck, Murphy's Law or a folk tale.

The falling of bread jelly side down is none of the items listed in the Myth; it is an application of physics. R. D. Edge ("Murphy's Law or Jelly-Side Down", *The Physics Teacher*, **26**, 392, 1988) has performed a detailed analysis of the bread falling problem, including effects of friction with the table as it slides off, the change in moment of inertia as the bread slides off the edge, energy transformations through the whole process and rotation as it falls to the floor. The process is too lengthy to reproduce here, but it is shown that, for a table of typical height and typically sized bread, the rotation of the bread during the time to fall is indeed such that the bread is jelly-side down when it hits the floor.

A much taller or much shorter table would change the situation, since the time for the bread to rotate would differ, but tables tend to be within a standard range of heights. Edge also shows that objects larger than about 60 cm in dimension or smaller than about 4 cm will land with the originally upward-facing side facing upward when they land.

2.) Centrifugal force is the Newton's Third Law reaction force to centripetal force.

If one uses the concept of centrifugal force (Myth #1 in Chapter 9 of *PBWM*), it is tempting to think of it as a Newton's Third Law reaction to the centripetal force, since it is equal in magnitude and opposite in direction. There is a serious flaw with this approach, however. Newton's Third Law pairs of forces *never act on the same object*. Centrifugal and centripetal forces are considered to act on the same object, the object moving in the circular path. Thus, they cannot be a Newton's Third Law pair of forces.

The Third Law reaction force to the centripetal force is a force outward on the agent that is pulling inward on the object moving in a circular path. Thus, the tension in the string whirling a rock in a circle is playing the role of a centripetal force. The Third Law reaction force is the outward force exerted on the string by the rock. Similarly, the Earth pulls outward on the Sun with a gravitational force as the Sun pulls inward on the Earth.

3.) Leap years occur every four years.

The need for leap year is due to the fact that the Earth does not revolve around the Sun in an even number of days. The popular explanation is that a leap year is necessary every four years, since the Earth takes $365\frac{1}{4}$ days to revolve around the Sun. Thus, an extra day is added to each year divisible evenly by 4. In reality, however, the Earth takes 365.2422 days to revolve, which is slightly different than the number given previously. This difference requires slight additional adjustments to be necessary to the year. The inclusion of a leap year *every* four years overcompensates for the error. To account for this, turn of the century years, such as 1700, 1800 and 1900, even though divisible by 4, are *not* leap years and have the normal 365 days. This correction overcompensates in the other direction, so another smaller correction is added. Turn of the century years divisible by 400 *are* leap years. Thus, the year 2000 is a leap year, the first turn of the century leap year since 1600. This final correction is still not exact, but close enough, since the remaining error is on the order of small, natural changes in the Earth's period around the Sun.

4.) Two identical cars are traveling toward each other at identical speeds, relative to the Earth, along a narrow roadway, one moving toward the east and one toward the west. They hit their brakes and start skidding at identical times and the coefficients of friction between the tires and the road are identical for each of the two cars. They crash at the midpoint of their initial positions. (Hint: The Earth is rotating.)

While it may be difficult to discern what is wrong with this statement, there is a subtle difference between the two cars due to the rotation of the Earth, as suggested in the Hint. The car traveling toward the East is moving in the same direction as the Earth's tangential velocity due to its rotation. Thus, the car's tangential velocity is the *sum* of that of the Earth and the ground speed of the car. For the car traveling toward the west, the tangential velocity is the *difference* between the Earth's tangential velocity and the ground speed of the car. Thus, the car traveling toward the east has a larger centripetal acceleration than the car traveling toward the west. This larger acceleration requires a larger centripetal force. The centripetal force on both cars is the sum of the gravitational force (down) and the normal force (up). (We will assume that the cars are traveling at the equator. The qualitative results are the same elsewhere, but would require more complicated calculations due to the change in radius of the circular motion and the variety of directions between the forces and accelerations.) Now, since the gravitational force on both cars is the same, the larger centripetal force for the eastward bound car can be accounted for by its having a *smaller normal force* than the westbound car. Since the eastbound car has less normal force, it has *less friction force* between the tires and the road. Thus, it cannot stop in as short a distance and *the collision will occur slightly east of the midpoint.*

5.) The launch area for the European Space Agency is in Europe.

Most European Space Agency (ESA) spacecraft are launched from a pad at Kourou, *French Guiana.* French Guiana is located in the northern part of *South America.* Why would the ESA want to have a launch pad so far from its home base? The answer is similar to that of Mystery #7 in Chapter 9 of *PBWM.* By taking advantage of the existing eastward velocity of the surface of the Earth, less energy is needed to launch a rocket into orbit if it is fired toward the east than toward the west. The tangential velocity of the Earth's surface is largest at the equator. Most of Europe is farther north than latitude 40°, so that a more southern location for launch is desirable. French Guiana is just slightly north of the equator, stretching from about 2° north to 6° north (Kourou is just north of the 5° latitude.). Thus, it is ideally located to take advantage of the equatorial tangential velocity of the Earth.

Chapter 8
Fluids

Mysteries:

1.) As an ice cube in a glass of water melts, does the level of the water in the glass rise, fall, or stay the same?

2.) Why are tennis balls stored in *pressurized* cans?

Mysteries:

3.) Cream is thicker than milk, right? Yet it *floats* on the top of the milk in the bottle (this Mystery may only make sense to *older* readers!). What's going on here?

4.) Why are canoes so easy to capsize?

5.) Why does hot water clean clothes better than cold water?

Mysteries:

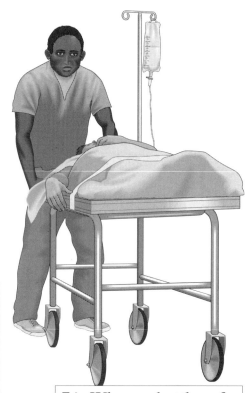

6.) Consider a drink "on the rocks". Alcohol is less dense than ice. So does the ice *float* in an alcoholic beverage?

7.) Why are bottles of intravenous fluid hung so high over the hospital bed?

8.) In 1984, and again in 1986, people living near lakes in a mountainous part of Cameroon were suffocated when the air was displaced suddenly by carbon dioxide. *How could this happen*?

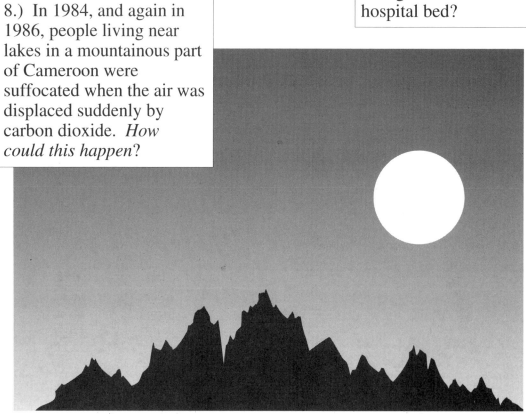

𝕸𝖞𝖘𝖙𝖊𝖗𝖎𝖊𝖘:

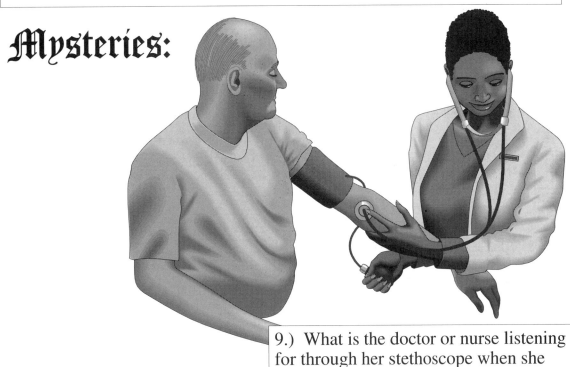

9.) What is the doctor or nurse listening for through her stethoscope when she takes your blood pressure?

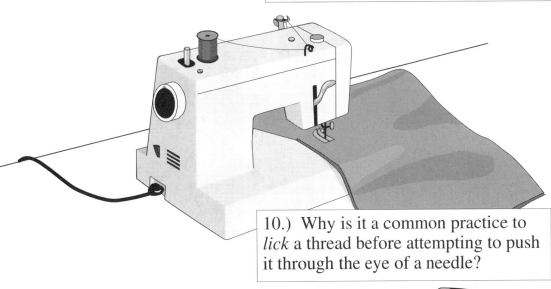

10.) Why is it a common practice to *lick* a thread before attempting to push it through the eye of a needle?

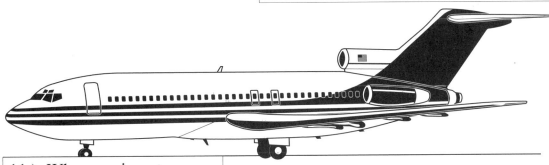

11.) Why are airport runways longer in Denver than in San Francisco?

Mysteries:

12.) Why are scuba divers instructed to *exhale* while ascending to the surface?

13.) You are at a party in a tall building, and you are holding an iced drink, in which the level of the liquid is at the brim of the glass. You enter an elevator which then accelerates upward. What happens to your drink?

Mysteries:

14.) If a helium balloon is released into the air, it rises upward until it finds an equilibrium position and comes to rest. A sinking submarine, on the other hand, simply sinks to the bottom, without ever finding an equilibrium position in the water. Why?

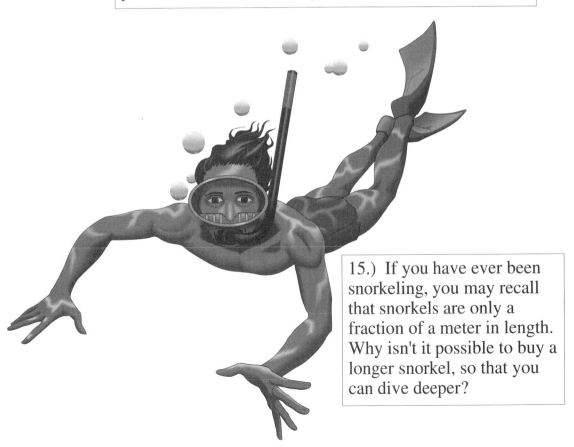

15.) If you have ever been snorkeling, you may recall that snorkels are only a fraction of a meter in length. Why isn't it possible to buy a longer snorkel, so that you can dive deeper?

𝕸𝖆𝖌𝖎𝖈:

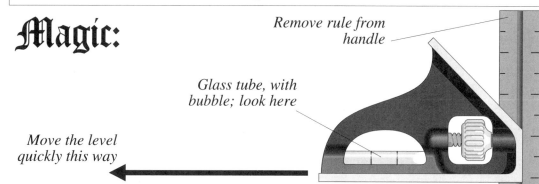

Remove rule from handle

Glass tube, with bubble; look here

Move the level quickly this way

The Trouble with Bubbles

Place a carpenter's level on a table and look closely at the bubble. If you don't have a carpenter's level, some adjustable squares, as pictured to the right, have a small leveling device built into the handle. The handle can be removed from the rule for this demonstration. Place the level or the handle from the adjustable square on a table. While watching the bubble, move the level quickly in a horizontal direction parallel to the glass tube. Which way does the bubble move?

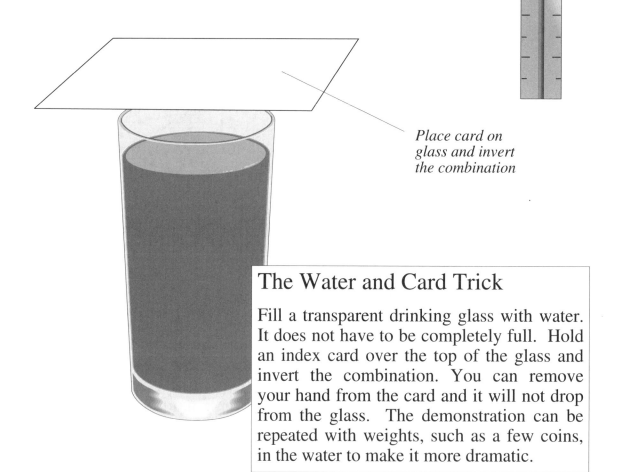

Place card on glass and invert the combination

The Water and Card Trick

Fill a transparent drinking glass with water. It does not have to be completely full. Hold an index card over the top of the glass and invert the combination. You can remove your hand from the card and it will not drop from the glass. The demonstration can be repeated with weights, such as a few coins, in the water to make it more dramatic.

𝕸𝖆𝖌𝖎𝖈:

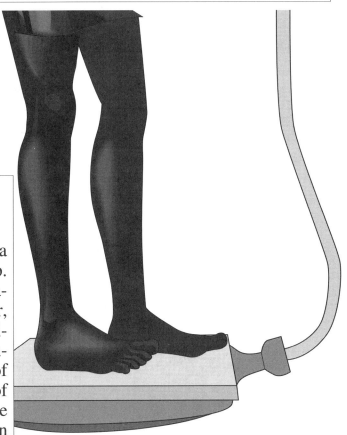

The Lifting Power of Water

Obtain a hot water bottle with a long tube attached to the top. Partially fill the bottle with water and lay it flat on the floor, holding the long tube vertically, as high as it will reach. Insert a funnel into the top end of the tube. Place a flat piece of wood on the hot water bottle and have a volunteer stand on the wood. As you pour water into the funnel, the volunteer will feel his or her body being raised.

Icing the Candle

Fasten a birthday candle to the bottom of a beaker and light the candle. Drop a few pieces of dry ice into the bottom of the beaker. The candle will go out in a few moments. Is this because of the drop in temperature?

𝔐𝔞𝔤𝔦𝔠:

The Magic Ice Cube

Fill two transparent glass containers, one with water and one with rubbing alcohol. Present these to an unsuspecting volunteer and drop an ice cube into each one. Do the ice cubes float?

WARNING - Rubbing alcohol is poisonous!

Place an ice cube in each glass

Alcohol

Water

Pressure in the Leg

A device which is becoming common in today's homes is a *sphygmomanometer*—a blood pressure meter. Use one of these devices to measure the blood pressure in a volunteer's arm and then repeat the measurement on his or her *leg* (at the calf) in a standing position. What do you find?

120 80

𝕸𝖞𝖙𝖍:

1.) Water is an incompressible fluid.

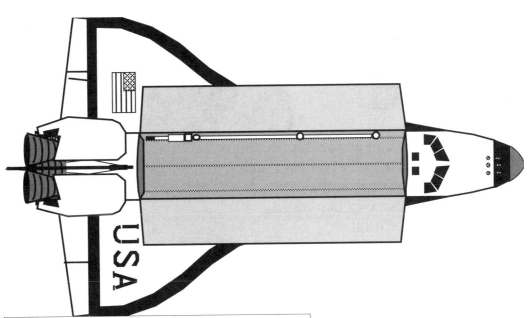

2.) Astronauts could maneuver across the outside surface of a spacecraft in orbit by using suction cups.

𝔐𝔶𝔱𝔥:

3.) The pressure on the bottom of a vessel containing a liquid is equal to the weight of the liquid divided by the area of the bottom.

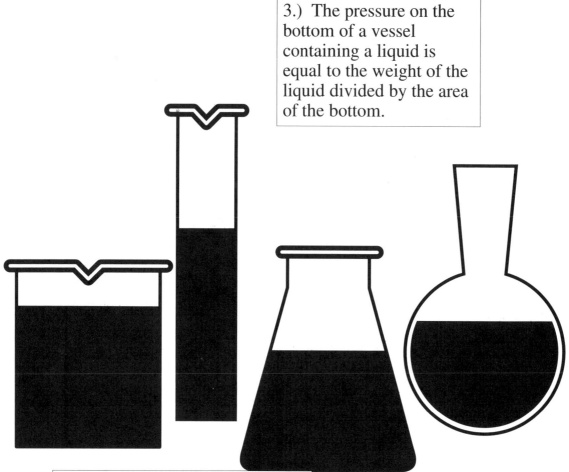

4.) Pressure in an incompressible fluid depends only on depth and does not depend on the cross sectional shape of the vessel holding the fluid.

Discussions; Chapter 8—Fluids

𝔐𝔶𝔰𝔱𝔢𝔯𝔦𝔢𝔰:

1.) As an ice cube in a glass of water melts, does the level of the water in the glass rise, fall, or stay the same?

This is a particularly meaningful question if the glass is full to the brim, so that the ice cubes project well above the lip of the glass. Will the water spill as the ice cubes melt? The answer is *no*. The density of the ice cube is smaller than that of water by some fraction which varies slightly depending on the characteristics of the water (salt water, distilled water, tap water, etc.). Let us assume that our ice has a density that is 92% of that of our water. Thus, 92% of the volume of the ice cube is submerged in the water. An alternate description of this situation is that the amount of water displaced is 92% of the volume of the ice cube. Let us imagine that that region of space occupied *by the part of the ice cube that is underwater* is an imaginary vessel into which we will place the water which results from the melting of the ice cube. Now, when the ice cube completely melts, what is the volume of the water into which it melts? Since the density of ice is 92% that of water, the volume of the water from the ice cube is 92% of the volume of the ice cube! Thus, this water perfectly fills our imaginary vessel, exactly to the level of the water outside the vessel. As a result, the water level in the glass *undergoes no change* during the melting of the ice cube.

2.) Why are tennis balls stored in *pressurized* cans?

The pressure inside a tennis ball is higher than atmospheric pressure. If tennis balls were not stored in pressurized cans, the large pressure difference between the inside of the ball and the outside would drive some of the air inside the ball to slowly leak out. Thus, balls stored for a long time before use would lose some of their liveliness. Maintaining a higher pressure on the outside of the ball during storage reduces the leakage and maintains the liveliness.

Once a ball has been removed from the pressurized can, the leakage of air from the ball can be minimized by *storing the ball in your freezer*. This will reduce the pressure of the gas in the ball and lessen the leakage rate.

3.) Cream is thicker than milk, right? Yet it *floats* on the top of the milk in the bottle (this Mystery may only make sense to *older* readers!). What's going on here?

This Mystery appeals to the possible confusion between *viscosity* (internal friction in the fluid) and *density* (mass per unit volume). The phrase "Cream is thicker than milk" is a reference to a *viscosity* comparison between cream and milk—cream is more viscous. *Density*, however, is an independent (though somewhat related) characteristic. Even though cream is *more viscous* than milk, it is *less dense* than milk. Thus, the cream floats to the top of the milk, according to Archimedes' Principle.

4.) Why are canoes so easy to capsize?

The stability of a floating object depends on the relative positions of the *center of gravity* and the *center of buoyancy*. The center of gravity is a relatively familiar concept to students of science, and represents a single point at which the weight of the floating object can be imagined to be applied. The center of buoyancy is perhaps not so familiar. It is the center of gravity *of the water which is displaced by the floating object.* Thus, the center of buoyancy is the point at which the buoyant force on the floating object can be imagined to be acting. In general, if the center of buoyancy is above the center of gravity, then the floating object is in equilibrium. This situation is shown on the left side of the diagram below for an object in water. The light-tinted cube is made of a low density material such as wood, while the dark material at the bottom is of higher density, such as metal. The overall density of the object is less than that of water, so that the system floats.

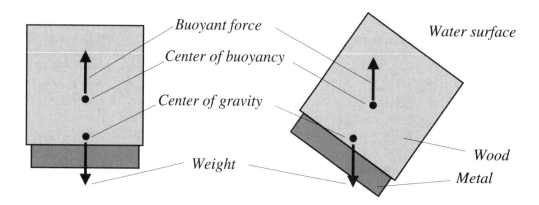

If the floating object were to tip over, as shown in the right side of the diagram, the two forces (weight and buoyant force) will exert a *restoring torque*, which will tend to rotate the floating object back to the equilibrium position. When the object tips, the shape of the water displaced changes, so that there is some shifting of the center of buoyancy. If the center of gravity and the center of buoyancy are well-separated, however, the floating position is quite stable.

The floating stability of ships is increased by incorporating *ballast* in the lower regions of the hull. By adding this large mass near the bottom of the ship, the center of mass is lowered, creating a larger restoring torque due to the weight and buoyant force when the ship tilts. The diagram above is a simplified model of a ship with ballast.

Now, what about the canoe? Because of the large area of the bottom of the canoe, and its relatively small weight, it does not sink very deeply into the water, even when occupied. As a result, the center of buoyancy is very close to the surface of the water. If the occupants of the canoe are sitting nice and low in the canoe, then the center of gravity of the system is also close to the surface of the water, but above the surface. The center of gravity is higher than the center of buoyancy, so that this is an inherently unstable position. If the occupant were to lean over (while sitting), the canoe will start to tip. In this case, the center of buoyancy shifts quite a bit toward the direction of the lean, due to the shape of the bottom of the canoe. As a result of this shift, there is a restoring torque which will keep the canoe from capsizing. This is shown in the diagram below.

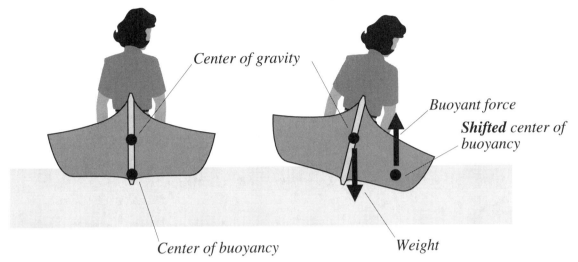

If the person in the canoe were standing, however, the center of gravity of the system is much higher, and there is a large separation of the two centers, with the center of gravity higher than the center of buoyancy. Now, if the person leans over, the center of gravity can move to the right by a distance larger than the center of buoyancy can shift, as shown below.

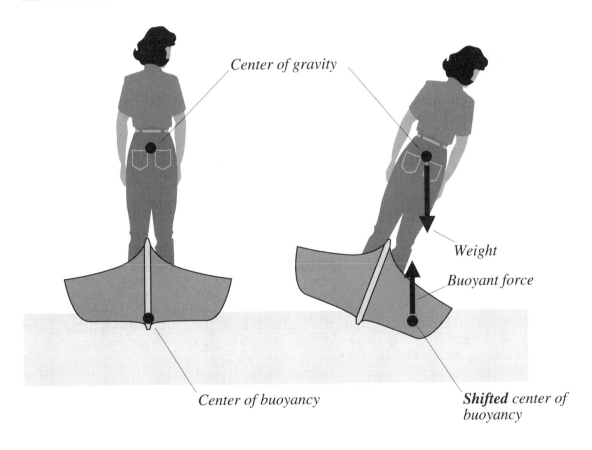

In this situation, notice that the two forces do not result in a restoring torque. The torque is such as to continue the original rotation and the result is the capsizing of the canoe.

An interesting application of these ideas is a research ship called FLIP (Floating Laboratory Instrument Platform). It can float in the normal orientation as well as a second orientation. If holding tanks in the rear portion of the ship are flooded, this ballast causes the stern of the ship to sink and it achieves a new stable orientation with the stern at the bottom and the bow at the top, projecting out of the water at 90° from the "normal" orientation. In this way, the stern is located about 100 m below the surface, allowing for studies of the water at this depth. A photograph of this vessel in its "flipped" orientation is available on page 454 of D. Halliday, R. Resnick and J. Walker, *Fundamentals of Physics*, 4th ed., John Wiley & Sons, New York, 1993.

5.) Why does hot water clean clothes better than cold water?

The success of water in cleaning clothes depends on the ability of the water to reach the particles of dirt in the threads of the cloth. Some of these particles of dirt are wedged in very tight corners and nooks between threads. In order for a water droplet to make contact with the dirt, the water surface would have to exhibit very large distortion as the water is pushed into the tight area. The surface tension of water is too high for the water surface to distort enough for the water to enter some of these very tiny regions. But *the surface tension depends on the temperature* of the water—the higher the temperature, the lower the surface tension. Thus, hotter water is more successful in entering these remote areas and "wetting" the particles of dirt.

Modern detergents can create the same effect in cold water by significantly reducing the surface tension of the water, removing the need for the water to be hot.

6.) Consider a drink "on the rocks". Alcohol is less dense than ice. So does the ice *float* in an alcoholic beverage?

In the Magic demonstration, The Magic Ice Cube, later in this chapter, an ice cube is placed in rubbing alcohol and it sinks, since the density of ice is larger than that of alcohol. Thus, should we expect the same result if we place an ice cube in an alcoholic beverage, such as whiskey or gin, making a drink "on the rocks"?

What we find is that the ice cube generally *floats* in this situation. An alcoholic beverage is only partially composed of alcohol. The "proof" rating on the bottle indicates the fraction (by volume) of the liquid which is alcohol, with the proof number being twice the percentage. For, example, a typical value for an alcoholic beverage is 80 proof, which means that 40% of the liquid is alcohol. Much of the remaining liquid is water. Thus, the overall density of the liquid can be larger than that of ice, so that the ice cube floats. The density of the liquid can be made even higher by incorporating "mixers" such as soda, tonic, etc., with the liquor.

What about a higher proof beverage? For example, Bacardi (Bacardi Corporation, San Juan, Puerto Rico) makes a rum which is 151 proof, or 75.5% alcohol. If an ice cube is dropped into a glass of this beverage, it sinks! The percentage of alcohol is so high in this particular rum that the overall density of the liquid is less than that of the ice.

7.) Why are bottles of intravenous fluid hung so high over the hospital bed?

The fluid in the bottle must enter the blood. The role of the intravenous needle is to provide a connection between the tube connected to the bottle and the blood vessel. The direction of the flow will depend on the pressure difference at the needle. If the blood pressure is higher than the fluid pressure, blood will leave the body and go into the tube. If the pressure in the tube is higher, fluid will flow from the tube to the blood stream, which is the desired result. This higher pressure in the tube is provided by hanging the bottle above the patient, resulting in additional pressure due to the depth of the fluid.

An interesting comparison can be made with blood *donations*. In this case, the receptacle for the blood is hung *below* the body, so that the pressure in the tube to the receptacle is lower than the pressure in the blood, resulting in the flow of blood out of the body.

8.) In 1984, and again in 1986, people living near lakes in a mountainous part of Cameroon were suffocated when the air was displaced suddenly by carbon dioxide. *How could this happen*?

A number of factors conspired to create this natural disaster, associated with the lakes near the villages in which the people lived, Lake Manoun in 1984 and Lake Nios in 1986. The first factor is that these lakes are very deep, having arisen from volcanic calderas. In a deep lake located in a temperate zone, variations in temperature will cause mixing of the water at various depths. For example, as the air above the lake cools, the water at the surface cools, becomes more dense than the water below, and sinks. This process provides a continuous circulation of water through various depths of the lake. The lakes in Cameroon, however, are located in a region of very little seasonal variation. This is the second factor that contributed to the disaster. As a result of both factors, the mixing process does not occur, so that water that is deep in the lake *stays* deep in the lake. The third factor is that the water deep in these lakes has absorbed carbon dioxide from springs entering the lakes near the bottom. Due to the large pressure at the bottom of the deep lakes, a large amount of carbon dioxide *can be* dissolved in the water. Due to the lack of circulation, a large amount of carbon dioxide *is* dissolved over long time periods and is not released by being brought to the surface.

This represents an explosive situation. If the pressure on the water containing the dissolved carbon dioxide were to be released, the carbon dioxide would suddenly come out of solution, just as when a soft drink can is opened. Here is where the fourth factor enters the picture. In 1984, a landslide on the shore of Lake Manoun caused rocks and dirt to fall into the lake, disturbing the layers of water that had not been previously mixed. The water containing the dissolved carbon dioxide was brought to a shallower depth, so that massive amounts of carbon dioxide were brought out of solution and floated to the surface as bubbles. Since carbon dioxide is more dense than air, the carbon dioxide released from the lake spread out from the lake along the ground, displacing the air as it spread. As the gas passed over villages, the inhabitants suffocated from lack of oxygen.

This tragedy was repeated in 1986 at Lake Nios, where an unknown event, possibly a volcanic tremor, caused a similar outpouring of gas, causing the deaths of 1700 people.

9.) What is the doctor or nurse listening for through her stethoscope when she takes your blood pressure?

When the blood pressure cuff is pumped up, it cuts off the flow of blood in the arteries and veins. As the pressure in the cuff is slowly reduced, a point is reached where the blood can just squeeze through the collapsed blood vessels. This flow is *turbulent*, and the chaotic movement of the blood through the vessel creates noise. This is what the doctor or nurse listens for. When the turbulent noise first appears, the systolic reading is taken. Similarly, when the turbulent noise disappears, representing smooth flow of blood once more, the diastolic reading is taken.

10.) Why is it a common practice to *lick* a thread before attempting to push it through the eye of a needle?

This technique is taking advantage of *surface tension*. When the thread is dry, the individual filaments tend to point in many directions, so that the end of the thread has a large effective cross section. If the thread is licked so as to be wet, the surface tension of the saliva pulls the filaments together, resulting in a smaller cross section, which is easier to push through the eye of a needle.

This effect can be demonstrated by looking at the effect of dipping an art brush in a glass of water. When the brush is in the water, the individual filaments have little attraction for each other, which can be seen by twirling the brush—the filaments move outward. When the brush is removed from the water, the filaments form a tight bunch, due to the effect of the surface tension.

11.) Why are airport runways longer in Denver than in San Francisco?

The design length of an airport runway depends on many factors. Some of these include the types of airplane and the length of the flight. Large, heavy aircraft require a longer runway in order to achieve the high speeds necessary for the lift on the wing to raise the large weight. For longer flights, more fuel must be carried, so, again, a longer runway is necessary to allow the aircraft to reach the necessary speed to raise the larger weight.

Let's assume that the aircraft and the length of flight are the same for the two airports mentioned. Why would there be a difference in the runway lengths? The primary reason for the difference comes from the difference in *elevation* of the two airports. Denver is at a much higher elevation than San Francisco, hence its nickname, the *Mile High City*. In fact, the Capitol building in downtown Denver is almost exactly one mile above sea level. Due to the higher elevation, the density of air in Denver is much less than it is in San Francisco, which is at sea level. With less dense air, the lift on the aircraft wings at takeoff is smaller for a given speed than the lift on an airplane at the same speed in San Francisco. Thus, the aircraft must reach a higher speed on the ground, requiring a longer runway to reach this speed. A similar effect requires a longer runway for landing also, since the aircraft must land at a higher velocity to keep it airborne during the landing process. The slowing down process then requires more distance on the ground.

An approximate rule of thumb for runway length correction is given by Horonjeff and McKelvey (R. Horonjeff, and F. X. McKelvey, *Planning and Design of Airports*, 4th ed., McGraw-Hill, Inc., New York, 1994), suggesting that the length be increased by 7% for each 1000 feet of elevation above sea level. Thus, for Denver, the runway length must be approximately $(1.07)^5 = 1.4$ times as long as (or, 40% longer than) a corresponding runway in San Francisco. Indeed, the newest runway at Denver is some 16,000 feet in length. In comparison, the required length for the airplane requiring the largest takeoff distance (the Boeing 747-400) at sea level is 11,100 feet (according to N. Ashford, and P. H. Wright, *Airport Engineering*, 3rd ed., John Wiley & Sons, New York, 1992). The Denver runway length is about 44% longer than this, so that the increase in elevation will be adequately addressed.

Another consideration for runway length is the *ambient temperature*. Using a reference temperature, which is a composite of various average temperatures (see Horonjeff and McKelvey, p. 367, for an equation), a correction for temperature can be calculated for a given location. In general, as the reference temperature increases, the runway length must also increase. This is due once more to the reduced density of air, this time a result of the higher temperature.

12.) Why are scuba divers instructed to *exhale* while ascending to the surface?

The large pressure changes associated with swimming underwater can have uncomfortable, and even fatal, results on the body. The problems associated with these pressure changes are often categorized as "squeezes", and such symptoms as *sinus squeeze, external ear squeeze, middle ear squeeze, face mask squeeze, lung squeeze* and *suit squeeze* can be found in books on skin diving (e.g., J. Reseck, *Scuba Safe and Simple*, Prentice-Hall, Inc., Englewood Cliffs, New Jersey, 1975).

One important consideration is the dependence of proper operation of the lungs on pressure balances between the air and the blood. Under normal conditions, the pressure of air in the lungs and the blood pressure have values that allow gas to flow *into* the blood, thus providing the source of oxygen that the body needs to survive.

As a scuba diver descends in water to even a modest depth, the external pressure on the body increases. In response, the pressure inside the body also increases. In particular, the *blood pressure also increases*. As the diver breathes from the scuba tank, the air in the lungs will also be at this increased pressure. Now, imagine that the diver ascends without exhaling. The air pressure in the lungs will remain relatively constant, while the body pressure and, in particular, the blood pressure will decrease. It is possible, even for modest depth changes, that the relatively high air pressure in the lungs can cause them to rupture and introduce air bubbles into the blood. If these bubbles are then carried to the heart or the brain, the diver could die. This situation is called an *air embolism*, and, according to Lee (O. Lee, *The Skin Diver's Bible*, Doubleday, New York, 1986), it is "without doubt the worst thing that can possibly happen to a diver, for air embolism is almost always fatal unless recompression and medical aid are immediate".

This danger is reduced by slowly exhaling as you ascend, thus keeping the lung and blood pressures equalized. See Mystery #15 for a related question.

13.) You are at a party in a tall building, and you are holding an iced drink, in which the level of the liquid is at the brim of the glass. You enter an elevator which then accelerates upward. What happens to your drink?

We appeal here to the *Principle of Equivalence* (see Chapter 22)—it is impossible to perform an experiment that will differentiate between a gravitational field and an accelerated reference frame. Thus, when the elevator accelerates upward, it is as if the gravitational field has increased in strength. You might be tempted to say that that will result in the ice cubes sinking more deeply in the fluid in the glass, causing the fluid to spill over the sides. But read carefully again Myth #4 in Chapter 13 of *PBWM*. In this Myth, we argued that large increases in gravity will not cause ships to sink. While the weight of the ice cubes in the drink will certainly increase, the pressure gradient in the fluid will also increase so that the buoyant force increases by the same factor as the weight. Thus, *the drink will be unaffected by the acceleration*!

14.) If a helium balloon is released into the air, it rises upward until it finds an equilibrium position and comes to rest. A sinking submarine, on the other hand, simply sinks to the bottom, without ever finding an equilibrium position in the water. Why?

The difference here is due to the *incompressibility* of water (well, almost—see Myth #1 in this Chapter) and the *compressibility* of air. The buoyant force applied by a fluid on an object is related to the pressure gradient over the vertical dimension of the object. This pressure gradient is a result of two factors—the variation in vertical height and the variation in density. The pressure gradient is often expressed as,

$$\Delta p = \rho g \Delta y$$

where ρ is the density of the fluid, g is the gravitational field and Δy is the height difference. This equation, however, is only true for fluids with a constant value for the density, which we call *incompressible fluids*. If the density varies with vertical position, the pressure varies in a more complicated way that requires knowledge of the functional dependence of the density with vertical position. We don't need to look at the complicated details here. We can just compare the behavior of the pressure in water and in air. As we move downward in water, the pressure increases solely because of the depth (ignoring the very small compressibility of water, discussed in Myth #1). Thus, the pressure *gradient* across the vertical dimension of the object (the submarine) remains constant. As a result, the buoyant force remains constant and, if the submarine were sinking to begin with, its weight must be larger than the buoyant force, and it will continue to sink.

Now, what about the balloon? As a helium balloon rises in the air, the pressure decreases. This decrease is due *both* to the decrease in "depth" in the atmosphere and the decrease in density. As a result, the pressure gradient over the vertical dimension of the balloon decreases. This results in a decreasing buoyant force as the balloon rises. Of course, the increasing size of the balloon, due to the decreasing external pressure, will result in an increase in the buoyant force, but this is not enough to compensate for the decrease due to the pressure gradient. Eventually, the buoyant force will decrease until it is equal in magnitude to the weight of the balloon. The net force on the balloon then goes to zero. It passes through this point with some momentum, so it may oscillate vertically for a short while as it transfers its kinetic energy to the air by means of the work done by the air friction. But eventually, it will come to rest at a certain height.

15.) If you have ever been snorkeling, you may recall that snorkels are only a fraction of a meter in length. Why isn't it possible to buy a longer snorkel, so that you can dive deeper?

This question is closely related to Mystery #12, in which a scuba diver fails to exhale while ascending. Let us think again about our negligent diver and imagine that he or she is a few meters under the surface of the water. As described in the discussion of Mystery #12, the body and the blood will exhibit relatively large pressures in this situation. The air in the lungs will also be at a large pressure.

Now, imagine that the diver places his or her mouth on one end of a very long snorkel, with the other end open to the atmosphere above the water surface. The high pressure air in the lungs will suddenly have a means of escape—through the snorkel and into the low pressure air above the water. As a result, the air in the lungs will lose pressure rapidly. This can cause the lungs to collapse (*pneumothorax*) and, if the pressure difference between the blood and the lungs is large enough, can cause blood to enter the lungs.

𝕸agic:

The Trouble with Bubbles

You will find that the bubble will move *in the direction of the acceleration*, forward while the level is speeding up and backward while it is slowing down. As the level speeds up, the fluid reacts as if there is an additional gravitational field applied opposite to the direction of the motion (the Principle of Equivalence, as in Mystery #13). Thus, there is a *pressure gradient* established, with the pressure increasing from the leading end of the fluid tube to the trailing end. This pressure gradient results in an additional buoyant force which pushes the bubble toward the front of the tube. When the level slows down, the pressure gradient reverses and the bubble moves toward the back.

The Water and Card Trick

This is a demonstration of the strength of the pressure of air. As the glass is inverted, a trapped volume of air is present in the bottom of the glass, which is now the highest part of the apparatus. As the water begins to fall out of the glass just after it is inverted, the trapped air expands. As a result, the pressure of the air drops. The water in the glass now feels a larger atmospheric pressure on the card from the bottom surface and a lower pressure on the top from the water and trapped air. As a result, the water is supported in the glass and does not fall out.

This demonstration also depends on the surface tension of water. The card does drop a small distance, so that a circular "edge" of the water is in contact with the atmosphere between the card and the cup. The distance is so small, however, that the surface tension is strong enough to prevent the water from leaking out from between the card and the cup.

The Lifting Power of Water

This is a demonstration that the pressure in a liquid depends only on depth for a cylindrical column (see Myths #3 and #4 in this Chapter for more discussion of this). The demonstration is surprising because observers will generally feel that the water will simply squirt out of the thin tube due to the weight of the person standing on the bag. On the contrary, pouring water into the tube results in the water entering the bag, even though the person is standing on it. A simple calculation will show that the pressure due to a column of water of height equal to the length of the tube is larger than the pressure due to the person standing on the bag. As a result, water enters the bag and lifts the person.

Icing the Candle

This demonstration depends on two factors: 1.) the density of carbon dioxide from the dry ice is larger than that of air; and 2.) the combustion process for the candle requires oxygen. As the dry ice sublimes, the resulting carbon dioxide gas begins to fill the beaker, pushing the lower density air upward and out of the container. Thus, the oxygen needed by the combustion process is removed from the beaker. The carbon dioxide cannot support combustion, so the candle flame dies. This is related to the fatal effects of carbon dioxide on the residents of Cameroon in Mystery #8 in this Chapter.

The Magic Ice Cube   WARNING—Rubbing Alcohol is poisonous!

You will find that the ice cube will float in the water, which is the expected result, but will sink in the alcohol. Since the alcohol appears just like water to the unsuspecting observer, the result is surprising. The specific gravity of ice is about 0.92 while the specific gravity of the rubbing alcohol commonly available is about 0.78 to 0.90, depending on the dilution of the alcohol with water. Thus, while the ice is less dense than water, it is more dense than alcohol, resulting in its sinking. For more discussion of this idea, see Mystery #6 in this Chapter.

Pressure in the Leg

Blood pressure is normally taken in the arm, since that is at the same approximate height as the heart. But the sphygmomanometer can be used to measure the pressure in the leg. If this is done, it is found that the pressure is higher when measured in the leg of a standing person than that measured in the same person's arm. This is due to the variation of pressure with depth, described by the following equation from Mystery #14 :

$$\Delta p = \rho g \Delta y$$

If we imagine that all of the blood in the body is a continuous fluid, filling up the vessels throughout the body, then there will be a variation of pressure with depth. It is just this variation that we are seeing in this Magic demonstration. By measuring the vertical distance between the points on the arm and the leg where the pressure is measured, a theoretical difference in pressure can be calculated with the equation above. The result in general is in relatively good agreement with the measured difference.

𝔐𝔶𝔱𝔥:

1.) Water is an incompressible fluid.

In performing calculations, it is often assumed that water is an incompressible fluid. While it is close to being incompressible, it is not *perfectly* incompressible.

We can express the *compressibility* (the inverse of *incompressibility*!) of a substance with a parameter called the *bulk modulus*, which is defined as follows:

$$B = -\frac{\Delta p}{\left(\dfrac{\Delta V}{V}\right)}$$

The negative sign indicates that the change in volume ΔV is negative for an increase in pressure Δp. The bulk modulus is a measure of how much pressure change is necessary to cause a certain fractional change in volume. Thus, a perfectly incompressible material would have an *infinite* bulk modulus.

The bulk modulus of water is 2.1×10^9 N·m^{-2}. This number is large, but it is not infinite. For comparison, the bulk modulus of steel is 1.6×10^{11} N·m^{-2}, so that water is easier to compress than steel, by about a factor of 75.

For additional comparison, we can use the Ideal Gas Law to calculate the bulk modulus for an ideal gas. If we assume that the temperature remains constant, the *isothermal* bulk modulus can be shown to be numerically equal to the pressure of the gas*. Thus, for a gas at atmospheric pressure, $B = p_{atm} = 1.01 \times 10^5$ N·m^{-2} . This is four orders of magnitude smaller than the bulk modulus for water, indicating the familiar fact that gases are significantly easier to compress than water.

---

*Using calculus,

$$pV = nRT \quad \rightarrow \quad p = \frac{nRT}{V} \quad \rightarrow \quad \frac{dp}{dV} = -\frac{nRT}{V^2} \quad \rightarrow \quad dp = -\frac{nRT}{V^2}dV$$

Then,

$$B = -\frac{dp}{\left(\dfrac{dV}{V}\right)} = -\frac{\left(-\dfrac{nRT}{V^2}dV\right)}{\left(\dfrac{dV}{V}\right)} = \frac{nRT}{V} = p$$

2.) Astronauts could maneuver across the outside surface of a spacecraft in orbit by using suction cups.

The operation of suction cups is another popular application of the myth of the "sucking force" (as discussed in Myths #1 and #3 in Chapter 12 of *PBWM*). It certainly feels like a suction cup is "holding onto" a surface. In reality, however, the suction cup operates by the same principle as a straw or a vacuum cleaner, in which a low pressure region is created and the higher pressure of the atmosphere succeeds in pushing the liquid up the straw or the dirt up the vacuum cleaner hose. As a suction cup is pressed against a surface by a force from a hand, some air is forced out from the interior space. As the hand is removed from the suction cup, its natural springiness causes it to begin to return to its original shape. Since the edge of the cup makes a tight fit against the surface, it is unlikely that there will be an exchange of air between the interior and the atmosphere—the air inside the cup is trapped.   As the material of the cup moves outward, the volume of trapped air is increased and, according to the Ideal Gas Law, the pressure of the trapped air drops.   Thus, the difference in pressure between the outside atmosphere and that of the trapped air is what pushes the cup tightly against the surface.

Now, let's imagine trying to use the suction cup on the surface of a spacecraft in orbit around the Earth. No matter how tightly you try to push the cup against the surface, you will not create a significant pressure difference between the inside of the cup and the outside, since there is virtually no air in the vicinity! Thus, the suction cup will simply drift away from the surface.

3.) The pressure on the bottom of a vessel containing a liquid is equal to the weight of the liquid divided by the area of the bottom.

This is only true *for a cylindrical vessel with its axis vertical*. Think about the following vessel shapes, where we are assuming that the cross sectional area of the bottom surface of each vessel is the same:

According to the traditional claim that the pressure depends only on the depth of the fluid (but see Myth #4), the pressure at the bottom of all three of these vessels will be the same. It is clear, however, that these vessels contain *different weights of fluid*. Thus, it certainly cannot be true to say that the pressure is the weight of the fluid divided by the area of the bottom surface. For a related discussion, see E. R. Dietz, "Vector Analysis and the Hydrostatic Paradox", *American Journal of Physics*, **59**, 89, 1991.

4.) Pressure in an incompressible fluid depends only on depth and does not depend on the cross sectional shape of the vessel holding the fluid.

Now, wait a minute, didn't we just use this claim to argue against the statement in Myth #3 above? Indeed, we did. And this statement is true in all situations involving *single* incompressible fluids. But what about a *mixture of immiscible fluids*, such as oil and water? What happens to the pressure on the bottom of the container *as the originally mixed fluids separate*?

To answer this question, let us first look at the rightmost vessel in the discussion of Myth #3. How can the pressure at the bottom be the same as in the other vessels, if there is less fluid to exert its weight on the bottom? The answer comes from a combination of *Pascal's Principle* and *Newton's Third Law*. Pascal's Principle tells us that the pressure in the fluid is exerted in all directions. Thus, the pressure in the fluid is exerted *upward* on the inward sloping sides of the vessel. By Newton's Third Law, then, the sides exert a *downward* force on the fluid. This force is just enough to account for the "missing weight" and the total force on the bottom of the container is the same as with the other shapes. It is an interesting exercise to argue this equality, which is made easier by considering a container which is formed from two joined cylinders of unequal radius, as we do below. The container with outwardly sloping sides (the middle vessel in the discussion of Myth #3) is even easier to handle. Imagine the cylindrical portion of the fluid directly above the bottom of the vessel. This fluid is supported directly by the bottom surface. Then, the portions of the fluid that are above the sloping sides are supported by the surfaces of the sides.

Now, what about the situation with immiscible fluids? We can simplify the argument by imagining the vessel with the shape shown to the right, filled with a *mixture* of two fluids.

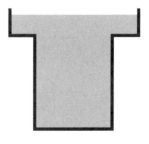

Now, let's redraw the diagram after we have waited a while and the immiscible liquids have separated. We have adjusted things (aren't we clever?) so that the ultimate dividing line between the liquids coincides with the break in the vessel walls, so that the final situation appears as follows:

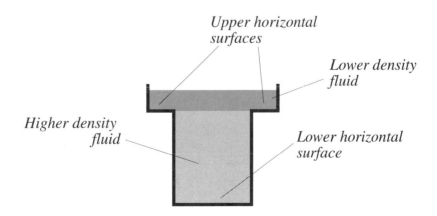

Upper horizontal surfaces

Lower density fluid

Higher density fluid

Lower horizontal surface

Now, let us consider the ring-shaped portion of the fluid that is above the *upper horizontal surfaces*, as indicated in the diagram. Compared to the previous figure, the weight supported by these surfaces is *smaller* than in the previous diagram, since the lower density fluid has migrated to the top. But since the vessel must be supporting the same total weight of fluid, the lower horizontal surface must then be supporting a *larger* weight than before. Thus, a larger force is distributed over the bottom surface and the pressure must necessarily be higher. As a result, we see that *the pressure at the bottom of this vessel has increased because of the separation of the immiscible fluids*!

It is also possible to show that the pressure *decreases* as the fluids separate in a vessel with *inwardly* sloping sides.

Further discussion of this concept can be found in A. Arons, *A Guide to Introductory Physics Teaching*, John Wiley & Sons, New York, 1990, pages 204 and 281-282.

Chapter 9
Temperature and Heat

Mysteries:

WARNING - Walking on hot coals is dangerous!

1.) How do firewalkers walk across hot coals without burning their feet?

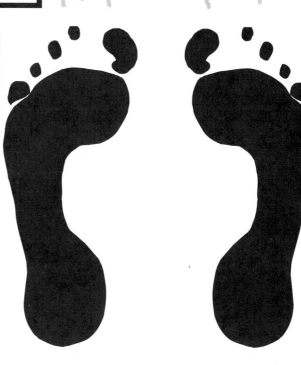

2.) Why is *steam* at 100°C more dangerous than *water* at 100°C?

DANGER

𝕸ysteries:

3.) Why is the climate on the coasts of a large continent more moderate than in the inland regions?

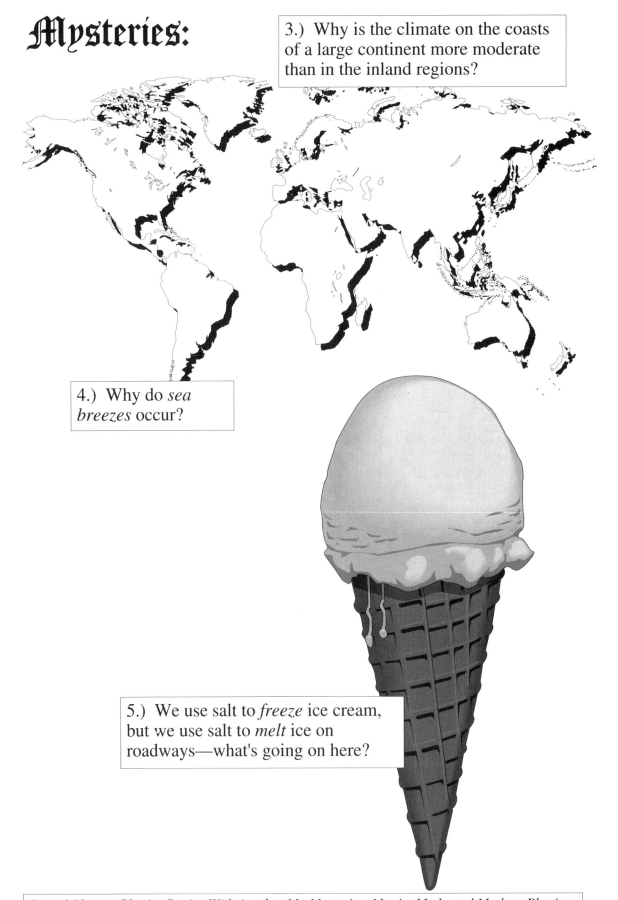

4.) Why do *sea breezes* occur?

5.) We use salt to *freeze* ice cream, but we use salt to *melt* ice on roadways—what's going on here?

𝔐ysteries:

6.) You are making cookies on a cookie sheet with turned up edges. When you remove the cookies from the oven, you find that the cookies near the edges are more well done than those near the middle. Why is this?

7.) Why do you never need to change the spark plugs in a diesel engine?

8.) Insulation is used in walls in a building to reduce conduction "losses". But wait a minute. Plain old air is a great thermal insulator. Why don't we just leave the walls empty and let the air do the job?

Mysteries:

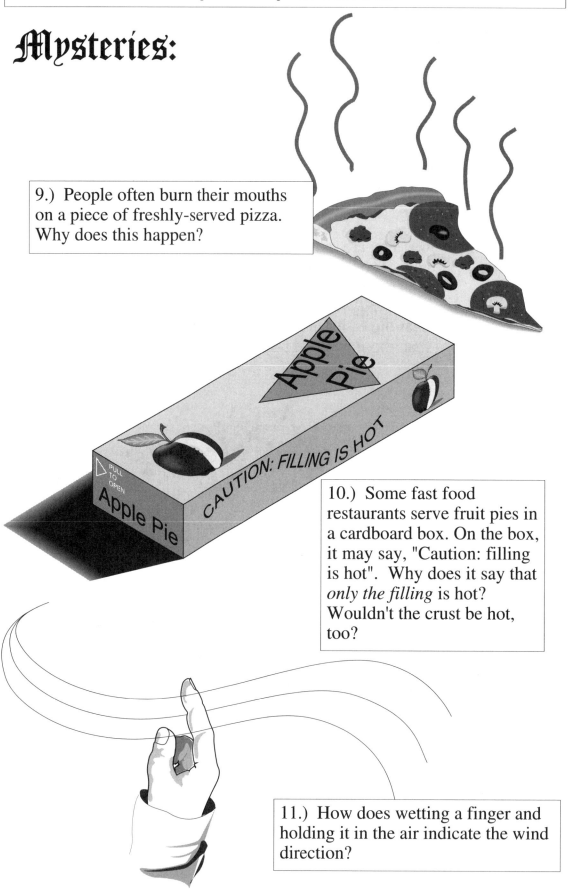

9.) People often burn their mouths on a piece of freshly-served pizza. Why does this happen?

10.) Some fast food restaurants serve fruit pies in a cardboard box. On the box, it may say, "Caution: filling is hot". Why does it say that *only the filling* is hot? Wouldn't the crust be hot, too?

11.) How does wetting a finger and holding it in the air indicate the wind direction?

Mysteries:

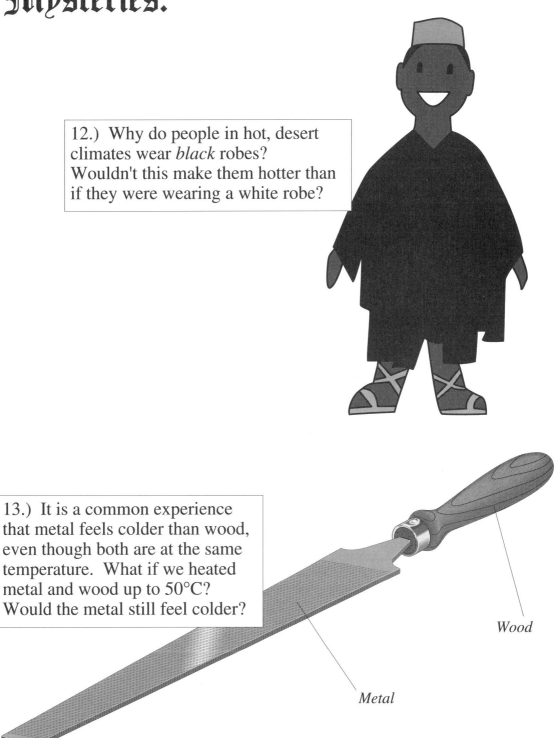

12.) Why do people in hot, desert climates wear *black* robes? Wouldn't this make them hotter than if they were wearing a white robe?

13.) It is a common experience that metal feels colder than wood, even though both are at the same temperature. What if we heated metal and wood up to 50°C? Would the metal still feel colder?

Wood

Metal

Mysteries:

14.) Putting your bare hand into a hot oven is uncomfortable but tolerable. But if you happen to touch a dish in that oven with your bare hand, it is very painful and can cause a nasty burn. Why is there this difference, when the air and the dish are at the same temperature?

15.) When your automobile engine overheats, some people suggest that you turn on the *heater*! Is this good advice?

𝕸ysteries:

16.) What is the hottest item in your house?

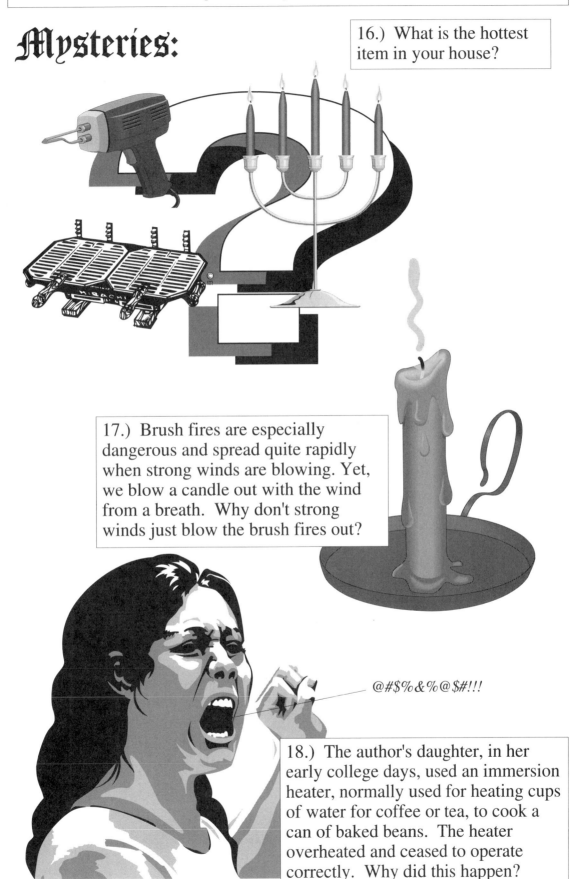

17.) Brush fires are especially dangerous and spread quite rapidly when strong winds are blowing. Yet, we blow a candle out with the wind from a breath. Why don't strong winds just blow the brush fires out?

@#$%&%@$#!!!

18.) The author's daughter, in her early college days, used an immersion heater, normally used for heating cups of water for coffee or tea, to cook a can of baked beans. The heater overheated and ceased to operate correctly. Why did this happen?

𝕸𝖆𝖌𝖎𝖈:

A Hot Band

Touch a rubber band to your lip or forehead and note its sensation of temperature. Stretch the rubber band and "measure" the temperature again—it should be warmer. Return the band to its original length and "measure" the temperature again—it is now cool. Why does this happen?

Touch here

The Jumping Coin

Place an empty glass beverage bottle in a freezer for a couple of hours. Remove the bottle and wet the edge. Place a coin, such as a dime, on top of the bottle so as to seal the opening. Wrap your hands around the bottle and observe the behavior of the coin.

𝔐agic:

Burning Metal

Using pliers or tongs, place two pieces of steel in a candle flame—a bolt and some steel wool (pull the steel wool apart, so that the filaments are separated). Does metal burn?

Fireblockers

Sit close to a fire in a fireplace and feel the warmth on your face. Close your eyes and note the feeling of warmth on your eyelids. Keeping your eyes closed, put on a pair of ordinary glasses. How do your eyelids feel now?

𝔐𝔶𝔱𝔥:

$$Q = mc\Delta T$$

1.) The specific heat of a substance is the amount of heat necessary to raise one gram of the substance by a temperature of 1°C.

2.) Window glass is a good thermal insulator.

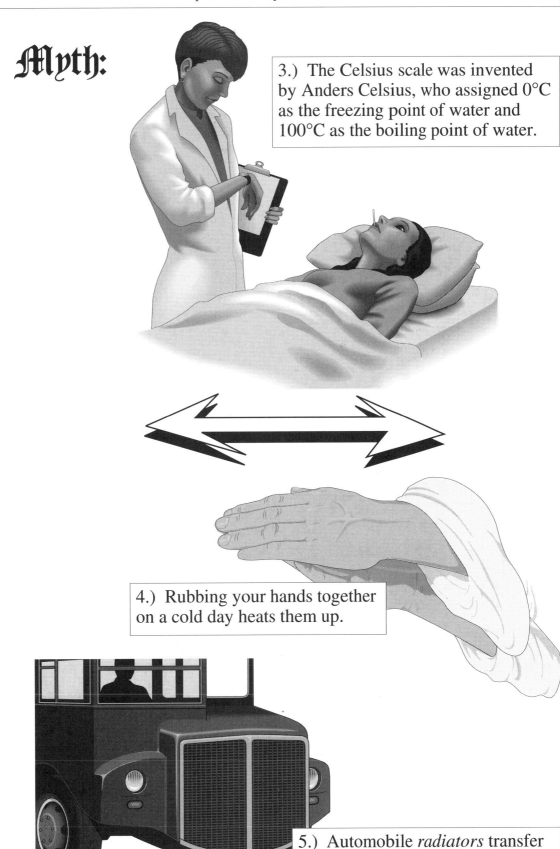

𝔐𝔶𝔱𝔥:

3.) The Celsius scale was invented by Anders Celsius, who assigned 0°C as the freezing point of water and 100°C as the boiling point of water.

4.) Rubbing your hands together on a cold day heats them up.

5.) Automobile *radiators* transfer energy by means of *radiation*.

𝕸𝖞𝖙𝖍:

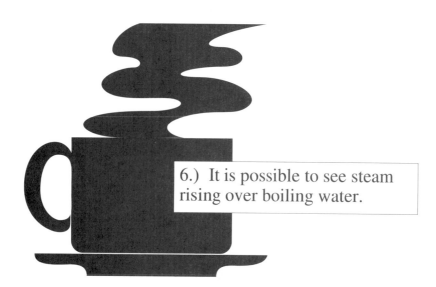

6.) It is possible to see steam rising over boiling water.

7.) Solids expand because the amplitudes of the molecular vibrations increase.

Myth:

8.) If you increase the temperature of the air in a room of a house, there is more internal energy in the air *in the room*.

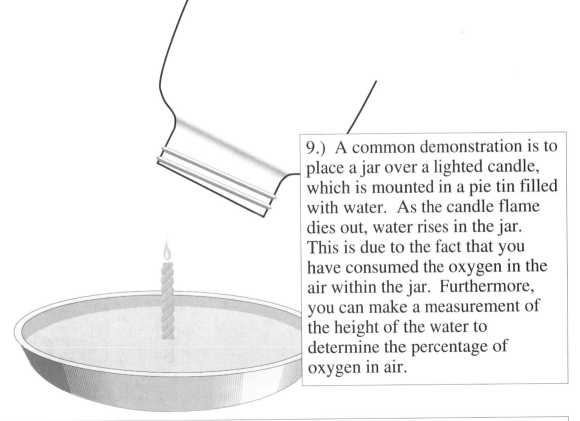

9.) A common demonstration is to place a jar over a lighted candle, which is mounted in a pie tin filled with water. As the candle flame dies out, water rises in the jar. This is due to the fact that you have consumed the oxygen in the air within the jar. Furthermore, you can make a measurement of the height of the water to determine the percentage of oxygen in air.

Myth:

10.) The higher the temperature of a hot skillet, the faster drops of water sprinkled on the skillet will vaporize.

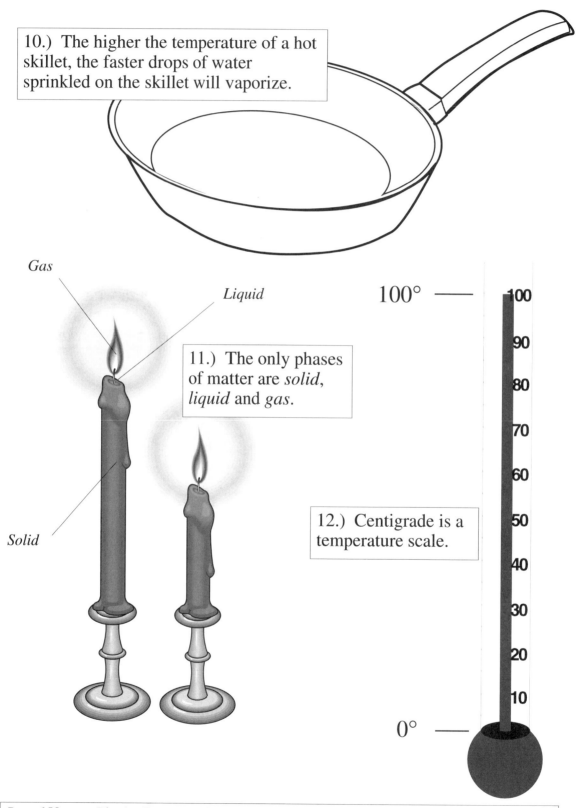

Gas

Liquid

11.) The only phases of matter are *solid*, *liquid* and *gas*.

Solid

100°

12.) Centigrade is a temperature scale.

0°

100
90
80
70
60
50
40
30
20
10

Discussions; Chapter 9—Temperature and Heat

𝕸𝖞𝖘𝖙𝖊𝖗𝖎𝖊𝖘:

1.) How do firewalkers walk across hot coals without burning their feet?
WARNING - Walking on hot coals is dangerous!

There are two major effects that help to prevent the burning of feet in this demonstration. The first is suggested by the fact that the firewalker walks *briskly* over the coals. The coals have relatively low heat capacity (see Myth #1) as well as relatively low thermal conductivity (see Myth #2). Thus, there is not much energy in the coals to be transferred and what energy is there transfers only slowly. As a consequence, if the contact time between the foot and the coals is short, little energy is transferred to the foot and a burn is avoided.

The second important consideration is the *Leidenfrost Effect*. This effect can be seen when drops of water are sprinkled onto a hot skillet. The drops form beads and dance around the skillet. When a drop first hits the hot surface, some water from its bottom surface vaporizes rapidly and forms a layer of gas under the drop. This layer of gas prevents the rest of the drop from actually touching the skillet surface. The suspended water forms a drop shape, due to the effects of surface tension. As the gas layer conducts heat from the pan to the drop, more water evaporates to sustain the gas layer. Meanwhile, the drop dances around under the effects of complicated forces from the bubbling and popping of the drop and others around it. Eventually, the drop no longer has enough liquid left to sustain the gas layer and the remaining drop falls to the surface and vaporizes. See Myth #10 in this Chapter for more discussion of this example.

A common application of the Leidenfrost effect is the wetting of a finger before touching it to a hot iron. A dry finger applied to the surface would result in a possible burn. With a wet finger, however, the Leidenfrost effect results in a thin layer of gas which prevents contact between the finger and the iron for the brief duration of the interaction.

In the case of firewalking, the walker generally has water on his or her feet, either from contact with wet ground or from sweat due to fear or excitement. Thus, when the foot contacts the hot coals, this water is vaporized and briefly forms a protective layer of water vapor. For more information, see J. R. Taylor, "Firewalking: A Lesson in Physics", *The Physics Teacher*, **27**, 166, 1989.

2.) Why is *steam* at 100°C more dangerous than *water* at 100°C?

This is due primarily to the very large heat of vaporization of water (2.3×10^6 J·kg^{-1}). Let us consider placing a hand in *water* first. If a relatively cold hand is brought into contact with water at 100°C, energy will flow from the water to the hand. As a result, the temperature of the water near the hand will immediately begin to drop, resulting in a decreasing flow of energy into the hand. Thus, although there is a large energy flow at the beginning, the flow rate drops and, if the amount of water is relatively small, a scald may be avoided.

If the cold hand is brought into contact with *steam* at 100°C, energy will begin to flow again. As energy leaves the steam, however, it does not *cool*, since the temperature remains constant as the steam condenses. Thus, the hand is surrounded by a gas that *remains* at 100°C. Due to the large heat of vaporization, the temperature will remain at 100°C for a large amount of energy flow, which translates to a relatively long time period. What's more, as the steam condenses, the pressure around the hand drops, causing more steam to be pushed into the region near your hand, providing a steady flow of 100°C steam to burn the hand.

Of course, an additional factor is that steam can be at a temperature higher than 100°C, making it even more dangerous.

3.) Why is the climate on the coasts of a large continent more moderate than in the inland regions?

This is one of the *long-term* effects of the interaction between the ocean and the atmosphere. Much of this interaction is based on the very different specific heats of water and air (see Myth #1 in this Chapter). Because of the very different densities of air and water, we will express the specific heats of the two substances in terms of energy per degree of temperature change *per unit volume*, rather than the more common ratio of energy per degree of temperature change *per unit mass*. Thus, we will look at a cubic centimeter of water adjacent to a cubic centimeter of air, which will be a meaningful model for analyzing the energy exchange process. In contrast, if we consider a *gram* of water adjacent to a *gram* of air, we would be looking at energy exchange between two volumes differing by almost a factor of 1000. With this proviso, then, the specific heats that we compare are $4.02 \text{ J} \cdot \text{K}^{-1} \cdot \text{cm}^{-3}$ for seawater and $0.0013 \text{ J} \cdot \text{K}^{-1} \cdot \text{cm}^{-3}$ for air. These differ by a ratio of more than 3000. Thus, as air begins to cool, energy can transfer from the ocean to the air to maintain the temperature of the air, with very little temperature change in the seawater. As a result, the ocean tends to keep the air at a temperature close to that of the water. For regions of land far from the ocean, this effect does not occur, since the specific heat of typical ground is much smaller than that of water, and the air temperature can become much colder. Temperature maps of the United States in winter show relatively warm temperatures along the coasts, while frigid temperature regions project far to the south in the middle portion of the country.

4.) Why do *sea breezes* occur?

This is one of the *short-term* effects of the interaction between the ocean and the atmosphere. Its explanation is similar to that in Mystery #3. During the day, the Sun provides energy to both the water and the land at a similar intensity. The specific heat of the water is relatively high, so there is a modest temperature increase. The lower specific heat of the land results in a larger temperature increase. Thus, the *air* over the land becomes warmer than that over the ocean. As a result, the buoyant force on the warmer air (due to the adjacent colder air) is larger than its weight, so that the warm air floats upward, by Archimedes' Principle. As a result, cool air from the ocean blows in toward the land—the sea breeze. At night, the situation reverses. The land cools faster than the ocean and the cooler air over the land blows out to sea as it pushes the warm air over the ocean upward.

5.) We use salt to *freeze* ice cream, but we use salt to *melt* ice on roadways—what's going on here?

This is not an inconsistency; in both cases, we wish to *lower the melting or freezing point* of water. (In normal situations, the melting and freezing points are the same. In some special situations, this is not true. For example, if water in a highly polished bowl is cooled, it can be taken to a temperature lower than 0°C without freezing, so that we have effectively lowered the freezing point. This is called *supercooled water*. If we start with ice and add energy, however, it will melt at 0°C—there is no superheated ice.) The addition of impurities to a pure substance has the effect of lowering the melting point. This is due to the interference which the impurity provides to the formation of the crystal lattice structure of the originally pure material. The impurity plays the role of providing a weaker bond than that between like molecules, and this weaker bond will break with the internal energy available at a temperature lower than the normal melting/freezing point.

A common use of mixing different materials to form another with new properties is the formation of *alloys*, which are mixtures of metals. For example, stainless steel is a mixture of iron, chromium and nickel that has the property of *not* rusting, as does ordinary iron. An alloy example closer to the spirit of this Mystery is that of *solder*, used for making electrical connections. It is a combination of lead and tin, with a melting point between 180°C and 190°C. In contrast, the individual melting points of lead and tin are 327°C and 232°C, respectively.

In the case of the ice cream freezer, the desire is to reduce the ice cream mixture to the freezing point and cause it to change its state to become frozen ice cream. The freezing point of ice cream is very close to that of water, since ice cream is largely made up of water. Thus, if we use unsalted ice, the ice-water mixture outside the ice cream container will come to equilibrium with the ice cream mixture inside and the ice cream will not freeze. We need the temperature of the ice-water mixture to be lower than that of the ice cream mixture, in order for energy to flow from the ice cream mixture and cause it to freeze. When the cold ice (temperature below 0°C) is mixed with salt, the resulting ice and salt water mixture comes to equilibrium at a temperature lower than 0°C, resulting in the required flow of more energy out of the ice cream and its resultant freezing.

There is another advantage to using an ice-water mixture over simple ice, in addition to the argument above. Since the ice-water mixture is a fluid, it can make better physical contact with the container holding the ice cream. Better *physical* contact results in better *thermal* contact, enhancing the flow of energy from the container.

The effect of using salt on snow-covered roadways is similar. As the salt combines with the water on the roadway from ice and snow, it lowers the melting point of the mixture. In the case where the ground temperature is only slightly below 0°C, then, the equilibrium temperature of the ice-salt-water mixture is lower than that of the ground. As a result, energy flows from the ground to the mixture, resulting in further melting of the ice and snow.

6.) You are making cookies on a cookie sheet with turned up edges. When you remove the cookies from the oven, you find that the cookies near the edges are more well done than those near the middle. Why is this?

This phenomenon occurs only for cookies sheets with turned-up edges. On a perfectly flat sheet, we do not see this effect. The primary method by which cookies cook in an oven is by conduction of heat into the dough from the hot air surrounding the cookies. In addition, since the cookie sheet is also at a high temperature, it is *radiating*, and the cookie dough absorbs some of this radiation. This absorption contributes to the cooking of the dough in combination with the conduction from the air. Radiation from parts of the cookie sheet underneath the cookies is either absorbed by the cookies or passes through them. Radiation from uncovered parts of *a flat sheet* does not pass through cookies, as shown below.

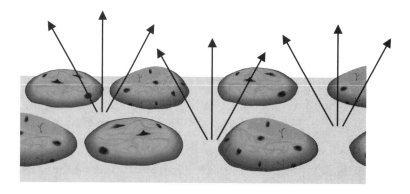

If the sheet has turned up edges, however, then some of the radiation from the turned up edges will enter the cookies near the edge as shown below. Thus, the cookies near the turned up edge will receive more energy per unit time than those near the middle and will brown faster.

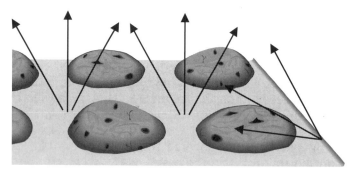

7.) Why do you never need to change the spark plugs in a diesel engine?

One never needs to change the spark plugs in a diesel engine because *there are no spark plugs*! The compression ratio of a diesel engine is so high (from 12:1 to 21:1, compared to a gasoline engine, with a typical compression ratio of 6:1 to 8:1) that the temperature of the mixture of fuel and air is high enough for combustion to take place without the assistance of a spark.

8.) Insulation is used in walls in a building to reduce conduction "losses". But wait a minute. Plain old air is a great thermal insulator. Why don't we just leave the walls empty and let the air do the job?

The problem with this suggestion is that air is a *fluid*. Let us imagine a wall cavity simply filled with air, as in the diagram below.

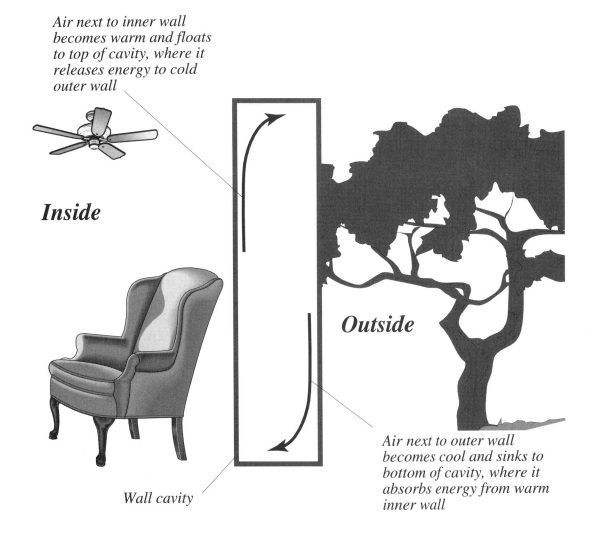

Air next to inner wall becomes warm and floats to top of cavity, where it releases energy to cold outer wall

Inside

Outside

Wall cavity

Air next to outer wall becomes cool and sinks to bottom of cavity, where it absorbs energy from warm inner wall

We will begin our thought experiment by assuming that all of the air in the cavity is at some initial temperature between that of the interior of the house and the lower temperature outdoors (we are assuming that it is winter). Now, the air near the inner wall will become warmer due to conduction of energy through the wall material. This warm air will be pushed upward by the buoyant force of the now cooler air near the outside wall. As the warm air begins to fill the top of the cavity, some of it is in contact with the outer wall, and energy will leave the air by conduction through this wall. Meanwhile, the cooler air, which has sunk to the bottom of the cavity, comes into contact with the inner wall. This air will now absorb energy from the inner wall and become warmer. It will start to float upward as it is pushed by the descending cooling air from the upper part of the cavity. This process will continue and we have established a *convection current* which carries energy from the inner wall to the outer wall by mass transfer, negating the insulation quality of the air. During the summer, the inner and outer temperatures reverse—it is warmer outside than inside. As a result, we again have the possibility of convection currents set up inside thick air-filled cavities, with the circulation proceeding in the direction opposite to that in the winter. This will result in energy being carried by convection from the outer walls to the cooler inner walls, fighting the effects of the air conditioning in the home.

How do we take advantage of the insulating characteristics of air but prevent the convection currents from occurring? We do this by making sure that the air *stays fixed in position*. This is done by filling the cavity with insulation. The main feature of the insulation is that it contains a very large number of air pockets. Thus, we have still filled the cavity with air, but the fibers of the insulation prevent the air from moving freely and establishing large scale convection currents.

9.) People often burn their mouths on a piece of freshly-served pizza. Why does this happen?

This phenomenon can be attributed to the relatively high specific heat (see Myth #1 in this Chapter) of the cheese, due mostly to the fact that the cheese has a high water content. As the cheese makes contact with your mouth, energy transfers from the cheese to your mouth, but the high specific heat results in a very slow temperature drop in the cheese. Thus, the temperature stays high while the cheese is in contact with your mouth, possibly resulting in a burn.

10.) Some fast food restaurants serve fruit pies in a cardboard box. On the box, it may say, "Caution: filling is hot". Why does it say that *only the filling* is hot? Wouldn't the crust be hot, too?

It is certainly true that the filling and the crust will be at approximately the same temperature. The filling will *seem* much hotter to the mouth, however, for the same reason as the cheese on the pizza in Mystery #9—the specific heat (see Myth #1 in this Chapter) of the filling is relatively high. Thus, the filling will remain at a high temperature even when it is in contact with the mouth, possibly resulting in a burn. The crust, on the other hand, is a flaky mixture of pastry and air bubbles, with a relatively low specific heat. When the mouth makes contact with the pastry, its temperature drops quickly, resulting in its *feeling* cooler than the filling.

In addition to the effect of the specific heat, the filling has a higher *thermal conductivity* than the crust, resulting in faster transfer of energy from the filling to the mouth.

Thus, there is a physics reason for the statement on the box, but it should more correctly read, "Caution: filling has relatively high specific heat and thermal conductivity". Despite this more correct statement of physics, perhaps there are marketing considerations which indicate that the statement should remain as it is.

11.) How does wetting a finger and holding it in the air indicate the wind direction?

This effect is a one-finger version of the *wind-chill factor*. As the wind blows over wet skin, it assists in the convection of energy away from the skin as discussed in Hot Breath? Cold Breath? in Chapter 14 of *PBWM*. The side of the finger facing into the wind will feel the effects of the convective energy transfer more than the side of the finger that is sheltered from the wind. Thus, the side of the finger which feels colder indicates the direction from which the wind is coming.

12.) Why do people in hot, desert climates wear *black* robes? Wouldn't this make them hotter than if they were wearing a white robe?

It is common experience to feel hotter in the summer sun when wearing a black T-shirt, for example, than when wearing a white T-shirt. Why would you possibly want to wear a black robe in the desert? The key word in the question is *robe*. A robe is a long garment that is *open at the bottom*, unlike a T-shirt. The black robe definitely absorbs more light than a white robe. This, in turn, warms the air inside the robe. By Archimedes' Principle, the warm air in the robe rises due to the buoyant force applied by the cooler air outside the bottom of the robe. Thus, cool air enters the robe through the open bottom. As a consequence, the desert dweller has a constant circulation of air which helps cool the body by convection. Measurements taken on both black and white robes show that the black robe has a higher surface temperature, but the temperatures of the air spaces inside both robes are the same. For more information on this effect, see A. Shkolnik, C. R. Taylor, V. Finch and A. Borut, "Why Do Bedouins Wear Black Robes in Hot Deserts?", *Nature*, **283**, 373, 1980.

13.) It is a common experience that metal feels colder than wood, even though both are at the same temperature. What if we heated metal and wood up to 50°C? Would the metal still feel colder?

The feeling of hotness or coldness depends on *energy flow* through the skin, not on the actual temperature. This was explored in Mystery #10 of Chapter 15 in *PBWM*. Thus, room temperature metal normally feels colder than wood because metal is a better thermal conductor than wood. The higher rate of energy flow out of the skin and into the metal results in the sensation that we describe as cold.

Now, if both the metal and the wood are at higher temperatures than that of the skin, energy will flow *into* the skin at a higher rate from the metal than from the wood. Thus, in this case, *the metal will feel hotter than the wood*. See Mystery #14 for another application of this effect.

14.) Putting your bare hand into a hot oven is uncomfortable but tolerable. But if you happen to touch a dish in that oven with your bare hand, it is very painful and can cause a nasty burn. Why is there this difference when the air and the dish are at the same temperature?

This situation is similar to that in Mystery #13. Air is not a good thermal conductor, so the flow of energy from the hot air into the skin is relatively low. The dish material is a much better thermal conductor, so that contact with the dish results in rapid energy flow into the skin, possibly resulting in a burn if enough contact time elapses.

15.) When your automobile engine overheats, some people suggest that you turn on the *heater*! Is this good advice?

The source of the energy for the automobile heater is the engine. The heating system draws energy from the water in the engine by means of heat exchangers and a forced air convection system (the fan!). Thus, if your engine overheats, it *is* a good idea to turn on the heater, as this will assist in drawing energy out of the engine and result in a faster drop in its temperature than with the heater off.

16.) What is the hottest item in your house?

The hottest item in your house is your *light bulb filament*. A 60 watt bulb has a filament temperature of approximately 2.7×10^3 K. This is why it glows with such brilliance (see Chapter 17 for discussions of glowing objects). This is hotter than a candle flame, which has regions as high as 1.7×10^3 K and much hotter than an electric stove burner at 800 K, which emits only a dull red glow. For more information on light bulb filaments, see H. S. Leff, "Illuminating Physics with Light Bulbs", *The Physics Teacher*, **28**, 30, 1990.

17.) Brush fires are especially dangerous and spread quite rapidly when strong winds are blowing. Yet, we blow a candle out with the wind from a breath. Why don't strong winds just blow the brush fires out?

Let us first consider what happens in blowing a candle out with a puff of air from the mouth. Continuous burning in a candle wick depends on the closeness of the hot gases in the flame to the liquid wax in the wick of the candle (See Mystery #4 in Chapter 7 in *PBWM*, for an explanation of the role of the wick in a candle.). Radiation from the hot gases vaporizes the wax to form the gaseous wax which is combustible. When a strong puff of air strikes the candle flame, the hot gases of the flame are blown away from the wick, reducing the energy input to the liquid wax in the wick. Thus, the liquid wax is not vaporized at a high enough rate to supply gaseous fuel for the flame and the fire is extinguished.

Now, what about the brush fire? In this case, when the strong wind blows hot gases away from a particular fuel source, *it blows the gases into new fuel sources*—neighboring brush. As long as there is brush available in the direction in which the wind is blowing, the flames will simply advance along that direction. Southern California has a serious problem with brush fires in the autumn, after the hot, dry summer has left brush parched and flammable. This problem is particularly dangerous when Santa Ana winds are blowing (Mystery #11, Chapter 15 in *PBWM*). When fires break out during this period, they advance in the direction in which the wind is blowing (south and west) until they reach one of two possible obstacles. One obstacle is a *firebreak*, which is a region of ground exhausted of fuel due to the firefighters' efforts in either digging up the region and turning under the brush, or by having set an earlier fire to deplete the region of available fuel. The second obstacle is the *ocean*, since it represents a lack of fuel.

18.) The author's daughter, in her early college days, used an immersion heater, normally used for heating cups of water for coffee or tea, to cook a can of baked beans. The heater overheated and ceased to operate correctly. Why did this happen?

Immersion heaters are designed to operate in an environment in which *convection currents* are established in the water being heated by the device, as discussed in Mystery #9 in Chapter 15 of *PBWM*. These currents carry energy away from the heater, and distribute the energy throughout the water. Thus, the temperature of the water remains below that which would cause damage. In the case of the baked beans, the high *viscosity* of this mixture reduces the possibility of effective convection currents being established. Thus, the energy transferred from the heater tends to stay in the region of food around the heater, being carried away only slowly by conduction. As a result, the temperature of the heater and this portion of the food simply increases until the heater is damaged.

𝕸𝖆𝖌𝖎𝖈:

A Hot Band

If you touch a metal spring to your forehead before and after stretching, you will feel no change in temperature. For a metal spring, the work done by stretching the spring (in terms of the energy continuity equation, the spring is the system and the force from the hands represents work from outside the system) manifests as spring potential energy after it is stretched. While a small amount of the work is stored as internal energy in the metal, due to the internal friction forces in the spring, this is not large enough to feel as a temperature increase.

Why does something different happen with a rubber band? In this case, the work done by stretching appears both as spring potential energy and as a significant amount of internal energy—enough to feel a significant temperature increase. The answer lies in the *Second Law of Thermodynamics*, as follows. Rubber consists of a chaotic mix of long, coiled molecules, whose axes lie in all directions relative to the body of the rubber band. Now, imagine that we stretch the rubber band out. The force of the pull tends to cause the coiled molecules to line up more nearly parallel with the length of the rubber band. This represents an increase in order of these molecules, or a *decrease* in entropy. The Second Law requires either an overall increase in entropy of the universe in a process or at least no change in the entropy (we will ignore any heat exchanges with the surroundings, so we can approximate the "universe" as simply the rubber band). If the rubber band is stretched quickly, then the stretching process is very close to adiabatic, and we approximate the net entropy change as zero. Thus, something must happen to compensate for the decrease in entropy due to the coils lining up. We can compensate for the decrease if *the molecules increase their vibrational motion*, so that their positions in the rubber are not so ordered. Increased vibrational motion is represented by more internal energy which, in turn, means that the temperature increases—this is what is felt on the forehead.

When the rubber band is allowed to return to its original length, the coiled molecules can become more disordered, resulting in an increase in entropy. Since the process is approximately adiabatic, as mentioned above, the overall entropy change should be close to zero. Thus, the increase in entropy of the molecules is accompanied by a decrease in entropy of the vibrations of the molecules. This decreased vibration represents a lower internal energy and a lower temperature—the rubber band drops in temperature as it returns to its original length.

A rubber band engine which uses this property of rubber bands is described by Feynman (R. P. Feynman, R. B. Leighton, and M. L. Sands, *The Feynman Lectures on Physics*, Addison-Wesley Publishing Co., Inc., Reading, Massachusetts, 1963). Although the engine has a low power output, it does demonstrate the effects of the changes occurring in the rubber. For a laboratory experiment on rubber band physics, see G. Savarino and M. R. Fisch, "A General Physics Laboratory Investigation of the Thermodynamics of a Rubber Band", *American Journal of Physics*, **59**, 141, 1991.

The Jumping Coin

When the bottle is removed from the freezer, the bottle and the air inside are at a low temperature. The wetting of the edge and the placing of the coin on the top seals the system, isolating the inside air from the outside atmosphere. The air inside the bottle will start to rise in temperature, due to conduction of energy through the glass walls of the bottle. This increase is aided by placing your (relatively warm) hands on the glass. As the temperature of the air rises, according to the Ideal Gas Law, the pressure will increase, since the volume is held constant. Eventually, the pressure will be high enough that the difference in force between the bottom of the coin and the top will exceed the coin's weight and lift the coin slightly away from the edge of the bottle. Thus, the coin will rise, allowing air to escape and reducing the pressure in the bottle to that of the atmosphere. The coin then falls back to the lip of the bottle, since the pressure has been released. This cycle repeats a number of times, with the coin continuing to jump up from the lip of the bottle until the air in the bottle is close to the temperature of the outside air.

Burning Metal

In both cases, we have placed steel in a flame. You will find, however, that the bolt does not burn, but the steel wool burns in a sparkling display. The difference is due to the *surface to volume ratio*. If you imagine an increasing radius r of a fixed length l of a cylindrical metal wire, the surface area increases in proportion to the radius ($A = 2\pi r l$), while the volume increases as the *square* of the radius ($V = \pi r^2 l$). Thus, the volume increases faster with radius than does the surface area. As an example, suppose the radius of a wire increases by a factor of 10. Then, the surface area of the wire is 10 times larger, but the volume within the surface is *100 times larger.*

Now, *the rate of transfer of energy into the metal depends on the surface area, while the rate of increase in temperature depends on the volume.* Thus, the thin strands of the steel wool can easily reach a high temperature due to the conduction of energy from the flame into a relatively small volume. For the bolt, however, even though more energy crosses the surface per unit time than for the steel wool filaments, the volume has increased by a larger percentage, and it takes much longer for the temperature of the metal to increase to the burning point. For a related phenomenon in the area of electricity, see Mystery #9 in Chapter 12.

Fireblockers

While there is obviously a significant amount of *visible* radiation from a fire in a fireplace, there is also a large rate of energy transfer in the *infrared* region of the electromagnetic spectrum. The warm feeling in your eyelids in front of a fire is due to the energy transferred to your eyelids by electromagnetic radiation *at all frequencies*. When the glasses are placed in front of the eyes, much of the infrared radiation is blocked, since glass and plastic are opaque to many wavelengths in the infrared region. Thus, the total amount of energy arriving at your eyelids per unit time is reduced and the lids feel cooler.

𝔐𝔶𝔱𝔥:

1.) The specific heat of a substance is the amount of heat necessary to raise one gram of the substance by a temperature of 1°C.

One problem with the statement given is related to the name specific *heat* (as well as a related parameter discussed below, *heat* capacity). It is unfortunate that these expressions have traditionally included the word *heat*. In reality, *any energy transfer mechanism* could appear on the left side of the equation—there is no need for it to be restricted to heat.

Consider the energy continuity equation (see Chapter 5), which is reproduced below,

$$\Delta KE + \Delta PE + \Delta U = W + Q + E_{MT} + E_S + E_{ER} + E_{ET}$$

Imagine a process in which there is no net change in kinetic or potential energy in the system. The only change is in the internal energy, so we represent the continuity equation as follows,

$$\Delta KE + \Delta PE + mc\Delta T = W + Q + E_{MT} + E_S + E_{ER} + E_{ET}$$

In this equation, we have let the internal energy be represented by $U = mcT$ (so that $\Delta U = mc\Delta T$), essentially measuring the internal energy by means of the temperature. If we ignore everything except Q on the right hand side, we obtain the equation in the diagram accompanying the Myth:

$$\Delta KE + \Delta PE + mc\Delta T = W + Q + E_{MT} + E_S + E_{ER} + E_{ET}$$

But, more generally, *any* of the transfer mechanisms on the right hand side of the equation could result in a temperature change of the object, and this change will be related to the specific *heat* of the material from which the object is made.

For example, if a bag containing lead shot is repeatedly dropped onto a concrete floor, the temperature of the lead will rise. The specific heat can be used to calculate the temperature increase, even though *there is no heat involved in the process at all*! In this case, the energy transfer mechanism is the *work* done by the floor in bringing the lead to rest each time after being dropped, so the continuity equation becomes,

$$\Delta KE + \Delta PE + mc\Delta T = W + Q + E_{MT} + E_S + E_{ER} + E_{ET}$$

Numerically, W is equal to the total work that the individual dropping the bag performed in raising the bag to its initial height a number of times.

We can also imagine other situations in which we raise the temperature of a material by some transfer or transformation mechanism other than heat. The coils of a toaster change temperature when the toaster is turned on due to energy transfer into the coils by means of *electrical transmission* and out of the coils by *electromagnetic radiation*:

$$\Delta KE + \Delta PE + mc\Delta T = W + Q + E_{MT} + E_S + E_{ER} + E_{ET}$$

where we have ignored, for the sake of simplicity, energy transfer out of the coils by conduction into the air.

The air-fuel mixture in a gasoline engine increases its temperature by means of a *chemical reaction* (combustion upon the firing of the spark plug):

$$\Delta KE + \Delta PE + mc\Delta T = W + Q + E_{MT} + E_S + E_{ER} + E_{ET}$$

In this case, there is no transfer across the boundary of the system (the air-fuel mixture), but rather a *transformation* of energy storage from potential to internal. Of course, there will be an immediate transfer of energy out the system after the combustion, as the mixture performs work on the piston.

As a final example, our bodies are just a little warmer due to the constant bombardment of *sound* to which we are constantly exposed!

There is another issue related to specific heat, based on two competing definitions that can be found in different written sources. Both definitions begin with a closely related parameter, the *heat capacity*. This is defined as the energy necessary to raise the temperature of a particular *system* or *object* by one degree. One definition of specific heat is then defined as *the energy necessary to raise one gram of the material by one Celsius degree*. This is found by dividing the heat capacity of the object by the mass of the object:

$$specific\ heat \equiv \frac{heat\ capacity}{mass}$$

The second definition introduces another parameter called *thermal capacity*, which is identical to the specific heat defined in the first definition. The specific heat in this case, however, is then defined as *the ratio of the thermal capacity of the material to that of water*.

$$specific\ heat \equiv \frac{thermal\ capacity\ of\ material}{thermal\ capacity\ of\ water}$$

The first definition is the more widely accepted one, and is more reasonable. One major problem with the second definition is that it results in a specific heat that is *dimensionless*. Thus, imagine incorporating this specific heat in the equation,

$$Q = mc\Delta T$$

Upon doing this, we find that the units will not work out correctly unless the units from the first definition of specific heat ($J \cdot kg^{-1} \cdot K^{-1}$) are "magically" attached to the number!

2.) Window glass is a good thermal insulator.

In fact, window glass is a particularly *poor* thermal insulator, as can be seen by placing your hand on the inside surface of a window pane on a cold day or night. Your hand will feel much cooler than when it is in the air of the room. So how can we keep houses warm in the winter with large expanses of glass in the windows?

The main agent in the insulation of windows is *the layer of air* that adheres to both sides of the glass in the window. The following approximate thermal conductivities, *k*, are found in tables of thermal properties of materials

Air: $k = 2.4 \times 10^{-2}$ $W \cdot m^{-1} \cdot K^{-1}$

Glass: $k = 1.3$ $W \cdot m^{-1} \cdot K^{-1}$

Air is a much better thermal insulator than glass, by about a factor of 50, and it is the thin layers of air that provide most of the insulation. On windy days, you may feel a chill in the house, since the layer of air on the outside of the glass is continuously blown away by the wind and the overall insulating properties of the glass and air layers are reduced.

The insulating properties of air can be exploited by incorporating *dual-glazed windows* in the design of a home. These windows consist of two panes of glass separated by a small air space. The air space serves as an excellent thermal insulator, which adds to the insulating characteristics of the adhered air on the outer edges. It might be tempting to try to improve the insulation qualities by moving the two panes of glass farther apart, resulting in a thicker blanket of trapped air. The problem with this approach, however, is that it is possible to set up a convection current between the panes of glass just like the convection current set up in the cavity in the discussion of Mystery #8. The maximum overall insulation quality occurs at a pane separation of about 2 cm, at which we have an effective thickness of air without a substantial probability of establishing a large-scale convection current. In some cold climates, the effective thickness of the air layer is increased further by using *triple-glazed windows*. Another consideration in going this route, however, is the balance of the cost of the more complicated window against the possible savings in heating bills.

3.) The Celsius scale was invented by Anders Celsius, who assigned 0°C as the freezing point of water and 100°C as the boiling point of water.

Anders Celsius (1701-1744) was a Swedish astronomer who was one of many people in the 1700's who were building thermometers. There was no standard temperature scale at that time. As a result, there were many scales and some thermometers were calibrated with a number of scales. There is one thermometer from 1754, which is housed in a museum in the Netherlands, which is calibrated with *eighteen* scales! This confusion among scales continued for quite some time, as evidenced by another eighteen scale thermometer in a museum in Rome, dated 1841.

Celsius devised a scale with 100 degrees between the freezing and boiling points of water, but *his scale was reversed from that in use today*. On Celsius' scale, the freezing point of water was 100° and the boiling point was 0°. His use of an inverted scale was influenced by a thermometer which he received from Joseph Nicholas Delisle, a French astronomer, whose thermometer scales were also inverted. The inverted scale can be traced back even further, to the beginning of the 1700's, with the work of John Patrick and Francis Hauksbee, both of England. Both of their thermometers had an inverted scale, which came to be known as the Royal Society scale in the 1720's.

The Celsius scale was changed to its present form after Celsius' death. There is some debate as to who actually performed the inversion, with the leading contenders being Daniel Ekström, Märten Strömer, and Carolus Linnaeus (later Carl von Linné), all of Sweden.

4.) Rubbing your hands together on a cold day heats them up.

This is an incorrect use of the word *heat*. Rubbing your hands certainly does cause their temperature to increase, as can be readily felt. But the energy transfer mechanism is *work* (due to the friction force between your hands), not heat.

5.) Automobile *radiators* transfer energy by means of *radiation*.

This name "radiator" implies that energy is transferred out of the automobile engine by *radiation*, which is incorrect. Energy is transferred out of the engine and into the "radiator" by *mass transfer*, in terms of the forced convection of the water-antifreeze mixture. Once the hot fluid is within the "radiator", the transfer mechanism is *conduction* into air blown by the fan across the large surface area of the "radiator". Once the energy is absorbed into the air, it leaves the "radiator" by *mass transfer* (convection), along with the mass of the moving air.

6.) It is possible to see steam rising over boiling water.

While you do see *something* over boiling water, it is not steam. *Steam is an invisible gas.* As the steam rises from the surface of the boiling water, it encounters cooler air. This causes the steam to condense into tiny water droplets. It is this fine mist of water droplets that forms the visible "gas" rising over boiling water.

7.) Solids expand because the amplitudes of the molecular vibrations increase.

This is a common "explanation" for thermal expansion, but it is incorrect. If the amplitude of vibration increases, but the *average separation* of the atoms does not, then there is no expansion. Conversely, if a solid expands, then the average separation distance between atoms must necessarily be larger than when the object is cooler. Let us imagine that a solid can be modeled as a collection of atoms connected by springs obeying Hooke's Law. Then, assuming perfect springs, the potential energy curve for a given atom (considering *only* its interaction with the nearest neighbor atom) would be a parabola described by $PE = \frac{1}{2} k(r - r_0)^2$, where k is the effective spring constant, r is the *instantaneous* separation between atoms and r_0 is the *equilibrium* separation between atoms. This potential is shown as the dark curve in the diagram below.

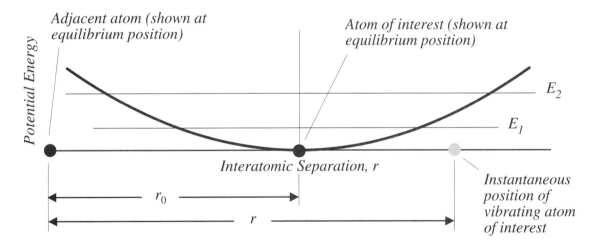

We imagine the atom of interest vibrating along the horizontal axis in the diagram. The horizontal lines across the diagram indicate two possible energies for the vibrating atom, with the higher energy, E_2, corresponding to a higher temperature than that for E_1. Notice, however, that at both temperatures, the average *position* of the atom is exactly in the middle of the diagram. Thus, its average *separation* from the atom at the left of the diagram is the same for both energies. As a result, the material at a higher temperature is no larger than when at the lower temperature—*there is no thermal expansion.*

This lack of thermal expansion is due to a deficiency in our model. While we can safely approximate the *very small* vibrations of atoms in a solid as simple harmonic, this is only an approximation. The atoms in a solid do not exactly obey Hooke's Law. The actual potential energy diagram for an atom in a solid looks more like that pictured below.

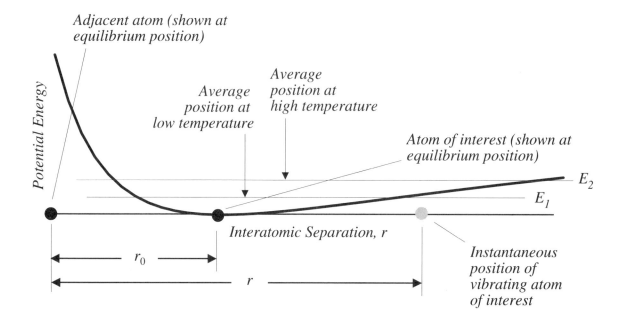

The shape of the curve toward the right of the diagram is modeled as an inverse dependence of the electric potential energy on distance between nearest neighbor atoms (for large separations). At the left of the diagram, corresponding to small interatomic separations, the sharp increase in the potential energy is due to the effects of the Pauli Exclusion Principle (see Myth #2 in Chapter 18). As the atoms are pushed together, the overlapping of the wave functions (see Chapter 18) results in the atomic systems moving to higher energy levels, causing the increase in the potential energy curve. The important feature to notice is that *the potential energy curve is not symmetric.* Thus, at a higher temperature, represented by the upper energy line labeled E_2 in the diagram, the average position of the atom of interest is further to the right than for energy E_1. Thus, *the average separation distance is larger* than at the lower temperature. This is the origin of the expansion of the solid—the <u>asymmetry</u> of the potential energy curve.

In a more sophisticated approach to a solid, we would incorporate the fact that atoms interact with more than just their nearest neighbors—in reality, each atom interacts with *all* other atoms in the solid. We would also include the fact that the solid is three-dimensional rather than one-dimensional, as in our model. These additions would not change the results, however, that we argued above in our nearest neighbor, one-dimensional model.

8.) If you increase the temperature of the air in a room of a house, there is more internal energy in the air *in the room*.

The part of this statement on which we want to focus is the phrase "in the room". Let us consider the relationship between the internal energy (U) and the associated temperature (T) for a gas such as the air in our room. We have:

$$U = nC_V T$$

where n is the amount of gas in moles and C_V is the molar heat capacity at constant volume.

Now, let us imagine adding some energy to the air in the room by means of a furnace or a portable heater. It would appear, from the above equation, that the internal energy in the room would increase along with the temperature. But this would only occur in a *sealed* room. In reality, there are many *leaks* in houses, due to small openings, so that a room in a house, or the house itself, is not a sealed system. As energy is added to the air, the pressure of the air will tend to increase. As a result, air will leak out of the room through the small openings in the walls, so that the pressure actually remains constant. In the equation above, then, the initial number of moles of gas, n, will not stay in the room.

Thus, let us write the above equation for the internal energy in the room *twice*, once for the situation *before* we add energy to the room and once *after* we add the energy. We have,

$$U_{before} = n_{before} C_V T_{before}$$

$$U_{after} = n_{after} C_V T_{after}$$

Note that these equations describe the internal energy *in the room* at the two times, *not the internal energy associated with the gas that was in the room at the beginning*—some of this gas has leaked to the outside.

The second step in the analysis involves the Ideal Gas Law, which we solve for the pressure of the gas:

$$pV = nRT \quad \rightarrow \quad p = \frac{nRT}{V}$$

Let us write this equation *twice*, once for the situation *before* we add the energy to the room and once for the case *after* the energy is added:

$$p_{before} = \frac{n_{before} R T_{before}}{V}$$

$$p_{after} = \frac{n_{after} R T_{after}}{V}$$

where we have indicated that the volume of the gas in the room does not change, since the room has rigid walls.

Now, because of the leakage of air through the walls, *the pressures before and after adding the energy to the room are the same.* Thus, from our Ideal Gas Law equations above,

$$p_{before} = p_{after} \quad \rightarrow \quad \frac{n_{before}RT_{before}}{V} = \frac{n_{after}RT_{after}}{V} \quad \rightarrow \quad n_{before}T_{before} = n_{after}T_{after}$$

Thus, the product of the number of moles of gas in the room and the temperature is a constant. Looking at our expression for internal energy, we note that the internal energy depends on this product and a constant, C_V. Thus, we see that we must have,

$$U_{before} = U_{after}$$

The internal energy of the air in the room *remains constant as the temperature increases.*

9.) A common demonstration is to place a jar over a lighted candle, which is mounted in a pie tin filled with water. As the candle flame dies out, water rises in the jar. This is due to the fact that you have consumed the oxygen in the air within the jar. Furthermore, you can make a measurement of the height of the water to determine the percentage of oxygen in air.

This is a common explanation for this effect, but it is incorrect. First of all, the flame dies out before all of the oxygen in the air in the jar can be consumed. Thus, any quantitative estimates of the percentage of oxygen in normal air are erroneous. Secondly, a large amount of the oxygen that is consumed reappears in the form of carbon dioxide. Replacing one gas with another is not going to reduce the pressure in the jar as it would if the oxygen disappeared.

So what is the correct explanation? As the jar is brought close to the candle flame, the hot gases from the combustion enter the jar and deliver energy to the cooler air in the jar, causing it to expand. Indeed, if the jar is lowered over the flame rapidly, bubbles can be seen escaping from the bottom lip of the jar. Once the flame is extinguished due to a reduced level of oxygen, two effects occur. First, the previously warmed gases cool, resulting in a lower pressure. Secondly, some of the water vapor which resulted from the combustion condenses, reducing the pressure further. With lowered pressure inside the jar, the difference between this pressure and the higher atmospheric pressure on the water surface outside the jar causes the water to rise in the jar. This reduces the volume of the gas in the jar and increases its pressure, until the internal and external pressures are equalized.

10.) The higher the temperature of a hot skillet, the faster drops of water sprinkled on the skillet will vaporize.

This is related to Mystery #1, in which we discussed the Leidenfrost Effect. If the temperature of the skillet is just above 100°C, drops of water sprinkled on the skillet will spread out and vaporize rapidly. But as the temperature *increases* to about 200°C, the drops tend to form beads and dance across the surface, as discussed in Mystery #1. At the lower temperature, the water droplet vaporizes slowly, and there is plenty of time for the resulting vapor to leak out from under the drop and escape. As a result, the rate of energy transfer into the remaining water is relatively high. At the higher temperature, the initial vaporization of the water is fast enough to create a layer of gas beneath the drop, which results in thermal insulation. This reduces the rate of energy transfer into the remaining water. Thus, *the drop lasts longer at the higher temperature than at the lower temperature*.

11.) The only phases of matter are *solid*, *liquid* and *gas*.

These are the common phases of matter that are often discussed. The candle in the diagram accompanying the Myth represents all three of these phases in action. The wax fuel is stored as the *solid* body of the candle. The fuel is delivered via the wick as a *liquid*. Once the wax has turned into a *gas*, it can participate in the combustion process. But the concept of a phase of matter has a much broader definition. In general, a phase of matter is any set of behaviors of the matter that changes abruptly with temperature. A common fourth phase of matter is a *plasma*. If a gas is raised to a high enough temperature, the atoms will dissociate, forming a gas of free electrons and ions. This is the plasma state of matter, which has very different properties than the neutral gas, particularly in terms of electrical and magnetic behavior, due to the charged particles.

There are other phases of matter. Ferromagnetism (see *PBWM*, Chapter 22) is a phase of matter. For a small number of materials, a permanent magnetized phase can exist, which clearly has different magnetic properties than the same material in the unmagnetized phase. If the temperature of a ferromagnet is raised beyond what is called the *Curie temperature*, the ferromagnetism disappears. The Curie temperature for the ferromagnetic phase is the analog to the melting point for the solid phase.

Another phase of matter is that of *superconductivity*. A superconducting material clearly has different electrical properties than a normal conductor. This phase of matter can be changed by raising the superconductor above its critical temperature.

Superfluidity in liquid helium is yet another example of a phase of matter. If the temperature of helium is lowered to about 2 K, a superfluid phase appears. The superfluid helium has distinctly different properties than the normal fluid.

12.) Centigrade is a temperature scale.

The Celsius temperature scale has also been called the Centigrade scale, due to the 100° difference between freezing and boiling. The Celsius name was officially adopted in 1948, to avoid confusion with a French angular unit, also called a centigrade. This unit is 0.01 of a right angle (as is the *grad*, an angle unit on many scientific calculators), so that 100 centigrade is equivalent to 90° (angular degrees, not temperature degrees!). The use of the Centigrade term for temperatures has hung on, but is dying out slowly.

Chapter 10
Vibrations and Waves

𝔐𝔶𝔰𝔱𝔢𝔯𝔦𝔢𝔰:

1.) Why do soldiers break step before marching across a bridge?

2.) If you are stuck in the sand or the snow, why does *rocking* your car back and forth help to extract you?

𝕸ysteries:

π??!!???

3.) The equation for the period of a mass on a spring contains π:

$$T = 2\pi\sqrt{\frac{m}{k}}$$

Wait a minute. The constant π is related to *circles*. Where's the circle in simple harmonic motion?

4.) Baseball and tennis players claim that there is a "sweet spot" on the bat or the racket, which represents a favored spot for the ball to hit. Is there any truth to such a spot?

𝕸𝖞𝖘𝖙𝖊𝖗𝖎𝖊𝖘:

5.) Earthquakes result in both longitudinal and transverse waves traveling through the Earth. In a band around the globe located between 105° and 142° from the epicenter of an earthquake, there is a *shadow zone* where the intensity of waves is very small. Why is this?

6.) During the 1985 Michoacán earthquake in Mexico, parts of Mexico City, *400 km from the epicenter*, were heavily damaged while other parts were relatively unharmed. Why was there damage so far from the epicenter and why was the damage so "spotty"?

7.) During the Loma Prieta Earthquake of 1989, part of the Nimitz Freeway in Oakland, a double decker construction, collapsed, with the upper roadway falling onto the lower roadway. Yet other portions of the same freeway, with the same construction, escaped unharmed. Why did this particular portion of the Nimitz Freeway collapse?

Mysteries:

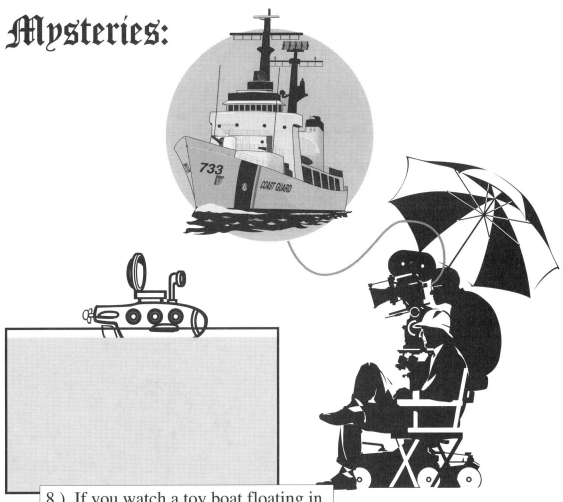

8.) If you watch a toy boat floating in a rough-water bathtub, the motion does not look realistic. There is something wrong with the way it bounces around. Yet, in the movies, *miniatures* of ships and other vehicles are used freely. Why do they look so good in the movies?

9.) Space Shuttle astronauts maintain radio contact with mission control. Is it possible to receive this communication on a home radio?

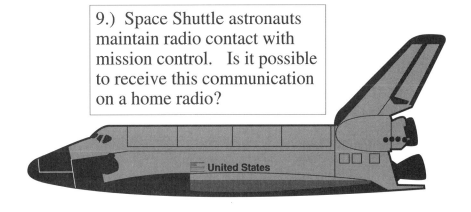

𝔐𝔞𝔤𝔦𝔠:

The Colored String

Set up a vibrating white string (using an AC magnetic driver, which invokes a 120 Hz wave in the string) in a room with fluorescent lights. Look carefully at the color of the string.

The Shimmering Tuning Fork

Set a tuning fork into vibration and hold it in front of the white screen of a computer monitor. Hold it in both a horizontal and vertical orientation. What do you notice?

𝔐𝔞𝔤𝔦𝔠:

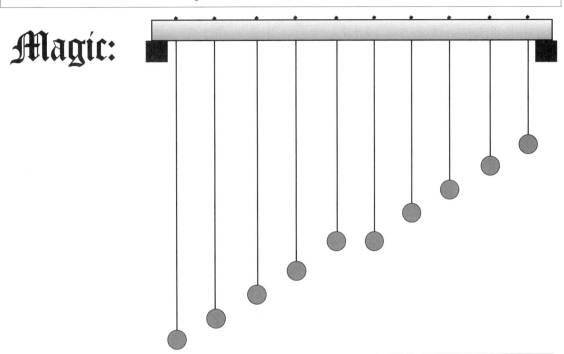

The Pendulum Resonator

Drill a number of holes through a short section of PVC plumbing pipe or a wooden dowel. Passing strings through the holes, set up a number of pendula of varying lengths. Adjust the lengths of two of the pendula in the middle to be the same, as shown in the diagram. Now, place the pipe or dowel on a support that will allow it to rock in reaction to the pendulum motion. Set one of the two matched pendula in motion and watch the motion of the others.

𝔐𝔶𝔱𝔥:

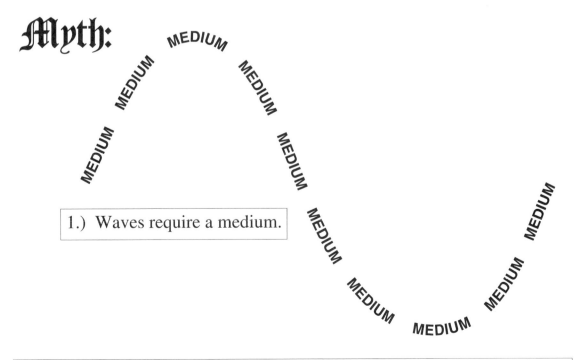

1.) Waves require a medium.

𝔐𝔶𝔱𝔥:

2.) Television stations can only be received on a television.

3.) If no earthquake occurs, that is equivalent to saying that an earthquake of magnitude zero on the Richter scale occurred.

4.) Waves experience a phase inversion of 180° upon reflecting from a rigid boundary.

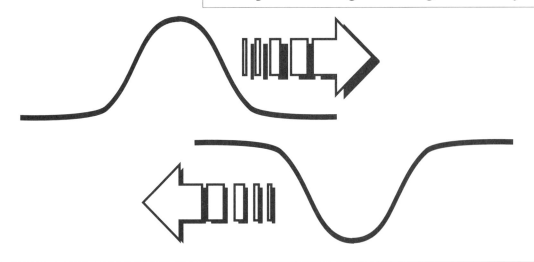

Myth:

5.) At one time, during the early years of the space program, a photographic company offered its ultrasonic ranging capability as a method for monitoring the distance between spacecraft during docking procedures.

6.) In the film, *The Poseidon Adventure* (Twentieth Century Fox, 1972), a ship traveling through open ocean is turned over by a passing tsunami.

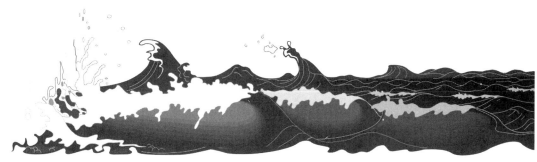

Discussions; Chapter 10—Vibrations and Waves

𝕸𝖞𝖘𝖙𝖊𝖗𝖎𝖊𝖘:

1.) Why do soldiers break step before marching across a bridge?

The steady footsteps of marching soldiers represent a periodic driving force to a bridge. If the frequency of this driving force were to match a natural frequency of the bridge, the bridge could be set into oscillation by *resonance*. Just such a situation occurred on April 14, 1831, when the Broughton suspension bridge in England collapsed while troops marched over it (a short description is available in *The Times* (London), April 15, 1831, page 3). Luckily, the river was low at the time and there were only 20 injuries and no deaths. Later investigations showed that the bridge was near failure anyway, but the resonance vibration induced by the marching soldiers caused it to fail even sooner than it otherwise would have.

Another bridge collapse, near Angers, France, in 1850, has been used as an example of a collapse due to resonance caused by troops marching in step (for example, see page 292 of H. C. Ohanian, *Principles of Physics*, W. W. Norton & Company, New York, 1994). Inspection of the newspaper accounts, however, indicates otherwise. There are a number of items relating to the collapse in *The Times* (London), from April 18, 1850 to April 23, 1850, that make for interesting reading, although there seems to be more politics than physics. The accident occurred when the 11th Regiment of Light Infantry was entering Angers just before noon on April 16. The 11th Regiment had apparently been the source of some concern to the French government, due to some raucous behavior. As an example of their disdain for the government, upon entering a town near Angers, and hearing calls of "Vivent les Rouges! Vive la Montagne!", the 11th Regiment soldiers answered with "a word of one syllable only, which is extremely expressive, though not sufficiently decent to repeat" (4/18/1850, page 6). At the time that the soldiers reached the bridge, "the wind blew violently from the east, rain fell in torrents, and a regular hurricane prevailed" (4/19/1850, page 6). "Reiterated warnings were given to the troops to break into sections, as is usually done, but the rain falling heavily at the time the warning was disregarded and the battalion advanced in close column" (4/20/1850, page 6). In the edition of April 22, 1850 (page 6), there is a quote from Lieutenant-Colonel Simonet, of the 11th Regiment, which indicates that *the lesson of Broughton had been learned*—"I entered on the fatal bridge, after having stopped the band, and broken the regularity of the steps, as is usual in such cases". In the April 23 edition (page 6), the President of the French Second Republic, Charles Louis Napoleon Bonaparte (the nephew of the more famous Napoleon) visits the scene and inspects the fallen bridge. The report states that "the wire ropes were found in some parts to have been completely rusted". In both the April 22 and April 23 editions, there is some inkling that there was some political sabotage involved in the incident—"You will have seen that it has been more than insinuated that the victims of the disaster of Angers were compelled to the fate that destroyed them from a political spite" and "It is curious that the same officer (Simonet) should have survived the terrible catastrophe which occurred at the battle of Leipsic, when Poniatowski and so many others were drowned in the Elster...".

From these accounts, it would seem that there are a couple of possibilities for the cause of the French collapse. The first is that there was indeed some political sabotage. The second is simply that the bridge was rusted badly and the wind caused the bridge to sway while it was overloaded with men frightened by the weather. In either case, there does not seem to be evidence that resonance was involved, and the quote from Simonet indicates that the effects of marching in step over bridges were well understood.

For a detailed analysis of bridge vibrations caused by walking, jogging and thronging humans, see J. E. Wheeler, "Prediction and Control of Pedestrian Induced Vibration in Footbridges", *Journal of the Structural Division, Proceedings of the American Society of Civil Engineers*, **108(ST9)**, 2045, 1982. For a prediction that a major bridge will collapse around the year 2000, based on a 30-year cycle of bridge failures, see H. Petroski, "Predicting Disaster", *American Scientist*, **81(2)**, 110, 1993.

2.) If you are stuck in the sand or the snow, why does *rocking* your car back and forth help to extract you?

If a car is stuck in the sand or snow, there is very little friction force between the tires and the sand or snow. The tires are sitting at the bottom of small depressions in the sand or snow formed by the weight of the car. Because of the very low friction force, the car cannot be lifted out of the depressions by using the engine in the normal manner—the tires simply spin. The tires can be freed from these depressions if the kinetic energy of the car can be increased to a large enough amount to account for the gravitational potential energy represented by the car rising up to the lip of the depression. We appeal to *resonance* here. Even though the force between the tires and the sand is small, the car can be removed if these small forces are repeatedly applied at a frequency which matches the natural frequency of the rocking of the car in the depressions. Eventually, as the energy of the oscillating motion increases, the amplitude of the oscillation of the car will be large enough that the car will roll out of the depressions.

3.) The equation for the period of a mass on a spring contains π:

$$T = 2\pi\sqrt{\frac{m}{k}}$$

Wait a minute. The constant π is related to *circles*. Where's the circle in simple harmonic motion?

There is no *apparent* circular motion in simple harmonic motion, so it might be difficult to understand how π applies to this motion. But imagine that we place an object on a horizontal rotating turntable and then use a flashlight to project the *shadow* of the object on a wall. If the turntable turns with a constant angular velocity, we will find that the shadow moves back and forth in simple harmonic motion! This arrangement is shown in the diagram on the next page.

Thus, the circle which we can identify with simple harmonic motion is the circular motion of an object whose projection is the simple harmonic motion that we observe. The *angular frequency* ω of the harmonic motion (equal to $2\pi f$, where f is the frequency

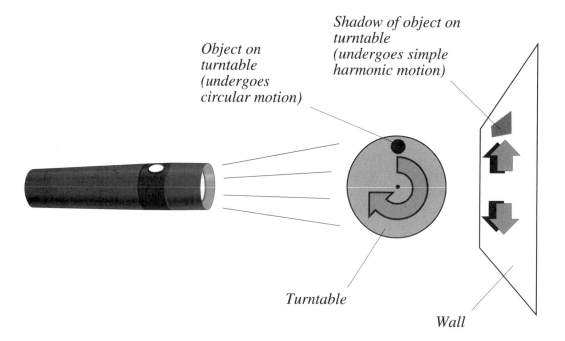

Object on turntable (undergoes circular motion)

Shadow of object on turntable (undergoes simple harmonic motion)

Turntable

Wall

of the oscillation), is the same as the *angular velocity* ω of the representative particle undergoing circular motion.

4.) Baseball and tennis players claim that there is a "sweet spot" on the bat or the racket, which represents a favored spot for the ball to hit. Is there any truth to such a spot?

Experimentation shows that there is a difference in the reaction of players, depending on where the ball strikes the sports implement. Thus, the concept of the sweet spot is valid as far as a subjective human response is concerned. There is some debate in the literature, however, as to the exact physical definition of the sweet spot. There are three competing definitions, each of which will be addressed below.

The baseball bat and the tennis racket are real examples of a *physical* pendulum. An idealized pendulum is a mass of zero size on the end of a massless rod. A physical pendulum represents a real object, with an extent in space. Imagine hanging a baseball bat or a tennis racket vertically from a point on the handle at which it is held while being used in a game. Now, imagine that we apply an impulsive force, as if the bat or racket is being hit by a ball, at various points along the body. In general, there will be a reaction force at the point of support. But there is one point, called the *center of oscillation*, for which there is no reaction force at the support. One can show that the distance between the center of oscillation and the support point is equal to the length of a simple pendulum that would have the same period of oscillation as the physical pendulum. Our interest here, though, is in the first-mentioned property of the center of oscillation—no reaction force at the support point. This is the first definition of the "sweet spot". Imagine that the bat or racket is supported in play and a ball hits the implement at the sweet spot. Then, there is no reaction force at the support point—*the hand(s)*. The presence of a reaction force at the hands is called the "sting" of the bat in baseball. The sweet spot is called sweet because there is no reaction force and, therefore, no sting.

A second definition of the sweet spot is related to *standing waves* established in the implement when it is struck by the ball. While the lowest frequency mode of oscillation is not unpleasant for the player, higher modes of oscillation appear to cause some discomfort. The higher modes of oscillation can be minimized in amplitude if the striking takes place at a *node* of the standing wave. Thus, the second definition of the sweet spot is that striking point among the nodes of the higher modes of oscillation that provides the most pleasant vibration at the hands, due to the minimization of the higher frequencies.

Some researchers refute these two definitions in favor of a third and claim that the important area on the racket or bat is more properly called the *power region*. This definition is based on the *coefficient of restitution*. The sweet "spot" is defined as that region of the implement for which the coefficient of restitution is higher than some minimum value. The description as the power region stems from the fact that it represents the area where the ball will rebound with the highest velocity.

For more information on the debate over the tennis racket sweet spot, see H. Brody, "Physics of the Tennis Racket", *American Journal of Physics*, **47**, 482, 1979; H. Brody, "Physics of the Tennis Racket II; The 'Sweet Spot'", *American Journal of Physics*, **49**, 816, 1981; H. Hatze, "Objective Biomechanical Determination of Tennis Racket Properties", *International Journal of Sport Biomechanics*, **8**, 275, 1992; H. Hatze, "Impact Probability Distribution, Sweet Spot, and the Concept of an Effective Power Region in Tennis Rackets", *Journal of Applied Biomechanics*, **10**, 43, 1994; and H. Brody, "How Would a Physicist Design a Tennis Racket?", *Physics Today*, **48(3)**, 26, 1995. For a discussion of the sweet spot for a baseball bat, see P. J. Brancazio, *SportScience: Physical Laws and Optimum Performance*, Simon and Schuster, New York, 1983, as well as H. Brody, "Models of Baseball Bats", *American Journal of Physics*, **58**, 756, 1990 and L. L. Van Zandt, "The Dynamical Theory of the Baseball Bat", *American Journal of Physics*, **60**, 172, 1992. For information on how the coefficient of restitution of the *baseball* affects fly balls, see D. T. Kagan, "The Effects of Coefficient of Restitution Variations on Long Fly Balls", *American Journal of Physics*, **58**, 151, 1990.

5.) Earthquakes result in both longitudinal and transverse waves traveling through the Earth. In a band around the globe located between 105° and 142° from the epicenter of an earthquake, there is a *shadow zone* where the intensity of waves is very small. Why is this?

This effect is evidence for the existence of a *liquid core* in the Earth. For locations on the Earth's surface that are at relatively small angular displacements from the epicenter, the earthquake waves travel entirely through the rocky mantle to reach these points. In the diagram on the next page, rays *1*, *2* and *3* represent such waves. The rays are curved due to refraction through the various density layers of the Earth's interior.

For points at larger and larger angular displacements from the epicenter, the waves must arrive at these locations by taking deeper and deeper paths through the mantle, as shown by the progression of rays from *1* to *3*. At a location 105° from the epicenter, a wave has just grazed the surface of the liquid core, as indicated by ray *4* in the diagram. Now, notice ray *5*, which is heading just slightly deeper than ray *4*. This ray *refracts* across the boundary into the liquid core. It then refracts again as it leaves the liquid core

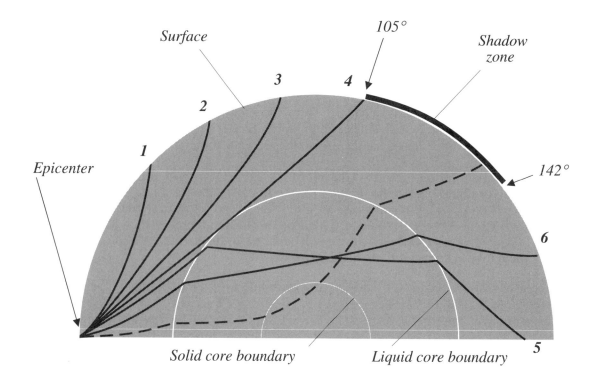

Surface

105°

Shadow zone

3

4

2

1

Epicenter

142°

6

Solid core boundary

Liquid core boundary

5

and ends up arriving at the surface of the Earth more than 180° from the epicenter. Now, imagine an even deeper ray, such as ray **6**. This ray encounters the liquid core at an angle closer to the normal than ray **5**, so the refraction is not so severe. Thus, this ray arrives at the surface at an angle less than 180°. If we continued to draw rays at deeper and deeper angles as they leave the epicenter (which we have not done, so as to keep the diagram from becoming too cluttered), we would find that the arrival at the surface would move toward smaller angles (as we saw for rays **5** and **6**), but *would reach a minimum at 142°*. Then, even though we continue to deepen the direction of the ray from the epicenter, the arrival point on the surface moves once again toward larger angles. Thus, the position at 142° is a minimum angle for refracted rays. This is very similar to the minimum angle reached by light rays refracting through a raindrop to form the rainbow, as discussed in Mystery #1 in Chapter 26 of *PBWM*.

The region between 105° and 142° is devoid of earthquake waves that have traveled through the interior, except for a small amount of energy arriving from rays that have *diffracted* from the outer edge of the liquid core or that have refracted through the inner *solid core*, as indicated by the dashed ray in the diagram. What's more, since the 142° position represents a minimum in the angle of rays refracted through the outer core, a relatively large amount of energy arrives at this location. The circle around the Earth located at 142° from the epicenter is called a *caustic circle*.

Some other considerations can be explored if one wishes to continue this investigation further. For example, the rays traveling through the Earth are of two types—*P* waves, which are longitudinal and *S* waves, which are transverse. The *S* waves do not travel through the liquid core, since the liquid will not respond to the shear force representing a transverse oscillation. If an *S* wave arrives at the boundary of the liquid core at an angle other than 90°, however, it can be interpreted as having both a longitudinal and a transverse component *relative to the normal* and the longitudinal component will pass into the liquid.

In addition to waves passing through the Earth, there are surface waves moving *around* the Earth. In studying the pattern of waves on a seismograph, all of these considerations, as well as others that have not been mentioned, must be kept in mind. The analysis of earthquake waves can be quite complicated. For a readable account of some of these considerations, see B. A. Bolt, *Inside the Earth*, W. H. Freeman and Company, San Francisco, 1982.

6.) During the 1985 Michoacán earthquake in Mexico, parts of Mexico City, *400 km from the epicenter*, were heavily damaged while other parts were relatively unharmed. Why was there damage so far from the epicenter and why was the damage so "spotty"?

The Michoacán earthquake continues to be studied and will for a long time. Two contributions to the damage in Mexico City have been described in the literature.

The first involves the fact that Mexico City is built on a *sedimentary basin*, as are many cities. In such a basin, the earthquake waves pass through *soil*, in which the velocity of propagation of the waves is slower than in solid rock. To address this situation, let us first think about ocean waves—either the usual waves or a tsunami. In the open ocean, the waves move quickly and have low amplitude. As a wave approaches the shore, it slows down and, since the energy carried in the wave is (almost) conserved, the amplitude increases; this is why waves pile up and break on the beach.

The same effect occurs when an earthquake wave moves into a region where the velocity of propagation is significantly slower—the amplitude (displacement *and* velocity) of the wave increases. In particular, earthquake waves move quite slowly through loose soil or mudfill. Thus, if a building rests on this type of soil, it can expect to see much more violent shaking than a building on solid rock. This is theorized as a contribution to the violent shaking in Mexico City, even though the epicenter was very far away.

An interesting effect related to soils in earthquakes occurred in 1923 in an earthquake in Kwanto, Japan. After the earthquake, a field of relatively loose soil was covered with *potatoes* that had previously been growing normally underground. The shaking of the soil had the same effect as shaking a can of mixed nuts (see The Anti-Gravity Brazil Nuts in Chapter 6 of *PBWM*), resulting in the Brazil nuts migrating to the top. The potatoes, which were larger than the typical soil particles, rose upward.

The second contribution suggested for the pattern of destruction in Mexico City, in which some areas were badly damaged and others were not, is the curved shape of the bedrock below the sedimentary basin. This leads to two possibilities. The first is standing waves set up in the basin, so that buildings located at antinodes would suffer more destruction than those at nodes. Also, the curved reflecting surfaces of the bedrock tended to focus, like a parabolic mirror, the earthquake waves at certain regions of the surface. For further discussion of this earthquake and its effects, see J. A. Rial, N. G. Saltzman and H. Ling, "Earthquake-Induced Resonance in Sedimentary Basins", *American Scientist*, **80**, 566, 1992.

7.) During the Loma Prieta Earthquake of 1989, part of the Nimitz Freeway in Oakland, a double decker construction, collapsed, with the upper roadway falling onto the lower roadway. Yet other portions of the same freeway, with the same construction, escaped unharmed. Why did this particular portion of the Nimitz Freeway collapse?

The portion of the Nimitz Freeway which collapsed was 100 km away from the epicenter of the Loma Prieta Earthquake. The general answer to the question as to why the collapse occurred is *resonance*. The earthquake frequency matched closely enough the natural frequency of the structure to cause it to undergo large vibrations which brought it to the ground. Adjacent portions of the freeway, however, had the same construction but were not destroyed. An understanding of this result can be found by looking at the ground on which the various portions were built. The portions of the freeway which survived were built on solid rock, while the destroyed portions were constructed on land which was relatively loose mudfill. The effect of soils on earthquake vibration amplitude is discussed in Mystery #6. Because of the difference in the medium through which the earthquake waves were passing, the vibration amplitude in the mudfill was *5 times as large* as that in the rock portions for frequencies in the range of 1 to 4 Hz and as much as 8 times as large for frequencies near 5 Hz. This larger amplitude of vibration was what caused the destruction of the portion that collapsed. For more details, see S. E. Hough, P. A. Friberg, R. Busby, E. F. Field, K. H. Jacob, and R. D. Borcherdt, "Sediment Induced Amplification and the Collapse of the Nimitz Freeway", *Nature*, **344**, 853, 1990.

8.) If you watch a toy boat floating in a rough-water bathtub, the motion does not look realistic. There is something wrong with the way it bounces around. Yet, in the movies, *miniatures* of ships and other vehicles are used freely. Why do they look so good in the movies?

This is an application of *scaling*. Since the toy boat is a miniature, we have scaled down the size, compared to a real boat, by some factor. Let us say that this factor is 100 —each linear dimension of the real boat is 100 times larger than that for the toy boat. When you are watching the bouncing of the boat, you are really making visual, but unconscious, determinations of the *frequency* at which it bounces. It appears to bounce around in the water much faster than a real boat. And indeed it does. Let us imagine that the bounces in the water can be modeled as simple harmonic. Then, it is clear that the bouncing frequency will be higher than normal because the *mass* of the toy boat has also been scaled down from the real boat. Since the mass is proportional to the volume, the mass will scale as the *cube* of the linear dimensions. Thus, if the linear scale factor is 100, the mass scale factor is the cube of this—10^6. Now, according to the principles of simple harmonic motion, the oscillation frequency is proportional to the square root of the mass. Thus, the scale factor for the oscillation *frequency* will be 10^3. This is a factor of 10 different from the scale factor for linear dimensions. This is why the toy doesn't look real—the bounces through a (vertical) linear dimension occur 10 times as fast as we are used to seeing for real objects.

We have performed this calculation with a simple volume-mass proportionality. In reality, the density of the material from which toys are made is usually much less than for real objects. In the case of the ship, for example, the real ship is made of metal, while the toy ship is likely to be made of plastic. This will enlarge further the scale factor for mass, making the non-realistic appearance even worse.

Now, how do we account for this in the movies? We could increase the mass of the boat, to try to bring the mass scale factor down to a reasonable value. The mass scale factor is so large, however, that it is likely that the toy boat will no longer float once all the extra mass is added! There is a better way; in the movies, we can do something that we cannot do with real-life observation of the toy boat. *We can slow down the time.* If we assume our numerical calculation above to be true, we can film the bouncing boat at 10 times the normal film speed. Then, when the movie is played back at normal speed, the effect is to cause time to slow down by a factor of 10. As a result, our bouncing frequency, which is normally 10 times too fast, appears to be correct in the movie and the ship looks real!

9.) Space Shuttle astronauts maintain radio contact with mission control. Is it possible to receive this communication on a home radio?

This item almost fits into the Myth section, since the communication used by the Space Shuttle is *just barely* radio. The frequencies used are in the "gray area" between radio and microwaves. There are three main frequency bands used for Shuttle communications. The primary launch, landing and spacewalk communications are in the *UHF band*, with several distinct frequencies in the range of 240 to 300 MHz (FM radio ranges from 88 to 108 MHz). These transmissions are frequency modulated voice signals and are relatively easy to intercept if one has the proper receiving equipment and the Shuttle is nearby during launch, spacewalk, or landing.

Another range of communication frequencies is in the *S band*, with frequencies ranging from 2000 to 2300 MHz. This is the primary communication band between the Shuttle and mission control but the signal is modulated by means of a process in which voice is multiplexed with telemetry data. Thus, it is not decipherable without very specialized receiving equipment.

A third range is in the *Ku band*, which is clearly in the realm of microwaves. The frequency is 15003 MHz, which is used for high transmission rate scientific data.

Thus, specialized equipment is necessary to *directly* receive Shuttle communications. On the other hand, a variety of radio amateurs receive the transmissions and rebroadcast them on frequencies more appropriate for amateur radio reception in the home. For information about these opportunities, see Chapter 8 in A. R. Curtis, *Monitoring NASA Communications*, Tiare Publications, Lake Geneva, Wisconsin, 1992.

𝕸agic:

The Colored String

You will see a color difference between the two sides of a given loop of string in the standing wave pattern. The top of one loop will be blue and the bottom will be yellow or orange. The adjacent loop will have these colors reversed. A color picture of this effect is available in E. Zwicker, G. Lietz, A. Behof, and M. Ellenstein, "Illuminating Standing Waves", *The Physics Teacher*, **24**, 449, 1986.

The effect is caused by the spectrum of light emitted by the fluorescent light tubes. There are two sources of light from the tubes. One is a discrete set of spectral lines emitted by the mercury vapor during the time periods surrounding the peaking of the AC voltage oscillation. This occurs at a frequency of 120 Hz, since there are two voltage peaks (one positive, one negative) in each cycle. The strongest line is a blue line at 435.8 nm. This is the light that provides the most illumination of the string when it is at one end of the oscillation, since the maximum displacement of the string also occurs at the same time and at the same frequency as the peak of the voltage. Thus, we have one extreme of the oscillation appearing blue.

The second source of light in the fluorescent tube is the fluorescent material on the inside surface of the glass envelope. This radiation is more continuous than the discrete mercury emission, and has its highest intensity in the orange-red region of the spectrum. The decay time for this radiation is longer than that for the mercury emission, so between the voltage peaks, the fluorescent tube is emitting primarily orange-red light. This is the light which illuminates the string at the other extreme of the motion, giving its orange-red appearance. In normal operation, the light from the two sources combines to simulate the color of sunlight. The string, vibrating at the same frequency as the light bulb, allows our eyes to resolve in space what cannot be resolved in time, similar to Circle of Light, in Chapter 24 of *PBWM*. Related to this demonstration, a color picture of a rotating *fluorescent* bulb is shown in the Zwicker, et al, article noted above. This picture clearly shows the separate blue and orange-red emissions. A wavelength spectrum for the fluorescent light bulb is available in R. D. Edge, "Why is the String Colored?", *The Physics Teacher*, **18**, 518, 1980.

P. D. Gupta ("Coloration on a String Vibrating in a Standing Wave Pattern", *The Physics Teacher*, **26**, 371, 1988) inserts a variable capacitor in the vibrator or the fluorescent light circuit in order to vary the phase between the string vibrations and the light emissions. With such an arrangement, the coloration of the string can be reversed or even eliminated with the appropriate adjustment of the capacitor.

For a demonstration in which standing string waves are established on a laser-lit optical fiber, see J. Abendschan and D. Speakman, "Laser-Enhanced Vibrating String", *The Physics Teacher*, **29**, 114, 1991.

The Shimmering Tuning Fork

The computer monitor screen is acting as a strobe light, since it is flickering, just slightly faster than most people can notice. As a result, the motion of the tuning fork appears to be slowed down.

The effects when the fork is held vertically or horizontally are quite different. The horizontally-held fork (with tines vibrating vertically) looks like a common stroboscope effect—the times appear to be vibrating slowly. The frequency of the apparent vibration depends on the relationship between the refresh rate of the monitor screen and the frequency of the fork.

The appearance when the fork is held vertically (with the tines vibrating horizontally) is more unusual—*the tines appear to be shaped like waves, and the waves move along the length of the tine*. This effect is suggested in the diagram to the right. The effect is strongest if the frequency of the fork is close to an integer multiple of the refresh rate of the computer monitor. For example, a fork with a frequency of 392 Hz exhibits a nice display against a monitor with a refresh rate of 66.7 Hz, since the ratio of the two frequencies is 5.88.

The reason for the wave shape of the tines is that the entire monitor screen is not illuminated at one time. The picture on the screen is swept out, one line at a time. Thus, as the monitor screen sweeps out its picture, it illuminates progressively lower portions of the fork. Each lower portion is more advanced·in its vibration than the previous portion. Since the frequency of the fork is higher than that of the monitor, several oscillations of the fork occur during a given sweep of the screen, and the fork appears to be bent into a wave shape.

A related effect can be seen by waving your hand in front of the screen. You will see *multiple images* of your hand. Compare this to waving your hand against the sky or other source of constant lighting. In this case, you will see images of your hand at the ends of its motion, due to the momentary stops it must make to reverse its motion, with a blur in between. When your hand is waved in font of the screen, the flashing of the screen illuminates your hand at various positions of its motion. The effect is different than that for the tuning fork, since you cannot wave your hand as fast as a tuning fork can vibrate!

This demonstration is described in J. W. Jewett, "Computer Monitor as Stroboscope for Tuning Forks", *The Physics Teacher*, **32**, 489, 1994. A similar demonstration using a television screen is described in D. P. Martin, "String Waves in Slow Motion", *The Science Teacher*, **59(3)**, 31, 1992, and G. E. Jones and J. L. Ferguson, "Easy Displacement versus Time Graphs for a Vibrating String: Tuning a Guitar by Television", *American Journal of Physics*, **48**, 362, 1980, in which waves on an elastic string are viewed. Similarly, in K. Brecher and K. Brecher, "The 'Videostrobe' Water Drop Gravimeter", *The Physics Teacher*, **28**, 108, 1990, a television is used as a strobe to view falling water droplets.

The Pendulum Resonator

All of the pendula should show some oscillatory motion. It should be clear, however, that the matched pendulum that was not initially set into motion exhibits the largest amplitude of oscillation. This is a *resonance* effect. When one of the matched oscillators is set into oscillation, energy is transferred effectively to the other. All of the other pendula are off resonance and will not absorb energy as efficiently from the initially oscillating pendulum. If you are able to quantify the amplitude in some way, you should be able to see the amplitude decreasing as you move away from the matched pendula in either direction, since the frequencies will be more and more different from the resonance frequency as the length of the pendulum both increases and decreases.

𝕸𝖞𝖙𝖍:

1.) Waves require a medium.

This statement is only true for *mechanical* waves, such as sound waves, earthquake waves or surface waves on water. *Electromagnetic* waves, of which light is a familiar example, do not require a medium; they can travel through empty space.

2.) Television stations can only be received on a television.

If you live in a region where television channel 6 (*broadcast* channel 6, not *cable* channel 6!) is in operation, you will be able to pick up the audio portion of the broadcast on an FM *radio*. The frequency of channel 6, by Federal standards, is in the range from 82 MHz to 88 MHz (Television stations have a 6 MHz bandwidth). The lowest frequency in the FM radio band is 87.9 MHz (This is called channel 100!). Thus, if the radio is tuned to the lowest frequency on the band, it is possible to detect the sound from channel 6.

There also other devices which are not complete televisions, but which can still receive television signals. Videocassette recorders, for example, have a television tuner, and can, therefore, receive and decode television signals. This is why you can watch one program while recording another—the videocassette recorder tuner sends its signal to the videotape for recording, while you watch the signal from the tuner in the television set. It is a common misunderstanding that a videocassette recorder records "from the television". This mistaken belief leads some people to feel that the television set must remain on while a recording is made.

In addition, there are devices which will receive and decode only the *audio* portion of a television signal, so that one can *listen* to television even if you are unable to watch it.

3.) If no earthquake occurs, that is equivalent to saying that an earthquake of magnitude zero on the Richter scale occurred.

This can be seen to be false if it is recalled that the Richter scale is a *logarithmic* scale. Thus, the *magnitude* of zero does not correspond to an *energy release* of zero. Consider one of the equations relating energy and magnitude from Myth #4 in Chapter 17 of *PBWM*:

$$\log E = 4.8 + 1.5M$$

where E is the energy released, in Joules, and M is the Richter magnitude. If we insert our desired value $M = 0$ in this equation, then,

$$\log E = 4.8 \quad \rightarrow \quad E = 6.3 \times 10^4 \text{ J}$$

which is equivalent to the kinetic energy achieved by a 1000 kg car being dropped to the ground from a height of about 6 meters.

Suppose we drop the car from a height lower than 6 meters. What is the equivalent Richter magnitude in this case? Since we now have an earthquake of magnitude lower than zero, the magnitude is *negative*! Suppose, for example, that a 68 kg person jumps from a 3 meter tall wall onto the ground. The kinetic energy just before striking the ground can be calculated to be about 2.0×10^3 J. Calculating the Richter magnitude associated with this energy gives us,

$$\log (2.0 \times 10^3 \text{ J}) = 4.8 + 1.5M \quad \rightarrow \quad M = -1$$

In practice, negative magnitudes are not used, since they represent very small individual releases of energy, which are generally overshadowed by the large number of such small events in normal life.

The concept of negative magnitudes is not restricted to the Richter scale, but is a feature of any logarithmic scale. For example, the apparent brightness of stars is described by a magnitude scale based on logarithms. But in this case, the scale is reversed from that for earthquakes. The *brighter* a star appears, the *lower* is its magnitude. Thus, the stars normally seen at night have small positive magnitudes, while larger positive magnitudes correspond to very faint stars. This is due to the origin of the magnitude scale in the astronomical observations of the Greeks and Romans, who classified stars into categories of brightness. The brightest stars were categorized with a magnitude 1 and the fainter stars were given higher numbered classifications. For objects brighter than stars, such as the Moon and the Sun, the magnitudes are negative.

An equation relating star magnitude and light intensity can be generated as follows. In an astronomy book, one can find the magnitude of the Sun as –26.8. It is also stated in such books that an increase of 5 orders of magnitude corresponds to a decrease in intensity by a factor of 100. Finally, we borrow the "Solar constant", $I = 1370$ W·m^{-2} from Myth #7 in Chapter 25 of *PBWM*. Now, the magnitude and intensity are related by a logarithmic equation similar to that for earthquake magnitudes. We write one with two unknown parameters, *a* and *b*:

$$\log I = a + bM$$

From the relationship for 5 orders of magnitude,

$$\log 100I = a + b(M - 5)$$

These last two equations can be combined to show that,

$$b = -0.4$$

Now, for the Sun,

$$\log (1370 \text{ W·m}^{-2}) = a + b (-26.8)$$

and, after substituting the value we found for b, we find,

$$a = -7.6$$

Thus, we have,

$$\log I = -7.6 - 0.4M$$

where I is expressed in units of $W \cdot m^{-2}$.

4.) Waves experience a phase inversion of 180° upon reflecting from a rigid boundary.

The mythical aspect of this statement is due to the fact that it is not true for <u>all</u> waves. It is true for *transverse* waves, but not for *longitudinal* waves. We can understand the phase inversion of transverse waves from Newton's Third Law. For example, imagine an upward pulse moving to the right on the string below, and approaching a rigid end. As the pulse arrives at the rigid end, the upward nature of the pulse results in an upward force on the support (if the end were free, the end would move up, then down). By the Third Law, then, the support exerts an equal and downward force on the rope, resulting in an inverted pulse moving to the left after the interaction.

Rigid end

Now, suppose the wave approaching a rigid end is longitudinal, such as a sound pulse approaching a solid wall. The absence of a phase inversion is easiest to see if we consider the pressure variation in the pulse. Let us assume that the pulse represents a disturbance of <u>increased</u> pressure. As this pulse hits the wall, the increased pressure will apply a larger than normal force perpendicular to the wall. In response, the wall will exert a larger than normal, Newton's Third Law force back on the air. This will result in an increased pressure pulse moving to the left. A high pressure region came in and a high pressure region left; there is no phase inversion!

If a sound wave reflects from a *non-rigid* boundary, there *is* a phase inversion of 180°. The rigid or non-rigid character of a boundary for a sound wave depends on the relative *acoustic impedances* of the media separated by the boundary (see Myth #6 in Chapter 14 for information on acoustic impedance). If a sound wave travels in air and arrives at an interface with water, the wave encounters an *increase* in acoustic impedance. This is an approximation to a rigid boundary, and there is no phase inversion. If the sound is created in water and arrives at an interface with the air at the water surface, the wave encounters a *decrease* in acoustic impedance, which approximates a non-rigid boundary. As a result, there *is* a phase inversion for the reflected wave.

5.) At one time, during the early years of the space program, a photographic company offered its ultrasonic ranging capability as a method for monitoring the distance between spacecraft during docking procedures.

This mechanism, which is discussed in Mystery #3 of Chapter 2 in *PBWM*, would have been useless, since the extremely thin air in the region of spacecraft orbits would not have allowed effective propagation of the *sound* waves used by these types of ranging systems.

6.) In the film, *The Poseidon Adventure* (Twentieth Century Fox, 1972), a ship traveling through open ocean is turned over by a passing tsunami.

In *The Poseidon Adventure*, a 7.8 magnitude earthquake causes a tsunami to be established in the East Atlantic Ocean. A measure of its speed is given in the dialog as 60 knots, which is about 70 miles per hour. This is far slower than a typical speed for a tsunami, which is measured in hundreds of miles per hour.

A tsunami is only dangerous when it interacts with the land. A tsunami in the open ocean is a very long wavelength wave (200 km or more) with a relatively modest amplitude (approximately 0.5 m). *It will pass by a ship unnoticed.* When a tsunami approaches the shore, it piles up and breaks, as discussed in Mystery #4 in Chapter 17 of *PBWM*.

There is a line in the movie that attempts to address the fact that an open-sea tsunami would be unnoticeable. As the tsunami approaches, the captain says, "It seems to be piling up in those shallows". Due to the wavelength of a tsunami, however, it would have to be an *extremely* large "shallows" to cause the effect in the movie.

Another problem with this scenario is the unlikely possibility that the ocean liner could float in a stable position *upside down*. Ships normally carry a great deal of ballast in the lower decks, as discussed in Mystery #4 of Chapter 8. If this ballast remains in the lower decks when the ship is upside down (of course, the lower decks are now the *upper* decks!), then the center of mass of the ship will be higher than the center of buoyancy. As a result, any deviation of the ship from the vertical would cause it to rotate back to the upright position.

Chapter 11
Sound

𝔐𝔶𝔰𝔱𝔢𝔯𝔦𝔢𝔰:

1.) If you hit glass bottles containing various levels of water with a metal spoon, the frequency of the sound <u>decreases</u> as the water level rises. But, if you blow across the top of the bottle, the frequency of the sound that you hear <u>increases</u> as the water level rises. Why is the behavior opposite in these two cases?

2.) The word *octave* has the stem *oct-*, meaning <u>eight</u>. Then why does a musical octave refer to *twelve* half-steps instead of *eight*?

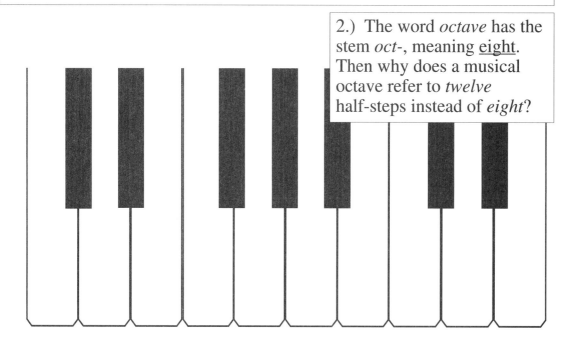

Mysteries:

3.) What is a sonic boom?

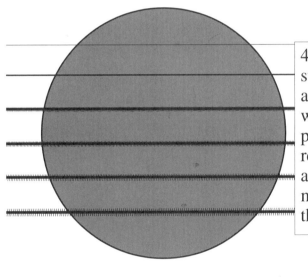

4.) The lower frequency strings on guitars and pianos are <u>wrapped</u> with additional wire to increase the mass per unit length and, thus, reduce the frequency. Why aren't these strings just made <u>thicker</u>? Wouldn't that have the same result?

5.) Why does sound travel faster in <u>moist</u> air?

𝕸𝖞𝖘𝖙𝖊𝖗𝖎𝖊𝖘:

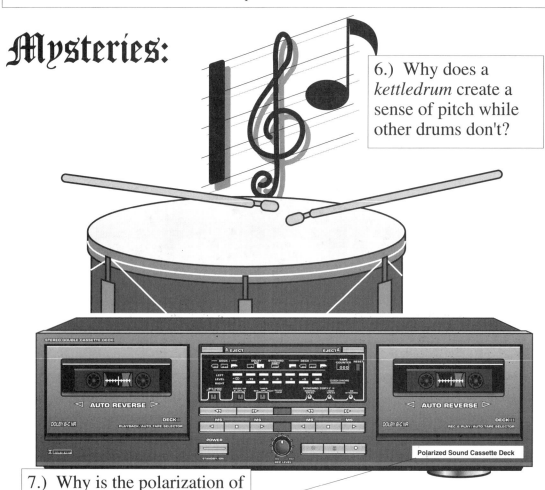

6.) Why does a *kettledrum* create a sense of pitch while other drums don't?

7.) Why is the polarization of sound waves not mentioned in physics books?

8.) When you connect your stereo speakers, you are warned that the polarity must be correct, or the bass will be weak. Why is this a consideration only for the bass?

Magic:

The Singing Aluminum Rod

Rub violin rosin on one hand. With the other hand, hold an aluminum rod, about 1 meter long, at the center. Rub the rosined hand along the rod in a direction away from the center. The rod will sing, quite loudly once you have practiced.

The Singing Wine Glass

Wet your fingers and rub them around the rim of a thin wine glass. The glass should ring with a loud clear tone. Try doing this with varying amounts of liquid in the glass.

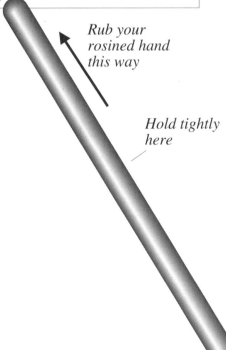

Rub your rosined hand this way

Hold tightly here

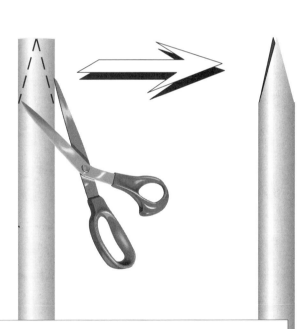

The Singing Straw

Cut off the ends of a plastic drinking straw in a V-shape, as shown in the diagram. Place the cut end in your mouth and blow—you will be able to obtain a razzy sound from the straw. You may have to experiment with pressure from your teeth on the straw to be successful. Once you can make a sustained sound, cut off, with the scissors, 1 or 2 cm sections from the flat end of the straw as you blow it—the frequency will rise as you cut it! Be careful not to cut off your nose!

𝔐𝔞𝔤𝔦𝔠:

Effects of Non-Linearity

Connect two function generators or oscillators to two loudspeakers, using amplifiers, if necessary to obtain sufficiently loud sounds. Set each oscillator on a frequency of 1000 Hz. Now, raise the frequency of one oscillator slowly. Listen for a sound <u>decreasing</u> in frequency!

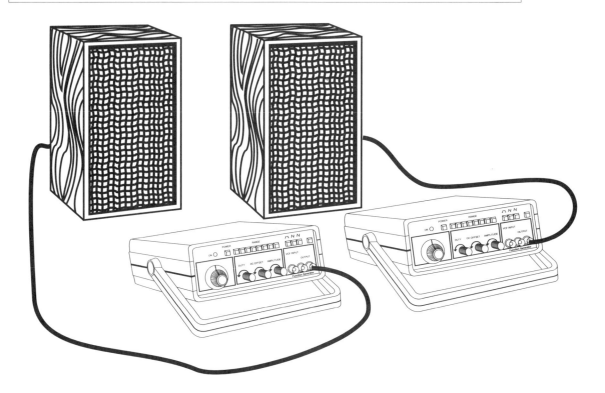

Sounds from Nothing??

Use the same equipment as in Effects of Non-Linearity, but connect both function generators to the *same* loudspeaker. Set each oscillator above the range of human hearing, say, at 25,000 Hz. Now vary the frequency of one of the oscillators, being sure *not* to bring it into the range of hearing. What do you hear?

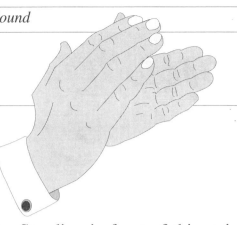

𝕸𝖆𝖌𝖎𝖈:

Staircase Reflections

All of the demonstrations on this page involve creating a sound near a structure and noting the nature of the sound coming back to you. Find a staircase with hard steps (not covered with carpet). Standing in front of this stair-case, at the bottom of the steps, clap your hands or make some other impulsive noise. You will be able to discern a *pitch* in response to the reflected sound. Why?

Sound Retroreflectors

If light is sent into a combination of three mirrors at right angles, forming the corner of a cube, it is reflected back along the same line—this is the construction for bicycle reflectors, for example. This effect can be observed for <u>sound</u> by finding a building with a face consisting of a large number of cement balconies arrayed on the wall of the building. Find such a building and make a loud sound near it. You should hear a distinct echo.

Piano Reflections

Hold the right hand pedal of a piano down and shout loudly. Listen to the sound coming back to you from the piano.

𝔐𝔞𝔤𝔦𝔠:

The Singing Quarter

Press the face of a quarter or other coin onto a piece of dry ice with your thumb. The coin will emit a shrill sound for a second or two.

Myth:

1.) Dogs have the highest range of hearing.

2.) In a table of decibels, a space shuttle launch is listed as 180 dB.

3.) The threshold of hearing is 0 dB.

Myth:

4.) Walking away from a sound source results in a decrease in intensity that varies as the inverse square of the distance from the source.

5.) The spectrum of a sound from a musical instrument allows us to identify the instrument.

Myth:

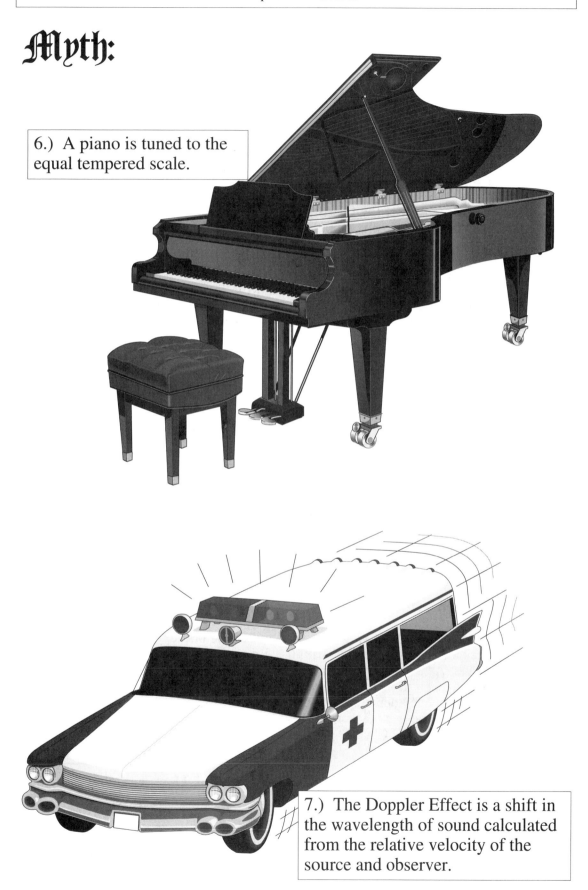

6.) A piano is tuned to the equal tempered scale.

7.) The Doppler Effect is a shift in the wavelength of sound calculated from the relative velocity of the source and observer.

Discussions; Chapter 11—Sound

𝕸𝖞𝖘𝖙𝖊𝖗𝖎𝖊𝖘:

1.) If you hit glass bottles containing various levels of water with a metal spoon, the frequency of the sound <u>decreases</u> as the water level rises. But, if you blow across the top of the bottle, the frequency of the sound that you hear <u>increases</u> as the water level rises. Why is the behavior opposite in these two cases?

The natural frequency of the glass bottle, as is the case with all vibrating systems, is related to a combination of the restoring force and the resistance to changes in motion. For example, for a common model of a mass on a spring, as related to the discussion in Mystery #3 in Chapter 10, the natural frequency is given by,

$$f = \frac{1}{2\pi}\sqrt{\frac{k}{m}}$$

where k is the spring constant (and is thus related to the restoring force) and m is the mass (which is the resistance to changes in motion).

Hitting a glass bottle with a spoon causes vibrations to be set up in the glass material of the bottle. The natural frequency of sustained vibrations is related to the restoring force, which depends on the elastic moduli of the glass material. The frequency also depends on the resistance to changes in motion, which is a combination of the density of the glass *along with the mass of the air and the water that are in contact with the glass.* If the water level in the bottle is raised, the additional water provides more mass loading due to the water in contact with the glass, *reducing* the natural frequency of vibration. (As another example of this phenomenon, listen to the sound of a struck metal bowl as you swish a small amount of water around the inside.)

Now, consider the effect of *blowing* across the top of the bottle. This causes vibrations of the *air cavity* in the bottle, unlike striking with a spoon, which caused vibrations in the glass material. As the water level rises, the air cavity decreases in size, which causes the natural frequency to increase. The air cavity is acting as a *Helmholtz resonator*, with the natural frequency depending on the volume of the cavity, the area of the opening, and the length of the neck. The behavior of a seashell as a Helmholtz resonator was discussed in Mystery #10 of Chapter 18 in *PBWM*.

2.) The word *octave* has the stem *oct-*, meaning <u>eight</u>. Then why does a musical octave refer to *twelve* half-steps instead of *eight*?

The octave is a combination of notes whose frequencies are in a ratio of 2:1. In the

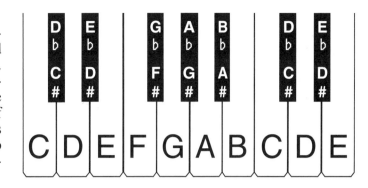

equal tempered scale of Western music, the octave is divided into twelve equal half-steps. The diagram to the right, showing the piano keyboard with the keys identified by the names of the notes, may be helpful in this discussion. The frequency ratio for a half-step in the equal tempered scale is:

$$\frac{f_{any\,note}}{f_{next\,lower\,note}} = \sqrt[12]{2} = 2^{\frac{1}{12}} = 1.059$$

Thus, for example, if we consider *concert A*, which is the A above middle C, and has an internationally accepted frequency of 440 Hz, the next highest note ($A^{\#}$ above middle C) has a frequency of,

$$\frac{f_{A^{\#}}}{440\,Hz} = 1.059 \quad \rightarrow \quad f_{A^{\#}} = 1.059(440\,Hz) = 466\,Hz$$

So where does the concept of *eight* come from, if there are *twelve* half-steps in an octave? If one plays a diatonic scale (on a piano, starting with a C, a diatonic scale is played by pressing all of the white keys up to the next C), from one note up to the note an octave higher, *eight notes* have been played. This is the origin of the *oct-* prefix.

3.) What is a sonic boom?

This is an extreme example of the *Doppler Effect*, as discussed in Mystery #5 in Chapter 18 of *PBWM* and Myth #7 in this Chapter. As noted there, sound waves moving away from and in the same direction as the source of the sound (such as the Space Shuttle shown in the diagram) will be compressed into a shorter wavelength, due to the fixed speed of sound in the air. If the speed of the source of the sound approaches the speed of sound in air, the waves are compressed into a very small region in front of the source. Thus, the energy of the wave is in a very small volume—there is a very high energy density. The result is often called a *shock wave*. The high energy density sound will spread away from the source of sound in a V-shape, just like the V-shaped wake of a motorboat moving through the water (this is a case of the source—the boat—moving *faster* than the waves in the water, resulting in what is called a *bow shock*). As this shock wave crosses the location of an observer on the ground, there is a sudden pressure pulse in the ear, which is heard as a sonic boom.

4.) The lower frequency strings on guitars and pianos are <u>wrapped</u> with additional wire to increase the mass per unit length and, thus, reduce the frequency. Why aren't these strings just made <u>thicker</u>? Wouldn't that have the same result?

It is true that using thicker strings would lower the frequency as well as using wrapped strings. The thicker strings, however, would introduce a defect in the sound as follows. In a thin string, oscillations result because of the restoring force that acts when the string is pulled to the side. This restoring force is the <u>tension</u> in the string; as the string is pulled to one side, the curving of the string results in components of the tension that will pull the string back toward equilibrium. For small oscillations of the string, a theoretical analysis of the action of the restoring force predicts a set of oscillation frequencies which are related as integral multiples of a fundamental frequency. This provides a combination of frequencies which results in a *musical* sound.

Now, suppose that the string is made thicker. Since the string is made of metal, it has <u>stiffness</u>, which is a tendency to return to a straight line shape. Imagine laying ordinary packaging string on a table in a curved shape—it will remain in that shape since it has negligible stiffness. But laying a piano string or a guitar string on the table in a curved shape and releasing it will result in it snapping back to a straight line, due to stiffness. Thus, stiffness represents an *additional restoring force* (added to the tension) which causes a musical string which is pulled away from equilibrium to return to equilibrium. A guitar or piano string pulled to the side will return due to the combined effects of tension and stiffness. Now, if the restoring force of the stiffness were simply an additive constant, then stiffness would just shift all standing wave frequencies of the string upward. But this is not the case. The effect of stiffness *increases as the curvature of the string is made larger*.

Consider the curvature of a guitar string in the first and twentieth harmonics, for example. In the first harmonic, the curvature is gentle, as shown below:

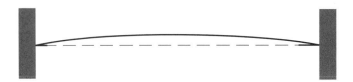

In the twentieth harmonic, however, the curvature must necessarily be greater, in order to fit nineteen nodes between the ends of the string:

Thus, the restoring force due to stiffness will have a greater effect in the twentieth harmonic than the first, due to the more severe bending of the string. In general, *the effect of the stiffness increases as the harmonic number increases*. Since the natural frequency depends on the restoring force, we see that each higher harmonic has its frequency raised *by an increasing amount* by the effects of the stiffness. As a result, we lose the integral relationship among the harmonics and the sound starts to represent a *noise* rather than a *musical* sound. This is an undesirable characteristic in a musical instrument.

These results can be minimized by wrapping the central wire with additional wire, which provides additional mass to lower the frequency without providing additional stiffness.

5.) Why does sound travel faster in <u>moist</u> air?

The speed of sound in a gas depends on the bulk modulus, B (see Myth #1 in Chapter 8), and the density, ρ, of the gas according to the following equation:

$$v = \sqrt{\frac{B}{\rho}}$$

In moist air, there are a large number of water (H_2O) molecules, which will occupy the space normally occupied by nitrogen (N_2) and oxygen (O_2) molecules. The water molecules are less massive than both nitrogen and oxygen molecules. Thus, the density of moist air is less than the density of dry air. As a result, according to the equation above, the speed of sound increases.

Conceptually, we can approach this from the role of mass as resistance to changes in motion. The less massive water molecules are easier to move from their equilibrium positions. Thus, when a disturbance due to a sound wave arrives, the water molecules respond more rapidly than the nitrogen or oxygen molecules, moving and communicating the disturbance to their neighbors.

6.) Why does a *kettledrum* create a sense of pitch while other drums don't?

Generally, two dimensional vibrating surfaces produce standing waves whose frequencies are not related by integer multiples. As a result, the combined sound of all the excited modes is a *noise*, rather than a *musical* sound. A noise creates no discernible pitch to a human, while a musical sound results in a definite pitch. Of course, these are extremes at the end of a spectrum. One can blow through one's lips and create a <u>noise</u> that results in a sense of pitch, and the pitch can be changed by altering the oral cavity or the shape of the lips. This noise has some frequencies which are much louder than others, which result in some sense of pitch for the sound.

As is the case with other musical instruments, the design and construction of kettledrums were developed from artistic considerations, and the scientific analysis came much later. While the understanding of kettledrums is still not complete, there are two major contributions to the sense of pitch in a kettledrum that are discussed. The first is the *kettle*. This is a closed air cavity (almost—there is a small hole at the bottom of the kettle) below the drumhead. This cavity has a natural frequency, just like the cavity inside a bottle, as discussed in Mystery #1. If a vibration frequency of the drumhead matches the frequency of the kettle, then the vibrations of the cavity will be excited and will provide feedback to the drumhead, reinforcing its vibration at that frequency. Some researchers argue, however, that the kettle is simply a *baffle*, preventing the air from sloshing back and forth from the top of the drumhead to the bottom, as in the spirit of the Magic demonstration, The Amplifying Poster, in Chapter 8 of *PBWM*. Blades (*Percussion Instruments and Their History*, Frederick A. Praeger, Publishers, New York, 1970) points out that "no appreciable difference in tone is perceptible whether the hole in the bottom of the shell is open or plugged", and claims that this suggests that there is little role of the kettle in the nature of the sound.

The second contribution arises from the location of the impact from the mallet. A vibration mode with an *antinode* near the strike point will be excited with a larger amplitude than a mode of vibration with a *node* near the strike point. If the drumhead is struck near the center, the lowest frequency mode of vibration is most likely to be excited. In this mode, the entire drumhead oscillates up and down. This mode is very quickly damped, since as the drumhead moves down, it must compress the air in the kettle (the hole at the bottom is small and cannot allow *rapid* passage of air). This represents a large amount of work done on the air, resulting in energy transferring out of the drumhead and into the air (as internal energy). The result is an unexciting dull thud. If the drumhead is struck at about one fourth of the diameter in from the edge, a higher mode is excited. In this mode, the drumhead vibrates in two pieces, on either side of a nodal line. Thus, since one side goes up while the other side goes down, there is little net change in in the volume of the air in the kettle. Although there may still be some air friction as the air sloshes back and forth, there is little need to compress the air. Thus, this mode of vibration lasts for a significant amount of time compared to the lowest mode.

The final consideration is to adjust the tension in the drumhead so that the frequency of this desired mode matches the natural frequency of the air cavity in the kettle. Thus, feedback from the kettle will result in the desired mode being louder than others that might also be excited by the one fourth diameter striking point. As a result, a single frequency rings out much louder than the others, giving the overall sound a frequency mixture that creates a sense of pitch in the listener.

For further information, A. H. Benade (*Fundamentals of Musical Acoustics*, Oxford University Press, New York, 1976) has a nice section on the kettledrum.

7.) Why is the polarization of sound waves not mentioned in physics books?

The polarization of a wave is only meaningful for *transverse* waves, since there are many choices of directions perpendicular to the velocity of propagation. For a *longitudinal* wave, such as a sound wave in air, the oscillation direction of the particles of the medium is established as parallel to the velocity of propagation—there are no choices. Thus, in a sense, all sound waves are polarized with the only possibility—along the direction of propagation!

For sound waves moving in a solid, we *can* have both longitudinal and transverse components (as discussed in Myth #3 in Chapter 18 of *PBWM*). In this case, we do have a possibility for polarization of the transverse component. This possibility for two polarizations of sound waves is included in the Debye Theory of specific heats of solids. See, for example, Chapter 14 in J. W. Rohlf, *Modern Physics from α to Z^0*, John Wiley & Sons, New York, 1994, for a discussion of this model. In addition, earthquake waves (see Mystery #5 in Chapter 10) are sound waves traveling through the Earth, with both transverse and longitudinal components.

8.) When you connect your stereo speakers, you are warned that the polarity must be correct, or the bass will be weak. Why is this a consideration only for the bass?

The problem has to do with the *interference pattern* set up by the stereo speakers, acting as two coherent sources of sound. We can address this question by calculating some wavelengths of sounds. Let us choose typical frequencies of bass and treble notes as 69 Hz (about C$^{\#}$, two octaves below middle C) and 690 Hz (about F above high C), respectively, since the speed of sound is conveniently divisible by these numbers. The wavelengths of these sound waves can be determined:

$$Bass: \quad \lambda = \frac{c}{f} = \frac{3.45 \times 10^2 \, \text{m} \cdot \text{s}^{-1}}{69 \, \text{Hz}} = 5 \, \text{m}$$

$$Treble: \quad \lambda = \frac{c}{f} = \frac{3.45 \times 10^2 \, \text{m} \cdot \text{s}^{-1}}{690 \, \text{Hz}} = 0.5 \, \text{m}$$

Now, if a given sound is emitted from both speakers, there will be interference effects between the waves arriving at your ears from the two sources. In a typical interference pattern, the distance between maxima and minima depends on the wavelength of the wave. For a typical stereo set-up and typically-sized listening room, the distance between maximum and minimum is approximately the same as the wavelength. Thus, for bass notes, the maxima and minima in the loudness of the sounds are separated by about 5 m. This is as large as, or larger than, the room! If the speakers are out of phase, then the region directly in front of the speakers will be a *minimum* and you might need to move farther from the center line than the room allows to reach the first maximum! Thus, the bass will be weak everywhere in the room. If the speakers are in phase, then the central *maximum* directly in front of the speakers will provide strong bass throughout a typical sized listening room.

On the other hand, the maxima and minima for the treble sounds will be separated by 0.5 m and by even smaller distances for higher frequencies. Thus, although there may be some variation in loudness of the high frequencies around the room, a small motion of the head will move the listener from a minimum to a maximum. For higher frequencies, the separations will be smaller than the size of the head, so it is likely that at least one ear will be close enough to a maximum to be satisfied.

This discussion has ignored the effects of *reflections* of the sound off the walls of the room, which will help to even out the sound at all frequencies.

Magic:

The Singing Wine Glass

The wine glass has a *natural frequency*, which is determined by its shape and its structural strength. When the finger is rubbed around the edge, it alternately sticks and slips along the surface, similar to the sticking and slipping of a bow on a violin string. The waveform of the waves transferred to the glass by this process is very complicated, containing many frequencies. At least one of these frequencies will be close to the natural frequency of the glass. The glass will start to vibrate, due to resonance, in response. The vibrations of the glass will provide feedback, enhancing the frequency component of the finger vibration that matches the natural frequency of the glass, so that a nice clear tone builds up.

For more information, see W. Rueckner, D. Goodale, D. Rosenberg, S. Steel and D. Tavilla, "Lecture Demonstration of Wineglass Resonance", *American Journal of Physics*, **61**, 184, 1993.

The Singing Aluminum Rod

The explanation of this effect is virtually identical to that in The Singing Wine Glass. The hand sliding along the rod alternately sticks and slips, providing a complicated waveform to the rod. The rod then resonates at its natural frequency.

One significant difference between the rod and the wineglass is that the rod acts as a *one-dimensional system*, unlike the complicated three-dimensional wine glass. This allows for additional investigations into holding the rod at other possible nodal points.

For information on measuring the speed of sound in aluminum rods and other solid materials with simple laboratory apparatus, see M. T. Frank and E. Kluk, "Velocity of Sound in Solids", *The Physics Teacher*, **29**, 246, 1991. For ideas on using the frequency of the singing rod to calculate Young's Modulus for aluminum, see J. E. Kettler, "Listening for Young's Modulus", *The Physics Teacher*, **29**, 538, 1991.

The Singing Straw

This is another one-dimensional system like The Singing Aluminum Rod, but the excitation mechanism is the flapping of the triangular shaped pieces at the end of the straw, rather than a stick-slip effect. The straw, acting as a resonant air column, provides feedback and results in a loud response at its natural frequency. As the straw is clipped to shorter lengths, its resonant frequency increases, which results in a sound of increasing frequency.

Effects of Non-Linearity

A perfectly linear acoustic device would exactly reproduce the waveform of the input signal. Thus, if a *perfect* electrical sine wave were introduced to a perfectly linear speaker, the output sound wave would be a *perfect* sine wave. This is an idealization. Real devices exhibit some degree of non-linearity, which results in some distortion of the output. This distortion results in additional frequencies added to the sound. This is similar to the additional frequencies introduced by modulating a pure wave, as discussed in Mystery #3 in Chapter 17 of *PBWM*. The additional frequencies introduced by distortion are integer multiples of the original frequency.

If *two* distorted waves are combined, non-linearity will also form *combinations* between the frequencies in the two waves. These are integer combinations, described in general as $mf_1 \pm nf_2$, where m and n are integers and f_1 and f_2 are the two original frequencies. This is what we are observing in this demonstration. An easily heard combination frequency is $2f_1 - f_2$. Thus, if both f_1 and f_2 are equal to 1000 Hz, the combination frequency is also 1000 Hz. Now, if f_2 is raised from 1000 Hz to 2000 Hz, notice that the combination frequency *decreases* from 1000 Hz to 0 Hz. The contrast between the increasing f_2 and the decreasing combination frequency makes the latter particularly easy to identify.

A question which arises in this demonstration is this—where is the non-linearity causing the combination frequencies to be produced? Is it in the *speaker* or the *ear*, both of which are non-linear acoustic devices? This can be explored by performing the activity with both sounds coming from one speaker and comparing this to the effect of having the sounds come from separate speakers. What's more, another question can be asked—are the combination frequencies formed in the *ear* or in the *brain*? This can be explored by repeating the activity with the sound coming from stereo headphones. One arrangement is to feed the two frequencies through a microphone mixer or other device with a mono/stereo switch. Then, it is easy to switch between combining the frequencies in each earpiece (mono) and keeping them separate (stereo). With the two source frequencies feeding into separate earpieces, the sounds do not combine until they enter the brain.

Sounds from Nothing??

You should be able to hear some quiet squeaks and other noises. Even though the *individual* frequencies are above the range of human hearing, some *combination* frequencies, as discussed in Effects of Non-Linearity, will be in the audio range. In this case, since the sounds are combined in the single loudspeaker, it is the non-linearity of the loudspeaker which causes the combination frequencies.

Staircase Reflections

When you clap your hands in front of the stairs, you will hear reflections from each of the stairs as they bounce the sound back to you. But each higher step is a little farther away. Thus, the reflection from each higher step will reach you a little later. As a result, your single clap will result in a *series* of echoes, equally spaced in time. Let's estimate the time between the echoes. Suppose that each step is 30 cm deep. Then, compared to the next lower step, the sound has to travel an additional 60 cm in its total trip from your hands to the step and back to your ears. Each successively higher step will result in an additional 60 cm of travel distance. Now, the time for sound to travel 60 cm is found easily:

$$\Delta x = v_{sound} \Delta t \quad \rightarrow \quad 0.60 \text{ m} = (345 \text{ m·s}^{-1}) \Delta t \quad \rightarrow \quad \Delta t = 1.7 \text{ x } 10^{-3} \text{ s}$$

The series of reflected sounds, each separated by this time interval will result in a *fre-*

quency, whose value is the inverse of this time interval:

$$f = (\Delta t)^{-1} = (1.7 \times 10^{-3} \text{ s})^{-1} = 5.8 \times 10^2 \text{ Hz}$$

This frequency is within the range of human hearing (it is between $C^{\#}$ and D above high C), so you will hear it and your brain will assign a pitch to this repeating sound!

Another example of this kind of effect can be discovered if you clap your hands while walking on a sidewalk under a horizontal concrete overhang. The sound will bounce up and down between the hard surfaces and your brain will assign a distinct pitch to the sound. It is interesting to move your ear close to the ground so that you are no longer near the midpoint between the ground and the overhang. Then you will hear two quick echoes (down and then up from ground) and two echoes separated by a longer time (up and then down from ceiling). With effort, you may be able to hear the effect on the apparent pitch. The author's son was quite embarrassed when his father would explore this effect when picking him up from day care.

Sound Retroreflectors

The physics behind this effect is the same as that of the optical retroreflectors in the description of the Magic demonstration. It is important to find a building with the balconies constructed as cubicles, with perpendicular concrete walls. The perpendicular surfaces will retroreflect the sound back to you. Be sure that you can *see* all three cement surfaces, so that the sound has a clear path back to your ears!

For further discussion of this effect and a related effect on a racketball court, see F. S. Crawford, "Cube Corner Retroreflectors for Sound Waves", *American Journal of Physics*, **59**, 176, 1991.

Piano Reflections

When the damper pedal is down, all of the strings are free to vibrate. When you shout into the piano, the sound of your voice will act as a driver for all the strings. Some of the strings will have natural frequencies that will match the frequencies in your voice. Others will not. Thus, by *resonance*, some of the strings will begin to vibrate and others won't. The result will be a sound coming back from the piano which is *an approximation of your voice*.

The Singing Quarter

Dry ice (solid carbon dioxide) is one of the few materials which *sublimes* at atmospheric pressure (see Mystery #4 in Chapter 15 of *PBWM*). As the relatively hot coin makes contact with the dry ice, some of the dry ice sublimes quickly. This create a high pressure area under the coin, which pushes the coin away. The motion of the coin away from the surface allows the gas to escape and the pressure of the gas in the region beneath the coin is reduced. As a result, the coin moves toward the surface again, causing more sublimation. The process then repeats. As a result, the coin vibrates back and forth, just above the surface of the dry ice. The sound that is heard is the result of this vibration. While this is occurring, energy from the coin conducts into the cold gas, and is carried away by convection when the gas leaves the area under the coin. Thus, the vibration is short-lived, as the temperature of the coin rapidly drops so that it can no longer cause the rapid sublimation necessary to sustain the process.

A related phenomenon is The Jumping Coin, in Chapter 9. This is a slower version of the effect, with the increase in pressure being due to increasing temperature in the air in the bottle and the release of pressure occurring when the coin jumps. Another similar phenomenon is the Leidenfrost Effect, discussed in Mystery #1 and Myth #10 in Chapter 9. In Myth #10, a drop of water in a hot skillet is supported by a layer of evaporated water, just as the coin in this demonstration is supported by the sublimed carbon dioxide.

𝔐𝔶𝔱𝔥:

1.) Dogs have the highest range of hearing.

It is a common joke in movies or television to see packs of dogs converging on the source of a high frequency sound. But there are a number of other animals whose ranges of hearing extend to higher frequencies. The upper end of a dog's range of hearing is 40-50 kHz, compared to that of a human of 20 kHz (at birth, with the upper end of the range falling as the human ages). Thus, the dog can certainly hear higher frequencies than the human, but another household pet, the *cat*, can hear even higher frequencies. Its range extends up to about 70 kHz. Both of these pale in comparison to the *bat*, which can hear frequencies as high as 100 kHz.

2.) In a table of decibels, a space shuttle launch is listed as 180 dB.

Since intensity decreases with distance from a sound source, a statement such as this has no meaning *unless the location of the receiver relative to the source is stated*. Is the 180 dB intensity level measured by someone standing right next to the space shuttle? Under it? 100 m away? Certainly the intensity level of a space shuttle being launched in Florida is not 180 dB according to someone at home in Texas!

Thus, this is not a complete definition of a particular intensity level. A better definition would include the distance between the source and receiver or would provide an example that would implicitly give this information. For example, "ordinary conversation" is often given as an example of an intensity level of about 60 dB. This is still not exact, but carries a stronger implication of the distance involved, since one imagines a conversation being carried on in a typical living room.

3.) The threshold of hearing is 0 dB.

In many tables of decibels, the 0 dB calibration is labeled as the threshold of hearing. Other levels are usually associated with common sounds in everyday life, such as rustling of leaves, whispers, normal conversations, jackhammers and rock bands. These higher level descriptions are relatively accurate, except for the notion of the distance from the source, as discussed in Myth #2. But the threshold of hearing is not a description of an external sound source, it is a description of a behavior of our hearing system. What most tables fail to point out is that the threshold of hearing is very dependent on the *frequency* of the sound, as discussed in Mystery #4 in Chapter 18 of *PBWM*. For pure tones of frequency about 2000 Hz, the threshold of hearing is relatively close to 0 dB. But the ear becomes less sensitive to frequencies above and below this range. This effect was studied in the early part of the twentieth century, using a large number of willing human subjects, and resulted in the *Fletcher-Munson curves* (after H. Fletcher and W. A. Munson, "Loudness, Definition, Measurement and Calculation", *Journal of the Acoustical Society of America*, **6**, 59, 1933) shown in the diagram below.

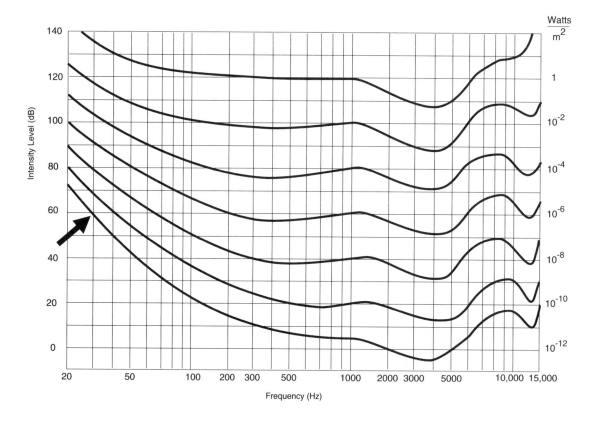

The vertical axis is intensity level in decibels (on the left) or intensity in watts per square meter (on the right). The horizontal axis is the frequency of the pure tone. All of these variables are *physical* descriptions of the sound. Along the dark lines, *the loudness of the sound was judged to be constant*, according to the experimental subjects. Loudness is a *psychological* variable. The lowest dark line on the graph represents the threshold of hearing.

It is clear from the curves that the loudness is highly frequency dependent. Notice, for example, that a 30 Hz tone has to have a physical intensity level of 60 dB just to be heard, as indicated by the dark arrow. Thus, the "threshold of hearing" at 30 Hz is 60 dB, not 0 dB!

Another intriguing feature of the curves is the dip that occurs at about 4000 Hz. This is due to a *resonance* in the auditory canal—the column of air between the pinna (the ear-lobe) and the eardrum. The length of this closed air column (i.e., closed at one end) is such that it has a natural frequency of about 4000 Hz, resulting in the extra sensitivity of the ear. As a closed air column, the auditory canal has another resonance at three times the fundamental, at about 12,000 Hz. The Fletcher-Munson curves show another dip in the curve near that frequency!

4.) Walking away from a sound source results in a decrease in intensity that varies as the inverse square of the distance from the source.

An inverse square dependence on distance is very familiar in physics: the behavior of the gravitational field around a spherical planet, the strength of the electric field around a point charge or a spherical charge distribution, the intensity of light from a spherical star, etc. Notice, however, in these examples, that the distribution of the mass, charge or source of radiation is stated—a point or a sphere. In the statement in the Myth, no such distribution for the sound source is stated, so that the statement is too general to be true.

It is indeed true that walking away from a *point* source of sound in the open air, such as a loudspeaker, will result in an inverse square dependence. But what if the source is a *line source*, such as a train, as suggested by the illustration, or a busy freeway? Then, we find a different dependence. In fact, the dependence of the intensity on distance for a line source is a *simple* inverse rather than an inverse square. This is the same dependence as that of an electric field near a line of charge, a fact that is useful in showing the unity of physical concepts. Planets tend to normally evolve as spheres, but we can *imagine* a very long line of mass; the gravitational field would then show the same simple inverse dependence with distance as the electric field and sound intensity examples.

5.) The spectrum of a sound from a musical instrument allows us to identify the instrument.

While there is some information about the instrument carried by the spectrum of its sound, this is not the whole story. In fact, the spectrum of the sound from a given instrument will be different for different notes. Thus, this can't be the entire story. There are other clues to the identification of the instrument. One of the most important clues is the *time behavior of the sound*. The time behavior can be divided into a number of steps, such as the *attack*, the *decay*, the *sustain*, and the *release*. A piano, for example, has a very sudden *attack*, as the key is struck. The sound immediately begins to *decay* away as energy is transferred away from the string vibration. Thus, there is no *sustain* in the piano sound. Once the damper pedal is released, there is a rapid decay in the *release* portion of the sound. Let us compare this to a clarinet. This instrument has a slower *attack* than the piano, since it takes a longer time for the standing sound wave to be established than a standing wave on the piano strings. There is little or no discernible *decay* after the attack. The clarinet will *sustain* a sound as long as the player continues to blow, since energy is being fed into the system continuously. Once the player stops blowing, there is a very quick *release* phase.

Another important clue to identification of instruments is the set of *noises* that various instruments make. These include the clicking of the piano action, the breathiness of the flute, the sound of fingers sliding on guitar strings, etc.

All of these clues *together*—the spectrum, the time behavior, and the noises—allow us to learn, over years of practice in a lifetime, to identify certain sounds as coming from certain instruments.

6.) A piano is tuned to the equal tempered scale.

The effect of stiffness in a vibrating string is to raise the harmonics of the string to frequencies higher than normal, as discussed in Mystery #4. It is impossible to remove stiffness altogether, and this effect is seen in the piano, which represents a large range of fundamental frequencies. Piano tuners match the frequencies of higher notes to those of harmonics of lower notes. The stiffness of these strings causes the harmonics to be raised, so that *the higher strings are tuned slightly sharper than they should be*. As this tuning continues up the piano keyboard, this "error" propagates until the highest notes may be as much as a third of a semitone too sharp, and the lowest notes similarly flat. This results in what is known as "stretched tuning". This may sound like it is a defect in piano tuning, which it is in a *physical* sense, but musical enjoyment is a *psychological* experience. If the piano is tuned electronically to exactly the tempered scale, audiences complain that high notes are too flat and low notes too sharp, since *we have become culturally accustomed to stretched tuning and now expect it for the proper piano sound*!

7.) The Doppler Effect is a shift in the wavelength of sound calculated from the relative velocity of the source and observer.

The problem with this statement lies in the claim that the *relative* velocity can be used to calculate the frequency shift. This is true for the Doppler Effect for light (see Mystery #3 in Chapter 22), but not for sound. The difference arises because sound requires a medium for its propagation and light does not. Thus, in the case of sound, individual velocities of the source and the observer can be identified, relative to the medium, which is the air. These individual velocities cannot be identified for light—only the relative velocity has meaning.

The equation for calculating the frequency shift in the Doppler Effect for sound is given below,

$$f_{observed} = \frac{v + v_{observer}}{v - v_{source}} f_{source}$$

where v is the speed of sound, $v_{observer}$ is the speed of the person listening to the sound, v_{source} is the speed of the source of the sound, f_{source} is the actual frequency emitted by the source, and $f_{observed}$ is the apparent frequency heard by the observer. This equation carries a sign convention for the direction of the velocity, such that speeds of the source or observer toward the other are positive, while speeds away from the other are substituted into the equation as negative numbers.

Let us perform two calculations to demonstrate the falsehood of the statement in the Myth. Suppose that the ambulance in the diagram accompanying the Myth were coming toward you at 25 m·s⁻¹ and emitting a sound of frequency 1000 Hz. You would hear an apparent frequency of,

$$f_{observed} = \frac{v + v_{observer}}{v - v_{source}} f_{source} = \frac{345\,\mathrm{m \cdot s^{-1}} + (0)}{345\,\mathrm{m \cdot s^{-1}} - \left(+25\,\mathrm{m \cdot s^{-1}}\right)}(1000\,\mathrm{Hz}) = 1078\,\mathrm{Hz}$$

Now, imagine that the ambulance stops moving but continues to emit the 1000 Hz tone. You start running toward the ambulance at 25 m·s⁻¹. Thus, the relative velocity between you and the ambulance is the same in this situation as it was in the previous situation. Is the apparent frequency the same? Let's calculate it:

$$f_{observed} = \frac{v + v_{observer}}{v - v_{source}} f_{source} = \frac{345\,\mathrm{m \cdot s^{-1}} + \left(+25\,\mathrm{m \cdot s^{-1}}\right)}{345\,\mathrm{m \cdot s^{-1}} - (0)}(1000\,\mathrm{Hz}) = 1072\,\mathrm{Hz}$$

Thus, the frequencies in the two cases are different, even though the relative velocities are the same. The difference arises from the origin of the frequency shift due to the different velocities involved in the effect. If the *source* of the sound moves, this causes a change in the *wavelength* of the sound. If the *observer* moves, this causes a change in the apparent *speed* of the sound. Let us consider a third situation, with the same relative velocity, but in which both objects are moving. Suppose the source and observer both move toward each other at 12.5 m·s⁻¹. Then, the apparent frequency is,

$$f_{observed} = \frac{v + v_{observer}}{v - v_{source}} f_{source} = \frac{345\,\mathrm{m \cdot s^{-1}} + \left(+12.5\,\mathrm{m \cdot s^{-1}}\right)}{345\,\mathrm{m \cdot s^{-1}} - \left(+12.5\,\mathrm{m \cdot s^{-1}}\right)}(1000\,\mathrm{Hz}) = 1075\,\mathrm{Hz}$$

which is yet another number.

We can provide another counterexample to the statement in the Myth which is unrelated to the above discussion. Suppose, for a given pair of velocities of the source and observer, that *the wind starts blowing*, with a component of its velocity parallel to the line connecting the source and the observer. This will alter the apparent speed of sound and, therefore, the apparent frequency. Thus, even though the relative velocity remains the same, the apparent frequency changes due to the wind!

Chapter 12
Electricity

𝕸ysteries:

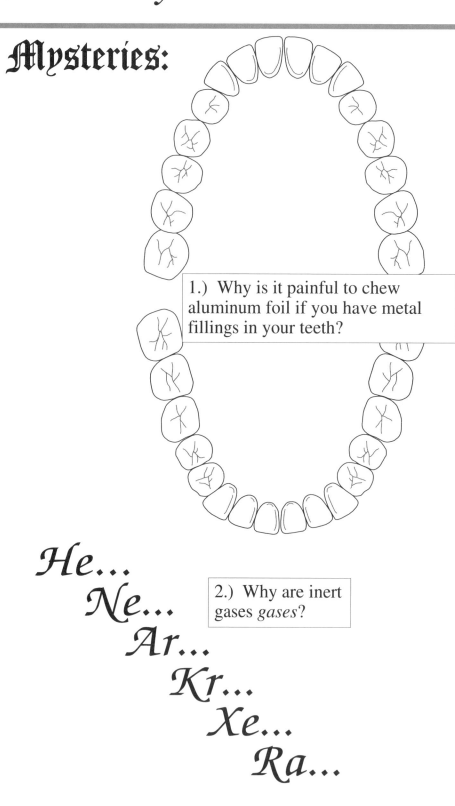

1.) Why is it painful to chew aluminum foil if you have metal fillings in your teeth?

He...
Ne...
Ar...
Kr...
Xe...
Ra...

2.) Why are inert gases *gases*?

Mysteries:

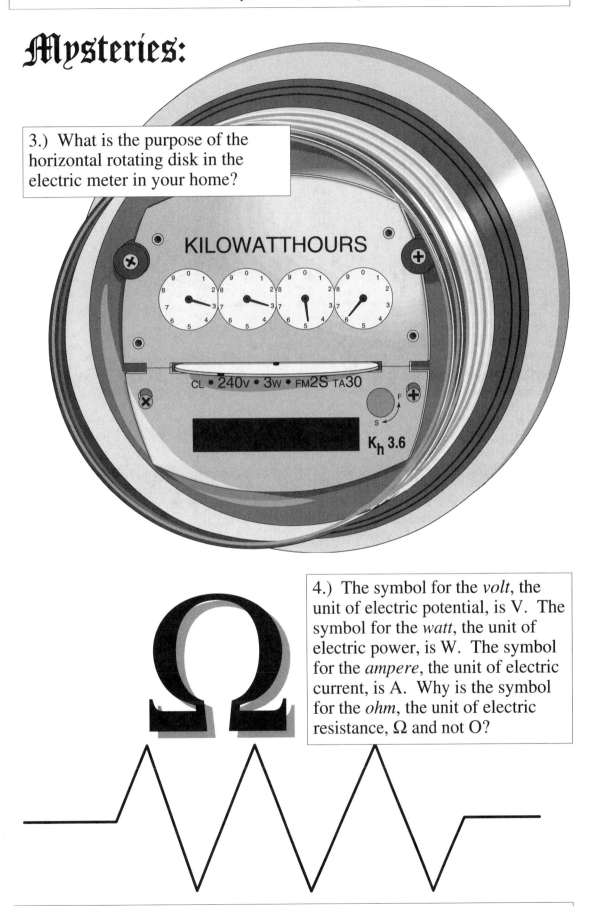

3.) What is the purpose of the horizontal rotating disk in the electric meter in your home?

KILOWATTHOURS

CL • 240v • 3w • FM2S TA30

K_h 3.6

4.) The symbol for the *volt*, the unit of electric potential, is V. The symbol for the *watt*, the unit of electric power, is W. The symbol for the *ampere*, the unit of electric current, is A. Why is the symbol for the *ohm*, the unit of electric resistance, Ω and not O?

Mysteries:

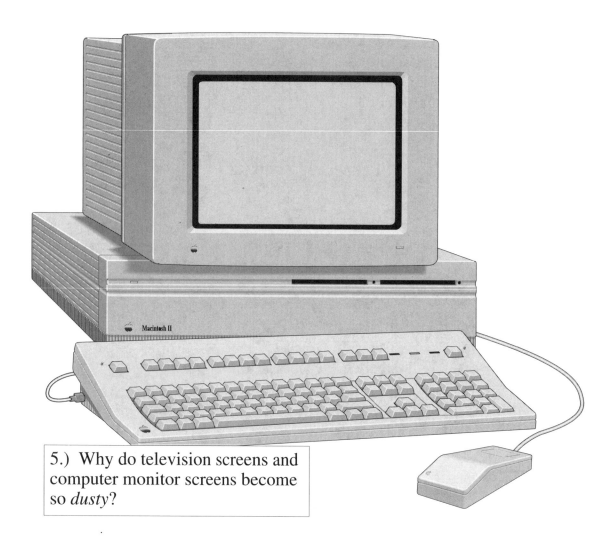

5.) Why do television screens and computer monitor screens become so *dusty*?

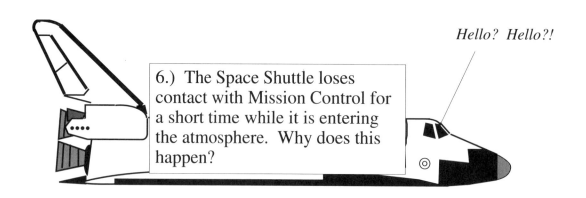

Hello? Hello?!

6.) The Space Shuttle loses contact with Mission Control for a short time while it is entering the atmosphere. Why does this happen?

Mysteries:

7.) In static electricity experiments, when objects are rubbed together, both objects that were rubbed together will attract small bits of paper or other material. Why is this?

8.) When watching television shows involving emergency rooms or paramedics, you may have noticed that, after using a defibrillator on a patient, the caregivers must *wait* before applying it again. *What are they waiting for*?

𝔐𝔶𝔰𝔱𝔢𝔯𝔦𝔢𝔰:

9.) Two wires, of identical lengths, but different diameters, are connected across a regulated power supply, so that each has the same potential difference between the ends. The wires are made of the same material and have a relatively low resistivity, so that they become warm as the current flows. *Which wire becomes hotter, the one with the larger or smaller diameter?*

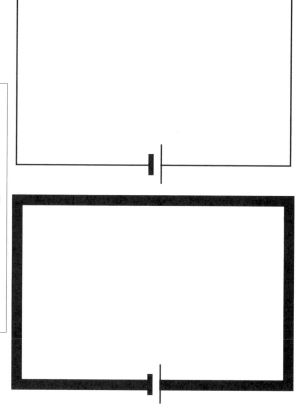

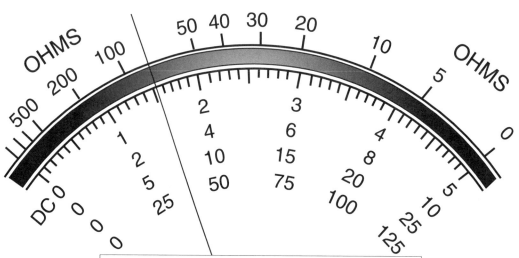

10.) Take a look at an analog multimeter. The voltage and current scales vary linearly across the face of the meter. But what about *the resistance scale*? The low values of resistance are spread out quite a bit on the scale, but the high values are all crunched together at one end. And the scale is *backward* compared to the current and voltage scales. Why is this?

𝔐𝔞𝔤𝔦𝔠:

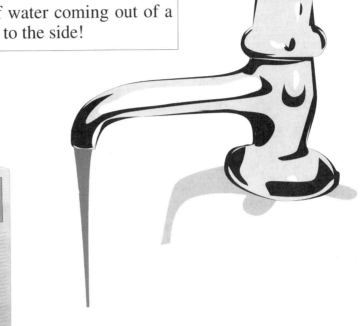

The Bent Water

On a dry day, comb your hair and hold the comb near a very thin stream of water coming out of a tap. The stream will bend to the side!

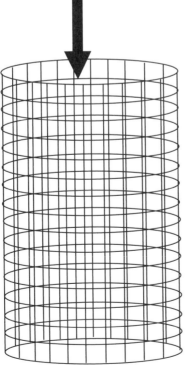

What a Fine Mesh You've Gotten Us Into This Time

Turn on a small portable radio so that it plays an AM station clearly. Now lower the radio into a coffee can or a cylinder made of wire mesh. What happens to the sound from the radio?

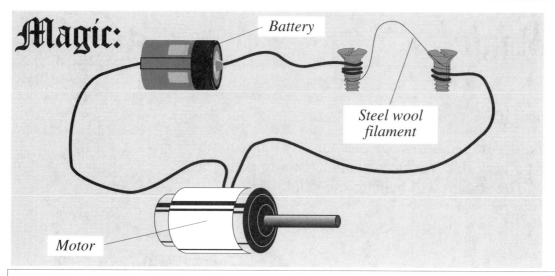

𝕸𝖆𝖌𝖎𝖈:

The Steel Wool Fuse I

Set up a simple circuit on a wooden board with a battery holder and a motor, but leave a gap in the circuit by wrapping the wire around two screws, as shown in the diagram. Strip off a filament of steel wool and complete the circuit by spanning the gap with the steel wool filament. Place the battery in the holder so that the motor begins to turn. Now grab the motor armature and stop its rotation. What happens to the steel wool filament?

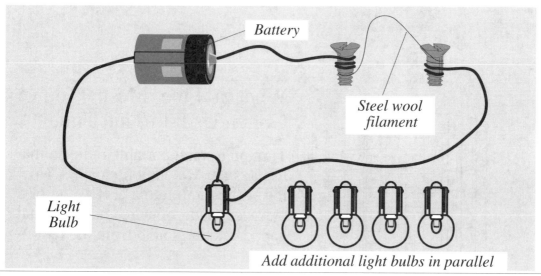

Add additional light bulbs in parallel

The Steel Wool Fuse II

Set up a simple circuit on a wooden board with a battery holder and a flashlight bulb, but leave a gap in the circuit by wrapping the wire around two screws, as shown in the diagram. Complete the circuit by spanning the gap with one filament of the steel wool. Place the battery in the holder so that the light bulb glows. Now add additional light bulbs *in parallel with the first*. What happens to the steel wool?

Myth:

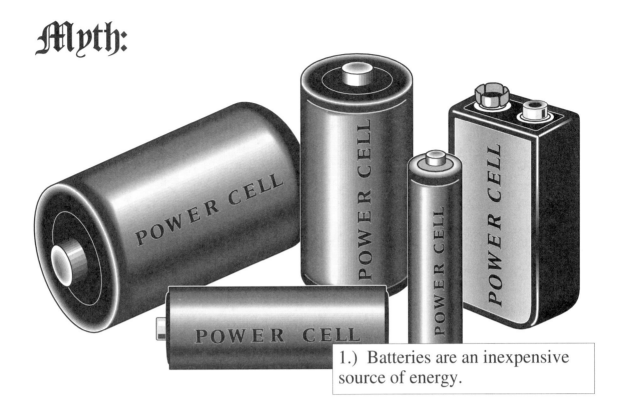

1.) Batteries are an inexpensive source of energy.

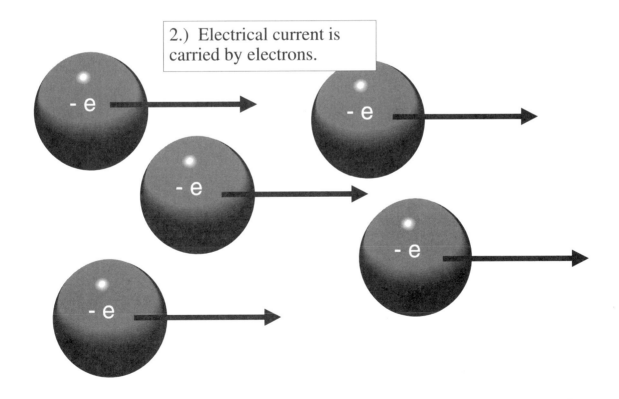

2.) Electrical current is carried by electrons.

Myth:

$$\sum_{j=1}^{N} I_j = 0$$

$$\sum_{j=1}^{N} \Delta V_j = 0$$

3.) Kirchhoff's rules are fundamental principles.

4.) Current takes the path of least resistance.

PATH OF
LEAST
RESISTANCE

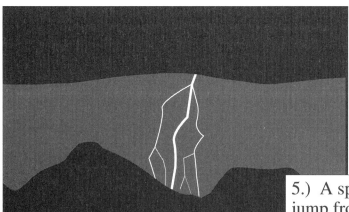

5.) A spark occurs when electrons jump from one object to another.

𝔐𝔶𝔱𝔥:

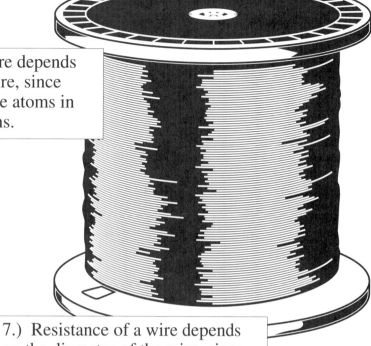

6.) Resistance of a wire depends on the length of the wire, since longer wires have more atoms in the way of the electrons.

7.) Resistance of a wire depends on the diameter of the wire, since thicker wires have more space in which the electrons can move.

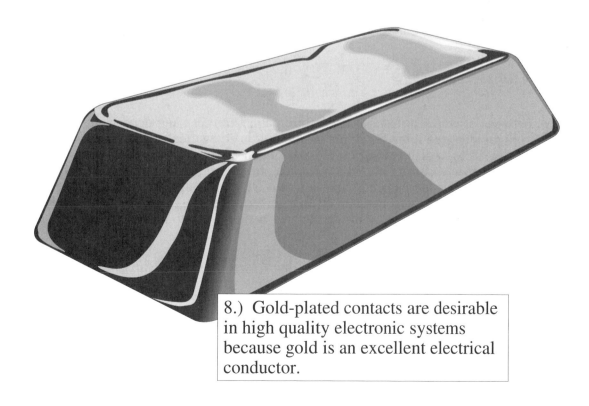

8.) Gold-plated contacts are desirable in high quality electronic systems because gold is an excellent electrical conductor.

Discussions; Chapter 12—Electricity

𝔐𝔶𝔰𝔱𝔢𝔯𝔦𝔢𝔰:

1.) Why is it painful to chew aluminum foil if you have metal fillings in your teeth?

This is an example of the difference in *Fermi levels* in the two metals—the aluminum foil and the metal in your fillings. A metal is a crystal lattice structure of positive ions with the electrons from these ions moving freely through the bulk of the metal. These free electrons give the metal its ability to conduct electricity. Let us imagine that we "build a metal" by gathering together a bunch of positive ions in a crystal lattice structure and then start adding electrons, up to the point where the metal becomes electrically neutral. We can imagine that the crystal lattice structure forms a box, into which we place the electrons (see Myth #1 in Chapter 18 for a discussion of the quantum particle in a box). As we add the electrons, one by one, to the box, they must go into higher and higher energy states, according to the Pauli Exclusion Principle (see Myth #2 in Chapter 18 for a discussion of this principle). By the time we add the last electron, energy states will be filled up to a level that we call the *Fermi level* or the *Fermi energy*. Let us assume that the temperature is absolute zero, so that we don't need to worry about thermal complications. If the temperature is other than zero, some electrons near the Fermi energy will be excited to levels higher than the Fermi energy, but the effect can be ignored for our purposes.

The Fermi energy varies from one metal to another. In particular, the Fermi energies in aluminum and the amalgam used to make fillings (usually consisting of silver, tin and mercury), are different. Thus, when the metals are placed in contact, as when aluminum foil is chewed, electrons can flow from the metal with the higher Fermi energy into the available energy states of the metal with the lower Fermi energy. This constitutes an *electric current*. It is this current in the teeth that provides the discomfort.

2.) Why are inert gases *gases*?

Forces between atoms of a material are electromagnetic forces and depend on electrical charges. In an idealized ionic bond, for example, it is energetically favorable (see Myth #7 in Chapter 18 for a discussion of this concept) for an electron transfer to occur from one atom to another, resulting in two ions which attract electrically. In a covalent bond, one or more electrons are "shared" between two atoms, resulting in a higher negative charge density between the atoms than elsewhere and an effective positive charge density in the vicinities of the atoms. This results in a bonding due to the electrical attraction between the negative and positive charge densities.

These types of bonding mechanisms are available for those atoms for which it is energetically favorable to transfer or share an electron. In general, these are atoms that have electrons in partially filled atomic shells outside of a closed shell or atoms with shells that are one or two electrons short of being filled. It requires energy to remove an electron that is bound to an atom (the *ionization energy*), but, if the electron is transferred to another atom, the energy released by the second atom in accepting the electron may be enough to supply the ionization energy (and possibly more). Thus, the overall energy of the atomic system is reduced by the transfer (the energy difference is transferred out of the system of the atoms by electromagnetic radiation—a photon). A covalent bond requires a bit more quantum physics to appreciate, but the fundamental idea is the same—the energy of the atomic system is reduced by the formation of the bond.

Now, what about the inert gases? These atoms have *closed atomic shells*. The electrons in these closed shells are very tightly bound (see Mystery #10, Chapter 19), so that a relatively large amount of energy is necessary to remove them. What's more, if an electron were transferred to another inert gas atom, it would be only weakly bound, since it would be added outside of a closed shell. As a result, it is not energetically favorable for this transfer to occur—*the transfer would require an input of energy*. Thus, electrostatic attractions between inert gas atoms generally do not occur. As with almost any statement, there are exceptions. For example, there are stable states of the He$_2$ molecule and a small number of other examples, such as XeF$_6$. There are extremely few such possibilities, however, compared to the possible molecules to be formed from other types of atoms.

We do have the possibility with the inert gases for a *dipole interaction*. As the positive and negative charges within the atoms fluctuate, there are instantaneous dipole moments formed. For neighboring atoms, the instantaneous dipole moment of one atom can induce a similar dipole moment in the other atom. Then, there is an attraction between the dipoles. This is called a *Van der Waals force*. It is very weak, since it depends on a dipole attraction, which is inherently weaker than straight electrical attraction (the net charge on the dipole is zero!) and the dipole moment is fluctuating continuously. Since the bonding is very weak between inert gas atoms, at room temperature, *they are gases*! At room temperature, the internal energy in the material is enough to prevent the weak bonds between atoms from forming. The temperature has to be lowered significantly before the weak Van der Waals force is strong enough to prevent the internal energy from tearing the atoms apart, so that a liquid can exist. This is demonstrated by the boiling points of the inert gases in the table below.

Element	Boiling Point (°C)	Melting Point (°C)
Helium	–269	-
Neon	–246	–249
Argon	–186	–189
Krypton	–152	–157
Xenon	–107	–112
Radon	–62	–71

Notice that the boiling point increases as we go deeper into the periodic table. This is a reflection of the fact that there are more charges involved in the higher atomic number atoms, resulting in a larger dipole moment and stronger Van der Waals forces.

The melting points of the inert gases show the same general trend as the boiling points. It is to be noted that there is no entry for the melting point of helium. See Mystery #2 in Chapter 18 for more discussion of this.

3.) What is the purpose of the horizontal rotating disk in the electric meter in your home?

There are two types of measuring devices for energy transfer (by electrical transmission) in your electric meter. The dials (usually four or five; the diagram accompanying the Mystery shows a meter with four dials) indicate the total energy transfer accumulated over a period of time since the dials all read zero. Thus, the dials are similar to the *odometer* in an automobile, since it indicates the number of miles that have accumulated since the car left the factory (or, for a very old car, since the *last* time the odometer read zero).

The horizontal disk is a measuring device which indicates the *rate* at which energy is being transferred into your home at the moment that you are looking at the meter. Thus, the horizontal disk is analogous to the *speedometer* in your automobile, which indicates an instantaneous rate at which you are accumulating miles. The horizontal disk is not quite so easy to read as your speedometer, however. Somewhere on your meter will appear a "Kh rating", with typical values being Kh 2, Kh 3.6 and Kh 7.2. These numbers correspond to the amount of energy, in watt-hours, transferred into your home *during one rotation of the disk*. Thus, if your Kh rating is 3.6 and the disk rotates once, the energy transferred into your home is 3.6 watt-hours or 0.0036 kWh. The instantaneous energy transfer rate is found by timing one rotation of the disk and dividing the Kh rating by the time. Thus, if one rotation of the disk on a Kh 3.6 meter takes 30 seconds, then the energy transfer rate (power) is,

$$P = \frac{0.0036\,\text{kWh}}{30\,\text{s}} = 0.00012\,\text{kWh}\cdot\text{s}^{-1} = 0.432\,\text{kWh}\cdot\text{h}^{-1} = 432\,\text{watts}$$

It is instructive to observe the rate of rotation of the horizontal disk both before and after activating a device with a large power input (toaster, electric oven, air conditioner, etc.), so as to appreciate its role as a detector for the rate of energy transfer. If the power calculation above is performed before and after turning on a device, an estimate of the power of the device can be made (assuming that no other automatically controlled devices turned on in the meantime). If the device has specifications listed on it, the calculated power rating can be compared with the listed power rating.

4.) The symbol for the *volt*, the unit of electric potential, is V. The symbol for the *watt*, the unit of electric power, is W. The symbol for the *ampere*, the unit of electric current, is A. Why is the symbol for the *ohm*, the unit of electric resistance, Ω and not O?

If the symbol used for resistance were O rather than Ω, there may be some confusion between the symbol for the unit and any zeroes on the end of the number. For example, does $R = 500$ represent fifty ohms, or five hundred, with the units omitted? In order to avoid this confusion, the Greek letter Ω (*ohm*-ega!) is used so that 50 Ω is unmistakably fifty ohms.

5.) Why do television screens and computer monitor screens become so *dusty*?

In a television picture tube, electrons are accelerated toward the front of the tube. As a result, the screen tends to become negatively charged. Dust coming near the screen becomes polarized by the electric field established in the region in front of the screen (see Mystery #7). This region is one of *non-uniform* electric field and, as a result, the dust is attracted to the screen. This attraction can be understood by realizing that the field is strongest near the screen. The positive end of the polarized piece of dust is closer to the screen than the negative end. Thus, the positive end feels a stronger attractive force than the repulsive force felt by the negative end. As a result, there is an overall attraction of the dust to the screen.

The effect of the charged screen can sometimes be felt by placing a hand or an arm near the screen and noticing that the hairs on your skin stand up. This charge will remain for a short time after the television is turned off and can be used as a test to determine if the television were turned off by children, who were supposed to be in bed, at the sound of the parents' key in the door.

6.) The Space Shuttle loses contact with Mission Control for a short time while it is entering the atmosphere. Why does this happen?

While the Space Shuttle is being braked by the atmosphere, the temperature of the air around the Shuttle is very high. This is due to the large amount of work that the air is doing to slow down the spacecraft. This high temperature causes the air molecules to ionize, forming a region of charged particles around the Shuttle. When radio waves from Mission Control encounter this region of charged particles, the waves are reflected, just like light and other electromagnetic waves are reflected from the free charges in a metal surface.

7.) In static electricity experiments, when objects are rubbed together, both objects that were rubbed together will attract small bits of paper or other material. Why is this?

When two objects, such as an amber rod and a piece of fur, are rubbed together, each of the objects becomes charged. When either object is brought close to a second, uncharged object, such as a bit of paper, the second object becomes polarized. Let us assume that we have brought a *positively* charged object, object 1, close to the second object, object 2, as shown below. If object 2 is a conductor, so that it contains free electrons that can move through the material, then these electrons will move toward the side of the object near object 1, leaving the other side of object 2 positively charged.

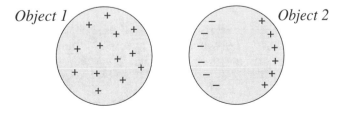

The electric field due to object 1 is non-uniform. It is strongest close to object 1. Thus, the negative charges in object 2 feel a stronger attractive force toward object 1 than the repulsive force on the positive charges. The result is an overall attractive force, similar to the attraction between the dust and the television screen in Mystery #5.

If object 2 is not a conductor, molecules in the object will become polarized due to the electric field from object 1, with a negative charge density arising on the surface of object 2 near object 1, as shown below.

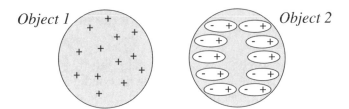

In the body of object 2, the negative charge in a given dipole is closer to object 1 than the accompanying positive charge. Thus, each negative charge is in a stronger electric field and feels a stronger force. As a result, we again have an overall attractive situation.

Now, imagine that we bring the other rubbed object, which is negatively charged, near object 2. The discussion above describes what happens in this case, also, except that the signs of the charges are all reversed—in the case of a conductor, electrons move *away* from the negatively charged object, as shown below.

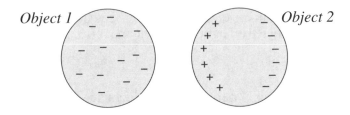

In the case of an insulator, a *positive* charge density arises on the side near the charged object, due to polarization:

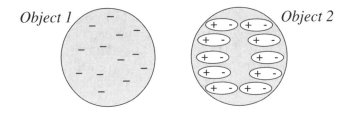

We again have an *attraction* between the negatively charged object and object 2, regardless of the electrical characteristics of object 2.

For a discussion of using metallic balloons as large "pith balls" for electrostatics experiments, see D. T. Kagan, "The Ultimate 'Pith Balls'", *The Physics Teacher*, **29**, 197, 1991.

8.) When watching television shows involving emergency rooms or paramedics, you may have noticed that, after using a defibrillator on a patient, the caregivers must *wait* before applying it again. *What are they waiting for?*

The intent of a defibrillator is to send a current through a patient's chest, in hopes of stimulating the heart to begin pumping again. The high current necessary to do this requires a relatively high potential difference, higher than a simple portable battery can provide. Thus, a battery is used with an oscillator and transformer circuit to store energy in a *capacitor*, similar to the operation of an electronic flash unit, as discussed in Mystery #12 of Chapter 18 in *PBWM*. The charging of the capacitor takes a relatively long amount of time, as a large amount of energy must be transferred from the battery to the capacitor. This is what the paramedics are waiting for—the complete charging of the capacitor. It is similar to the wait for the capacitor to charge in an electronic flash unit, although the wait for the flash is shorter, since the required energy is lower.

Another similar, but non-electrical, example is the common household *toilet*. Water must be stored in the tank to be released during a flush. It takes some time for the water to fill the large tank from the relatively narrow supply line. This is analogous to the wait for the flash unit or the defibrillator. Once a flush has occurred, a subsequent flush cannot happen until after the prescribed waiting time for the tank to fill.

9.) Two wires, of identical lengths, but different diameters, are connected across a regulated power supply, so that each has the same potential difference between the ends. The wires are made of the same material and have a relatively low resistivity, so that they become warm as the current flows. *Which wire becomes hotter, the one with the larger or smaller diameter?*

The analysis of this question will require a number of steps. Let us first compare the *resistances* of the two wires, where we use the relationship between resistance, R, resistivity, ρ, length, l, and cross sectional area A. We will compare the resistances by means of a ratio:

$$\frac{R_l}{R_s} = \frac{\left(\dfrac{\rho l}{A_l}\right)}{\left(\dfrac{\rho l}{A_s}\right)} = \frac{A_s}{A_l} = \frac{\pi r_s^2}{\pi r_l^2} = \left(\frac{r_s}{r_l}\right)^2$$

We have used the subscript "*l*" for the *large* (diameter) wire and "*s*" for the *small* wire. Thus, the thinner wire has the larger resistance.

Now, let's calculate the ratio of *power* dissipated in each wire, which will represent the rate at which energy is delivered to the wires by electrical transmission and is stored as internal energy in the wires:

$$\frac{P_l}{P_s} = \frac{I_l \Delta V}{I_s \Delta V} = \frac{\left(\dfrac{\Delta V}{R_l}\right)\Delta V}{\left(\dfrac{\Delta V}{R_s}\right)\Delta V} = \frac{R_s}{R_l} = \left(\frac{r_l}{r_s}\right)^2$$

where we have incorporated the result for the ratio of resistances from before. Thus, the larger wire has more energy delivered to it per unit time. Does that mean that it becomes hotter? Not necessarily. The larger wire has more energy delivered per unit time, but it also has more mass to absorb that energy.

Our next step, then, is to relate the mass of each wire to the energy necessary to raise its temperature. We do that by using a modification of the commonly seen $Q = mc\Delta T$ (see Myth #1 in Chapter 9), rewriting it, from the energy continuity equation, as $E_{ET} = mc\Delta T$, since the transfer mechanism is electrical transmission. Thus, we set up a ratio of temperature changes in the wire material:

$$\frac{\Delta T_l}{\Delta T_s} = \frac{\left(\dfrac{(E_{ET})_l}{m_l c}\right)}{\left(\dfrac{(E_{ET})_s}{m_s c}\right)} = \frac{(E_{ET})_l}{(E_{ET})_s}\frac{m_s}{m_l}$$

If we multiply top and bottom of this ratio by the time interval Δt during which the energy transfer takes place, then we can express the ratio in terms of the power delivered to each wire:

$$\frac{\Delta T_l}{\Delta T_s} = \frac{(E_{ET})_l}{(E_{ET})_s}\frac{m_s}{m_l}\frac{\Delta t}{\Delta t} = \frac{P_l}{P_s}\frac{m_s}{m_l}$$

Now, we have already calculated the ratio of powers, so we substitute, and also express the mass in terms of density and volume:

$$\frac{\Delta T_l}{\Delta T_s} = \frac{P_l}{P_s}\frac{m_s}{m_l} = \left(\frac{r_l}{r_s}\right)^2 \left(\frac{D\pi r_s^2 l}{D\pi r_l^2 l}\right) = 1$$

where we have used the symbol D for density (instead of the commonly used ρ), to differentiate it from the *resistivity* which was used earlier. Thus, the temperature change ratio comes out to be *one*, suggesting that both wires reach the same temperature! But the story does not end here. The temperature change would be the same if the energy delivered to each wire *stayed in the wire*. But wires are generally in contact with air. As a result, energy can *conduct* from the surface of the wire to the air. The larger wire has more surface area through which energy can conduct, but the important factor is the *surface to volume ratio*. As the radius of a wire increases, its surface area increases by *r*, but its volume increases by r^2 (see the Magic demonstration Burning Metal in Chapter 9 for another example of this effect). Thus, even though the larger wire has more surface area, it has a proportionally larger volume to be cooled than the smaller wire. Thus, the smaller wire is more effective at cooling itself by conduction of energy into the air, and *the larger wire will become hotter*.

What if this activity were performed in the vacuum of empty space, so that the possibility of conduction of energy into the air were removed? We still have the possibility of *radiation* from the wire. The power of radiation emitted is governed by the Stefan-Boltzmann Law, described in the Concepts section of Chapter 17. The important consideration in this application is that the power radiated away depends on the surface area. Thus, we have the same consideration of surface to volume ratio that we have for conduction. The larger wire has more area to radiate, but has even more volume to cool than the smaller wire. Thus, once again, the larger wire will become hotter.

For a discussion of the surface to volume effect in the context of thermal equilibrium in the body of an elephant, see A. A. Bartlett, "How to Cool an Elephant", *The Physics Teacher*, **29**, 196, 1991.

10.) Take a look at an analog multimeter. The voltage and current scales vary linearly across the face of the meter. But what about *the resistance scale*? The low values of resistance are spread out quite a bit on the scale, but the high values are all crunched together at one end. And the scale is *backward* compared to the current and voltage scales. Why is this?

The quantity that an analog meter measures is *current*. Inside the meter is a *galvanometer*, which consists of a small coil of wire between the poles of a magnet. When a current passes through the coil, a magnetic torque causes the coil to rotate. As it rotates, it stretches a spring. Thus, the coil reaches an equilibrium position, at which the torque of the spring and the magnetic torque are equal and opposite. If more current passes through the coil, the magnetic torque increases and the coil rotates to a new equilibrium position. If the current decreases, the larger spring torque pulls the coil back until another equilibrium position is established. By attaching a needle to the coil and adding a calibrated background against which the needle is viewed, the galvanometer can be calibrated to measure current.

If the meter is to be used as an ammeter, it is placed in the circuit to be measured and the galvanometer (along with some shunt resistances to change the scale) simply measures the current. As a voltmeter, the galvanometer (with a different combination of series resistances) is placed in parallel with the component whose voltage difference is to be measured. The voltmeter "borrows" a small amount of current from the circuit, which is measured by the galvanometer. In concert with the series resistances, the scale can be calibrated in volts, so that, even though the meter is measuring current, it can be used to measure potential difference.

Since the magnetic torque is proportional to the current, the rotation of the coil is linear in current. Thus, the current scale on the meter is linear. Now, potential difference is proportional to current ($\Delta V = IR$). Thus, if the meter is used as a voltmeter, the voltage scale is also linear. The voltmeter and ammeter both measure *dynamic* parameters in the circuit—the circuit must be operating in order for values of the current and voltage difference to exist. But what about the ohmmeter? This measures a *static* parameter—a resistor has a resistance regardless of whether there is a current flowing through it or not. A similar situation exists for the familiar form of Newton's Second Law, **F**= *m***a**. The variables **F** and **a** are dynamic—they may change with the motion. The parameter *m*, the mass of the object, is static—there is a mass whether or not the object is moving, and the mass remains constant. Since we wish to measure a static parameter, the ohmmeter must have its own power source—a battery of known emf $\mathscr{E}$. This battery causes a current to flow through a resistance R placed between the leads of the ohmmeter, and the galvanometer measures the current. This current is given by,

$$I = \frac{\mathscr{E}}{R + R_{int}}$$

where R_{int} is the internal resistance of the ohmmeter itself. Now, notice that the largest current will result when $R = 0$. As R increases, the current will decrease. *This is the reason that the resistance scale is backward*—remember that the galvanometer is really measuring current; it is simply *calibrated* in ohms. Notice also that the current varies *inversely* with resistance R. *This is why the scale is non-linear.*

𝔐𝔞𝔤𝔦𝔠:

The Bent Water

This demonstration shows the attraction between a charged object (the comb) and an uncharged object (the water stream), as discussed in Mystery #7. In this case, the attraction is strong enough to deflect the stream of water from its normally straight down path in the gravitational field of the Earth.

What a Fine Mesh You've Gotten Us Into This Time

You will find that the sound from the radio *disappears* when it is lowered into the wire mesh or can. This is a demonstration of the electromagnetic *shielding* effects of metals. We are familiar with the effect of shining the electromagnetic radiation that we call visible light on a metal surface—it reflects. We find the same effect when allowing radio waves, which are also electromagnetic in nature, to strike the metal surface of the can or mesh. In addition to the reflection, there is some refraction into the metal, but the refracted waves only proceed for a *very* small distance, with rapid attenuation.

The mesh used in this demonstration has holes which are smaller than the radio wavelengths, so that the mesh appears to be a solid piece of metal, as discussed in Mystery #1 in Chapter 16. Screening of this sort is often used to shield instruments or even entire rooms from electromagnetic radiation.

The Steel Wool Fuse I

It is very likely that the steel wool will burn with bright sparks. When the motor shaft turns normally, the current which flows through the motor is that due to the potential difference applied across the resistance of the motor minus that from the back emf induced by the coils of wire turning in the magnetic field. A discussion of back emf is available in Mystery #7 in Chapter 23 of *PBWM*. The result is that the net flow of current is relatively small.

When the motor armature is grasped, the back emf no longer exists and the current depends only on the applied potential difference and the resistances of the motor and steel wool. As a result, the current will *increase*, enough so that the steel wool filament will become very hot and burn.

The Steel Wool Fuse II

As additional light bulbs are added in parallel with the first, more and more current is drawn from the battery. This can be understood either from the point of view that more paths are being made available for the current, or from the fact that the total resistance of the circuit is decreasing. Eventually, the current will be high enough to raise the temperature of the steel wool filament high enough for it to burn.

𝔐𝔶𝔱𝔥:

1.) Batteries are an inexpensive source of energy.

In order to assess this statement, let us establish a standard against which costs can be compared. We will use the cost of household electricity as our standard. The cost of "electrical energy" varies from place to place, but let's choose a typical value of 10¢ per kilowatt-hour. A kilowatt hour is easily shown to be equal to 3.6×10^6 Joules. Thus, household electrical energy has a per unit cost of,

$$\frac{\$0.10}{3.6 \times 10^6 \text{J}} = 2.8 \times 10^{-8} \, \$ \cdot \text{J}^{-1}$$

Let's compare this to the cost of energy from a battery. A flashlight D cell provides a potential difference of 1.5 volts and will typically supply 375 mA of current for about six and a half hours. Thus, the total energy output is,

$$\Delta E = P\Delta t = (I\Delta V)(\Delta t) = (375 \times 10^{-3} \text{A})(1.5 \text{V})(6.5 \text{h})(3600 \, \text{s} \cdot \text{h}^{-1}) = 1.3 \times 10^4 \text{J}$$

If we approximate the cost of a D cell as $1.00, then our cost per energy unit is,

$$\frac{\$1.00}{1.3 \times 10^4 \text{J}} = 7.7 \times 10^{-5} \, \$ \cdot \text{J}^{-1}$$

This cost is *more than 2700 times the cost of household electricity*, or, $270 per kilo-watt-hour, if we consider our typical value of household electricity! A D cell is clearly an expensive source of energy!

The situation becomes even worse for smaller batteries, such as mercury, silver or lithium batteries for watches and cameras. For example, the total energy output of a watch battery costs *five to six orders of magnitude* more per energy unit than household electricity. This would give a cost of $10,000 to $100,000 per kilowatt-hour! Despite these exorbitant costs, the small amount of energy needed and the convenience of these types of energy sources outweigh the financial considerations.

2.) Electrical current is carried by electrons.

While this is a common situation in metal wires, there are other situations in which electrical current can be carried by other agents. For example, in a semiconductor, electrical current is carried both by electrons and *holes*, which are electron vacancies. The holes act just like positive charge carriers. In an electrolytic solution, electrical current is carried both by negative and positive ions, as in the Magic demonstration, The Magic of Salt, in Chapter 21 of *PBWM*. In this demonstration, salt dissociates into sodium and chlorine ions, each of which act as current carriers in the solution.

3.) Kirchhoff's rules are fundamental principles.

While Kirchhoff's rules are important and useful for analyzing complicated circuits, they are applications of more fundamental principles to the situation of current flowing in an electrical circuit. The first rule is that of current flowing into a junction point:

$$\sum_{j=1}^{N} I_j = 0$$

where N is the number of wires entering the junction and I_j is the current flowing into (or out of) the junction in the jth wire. Using the definition of current as the time rate of flow of electric charge, we can rewrite this equation as follows:

$$\sum_{j=1}^{N} \frac{\Delta q_j}{\Delta t} = 0 \quad \rightarrow \quad \sum_{j=1}^{N} \Delta q_j = 0$$

The second equation is obtained by multiplying the first by the common factor of the time interval, Δt, during which the charges move. The final equation states that the sum of all of the charge transfers at the junction is zero (Δq is positive for charge entering the junction, negative for charge leaving). This is a special case of the *continuity equation* for charge (see page 77 in *PBWM*), in which charge cannot be stored in the system in any way. As such, Kirchhoff's first rule is equivalent to the fundamental principle of *conservation of charge*.

The second of Kirchhoff's rules relates to the potential differences across circuit elements as one traverses a closed loop in the circuit:

$$\sum_{j=1}^{N} \Delta V_j = 0$$

where ΔV_j is positive for "sources" of potential difference, such as batteries, and negative for potential difference "drops" across resistive elements (unless the direction of travel around the loop is reversed, in which case the signs are reversed also). Now, the potential difference across a circuit component is related to the difference in electrical potential energy across the component as follows:

$$\Delta PE_E = q \, \Delta V$$

Thus, if we imagine a charge q moving completely around the loop, we can rewrite Kirchhoff's second rule as:

$$\sum_{j=1}^{N} \frac{\Delta PE_{Ej}}{q} = 0 \quad \rightarrow \quad \sum_{j=1}^{N} \Delta PE_{Ej} = 0$$

where the second equation is obtained by multiplying the first by the common factor of the charge, q, which moves around the loop. Thus, Kirchhoff's second rule simply states that the sum of the potential energy changes is zero for traveling around a closed loop. This is a special case of the *continuity equation* for energy (which we have discussed in Chapter 5 of this book as well as Chapter 7 of *PBWM*), in which energy can not be stored in the system in any way. As such, Kirchhoff's second rule is equivalent to the fundamental principle of *conservation of energy*.

4.) Current takes the path of least resistance.

In a circuit containing many possible paths for current to take, it does not choose the path of least resistance, it flows through *all available paths*. The amount of current flowing in each path depends on the relationship between the resistance in the path and the overall equivalent resistance of the circuit.

5.) A spark occurs when electrons jump from one object to another.

A spark is initiated by the ionization of air molecules in the presence of an electric field. The ionization is not necessarily caused by the electric field. Ionization can occur due to random collisions between molecules. Once a molecule is ionized, however, an electric field will accelerate the ion and the electron, causing them to collide energetically enough with other molecules to ionize them, resulting in a cascade of ionizations and a significant current carried by both electrons and ions. This current can neutralize the charged objects, thus removing the electric field. This process all occurs in a very short time and is seen as a *spark*.

Notice that electrons do not necessarily transfer from one charged object to the other. The electrons carrying the current may only travel a short distance through the air before the charge is neutralized and the current stops flowing. The important entity bridging the gap between the two objects is the *electric field*. The ionization is most likely to begin where the field is strongest, since the randomly created electrons and ions will have sufficient energy in these regions to ionize other molecules.

6.) Resistance of a wire depends on the length of the wire, since longer wires have more atoms in the way of the electrons.

The resistance of a wire to the flow of electrons, if we consider the electrons as particles (ignoring their wave behavior, as discussed in Chapters 17 and 18), stems from collisions that the electrons experience with the crystal lattice ions in the wire. The Myth suggests the erroneous understanding that the electrons flowing in a wire move along its entire length. With this erroneous approach, since there are more ions in the way, there are more collisions and more resistance. In reality, the drift velocity of electrons in wires is extremely small, on the order of 10^{-5} m·s^{-1} in a typical household wire carrying 100 mA of current. Thus, electrons near one end of the wire will have no way of detecting the addition of atoms due to lengthening the wire at the other end.

The increase in resistance for a longer wire is due to the fact that the potential difference between the ends of the wire is extended over a larger distance. This causes a *weaker electric field* in the wire, resulting in a slower drift velocity for the electrons. As a result, the same potential difference applied to two wires of unequal lengths results in different currents, which is described by saying that the wires have different resistances.

The idea discussed in the first paragraph, that of electrons traveling the entire length of the wire, leads some students to misconceptions about circuits. For example, why does a light turn on *right away* if it takes several minutes for the electrons to move from the switch to the light bulb? How can we talk on telephones across the country if it would take *weeks* for the electrons to move that distance? The important consideration, of course, is that the changes in electric field move *at the speed of light*. Thus, if we talk into a telephone receiver at one end of the country, the resulting change in electric field is almost instantaneous in the receiver at the other end, and that change in electric field will apply forces to electrons *that are already present* in the receiving equipment.

7.) Resistance of a wire depends on the diameter of the wire, since thicker wires have more space in which the electrons can move.

While there may be more cross-sectional area in a thicker wire, there are proportionally more electrons to move through this larger area. Thus, each electron experiences the same ion density for collisions as any other electron, regardless of the size of the wire.

The decrease in resistance stems from the simple fact that there are *more electrons to carry the current*. The current in the wire depends on the drift speed of electrons, which is independent of the diameter, and the number of electrons, which is highly dependent on the diameter. Thus, as the diameter increases, more electrons contribute to the current, the current for a given potential difference is larger, and the resistance is smaller.

8.) Gold-plated contacts are desirable in high quality electronic systems because gold is an excellent electrical conductor.

Let's see how good a conductor gold is. If we consult a table of resistivities, we find the following:

Gold: $\rho = 2.24 \times 10^{-8} \ \Omega\cdot m$

Copper: $\rho = 1.68 \times 10^{-8} \ \Omega\cdot m$

Thus, gold is *more resistive* than copper, which is the metal used in most "ordinary" wiring. So why would we want to use gold contacts?

The reason that gold is used for contacts in high quality electronic systems is that it does not participate in chemical reactions with the air with which it is in contact. Thus, it will not develop a surface coating of an oxide compound which would increase the resistance between the pieces of metal in contact. Copper, even though a better conductor than gold, forms an oxide which will result in higher resistance at the contact.

Silver is the best conductor ($\rho = 1.59 \times 10^{-8} \ \Omega\cdot m$), but it also forms a surface layer (seen as *tarnish* on silver kitchen implements) when exposed to air.

Chapter 13
Magnetism

𝕸ysteries:

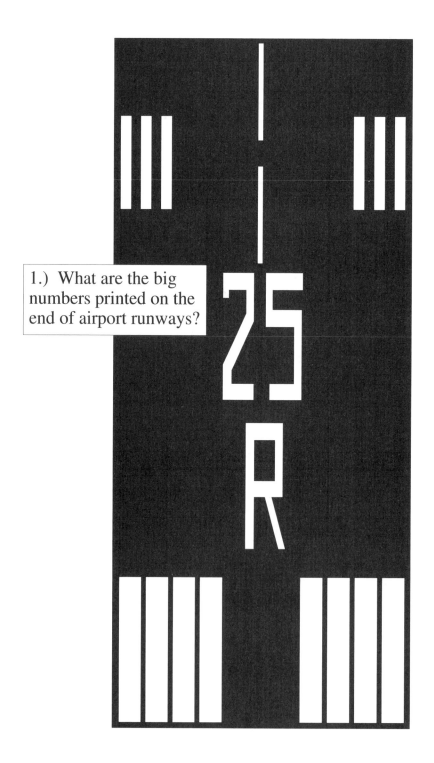

1.) What are the big numbers printed on the end of airport runways?

Mysteries:

2.) Why does the magnetic field of the Earth show periodic reversals?

3.) When a switch in a circuit carrying a relatively large current is opened, a spark is likely to occur between the metal parts of the switch. Yet, as the switch is closed, no such spark occurs. Why?

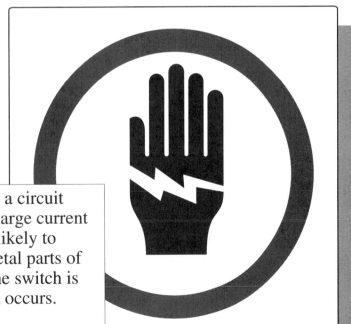

Electrical Hazard

𝔐𝔶𝔰𝔱𝔢𝔯𝔦𝔢𝔰:

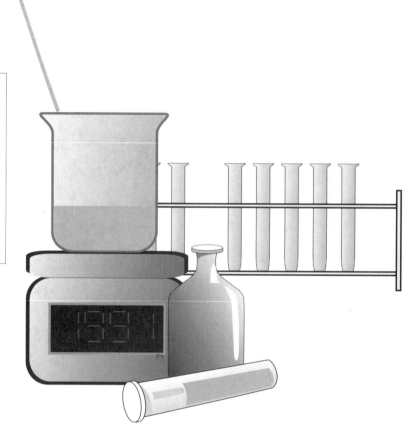

4.) A *scale* (spring, bathroom, etc.) measures weight. A *balance* (equal arm, triple beam, etc.) measures mass. What does a *digital electronic balance* measure?

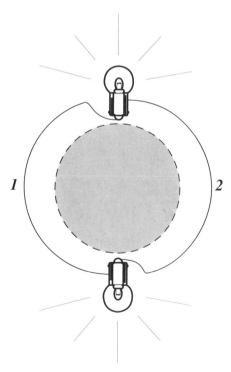

5.) Suppose that you are powering light bulbs in the circular loop of wire to the left by establishing a changing magnetic field in the shaded region within the loop. Both bulbs will light. Suppose that you now short out the bulbs, by attaching a wire between points *1* and *2*, with the wire not passing through the magnetic field region. What happens to the bulbs now?

𝕸𝖆𝖌𝖎𝖈:

The Magnetic Files

Move a compass vertically from the top to the bottom of a filing cabinet that has been in place for a long time. What do you notice?

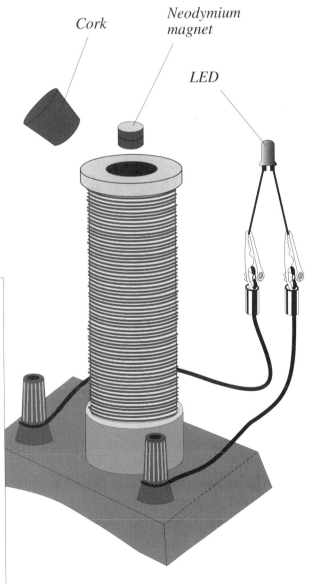

Cork

Neodymium magnet

LED

Powering an LED by Shaking

A common piece of laboratory apparatus in a physics stockroom is a coil of wire mounted on a hollow wooden form. Attach a light emitting diode across the terminals of such a coil. Stuff a tissue into the coil and push it to the bottom. Now drop a neodymium magnet into the coil, place your finger or a cork over the hole at the top and shake! The LED will flash.

𝕸𝖞𝖙𝖍:

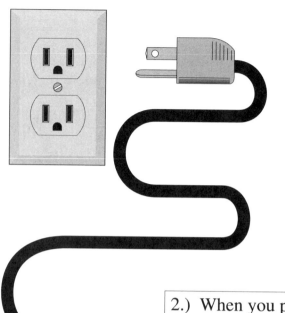

1.) A generator produces an AC potential difference.

2.) When you plug a device into your wall outlet, you connect your device to wires running all the way to the power station.

Electron in wire

Outer electron

3.) If an electron moves parallel to a current-carrying wire at the same speed as the drift speed of electrons in the wire, the magnetic force between the electron and the wire disappears, since, in the rest frame of the wire electrons, the outer electron is not moving.

Discussions; Chapter 13—Magnetism

Mysteries:

1.) What are the big numbers printed on the end of airport runways?

The numbers are for the benefit of the pilots of landing aircraft and represent the direction of the runway with respect to the magnetic field of the Earth. The numbers are obtained by dividing the angle (in degrees, measured clockwise from magnetic north) between magnetic north and the direction in which the plane lands on the runway by *ten*. Thus, a runway on which an airplane lands while traveling due east (at a location where magnetic north is in the geographic north direction) would have a marking of 9 (90° divided by 10). The other end of the runway, which would be seen by a plane landing while traveling due west, would be marked 27. If there are a number of parallel runways, an additional *letter* is used to differentiate them, representing the relative position of the runway. For example if there are three parallel runways in the east direction, the west ends will be marked 9L, 9C, and 9R, where the letters represent *left*, *center* and *right*, respectively. If there are more than three parallel runways, they are differentiated by marking one with a number corresponding to rounding the magnetic heading *down* to the nearest 10° and others by rounding *up* to the nearest 10°. Thus, for example, the west ends of four east-west runways might be marked 9L, 9R, 10L and 10R (the latter two could also be 8L and 8R if the runway heading is *exactly* 90°).

2.) Why does the magnetic field of the Earth show periodic reversals?

The reversals of the Earth's magnetic field are well documented in the magnetization of material on the Earth's surface (for details on this documentation, see, for example, J. D. A. Piper, *Paleomagnetism and the Continental Crust*, Halsted Press, New York, 1987 or D. H. Tarling, *Paleomagnetism*: *Principles and Applications in Geology, Geophysics and Archaeology*, Chapman and Hall, London, 1983). These records show that reversals occur at a relatively random frequency which averages about 3 reversals every million years. Each reversal takes place over a period of from 1,000 to 10,000 years and the magnitude of the field drops to less than 20% of its stable value during the reversal.

In addition to reversals, there is some evidence for occasional magnetic *excursions*, in which the magnetic pole moves away from its normal position, but then returns without a polarity reversal.

In *PBWM*, the discussion of Mystery #2 in Chapter 22 indicated that the source of the Earth's magnetic field is not at present fully understood. The same can be said for magnetic reversals and excursions. This is a field of continuing research (pun intended!).

3.) When a switch in a circuit carrying a relatively large current is opened, a spark is likely to occur between the metal parts of the switch. Yet, when the switch is closed, no such spark occurs. Why?

This is an example of Faraday's Law. It is especially evident when there is a relatively large amount of *inductance* in the circuit. When current is flowing through the switch and the switch is opened, the collapsing magnetic fields in the circuit induce a current in the original direction—that is, the circuit attempts to "keep the current going". Thus, for very large initial currents, the current can be maintained over the air gap between the metal portions of the switch for a short time. This is the spark that is seen.

For the reverse process, when the switch is closed, there is no current flowing initially. Thus, there is no magnetic induction occurring until after the switch is closed and, of course, the air gap is no longer present. Thus, no spark is seen.

4.) A *scale* (spring, bathroom, etc.) measures weight. A *balance* (equal arm, triple beam, etc.) measures mass. What does a *digital electronic balance* measure?

Bathroom scales employ a spring to provide a force to act against the downward force of an object placed on the scale. Thus, the bathroom scale responds directly to the force applied to the scale by the object. An equal arm balance compares the gravitational force on an object in a pan on one end of the beam with the force on standard masses on a pan on the other end of the beam. A triple beam balance compares gravitational torques between the side of the beam with the object and the other side with sliding masses. As long as the gravitational field values at all locations of a beam balance are the same, the device will still be balanced if it is moved to the Moon or some other region of different gravitational field. Thus, the beam balance measures mass.

A digital electronic balance is a box with a pan on the top and a digital readout. It is impossible to know how to answer the question posed in the Mystery without knowing what is inside the box. Inside the box is a *beam*, with the external pan on one end. We might be tempted to say at this point, "Aha! It's a beam balance—it measures mass!", but be careful. At the other end of the beam is a *coil of wire, in the field of a magnet*, similar to the construction of a loudspeaker voice coil. The goal of the magnet-coil combination, along with the associated electronics, is to keep the beam in a *horizontal position*. If a mass is placed on the external pan, the pan end of the beam goes down and the coil end goes up. A light source-photocell assembly at the coil end detects that the end has risen and sends a signal to the feedback electronics. The feedback circuits increase the current in the coil, resulting in a magnetic force on the coil in the downward direction, pulling the coil end of the beam back down. Once the photocell indicates that the beam is back in equilibrium in a horizontal position, the current flowing in the coil is measured and, according to calibration in the electronics, the appropriate reading is output on the digital readout. The heavier the object on the pan, the larger is the current necessary to bring the beam into a horizontal position and the readout increases accordingly.

This is similar to what one does on a mechanical beam balance. In the mechanical case, the beam is returned to the horizontal by adding more mass or sliding masses farther out on the beam to increase the torque. This role is played by the magnetic force in the digital balance. Despite this similarity, while the mechanical beam balance measures *mass*, the digital balance measures *weight*. If the digital balance is taken to the Moon, the gravitational force on a given mass on the pan decreases. The magnetic force at the other end, however, *has nothing to do with gravity*. There is a smaller force on the pan end, so a smaller current is required to balance it and the readout will be smaller. Some digital balances have a capability of allowing for this by incorporating a test mass for calibration in different gravitational fields, but the fundamental nature of the instrument is such that it measures weight.

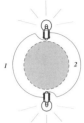

5.) Suppose that you are powering light bulbs in the circular loop of wire to the left by establishing a changing magnetic field in the shaded region within the loop. Both bulbs will light. Suppose that you now short out the bulbs, by attaching a wire between points *1* and *2*, with a wire not passing through the magnetic field region. What happens to the bulbs now?

The effect on the light bulbs depends on which side of the magnetic field region the wire lies. Suppose that the two points are shorted by passing a wire along the bottom of the diagram, as shown to the right. Then *the bottom light bulb will go out and the top bulb will continue to glow*.

This can be understood from a consideration of the loops of wire in the diagram. The loop consisting of the lower light bulb and the shorting wire is a closed loop outside of the region of changing magnetic field and not enclosing the region of changing magnetic field. There is no magnetic flux passing through this loop. Thus, the total induced emf in this loop must be *zero*. If we split the loop into two pieces, with piece *A* representing the wire and bulb path between points *1* and *2*, and *B* representing the shorting wire path between points *1* and *2*, then

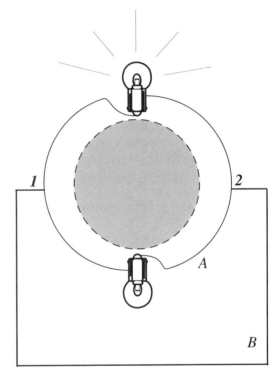

$$\Delta V_A + \Delta V_B = 0 \quad \rightarrow \quad \Delta V_A = -\Delta V_B$$

Since path *B* is the shorting wire, there is no potential difference across it, since we assume that it has no resistance. Then, according to the above equation, there is no potential difference across the path containing the light bulb, path *A*. Thus, the light bulb does not light.

A related question is the following. Consider the circuit shown to the right, consisting of two resistors and two voltmeters, outside of a region of changing magnetic field. The voltmeters are connected *between the same points*, so that a first guess would be that both meters read the same value. Is this true?

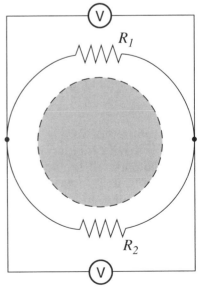

The first guess *is not true*. No matter what the values of R_1 and R_2, the signs of the voltmeter readings are opposite, and, unless $R_1 = R_2$, the magnitudes are different. The solution to this problem depends on the loop arguments stated above and is available in R. H. Romer, "What Do 'Voltmeters' Measure? Faraday's Law in a Multiply Connected Region", *American Journal of Physics*, **50**, 1089, 1982.

𝔐agic:

The Magnetic Files

File cabinets tend to remain in a given location for a long period of time. In addition, metal file cabinets are made of steel, which is ferromagnetic. Thus, the ferromagnetic material in the file cabinet is immersed for a long period of time in the magnetic field of the Earth. As a result, the cabinet becomes magnetized! In the location of the United States, the magnetic field lines have a downward component. Thus, *in the idealized case*, the lower part of the cabinet tends to become a North pole, while the top becomes a South pole. In reality, you may not see this *ideal* effect, but you will see *some* effects on the compass as you move it along the vertical dimension of the file cabinet.

Powering an LED by Shaking

The magnet moving around inside the coil will induce an emf in the coil, resulting in the flashing of the LED when the emf is induced in the correct direction for the diode to pass current. The demonstration is particularly vivid if a *bicolor* LED is used, so that different colored flashes will result, depending on which way the emf is induced. For more information, see J. W. Jewett and D. Johnson, "Demonstrating Induced Voltages with an LED", *Journal of College Science Teaching*, **20**, 196, 1992 and C. Lopez and P. Gonzalo, "Using LED's to Demonstrate Induced Current", *The Physics Teacher*, **27**, 218, 1989.

𝔐yth:

1.) A generator produces an AC potential difference.

The common type of electrical generator, as used in power generation stations, consists of a coil of wire rotating in a magnetic field. These types of generators do indeed produce a potential difference which alternates in time. Since these types of generators are so common, it is often assumed that a generator produces an AC potential difference. But it is not hard to imagine a generator which will produce not only a DC potential difference, but a *constant* DC potential difference. Consider the diagram on the next page, which shows a solid metal disk rotating in a magnetic field. By means of a right hand rule, one can convince oneself that electrons in the metal will feel a force to the outer rim of the disk. By attaching a wire between the center of the disk and a sliding contact at the edge, a constant DC current will flow through the wire when the disk is rotated.

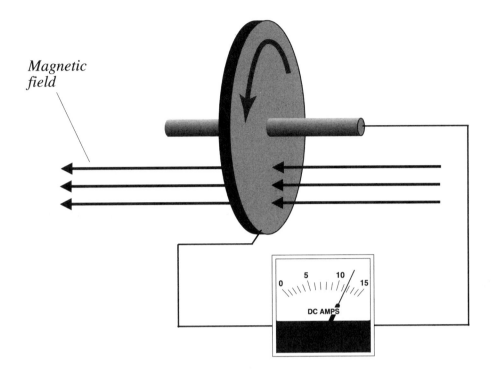

This configuration is actually that of the first generator invented, by Michael Faraday in the 1830's.

2.) When you plug a device into your wall outlet, you connect your device to wires running all the way to the power station.

At several places between your home and the power station, there will be *transformers*, which will step up or step down the potential difference, as discussed in Mystery #3 in Chapter 23 of *PBWM*. There is no *electrical* link between the primary and secondary coils of a transformer, only a *magnetic* link. Thus, the device that you plug into your wall outlet is only connected by wires to the nearest transformer to your home.

3.) If an electron moves parallel to a current-carrying wire at the same speed as the drift speed of electrons in the wire, the magnetic force between the electron and the wire disappears, since, in the rest frame of the wire electrons, the outer electron is not moving.

In this situation, there will be no relative velocity between the electrons in the wire and the outer electron. There *will* be a relative velocity, however, between the outer electron and the *positive lattice ions* in the metal wire. Thus, there will still be a magnetic field, due to the relative motion of the positive particles, and, therefore, a magnetic force on the outer electron.

Chapter 14
Optical Phenomena

𝔐𝔶𝔰𝔱𝔢𝔯𝔦𝔢𝔰:

1.) In an episode ("Deadly Dreams") of the television series *MacGyver* (Paramount Pictures, 1985-1992), MacGyver wanted to see through a frosted glass door. He performed this feat by rubbing motor oil on the glass. Why did this make the glass transparent?

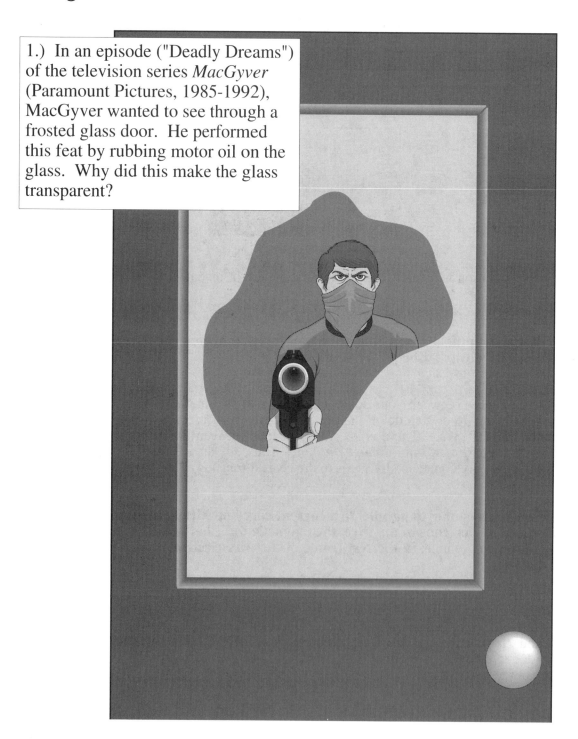

𝔐ysteries:

2.) Shadows on the Moon are much darker than shadows on the Earth. Why?

3.) When the Moon is a thin crescent, you can see the rest of the Moon dimly lit. Why?

Mysteries:

4.) A picture of a comet normally shows a *tail*. But sometimes comets have *two* tails. Why is this?

5.) Sometimes in the late afternoon, it is possible to see a number of rays of light coming from the Sun through the clouds. They diverge from the location of the Sun in the sky. Now, wait a minute. The Sun is extremely far away. How can we see *diverging* rays from such a distant source?

Mysteries:

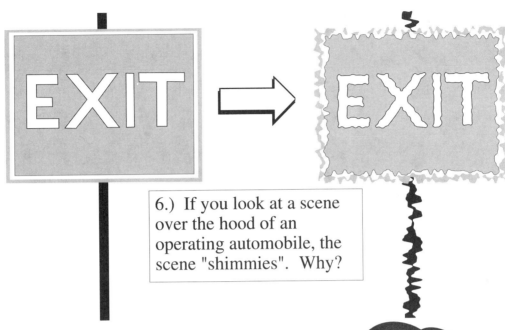

6.) If you look at a scene over the hood of an operating automobile, the scene "shimmies". Why?

Magic:

Identical Coins?

Place two glasses next to each other. Place an identical coin in the bottom of each glass. Fill one glass with water. Look down into the glasses, one eye into each glass. Are the coins the same size?

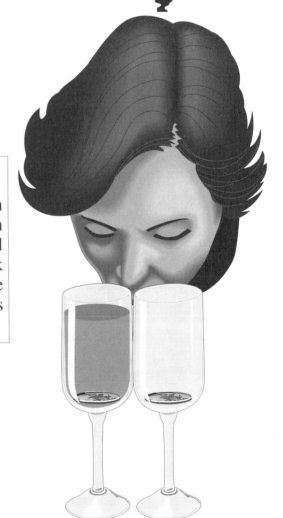

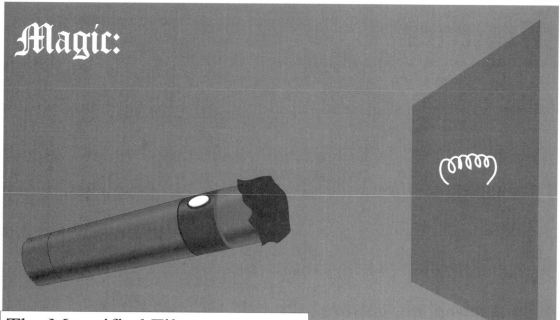

Magic:

The Magnified Filament

Poke a small hole in a piece of black construction paper. Place the paper over the face of a flashlight and project the light through the hole onto a wall in a darkened room. You will be able to see an enlarged image of the filament of the flashlight bulb on the wall.

Mirages on the Wall

A dark wall facing the Sun can be used to see a mirage. Place a bright object near the wall and stand a few meters along the wall from the object. Look back toward the object, along a line almost parallel to the wall but slightly toward it and you will (with luck!) see a mirage of the object.

Myth:

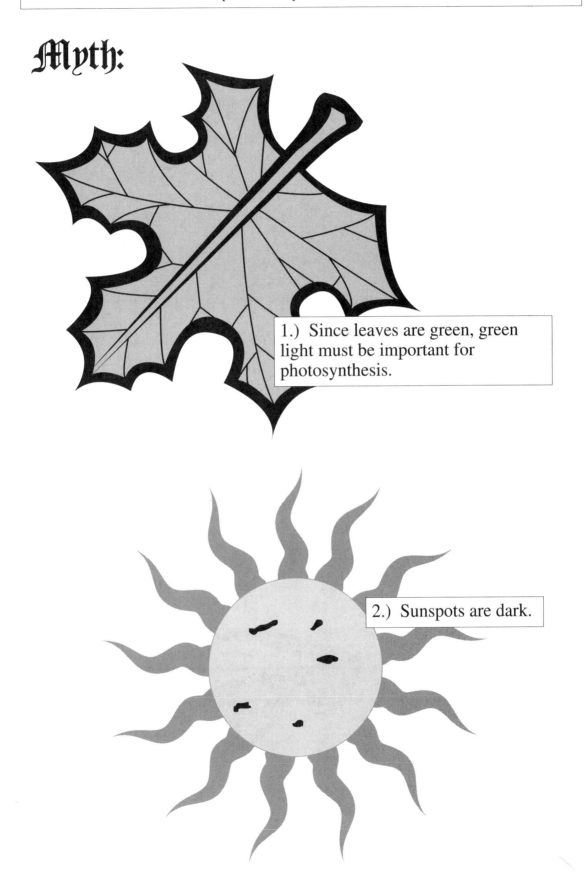

1.) Since leaves are green, green light must be important for photosynthesis.

2.) Sunspots are dark.

𝔐𝔶𝔱𝔥:

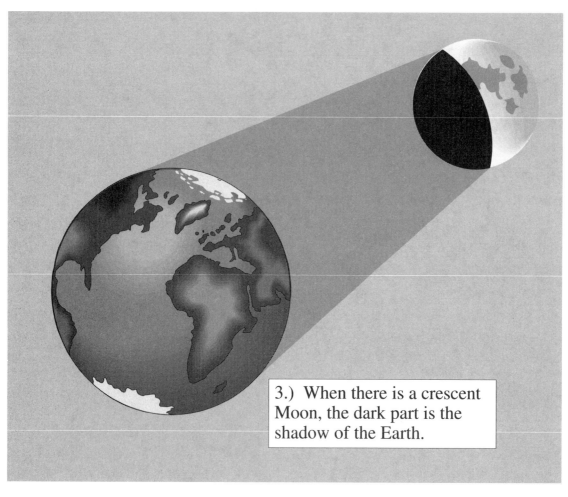

3.) When there is a crescent Moon, the dark part is the shadow of the Earth.

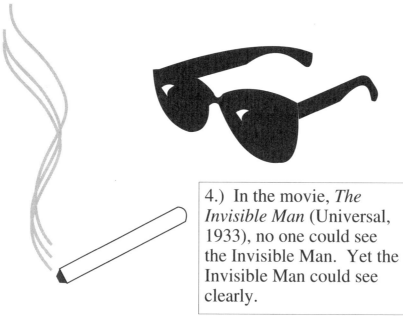

4.) In the movie, *The Invisible Man* (Universal, 1933), no one could see the Invisible Man. Yet the Invisible Man could see clearly.

𝔐𝔶𝔱𝔥:

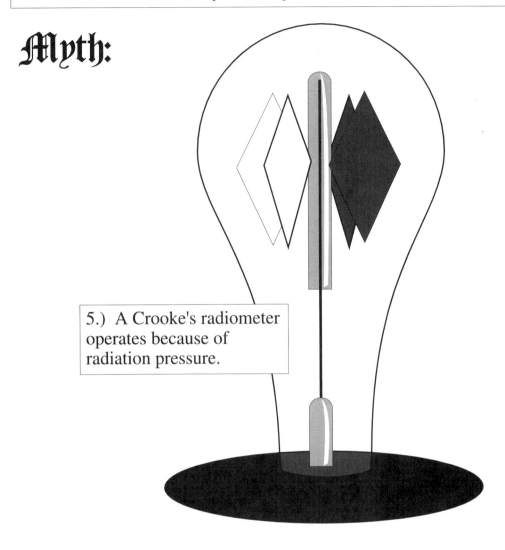

5.) A Crooke's radiometer operates because of radiation pressure.

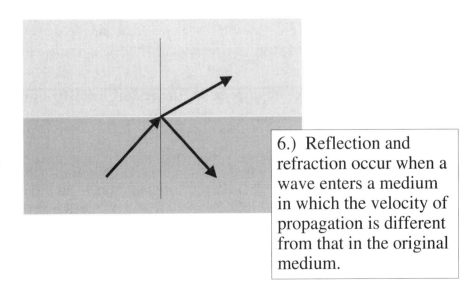

6.) Reflection and refraction occur when a wave enters a medium in which the velocity of propagation is different from that in the original medium.

Discussions; Chapter 14—Optical Phenomena

𝔐𝔶𝔰𝔱𝔢𝔯𝔦𝔢𝔰:

1.) In an episode ("Deadly Dreams") of the television series *MacGyver* (Paramount Pictures, 1985-1992), MacGyver wanted to see through a frosted glass door. He performed this feat by rubbing motor oil on the glass. Why did this make the glass transparent?

Frosted glass results in a blurry image of an object seen through it, as discussed in Mystery #12 of Chapter 25 of *PBWM*. The rough surface of this glass scatters light passing through in all directions, resulting in the blurriness. Now, let's consider the oil. As discussed in The Magical Glass Repairing Fluid in Chapter 26 of *PBWM*, the indices of refraction of Pyrex glass and vegetable oil are very close to each other. The indices of window glass and motor oil are not *as* close, but still close. Thus, when MacGyver rubbed the oil on the frosted glass, the oil filled in the valleys between the "bumps" on the frosted glass. When the light rays passing through the glass encountered a surface of a bump, the oil on the other side of the boundary had almost the same index of refraction. Thus, there was very little optical interface between the glass and the oil. As a result, there was little refraction, and the light rays passed through with minimal change in direction, giving a reasonably clear image.

2.) Shadows on the Moon are much darker than shadows on the Earth. Why?

Ideally, a shadow represents the complete blockage of light from a source such as the Sun. A large object on the Earth will display an approximation to such a shadow. If the same object is transported to the Moon, it is noticed that the shadow is significantly darker. On the Earth, the atmosphere performs a significant amount of scattering—this is the reason for the blue sky (Mystery #3, Chapter 25 of *PBWM*). Thus, light is traveling through the atmosphere in all directions. As a result, some light enters the shadow region of our large object *from the side* and reduces the darkness of the shadow. On the Moon, the absence of an atmosphere precludes this scattered light and the shadow is extremely close to a complete absence of light.

3.) When the Moon is a thin crescent, you can see the rest of the Moon dimly lit. Why?

This phenomenon is called *Earthshine*. When you are looking at a thin crescent Moon in the evening, the Sun is located generally in the direction in which you are facing, but below the horizon. Light from the Sun will strike the Earth and some will reflect from the surface. In turn, some of this reflected light will strike the Moon and reflect off its surface. Some of this light, in turn, will travel back to Earth and enter your eye. Thus, the dark region of the Moon will appear to be dimly lit by this light which has made reflections off both bodies. This effect is present whenever the Moon is not full, but the dim light is not visible against the bright light of anything but a thin crescent.

4.) A picture of a comet normally shows a *tail*. But sometimes comets have *two* tails. Why is this?

The two tails of some comets consist of different types of particles that are released from the surface of the comet due to energy input from the Sun. One tail, the *Ion Tail*, is directed away from the Sun (not *exactly* away, but very close to the direction away from the Sun, with the angular deviation depending on the solar wind velocity and the comet orbital velocity). This tail is due to ions (non-neutral atoms) that are forced away from the comet by the *Solar wind*, which is a stream of fast-moving ions projected radially from the Sun. The second tail is the *Dust Tail*. This is due to particles of dust that are released from the comet's surface. These particles are too heavy to be affected in the same way by the Solar wind. As they are released, they are in the same orbit as the comet. As light from the Sun reflects from the dust particles, they are subject to *radiation pressure* from this light. As a result of this and ion pressure, these particles continue to move in orbit around the Sun, but are constantly pushed slowly outward. The result is a curving tail forming behind the comet, as shown in the diagram below.

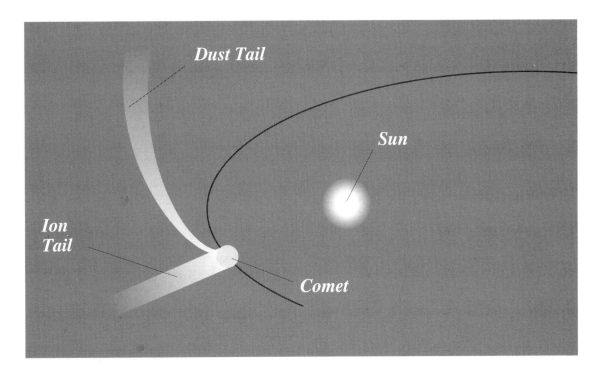

5.) Sometimes in the late afternoon, it is possible to see a number of rays of light coming from the Sun through the clouds. They diverge from the location of the Sun in the sky. Now, wait a minute. The Sun is extremely far away. How can we see *diverging* rays from such a distant source?

These are called *crepuscular rays*, referring to their appearance in the late afternoon (animals which are active at twilight are called *crepuscular*). They appear when there is smoke, fog or other particles in the air to scatter the light, so as to make the rays visible. They often appear after a rainstorm, when water droplets provide the scattering. In addition, the sunlight must come through clouds so that there is contrast between the part of the atmosphere providing scattered sunlight and the part where the light is blocked by the cloud. Now, why do the rays appear to diverge? Since the Sun is so far away, the rays coming toward your eyes are indeed parallel. But, because the Sun is low on the horizon, you are looking almost right along the rays of light. Thus, *they appear to diverge from a "vanishing point"* (to use an artistic metaphor). The same effect occurs when you are standing on railroad tracks. Because you are close to the tracks, looking along them, they appear to diverge from a point far in the distance. But, if you could hover far above the tracks, you would see that they are indeed parallel.

For color photographs of crepuscular rays, see R. Greenler, *Rainbows, Halos, and Glories*, Cambridge University Press, Cambridge, 1980.

6.) If you look at a scene over the hood of an operating automobile, the scene "shimmies". Why?

Energy rises from the engine by convection in the air. The index of refraction of the air is a function of temperature. Thus, as you look through air which is experiencing turbulent temperature changes due to the convection, the light from a source on the other side of this air suffers random variations in refraction, resulting in the shimmying effect.

This is closely related to the twinkling of stars, which was discussed in Myth #1 in Chapter 26 of *PBWM*.

𝔐agic:

Identical Coins?

The coin at the bottom of the water-filled glass will appear to be slightly larger than the other coin. This is due to the refraction of the light from the coin as it leaves the water. The diagram below shows the paths of some of the light rays coming from a point on the coin.

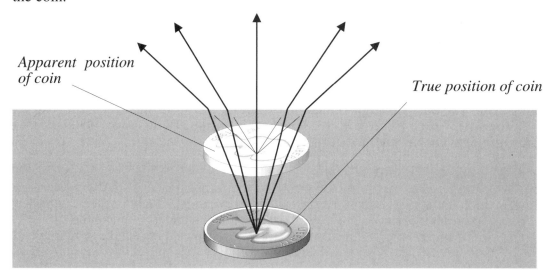

Apparent position of coin

True position of coin

As light rays leave the water, they bend away from the normal, and seem to be coming from a point higher in the water than the actual source of the light. Thus, the image of this point on the coin is higher in the water than the actual point. Every point on the coin will have an image that is raised in this way. Thus, the coin will appear as if it has been brought closer to the eye looking into the glass. Since it has effectively been brought closer, it will appear larger.

This a common phenomenon when looking into water. Swimming pools and streams appear to be shallower than they are due to this effect.

The effect can be magnified somewhat by looking into the glasses (without the coins) at an angle and focusing on the bottom of the glasses, as suggested in the diagram below. It will appear that the glass with water is significantly shallower than the empty glass.

The Magnified Filament

This could be called an "inverse pinhole effect". In a pinhole camera, light from outside of a closed box passes through a pinhole in the side of the box. As a result, a small image of the scene can be captured, over a length of time, on a piece of film on the side of the box opposite the pinhole.

In this demonstration, the source of light is "inside the box"—it is the filament of the flashlight. The light from the filament passes through the pinhole and is projected onto a screen, resulting in an *enlarged* image of the filament. The size of the image will depend on the ratio of the distances from the pinhole to the screen and from the pinhole to the filament. The image can be enlarged by moving the flashlight away from the screen, but the intensity of the image will decrease.

Mirages on the Wall

The formation of this mirage is analogous to that formed by dark roadways on sunny days, as discussed in Mystery #5 of Chapter 26 of *PBWM*. The dark wall absorbs a large fraction of the energy of the incident sunlight, raising its temperature significantly. As a result, the air in contact with the wall increases in temperature and there is a temperature gradient perpendicular to the wall. The temperature of the air near the wall is high and the temperature decreases as one moves away. This provides the corresponding gradient in the index of refraction of the air to refract light approaching the wall at grazing incidence so that it "misses" the wall and deviates away into the eye of the observer. As a result, the observer sees an image of the light source as if it were "inside" the wall.

For a method of using the computer to demonstrate mirages, see J. F. Davis and T. B. Greenslade, "Computer Modeling of Mirage Formation", *The Physics Teacher*, **29**, 47, 1991.

𝔐𝔶𝔱𝔥:

1.) Since leaves are green, green light must be important for photosynthesis.

Leaves appear to be green because the reflected light from the surface of the leaf is primarily green. Thus, the leaf is *rejecting* the green light, so it must not be important to the process of photosynthesis.

The light absorption in green plants is performed primarily by two types of chlorophyll, called chlorophyll *a* and chlorophyll *b*. Each of these complex molecules has two energy states above the lowest state that can be excited by visible photons (see Chapters 18 and 19 for more discussion of energy states and their excitations). The range of wavelengths for absorption for both molecules is about 640 nm to 680 nm for the first excited state and about 400 nm to 460 nm for the second state. The first range corresponds to the red region of the spectrum and the second to the blue region. There is virtually no absorption, due to the absence of appropriate excited states, in the green range of the spectrum, resulting in the reflection of green light and the green color of leaves.

For graphs of the absorption spectra of chlorophyll, see D. W. Lawlor, *Photosynthesis: Molecular, Physiological and Environmental Processes*, 2nd ed., Longman Scientific & Technical, London, 1993.

2.) Sunspots are dark.

Sunspots appear as dark regions on the surface of the Sun, but this is only *relative*. If you could bring a sunspot by itself into a room, it would be blindingly bright. On the Sun, the sunspot is a region that is at a lower temperature than the rest of the Sun and, therefore, looks darker *only by comparison*.

3.) When there is a crescent moon, the dark part is the shadow of the Earth.

This is a common misconception and demonstrates the failure of many people to think about where the Sun is when the Moon is in the crescent phase. A few moments' thought will reveal that, when the Moon is in the crescent phase, the Sun is in the same general direction as the Moon, since it is lighting up the "back side" of the Moon (see Mystery #3 for more discussion). Thus, the Earth is not between the Sun and the Moon at this time and there is no possibility of the Earth casting a shadow on the Moon. (When the Earth does cast a shadow on the Moon, we call it a *lunar eclipse*.) The dark part of the Moon is due simply to the fact that it is not lit by the Sun.

4.) In the movie, *The Invisible Man* (Universal, 1933), no one could see the Invisible Man. Yet the Invisible Man could see clearly.

If the Invisible Man were to be truly invisible, then all light incident upon him would pass through him without being absorbed or reflected—he would be perfectly transparent. In order for him to see, however, his eyes would have to absorb light. But, if his eyes absorbed light, than people would be able to see that light did not transmit perfectly through the region of his eyes, which would allow his position to be detected. Thus, the *truly* invisible man must be *blind*.

5.) A Crooke's radiometer operates because of radiation pressure.

A Crooke's radiometer typically consists of four vanes, each with a white side and a black side, mounted on a rotor suspended from a needle point, resulting in very low rotational friction. The assembly is housed in a glass bulb. When light shines on the vanes, the assembly begins to rotate. If we consider a photon description of light (see Chapter 17), we can imagine photons reflecting from the white sides and being absorbed into the black sides. Thus, the photons striking the white sides should exert more force on the vane than those striking the black sides. This is analogous to the situation with the happy and sad balls in The Happy and Sad Block-Knockers in Chapter 6. The "reflected" happy ball exerts more force (and knocks the block over) while the sad ball exerts less. Thus, we might expect that the direction of rotation would be such that the black sides of the vanes are leading and the white sides trailing, due to the larger total force on the white sides.

A close look at an operating radiometer shows that *just the opposite is true*—the white sides lead and the black sides trail. This is due to the fact that there is *air* in the radiometer. The effect of the air dominates over the radiation pressure. Since the black sides of the vanes absorb more energy than the white sides, the black sides become hotter. By conduction, the air in contact with the black sides becomes hotter than that in contact with the white sides. As a result, the pressure of the air just next to the black sides is larger than the pressure in the air just next to the white sides. Thus, there is a pressure difference across each vane, in a direction so as to apply a force in the direction so that the white sides lead in the rotation.

The opposite rotation can be induced in the radiometer by creating an environment in which there will be a net flow of energy *out* of the vanes. This can be done by placing the radiometer in a freezer or by spraying the bulb with electronic component cooler. The result is that the rotation will be such that the black sides lead! While the observer may be tempted to explain this via photon pressure, since it is consistent with the direction predicted by such, this hypothesis is incorrect again, especially since the rotation in this case does not require the application of light!

Let us consider the radiation from the vanes in this situation. The black sides will have a higher emissivity than the white sides and will thus radiate energy at a higher rate. Thus, the black sides will cool faster, the air in contact with the black sides will cool faster by conduction and will exert less pressure than the air on the white sides. As a result, the force will be in a direction such that the rotation has the black side leading. This will continue as long as the temperature of the radiometer is significantly above that of the environment. After a while, equilibrium will be reestablished and the rotation will cease.

An application in which photon pressure *is* the primary mechanism is that of *space sailing*. A space sailcraft has a very large and reflective sail of very low mass oriented perpendicularly to the Sun, so that reflected photons will apply a pressure to accelerate the craft. Calculations show that an efficient sailcraft could reach the planets in times comparable to a spacecraft powered by rocket engines. For more information, see J. L. Wright, *Space Sailing*, Gordon and Breach Science Publishers, Philadelphia, 1992.

6.) Reflection and refraction occur when a wave enters a medium in which the velocity of propagation is different from that in the original medium.

This is a standard statement that will not cause us trouble in optics. But it is a special case of a more fundamental principle of wave behavior. The more general principle is this: the division of incident energy into reflected and transmitted portions will occur when a wave enters a medium in which the *impedance* is different from that in the first medium.

The concept of *acoustic* impedance was discussed in Myth #6 in Chapter 18 of *PBWM*. Acoustic impedance is a measure of the opposition that the medium offers to the propagation of a sound wave. If the wave enters a second medium with a different impedance, there will be some reflected energy and some transmitted energy. The acoustic impedance of a medium is given by,

$$Z_{acoustic} = \rho v$$

where ρ is the density of the medium and v is the velocity of propagation of acoustic waves. This suggests that there exists the possibility of an interface between two media such that the velocity of propagation will change across the interface, but there will be no change in impedance. This would require that the density change across the interface be opposite in sign to that of the velocity change and of a value such that the product of velocity and density remains constant. Thus, in this case, *there would be no reflection of energy at the interface, even though there is a velocity change.* All of the energy would be transmitted. There would still be a change in direction of the wave propagation, however, since the direction of propagation is determined by Snell's Law, which depends only on velocity, not impedance.

This is not a consideration in optics, since electromagnetic radiation does not require a medium for propagation. Thus, a velocity change across an interface is sufficient for both reflection and refraction to occur. Conversely, if there is no velocity change, there will be no reflection, as seen in the Magic demonstration, The Magical Glass Repairing Fluid in Chapter 26 of *PBWM*.

For mechanical waves, however, the distinction between a velocity change and an impedance change is a consideration. As an example, exploration geologists often establish seismic waves with an explosive or impulsive source and look for reflections from interfaces between layers of different materials under the ground. Some of these interfaces are "hidden" from this strategy, in the sense that, although there may be a velocity change across the interface, there is no impedance change, and the interface will not appear on the resulting underground structural diagram for the region.

Chapter 15
Image Formation

Mysteries:

1.) If you are standing on second base in a baseball game, the batter appears much smaller than the pitcher and it is clear that the pitcher and batter are far apart. A common camera angle for the television coverage (or for a zoom lens on a video camcorder or still camera) at a baseball game is from center field, looking into the pitcher-home plate area. From this view, the pitcher and batter seem to be very close to the same size, and very close to each other. Why is this?

2.) Sometimes you see older pictures of doctors wearing a mirror on their head, with a hole in it (the mirror, not the head). What is the purpose of this mirror?

𝔐ysteries:

3.) A typical lens for a camera is described as "38 mm". What does this measurement mean?

4.) Another lens available for cameras has a focal length of 200 mm. Why is this a *telephoto* lens? That is, why does it magnify the image?

5.) During the construction of the newly-legalized casinos in Atlantic City in the late 1970's, a curious accident occurred. One casino was designed with an external wall of reflective plastic panels. Unfortunately, the panels were slightly larger than the openings into which they were to be placed. The construction workers bowed the panels slightly, so that they would fit. The next day, several spots on the wooden boardwalk next to the casino seemed to spontaneously erupt into flame. Why did this happen?

𝔐𝔞𝔤𝔦𝔠:

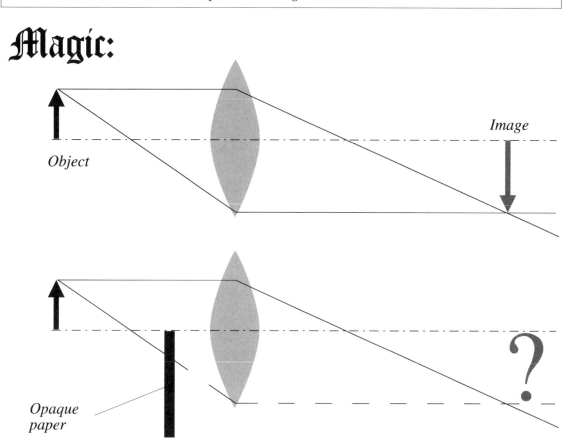

Object

Image

Opaque paper

The Halves and the Halve-Nots

Set up an object-lens-screen system so that a real image is projected clearly on the screen. Now, cover half of the lens with opaque paper. What happens to the image—does half of it disappear?

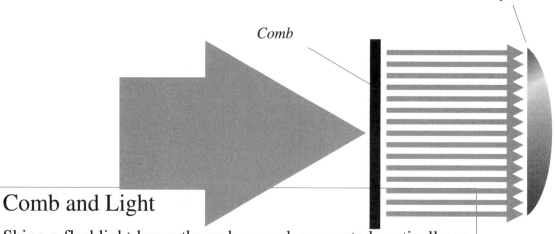

Comb

Spoon

Comb and Light

Shine a flashlight beam through a comb supported vertically on a piece of paper. This will provide a bundle of near-parallel rays appearing on the paper. Place a spoon in the path of the rays and observe the effects.

Magic:

The Constant-Sized Face

Stand in front of your bathroom mirror. Use a piece of soap or a washable marker to draw a circle on the mirror around the image of your head. Now, move away from the mirror, keeping your face centered in the circle. How does the size of the circle compare to the size of the image of your head as you walk away?

Myth:

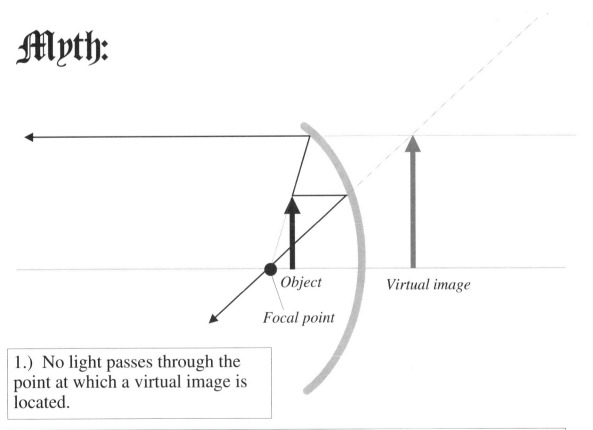

Object

Focal point

Virtual image

1.) No light passes through the point at which a virtual image is located.

𝔐𝔶𝔱𝔥:

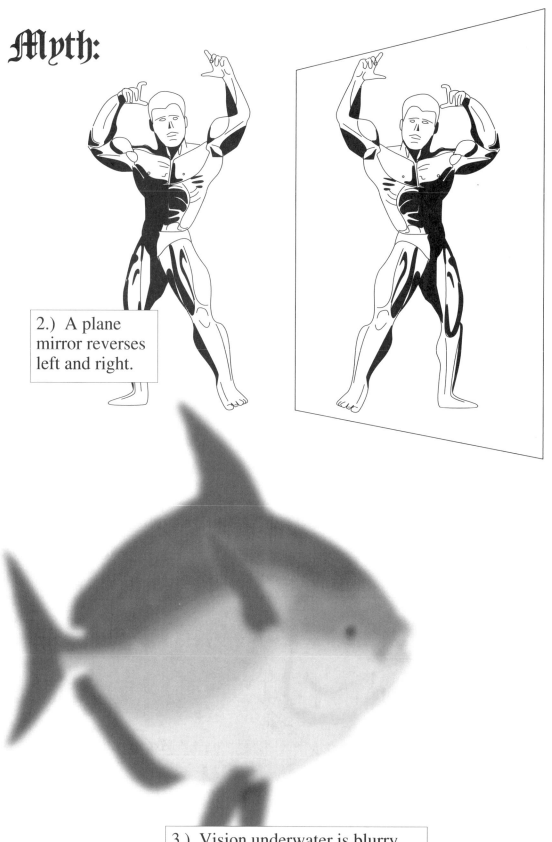

2.) A plane mirror reverses left and right.

3.) Vision underwater is blurry.

Discussions; Chapter 15—Image Formation

𝔐𝔶𝔰𝔱𝔢𝔯𝔦𝔢𝔰:

1.) If you are standing on second base in a baseball game, the batter appears much smaller than the pitcher and it is clear that the pitcher and batter are far apart. A common camera angle for the television coverage (or for a zoom lens on a video camcorder or still camera) at a baseball game is from center field, looking into the pitcher-home plate area. From this view, the pitcher and batter seem to be very close to the same size, and very close to each other. Why is this?

When you are standing on second base, the batter at home plate is twice as far away as the pitcher. As a result, the batter subtends half the visual angle as the pitcher and will appear half as high. When viewed from the center field fence, let us estimate the batter to be 400 feet away and the pitcher is then 400 ft – 60.5 ft = 339.5 ft away (60.5 feet is the distance from home plate to the pitcher's mound). Thus, the batter will subtend an angle that is $^{339.5}/_{400} = 0.85$ as large as the pitcher. Thus, the pitcher and batter look similar in size from this point of view. When the telephoto lens on the television camera is used, the scene appears to be closer, but *the relative sizes of the two players remain the same.* The viewer's brain has difficulty interpreting this result, since it appears to be viewing the scene from a close position, such as second base, but the relative sizes of the two players are incorrect for such a viewing position.

The same effect occurs for zoom lenses on cameras and strong pairs of binoculars. In particular, if strong binoculars are used to view a scene where people are close together, such as performers on a stage, the individuals that are seen to be behind others, due to being partially obscured, sometimes will look bigger than those in front! This is a psychological trick related to the expectation that the relative size should depend on the distance from the observer. When the people farther away look bigger than expected from prior viewing experience, the brain makes them look even bigger!

For a simple lens combination to show the zoom lens effect, see L. Kowalski, "On Field Lenses", *The Physics Teacher*, **30**, 366, 1992.

2.) Sometimes you see older pictures of doctors wearing a mirror on their head, with a hole in it (the mirror, not the head). What is the purpose of this mirror?

Mirrors such as that described in the Mystery were used by many doctors in the past. Today, the mirrors have been replaced in most doctors' toolkits with battery operated light sources.

The mirror is used to reflect light into the mouth, nose, ears, etc., of a patient. The mirror can be worn over the eye, so that the doctor can look through the hole. The position of the doctor's head is then adjusted so that the mirror is oriented to reflect light from behind the patient's head into the appropriate area.

This set-up is shown in the diagram below, in which a doctor is using the mirror to reflect light into the mouth of a patient.

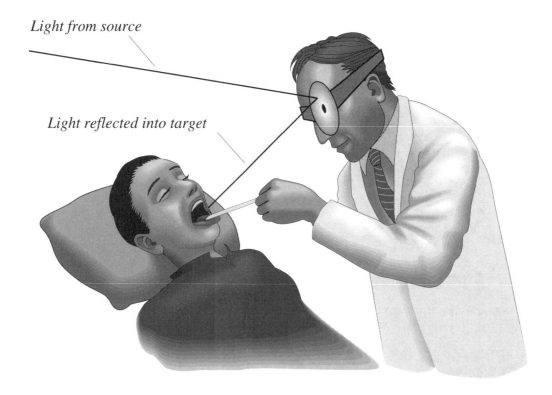

Light from source

Light reflected into target

3.) A typical lens for a camera is described as "38 mm". What does this measurement mean?

This measurement is the *focal length* of the lens. Thus, when the lens is focused on a very distant object, the distance between the film and the lens is 38 mm. In reality, high quality camera lenses are combinations of several elements, so that they can not be described as thin lenses, like the lenses in most textbook examples. Thus, some single point in the combination of lenses serves as the reference from which the distance of 38 mm is measured.

4.) Another lens available for cameras has a focal length of 200 mm. Why is this a *telephoto* lens? That is, why does it magnify the image?

The magnification of an image produced by a lens can be shown by geometry to be as follows:

$$magnification = -\frac{image\,distance}{object\,distance}$$

where the negative sign indicates that the image is upside down for the normal situation of a real image formed by the lens, as is the case with a camera lens.

Consider a normal 38 mm lens focused on a very distant object. As discussed in Mystery #3, the lens is then located 38 mm from the film. Now, imagine replacing the 38 mm lens with the 200 mm lens. If we focus this lens on the same distant object, the lens will be 200 mm from the film. Thus, the replacement of the lens has the effect of *increasing the image distance*—the distance between the lens and the film. From the relation above, we see that increasing the image distance while holding the object distance constant results in a larger magnification. Thus, the 200 mm lens has a larger image on the film than the 38 mm lens—it acts as a *telephoto lens*.

5.) During the construction of the newly-legalized casinos in Atlantic City in the late 1970's, a curious accident occurred. One casino was designed with an external wall of reflective plastic panels. Unfortunately, the panels were slightly larger than the openings into which they were to be placed. The construction workers bowed the panels slightly, so that they would fit. The next day, several spots on the wooden boardwalk next to the casino seemed to spontaneously erupt into flame. Why did this happen?

When the reflective panels were bowed in order to fit into the openings, they became *concave mirrors*. The next day, when the Sun shone on the panels, the concave reflecting surfaces focused the sunlight onto small regions of the wooden boardwalk, enough to start a number of small fires.

For a similar situation on the rooftop of a university building, caused by reflections from sagging window glass, see F. E. Domann, "Damaging Reflections", *The Physics Teacher*, **31**, 190, 1993.

𝔐𝔞𝔤𝔦𝔠:

The Halves and the Halve-Nots

Many observers of this demonstration will predict that half of the image will disappear, using the mistaken concept that one half of the lens forms the upper half of the image while the other half of the lens forms the bottom half. In reality, light rays from *every point on the object* pass through *every point of the lens*. Thus, every part of the lens is capable of, and participates in, the formation of an image. In the case of covering half of the lens, we would see a small but noticeable drop in *brightness* of the image (since we have blocked half of the light), but the image would be complete. We could form an image even if we covered up almost the entire lens, leaving only a small opening. In this case, the brightness of the image would be severely reduced, but the entire image would still be present.

Comb and Light

The comb and flashlight combination provides a crude device for establishing a set of (almost) parallel light rays, as seen on the paper. When these rays strike the spoon, which is a crude approximation of a spherical mirror, they are (approximately) focused at a point that we call the *focal point*.

The Constant Sized Face

If you perform this activity, you find that your face always just fills the circle. Let us suppose that you double your distance from the mirror. The circle is now twice as far away and appears to have half the angular diameter that it had at your original position. Your image in a plane mirror is as far behind the mirror as you are in front of it. Thus, if you double your distance from the mirror, you also double your distance from your image. As a result, the image of your face is half as big (in each dimension) as it was initially. Thus, your face is half as big and the circle is half as big—your face still fits in the circle. The same argument can be made for any change in your distance from the mirror.

If you move your face very close to the mirror, you may find that there is some difference in the amount of your face that just fills the circle. This is due to the fact that your reflection occurs on the silvered *back* side of the glass, while the soap ring is on the *front* surface. In addition, the depth of your face (ears to nose) is a large fraction of (if not larger than) the distance from your face to the mirror in this situation, causing some distortion of the image.

For another activity related to images in plane mirrors, see D. R. Lapp, "Determining Plane Mirror Image Distance from Eye Charts", *The Physics Teacher*, **31**, 59, 1993.

𝔐𝔶𝔱𝔥:

1.) No light passes through the point at which a virtual image is located.

This statement is true in the case of a virtual image formed by a single *mirror*, as in the diagram accompanying the Myth. The virtual image in this case is "behind" the mirror (on the side opposite to the object), and light cannot pass through the mirror. Consider the construction on the next page, however, for a virtual image formed by a *diverging lens*. If the object is represented by an arrow, as is commonly done, with its base on the lens axis, then a typical ray diagram for the formation of the image of the tip of the arrow is as shown.

The object is the dark arrow to the left. The construction shows two rays leaving the tip of the arrow. The upper ray, ray *1*, is directed toward the focal point on the opposite side of the lens. Thus, it proceeds out of the lens parallel to the axis. The light line parallel to the axis to the left of the lens is the direction from which the outgoing ray seems to come. The lower ray, ray *2*, leaves the tip of the arrow, passes through the center of the lens and is undeflected. The resulting image can be located by placing its tip at the intersection of ray *2* and the apparent direction of ray *1*, as shown in the diagram. This is a virtual image, but note that *ray 2 passes through the image point.*

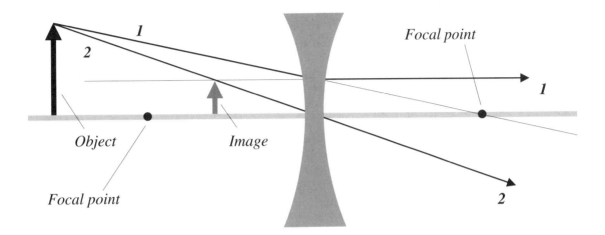

Thus, there *are* possibilities for virtual images through which a light ray passes. The definition of a virtual image should not refer to the absence of light rays passing through the image point. A more proper definition of a virtual image is simply that type of image that is obtained when the output rays of the lens (or mirror) are *diverging* from the image point.

What's more, a proper definition of a *real* image cannot include a phrase such as "a point through which light passes", since the above construction is an example of such a point, but represents a virtual image. This real image definition can be made more strict by including the requirement that *an arbitrarily large number of rays* must pass through the image point. On the other hand, a real image can also be defined as that type of image that is obtained when the output rays of the lens (or mirror) are *converging* to the image point.

2.) A plane mirror reverses left and right.

This is a common statement and has generated much discussion in the literature. Some of this discussion is referenced below for the interested reader.

If one attempts to impose the idea of reversal of left and right, then it is difficult to argue that there should not be an up and down reversal, also, since there is nothing special about the horizontal direction (left-right) compared to the vertical direction (up-down). It is clear, however, that there is no apparent up-down inversion—your feet don't appear in an image at the location of your head. On the other hand, if one lies down parallel to a mirror surface and looks in the mirror, there *is* an *apparent* up-down inversion. If you are lying on your left side and raise your right hand, your image is lying on its right side and raising its left hand. Since you are positioned horizontally, this appears to be an up-down inversion.

In reality, the inversion process in a mirror reflection is a *front-back* inversion. If you stand facing a mirror and imagine a positive *z*-axis leaving your stomach and pointing toward the mirror, the reflected *z*-axis is leaving the stomach of the image and coming toward you. This inversion of the *z*-axis results in a change in *handedness* of the reflection compared to the object. For example, if an analog clock is held in front of a mirror, the image of the clock will be seen to be running in the counterclockwise sense. If a corkscrew is held in front of the mirror, the sense of rotation as one moves along the axis of the corkscrew will be opposite in the image from that in the object. It is this inversion of the handedness that causes your left hand to appear as a right hand in the image.

For more discussions on this idea, see I. Galili, F. Goldberg and S. Bendall, "Some Reflections on Plane Mirrors and Images", *The Physics Teacher*, **29**, 471, 1991; T. H. Ansbacher, "Left-Right Semantics?", *The Physics Teacher*, **30**, 70, 1992; I. Galili, S. Bendall and F. Goldberg, "Author's Response to 'Left-Right Semantics?'", *The Physics Teacher*, **30**, 70, 1992; and I. Galili and F. Goldberg, "Left-Right Conversions in a Plane Mirror", *The Physics Teacher*, **31**, 463, 1993.

3.) Vision underwater is blurry.

As discussed in Myth #6 of Chapter 26 in *PBWM*, the major refraction in the eye occurs at the air-cornea interface. For an eye with perfect vision, the light rays focus on the retina due to this refraction, with some fine-tuning assistance from the lens. When this eye is opened underwater, there is less of a difference between the indices of refraction of the water and the eye than there was between the air and the eye when the eye was opened in air. Thus, there is less refraction, and the focusing of the light rays occurs *behind* the retina. The result is that the image is blurry.

Now, let us consider a *near-sighted eye*. Eyes with this defect (*myopia*) are elongated along the optic axis, so that light rays refracted by the normal air-cornea interface are focused in front of the retina. By the time the light rays reach the retina, they have diverged again and the image is blurry. Individuals with this eye problem wear *diverging* lens, which move the focusing point back onto the retina. Now, if a near-sighted individual opens his or her eyes under water, the reduced difference in the index of refraction will move the image farther from the cornea, just as discussed above. For a certain degree of myopia, this could actually move the image from its defective position, in front of the retina, *onto* the retina, so that this person can see more clearly underwater than in air!

Chapter 16
Physical Optics

Mysteries:

1.) Some satellite dishes are mesh-like rather than solid. Why don't the signals from the satellite simply pass through the holes?

2.) Some African tribesmen claim to be able to see the moons of Jupiter with the unaided eye. Is this possible?

𝕸𝖞𝖘𝖙𝖊𝖗𝖎𝖊𝖘:

3.) When you drive under an underpass or into a short tunnel while your AM radio is playing, you hear lots of static or a loss of the signal. Yet, you hear no such effect if you are playing FM radio. Why is this?

...coming to you loud and clear - KMMM-FM

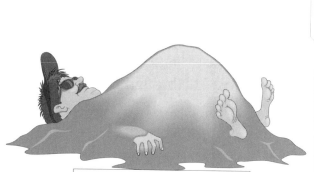

4.) Many people feel that they can not become sunburned on a cloudy day. Why *can* you be sunburned even if the sky is cloudy?

5.) Why do you feel the "heat" of the Sun through a window, yet you do not become sunburned?

Mysteries:

6.) Sonic booms are relatively common. How about "optical booms", that is, an *optical shock wave*?

Magic:

Wax paper

Crossed polarizers

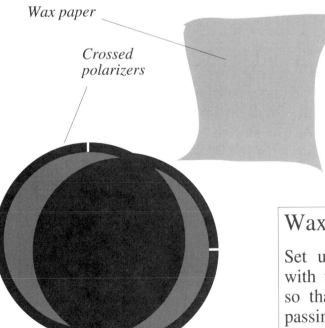

Wax Paper Polarization

Set up two polarizing filters with their axes perpendicular, so that light is blocked from passing through the pair. Now, insert a piece of wax paper between the filters. What happens?

Magic:

LCD Polarization

Look at a liquid crystal display (LCD) on a watch, gas station pump, or calculator through a polarizing filter. Rotate the filter—is the light from the display polarized?

What's Between the Slit and the Screen?

Set up a double-slit interference pattern by shining a laser or other monochromatic source of light through a double slit. Now, introduce chalk dust or smoke *between* the slit and the screen. What do you see?

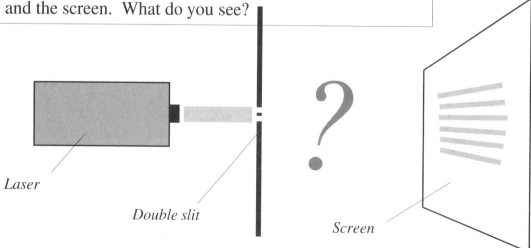

Laser

Double slit

Screen

𝔐𝔞𝔤𝔦𝔠:

Circle Interference

Print out a large number of concentric circles, using a drawing program on a computer, or by photocopying the circles below. Prepare one copy of the circles on paper and one on a transparency (or both on transparencies if you wish to display the result on an overhead projector). Now, place the transparency on top of the paper, with the centers slightly displaced.

𝕸𝖆𝖌𝖎𝖈:

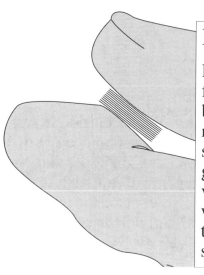

Finger Interference

Place your thumb and fore-finger very close together, but not touching. Look at a room light through the very small slit between these fingers, holding the fingers very close to your eye. You will see dark lines between the fingers, parallel to their surfaces.

𝕸𝖞𝖙𝖍:

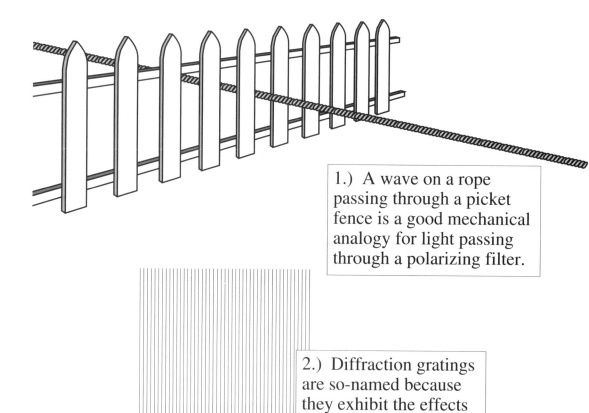

1.) A wave on a rope passing through a picket fence is a good mechanical analogy for light passing through a polarizing filter.

2.) Diffraction gratings are so-named because they exhibit the effects of diffraction.

Discussions; Chapter 16—Physical Optics

𝔐𝔶𝔰𝔱𝔢𝔯𝔦𝔢𝔰:

1.) Some satellite dishes are mesh-like rather than solid. Why don't the signals from the satellite simply pass through the holes?

This question is very similar to that in Mystery #1 of Chapter 25 in *PBWM*, which related to the failure of microwaves to leak out of the holes in the microwave oven door. As discussed there, a wave impinging on an object or an aperture that is much smaller than the wavelength of the wave will not be affected by the object or aperture. Thus, for radio waves, the holes in the meshlike antenna dish are very small, since radio wavelengths are typically measured in meters or even longer. The dish "looks" solid to the waves. Thus, it is advisable to build the antenna as a mesh, in order to reduce weight and expense, rather than as a solid piece of material.

2.) Some African tribesmen claim to be able to see the moons of Jupiter with the unaided eye. Is this possible?

There are two considerations that need to be addressed to respond to this Mystery:

- Do the orbits of Jupiter's moons subtend a large enough angle to be seen from Earth, based on human visual acuity?

- Can the individual moons of Jupiter be spatially resolved, given the diffraction which occurs as light enters the pupil of the eye?

To respond to the first consideration, let us calculate the angle subtended by the system of Jupiter and its moons. The four largest moons of Jupiter are Callisto, Europa, Ganymede and Io. Let us maximize the angle subtended by the system by choosing the two moons with the largest orbital radii, which also happen to be the two largest moons— Callisto, with a mean orbital radius of 1.88×10^9 m, and Ganymede, at 1.07×10^9 m. Thus, the maximum separation of these two moons, if they are on opposite sides of Jupiter, will be,

$$maximum\ separation = 1.88 \times 10^9 \text{ m} + 1.07 \times 10^9 \text{ m} = 2.95 \times 10^9 \text{ m}$$

We will also maximize the opportunity to see the moons by imagining that the observer is viewing them when Earth and Jupiter are as close together as possible. Thus, we assume that both planets are on the same side of the Sun, so that the distance between them is the difference in their orbital radii, choosing the minimum orbital radius for Jupiter and the maximum for Earth:

$$minimum\ distance\ between\ planets = 4.60 \times 10^{11} \text{ m} - 1.52 \times 10^{11} \text{ m} = 3.08 \times 10^{11} \text{ m}$$

Now, the angle subtended by the largest separation of the moons, in radians, is,

$$\theta = \frac{separation}{distance} = \frac{2.95 \times 10^9 \text{ m}}{3.08 \times 10^{11} \text{ m}} = 9.6 \times 10^{-3}$$

As discussed in Myth #8 of Chapter 27 in *PBWM*, the minimum angle for human visual acuity is about 3 x 10^{-4} radians. Thus, the angle subtended by the moons of Jupiter calculated above is larger than this minimum.

The second consideration involves the ability to resolve the separate sources of light as the light diffracts upon entering the pupil. This can be considered to be a test of the *Rayleigh criterion* for resolving closely spaced sources of light. If light from two sources passes through an aperture, each source will generate a diffraction pattern. For a circular aperture, the diffraction minima and maxima will be described by a *Bessel function*, which is a common mathematical function which appears in the solutions to problems with circular geometry. Using a Bessel function, it can be shown that the first minimum in the diffraction pattern is located at an angular position, given by,

$$\sin\theta = \frac{1.22\lambda}{a}$$

where *a* is the diameter of the circular aperture and 1.22 is a number related to the first zero of the Bessel function (as an analogy, 0.5π, in radians, is the first zero of the cosine function). The Rayleigh criterion for resolution of two sources is that the sources can *just be resolved* if the first minimum in the diffraction pattern of one source coincides with the maximum in the pattern of the second source. Since we generally apply this to objects that are very close together, the angle θ is small, so that we can approximate $\sin\theta$ as equal to θ, measured in radians. Thus, the Rayleigh criterion for resolution is that the angular separation between two light sources is that the angle must be larger than,

$$\theta = \frac{1.22\lambda}{a}$$

Now, let's determine the angular separation needed to resolve two light sources for which light passes through the *pupil of the eye*. We will estimate the pupil diameter at night as 7.0 mm and choose a wavelength of light in the middle of the visible range, say, 550 nm. Then, the limiting angle of resolution, in radians, is,

$$\theta = \frac{1.22\lambda}{a} = \frac{1.22\left(550\times10^{-9}\,\text{m}\right)}{7.0\times10^{-3}\,\text{m}} = 9.6\times10^{-5}$$

This is smaller than the angle subtended by Jupiter's moons calculated above. Thus, according to this criterion, the moons can be resolved, given the optimum conditions described above.

There are other considerations, however. For example, can the relatively dim moons be seen against the bright nearby sphere of Jupiter? When all considerations are included, many of which are approximate, the moons are close to the limit of vision and someone with *extremely sharp vision* may be able to just barely see the moons.

3.) When you drive under an underpass or into a short tunnel while your AM radio is playing, you hear lots of static or a loss of the signal. Yet, you hear no such effect if you are playing FM radio. Why is this?

Let us respond to this question by calculating typical wavelengths for AM and FM radio waves. Let us use typical midrange carrier frequencies of 1000 kHz for AM and 100 MHz for FM. We can calculate the wavelengths using the relationship between wavelength, frequency and velocity of propagation. The wavelengths associated with these carrier waves are as follows:

$$AM: \quad \lambda = \frac{c}{f} = \frac{3 \times 10^8 \, \text{m} \cdot \text{s}^{-1}}{1000 \times 10^3 \, \text{Hz}} = 300 \, \text{m}$$

$$FM: \quad \lambda = \frac{c}{f} = \frac{3 \times 10^8 \, \text{m} \cdot \text{s}^{-1}}{100 \times 10^6 \, \text{Hz}} = 3 \, \text{m}$$

If we consider a typical opening of a tunnel or an underpass as an aperture in the ground, we see that the opening is much smaller than AM radio wavelengths, but larger than FM wavelengths. Thus, the AM waves tend not to "see" the aperture, in the spirit of the discussion of Mystery #1, and will reflect off the ground around the opening. This results in the loss of signal as the automobile enters the opening. On the other hand, the FM waves are smaller than the aperture and will propagate into the opening or the tunnel easily. Thus, the FM signal remains strong.

4.) Many people feel that they can not become sunburned on a cloudy day. Why *can* you be sunburned even if the sky is cloudy?

Psychologically, one feels that he or she cannot become burned if the Sun cannot be seen or its warmth felt. But *seeing* the Sun depends on *visible* radiation, which is effectively blocked by clouds. *Feeling* the warmth of the sunlight on the skin is due mainly to infrared radiation, which is also effectively blocked by the clouds. Sunburn, however, is caused by *ultraviolet* radiation, to which the clouds are relatively transparent. Thus, the ultraviolet radiation can pass through the clouds and burn your skin. Individuals will often stay outdoors without sunblock or other protection longer on cloudy days, resulting in a nastier burn than on clear days.

5.) Why do you feel the "heat" of the Sun through a window, yet you do not become sunburned?

When sunlight shines through a window onto your skin, your skin feels warm. This is due to the fact that the glass is relatively transparent to the red and near infrared portion of the electromagnetic spectrum and your skin is particularly absorptive at these frequencies. Thus, a relatively large amount of energy is transmitted through the glass and absorbed by the skin, giving you the warm feeling. On the other hand, as mentioned in Mystery #4, sunburn is due to *ultraviolet* radiation. The window glass is relatively opaque to ultraviolet radiation. Thus, even though your skin feels warm, it will not become burned by the sunlight.

6.) Sonic booms are relatively common. How about "optical booms", that is, an *optical shock wave*?

A sonic boom occurs when an object moves as fast as the speed of sound waves in the medium through which it is traveling, as discussed in Mystery #3 in Chapter 11. The first response to the possibility of *optical booms* might be that these would be impossible, since no material object can travel with the speed of light. This response is true if we only consider motion of objects through a vacuum. But what about the motion of objects through a *material*? In this case, the speed of light is less than that in the vacuum, so that it is possible that an object could move through the material faster than the speed of light in that material.

This can occur for highly energetic electrons passing through a transparent material, such as water used for cooling nuclear reactors or in particle detectors. The result is called *Cerenkov radiation*. It was noticed by Marie Curie in 1910 in bottles of concentrated radium solutions. Experimental analysis and theoretical hypotheses did not occur until the late 1920's and early 1930's, including the work of P. A. Cerenkov, after whom the effect is named. It is often described as an electromagnetic shock wave that is emitted by the electron as it moves through the material. This is a little misleading, however, since the radiation does not actually come from the electron.

If we imagine an electron passing through a medium *with a uniform velocity*, it should not radiate. This is not a surprise for the constant velocity electron, but we also need to consider the effect on the *medium* as the electron passes by. The negatively charged electron will polarize the atoms of the medium, and attract the positive "end" of the polarized atom and repel the negative "end". This effect is shown below for an electron (black circle) moving slowly ($v < {}^{c}/_{n}$, where n is the index of refraction of the material) to the right.

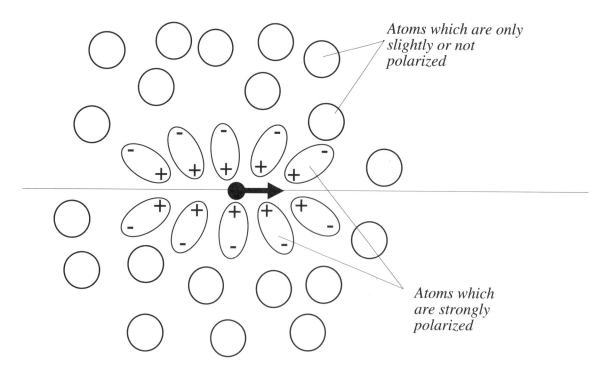

Atoms which are only slightly or not polarized

Atoms which are strongly polarized

In this situation, the disturbance in the polarized molecules is *symmetric* about the charge—the picture looks the same forward and backward and in all directions perpendicular to the direction of motion. There is no net polarization seen from a large distance from the electron. Due to this symmetry, *no energy is radiated* as the atoms become polarized, rotate as the charge passes, and lose their polarization.

Now, consider the situation with the electron moving very rapidly, so that $v > {}^c/_n$. Since the atoms can only receive the "signal" to become polarized at the speed of light (in the medium), the electron moves more rapidly through the material than does the disturbance in the polarization. Thus, the atoms ahead of the electron do not become polarized *until the electron is very close to them*, and the situation loses its forward-backward symmetry, as suggested in the diagram below.

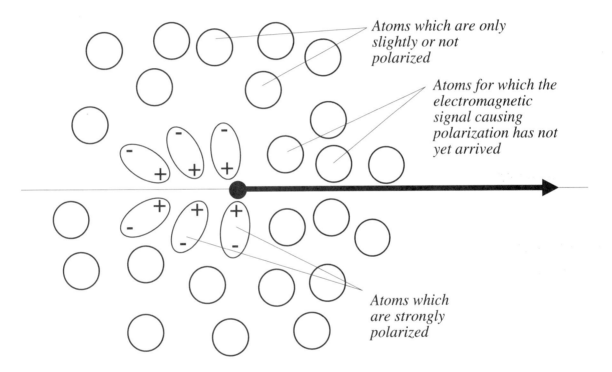

Atoms which are only
slightly or not
polarized

Atoms for which the
electromagnetic
signal causing
polarization has not
yet arrived

Atoms which
are strongly
polarized

Thus, the region around the electron now has a *net* polarization and the establishment and relaxation of this polarization as the electron passes results in radiation—Cerenkov radiation.

By using a Huygens wavelet construction, it can be shown that the radiation is emitted in a cone projected in the forward direction, at an angle θ (with respect to the velocity vector) given by,

$$\cos\theta = \frac{c}{nv}$$

where v is the particle velocity.

For a comprehensive discussion of many aspects of Cerenkov radiation, see J. Jelley, *Cerenkov Radiation and Its Applications*, Pergamon Press, New York, 1958.

Magic:

Wax Paper Polarization

This sounds very similar to a popular demonstration in which a third polarizer is inserted between two crossed polarizers, resulting in the transmission of light. The explanation is different, however, since wax paper is not a polarizer. In fact, the wax paper is acting as a *depolarizer*. When light scatters a number of times in a material, any initial polarization is lost, since the scatterings can be in any random direction. This was discussed in the Magic demonstration Polarization in the Streets in Chapter 28 of *PBWM*. In the wax paper demonstration, light from the first polarizer enters the wax paper and is scattered a number of times before exiting the paper. As a result, the initially polarized light going in to the paper comes out unpolarized. Thus, there is some light coming out of the wax paper which will be polarized along the axis of the second polarizer, which is oriented perpendicularly to that of the first polarizer. As a result, some light does come through the combination.

LCD Polarization

The operation of a liquid crystal display was discussed in Mystery #3 of Chapter 28 in *PBWM*. The polarization of light is important to this operation and *the light reflected from the display is polarized*. Thus, when the reflected light is viewed through a polarizing filter, there will be some orientations of the filter for which the view of the display will be blocked.

What's Between the Slit and the Screen?

A typical diagram describing the generation of a two-slit interference pattern is shown below. Rays from each of the two slits are drawn from the slits to a point on the screen. Geometrical arguments are then made to generate an expression for the difference in path length as function of the angle θ. If the path length difference is an integral number of wavelengths, there will be constructive interference at the point on the screen. If the difference is an odd integral number of half wavelengths, we will have destructive interference.

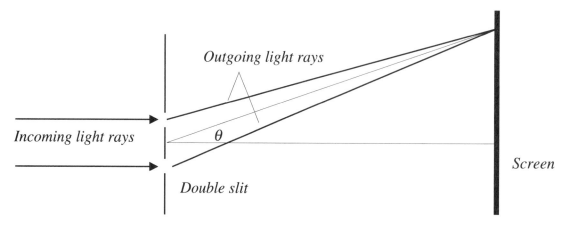

This diagram implies that *the interference does not take place until the light rays combine at the screen.* This would suggest that there is no effect of interference *between* the slit and the screen. If the activity is performed, however, it is clear that there *are* regions of light and dark extending all the way from the slit to the screen, as suggested in the diagram below.

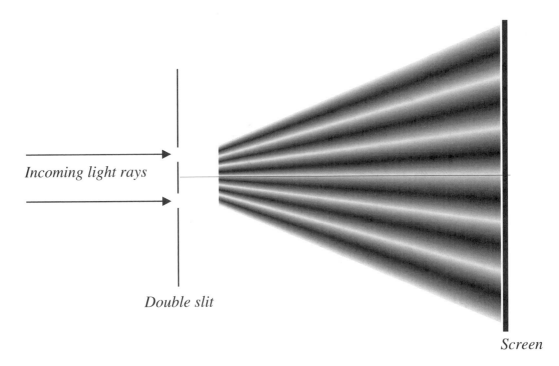

Incoming light rays

Double slit

Screen

The geometrical argument above is purely a ray argument and does not reflect the wave nature of light. This is why it predicts the incorrect result in this activity. If we include the wave nature of light, we would imagine each slit being a source of spherical wavefronts, according to Huygens' Principle. Then, the waves from the two slits would interfere *everywhere* to the right of the slits in the diagram above. This would give a construction showing lines of constructive and destructive interference, similar to the standard picture of interference from two sources in a ripple tank. This type of pattern is simulated by a pair of sets of concentric circles as seen in the results of the next Magic demonstration, Circle Interference.

The diagram above indicates only the interference maxima and minima from the double slit. In addition, when the demonstration is performed, you will also be able to observe the superimposed *diffraction* minima from each slit as broad regions of darkness in the pattern.

Circle Interference

The circles will represent the circular wavefronts from a wave source emitting in all directions. When two such arrays of circles are overlaid with a slight displacement, the combination is analogous to two wave sources slightly displaced, and an interference pattern should develop. We can see the interference pattern in the overlaid display shown below, with the centers displaced vertically. If we imagine that the white portions of the circles are crests, with the dark areas being troughs, then we see bright regions coming from the pair of sources, representing constructive interference between wave crests. Notice that the areas in the horizontal directions from the two sources are bright, representing the zeroth order constructive interference. Between the bright areas are darker regions, where crests and troughs are combining to produce destructive interference.

Compare this diagram to that in the previous Magic demonstration, What's Between the Slit and the Screen?, as there is a strong link between the two.

Finger Interference

The space between the fingers acts as an aperture for the light passing through. If the fingers are very close but not touching, the aperture approximates a *single slit*. As a result, you see an interference pattern of light and dark bands when the fingers are close enough together.

𝕸𝖞𝖙𝖍:

1.) A wave on a rope passing through a picket fence is a good mechanical analogy for light passing through a polarizing filter.

This can be a valuable analogy for conveying the spirit of the action of a polarizing filter. The picket fence contains long *boards*, lined up parallel to each other in a certain direction. The polarizing filter contains long *molecules*, lined up parallel to each other in a certain direction. It should be kept in mind, however, that the analogy is not perfect. A picket fence passes rope waves that are polarized in the *same* direction as the boards. A polarizing filter, however, passes electromagnetic waves whose electric field vectors are polarized *perpendicularly* to the stretched molecules in the filter. For more information on the processes occurring in polarizing filters, see the Concepts section of Chapter 28 in *PBWM*.

2.) Diffraction gratings are so-named because they exhibit the effects of diffraction.

A diffraction grating is a series of slits through which light passes and forms a pattern of maxima and minima on a distant screen. While diffraction is important for explaining why light traveling toward the slits spreads out after passing through the slits (which occurs for a single slit, too), it is the phenomenon of *interference* which produces the pattern of maxima and minima. Thus, it should more properly be called an *interference grating*.

Chapter 17
Early Modern Physics

𝕸ysteries:

1.) Why does your electric stove burner glow red?

2.) Why are pupils black?

Mysteries:

3.) Energy takes 8 minutes to reach the Earth (by the transfer mechanism of electromagnetic radiation) from the surface of the Sun. How long does the energy take to travel from the *center* of the Sun to the *surface*?

4.) Why do clear winter nights seem colder than cloudy nights?

Mysteries:

5.) Why does velvet look so black?

6.) When nuclear explosions take place high in the atmosphere, an *electromagnetic pulse* is generated, which can knock out communications and other electrical circuits on the surface. What is the origin of this pulse?

7.) Why are *pockets* of coals in the glowing embers from a fire so bright compared to the coals themselves?

𝔐𝔞𝔤𝔦𝔠:

The Razorblade Blackbody

A good approximation to a blackbody can be made by stacking 50 to 100 double edge razor blades on top of each other. They can be held together with bolts through the holes in the center. Looking into the edges will result in a sensation of blackness that is quite surprising.

WARNING - Razor blades are very sharp!

The Filament Spectrum

This activity uses a showcase light bulb, which is cylindrical in shape, has a clear glass envelope and whose filament is linear and several centimeters in length. These types of bulbs are used in music stand lights, picture frame lights and showcases. Turn on such a light bulb in a lamp connected to a variable rheostat. With the rheostat set at a very low voltage, view the light bulb through a diffraction grating. As the voltage is turned up, note how the display through the diffraction grating changes.

𝕸𝖆𝖌𝖎𝖈:

Coffee Can Blackbody

Obtain a coffee can, or mixed nut can, with a plastic lid. Paint the top of the lid with a dull black paint. Now place the lid on the can and poke a small hole in the lid with a pin, tack or nail. Notice the difference between the blackness of the hole and that of the paint.

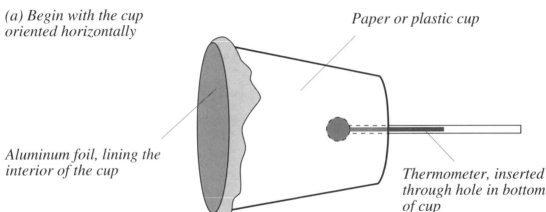

(a) Begin with the cup oriented horizontally

Paper or plastic cup

Aluminum foil, lining the interior of the cup

Thermometer, inserted through hole in bottom of cup

The Paper Cup Infrared Detector

Line a paper or plastic cup with aluminum foil. Poke a hole through the bottom and insert the bulb end of a weather thermometer or, better yet, a thermocouple attached to a digital temperature measuring device. Take the apparatus outside on a *clear* night, hold the axis of the cup in a horizontal orientation, as in diagram (*a*), and let it come to thermal equilibrium with the night air. Record the temperature. Now, point the cup opening toward the sky (*b*) and take another reading. Turn the cup over and point the opening at the ground (*c*). Take a final reading. How do the three temperature readings compare?

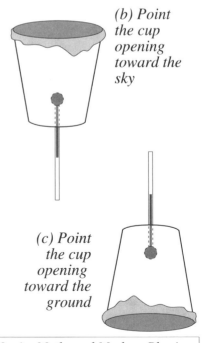

(b) Point the cup opening toward the sky

(c) Point the cup opening toward the ground

𝕸𝖞𝖙𝖍:

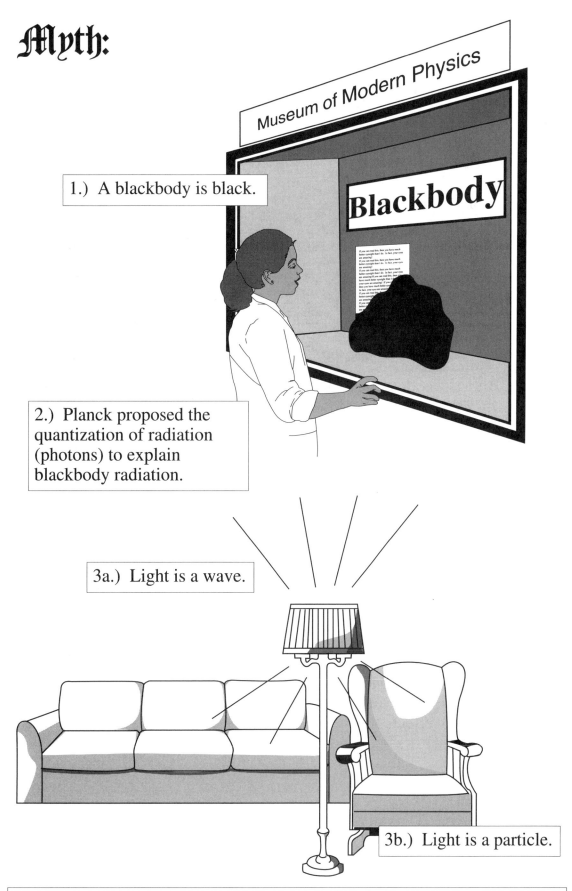

Museum of Modern Physics

1.) A blackbody is black.

Blackbody

2.) Planck proposed the quantization of radiation (photons) to explain blackbody radiation.

3a.) Light is a wave.

3b.) Light is a particle.

𝕸𝖞𝖙𝖍:

4.) Blue is a cool color.

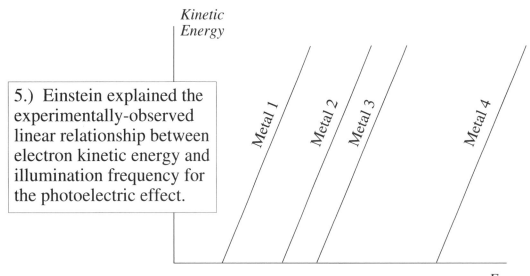

Kinetic
Energy

5.) Einstein explained the experimentally-observed linear relationship between electron kinetic energy and illumination frequency for the photoelectric effect.

Metal 1

Metal 2

Metal 3

Metal 4

Frequency

Concepts of Early Modern Physics*

In the latter part of the nineteenth century, there were several phenomena which could not be adequately explained by means of classical physics. In addition, the last few years of the century brought new discoveries which would require new ideas in physics for their explanation—X-rays, radioactivity, and the electron, for example. One of the phenomena which resisted classical attempts at explanation was that of *thermal radiation*, or *blackbody radiation*. It was well known that electromagnetic radiation was emitted by an object with a non-zero temperature and that the character of the radiation varied with temperature. An idealized radi-

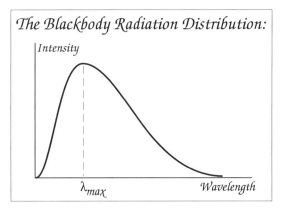

The Blackbody Radiation Distribution:

ating body is described as a perfect absorber of radiation, leading to the name of a *blackbody*. In order to maintain thermal equilibrium, this object will continuously emit radiation at the same rate that it receives radiation. The emitted radiation will exhibit a certain distribution among wavelengths. A typical distribution of emitted wavelengths is shown in the diagram above.

The variation of the emission with temperature is described by two laws. The first is the *Stefan-Boltzmann Law*, which expresses the behavior that the total power (*P*) of radiation emitted for an *ideal* blackbody varies as the fourth power of the Kelvin temperature (*T*):

> *The total power of emitted radiation increases rapidly with temperature.*

$$P = \sigma A T^4$$

In this expression, *A* is the surface area of the emitter and σ is the *Stefan-Boltzmann constant* ($\sigma = 5.67 \times 10^{-8}$ W·m^{-2}·K^{-4}). For real objects, the above expression has an additional factor, ε, the *emissivity* of the surface, which also may be a function of temperature. The emissivity of a blackbody is 1, while the emissivities of real objects are less than 1.

> *The peak in the wavelength distribution moves toward shorter wavelengths as the temperature increases.*

The second description of blackbody behavior is given by *Wien's Law*, which indicates that the wavelength at the peak in the distribution (λ_{max}) varies inversely as the Kelvin temperature (*T*):

$$\lambda_{max} T = 2.9 \times 10^{-3} \text{ m·K}$$

The peak for room temperature objects is in the far infrared region of the spectrum and moves toward the visible with increasing temperature.

---

*As noted in the Preface, the chapters on *modern physics* in this book will include a Concepts section. The concepts related to *classical physics* have been discussed in the Concepts section in each chapter of PBWM.

Concepts of Early Modern Physics (continued)

Classical attempts to describe the shape of the wavelength distribution and these temperature behaviors were unsuccessful. It was not until 1900 that Max Planck developed a proposal which led to a successful match between theory and the experimental distribution curve. This proposal was based, however, on a controversial assumption that the oscillating sources of the radiation within the blackbody could only emit energy in amounts proportional to their oscillation frequency, *f*, as follows:

$$E = hf$$

where *h* is *Planck's constant*:

$$h = 6.63 \times 10^{-34} \text{ J·s} = 4.14 \times 10^{-15} \text{ eV·s}$$

The quantization of energy was a radical break from physics tradition, but was given further credence in 1905 when Einstein extended the idea to explain another phenomenon which resisted classical attempts—the *photoelectric effect*. In this phenomenon, electrons are ejected from a clean metal surface when the surface is irradiated with light of an appropriate frequency. The classical theory describes the electrons as absorbing energy continuously from the incoming electromagnetic waves until an electron has absorbed enough energy to break free from the metal. This explanation would predict the following behavior:

1.) In very dim light, there would be a significant time delay between onset of the light and ejection of electrons.

2.) The kinetic energy of the ejected electrons would increase as the intensity of the light increases.

3.) The kinetic energy of the ejected electrons would have no dependence on the frequency of the light.

In reality, the experimental results show exactly the *opposite* of *all three* of these behaviors; there is *no time delay*, and the kinetic energy depends on the *frequency*

> *The photoelectric effect is a one photon – one electron interaction.*

and not on the *intensity*. Einstein's insight was to describe the radiation as being quantized, with packets of energy given by the same expression as Planck's: *E = hf*. We now call these packets of energy *photons*. The photoelectric effect, then, is a one photon–one electron interaction. If the frequency is high enough, the photon has enough energy to eject the electron. Any surplus energy over that needed to break the electron free from the metal appears as kinetic energy. We can generate from the energy continuity equation (see Chapter 7 in *PBWM* and Chapter 5 in this book) the same equation that Einstein proposed. If we imagine the system of one electron and the metal in

Concepts of Early Modern Physics (continued)

which it resides, the energy transferred into the system by electromagnetic radiation (the photon) is stored as increased electrical potential energy of the system and kinetic energy of the electron. Thus,

$$\Delta KE \ + \ \Delta PE \ + \ \Delta U \ = \ W \ + \ Q \ + \ E_{MT} \ + \ E_S \ + \ E_{ER} \ + \ E_{ET}$$

The amount by which the kinetic energy of the system increases is the kinetic energy of the ejected electron. We assume that the electron leaves with no additional scattering, so that it has the maximum kinetic energy that it can have. The amount by which the potential energy of the system is increased is called the *work function*, which is often given the symbol ϕ. The energy transferred into the system by electromagnetic radiation is the energy of one photon. Thus, our continuity equation becomes,

$$KE_{max} \ + \ \phi \ = \ hf$$

which is just the equation generated by Einstein.

The concept of *particles* of light was hard for physicists to swallow. One test of this idea was *Compton scattering*. While visible light will only penetrate slightly into the surface of a metal, X-rays are able to penetrate deeply into the metal.

> *The Compton Effect shows photons "bouncing" off electrons like billiard balls.*

Thus, we can imagine an X-ray photon interacting with a free electron in the metal, scattering through some angle, and leaving the metal. If the light actually is behaving as a particle, then we should be able to apply conservation of momentum and energy to the scattering event and predict the energy (and, therefore, the frequency and the wavelength) of the scattered photon as a function of the scattering angle. Compton reported on the results of this experiment in 1923, and found that there was excellent agreement between experiment and theory, giving strong additional evidence for the particle nature of light.

In 1924, deBroglie published a Ph.D. thesis in which he proposed that, if light behaves as a particle, then particles of matter should also behave as waves. Following from the relationship between the wavelength and momentum of a photon, the *deBroglie wavelength* of a particle is given by:

$$\lambda = \frac{h}{p}$$

where p is the momentum of the particle. This wavelike character of a particle was quickly verified in the experiments of Davisson and Germer, who observed the *diffraction* of *electrons* in a nickel crystal.

Discussions; Chapter 17—Early Modern Physics

𝔐𝔶𝔰𝔱𝔢𝔯𝔦𝔢𝔰:

1.) Why does your electric stove burner glow red?

This is a nice home demonstration of thermal radiation. At room temperature, the burner is emitting a small amount of radiation, which peaks in the infrared. Thus, it does not appear to be glowing to our eyes. When its temperature is increased, more radiation is emitted (according to the Stefan-Boltzmann Law) and the peak of the radiation moves toward the visible (according to the Wien Law). The graph below shows this behavior. The dotted lines indicate the extent of the visible range of wavelengths in air. Notice that, for the curve representing the hot burner, much more radiation is emitted at the red end of the visible spectrum than at the violet end. The result is that the burner appears red—"red hot".

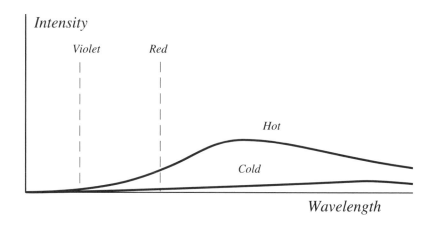

If we imagined a stove with an unlimited supply of input power, we could increase the temperature of the burner even higher. As the temperature reaches a high enough value so that the peak of the curve enters the visible range (we ignore the inevitable *melting* of the burner!), the burner would appear "white hot". For further increases in temperature, the burner would begin to look "blue hot". See Myth #4 in this Chapter for more discussion of these ideas.

2.) Why are pupils black?

This is an example of a popular model for a blackbody—a small hole leading into a cavity in a piece of material. This model was used in theoretical analyses of the blackbody theory, since the hole acts as an almost perfect absorber—light entering the hole bounces around, reflecting off the interior walls of the cavity and has little probability of "finding" the hole again. That light which does leave the hole is in thermal equilibrium with the walls of the cavity. Thus, this *cavity radiation* is treated as a model for blackbody radiation.

Now, the pupil is a *relatively small hole leading into a larger cavity*. Light entering the pupil tends to be absorbed by the retina, resulting in vision. Some light may reflect off the retina but will likely be absorbed by some other part of the retina. The retina is also emitting radiation, but this radiation is representative of the temperature of the retina and is thus peaked in the infrared. As a result, the eyes of someone looking at someone else's pupils are not sensitive to the radiation being emitted and the pupils appear black.

3.) Energy takes 8 minutes to reach the Earth (by the transfer mechanism of electromagnetic radiation) from the surface of the Sun. How long does the energy take to travel from the *center* of the Sun to the *surface*?

Surprisingly, the energy takes some *10 million years* to travel from the center to the surface! Much of this time is spent near the center, where the temperature and density of material are both extremely high. The energy transformed by the nuclear fusion reactions occurring in the solar core is transferred in the form of gamma ray photons. Because of the high density of material in the solar core, these photons travel, on the average, only a fraction of a centimeter before undergoing a scattering event. The scattering events are *Compton scatterings*, from electrons, protons and a few slightly heavier atomic nuclei. Due to the large number of scattering events, the motion of the photons is random, with many of them going toward the center of the Sun as well as away from it. There is a temperature gradient (although the temperature change is <u>very small</u> over the mean free path of a photon), with the temperature decreasing as one moves away from the center. As a result, there is a net flow of energy away from the center. Due to the extremely large number of scattering events, however, this migration is very, very slow, resulting in the large amount of time mentioned in the opening sentence.

At some distance from the center of the Sun, the temperature will be low enough for electrons and nuclei to remain bound together as atoms. At a level where the temperature is low enough for atoms to exist, the solar material becomes *opaque*—the photons will be absorbed by the atoms. Now, the photons experience a continuous cycle of absorption and re-emission from these atoms. If it were not for another transport mechanism, the energy might be stopped at this point. The new transport mechanism is *convection*. In the region where the opacity of the solar material begins, the energy transfer rate (by the mechanism of electromagnetic radiation) drops rapidly. Thus, energy does not reach the higher layers by this process and the temperature drops faster with radial distance than it did in the lower layers. As a result, we have hot gas closer to the center of the Sun than the cooler outer layers of gas. We now invoke Archimedes' Principle, and realize that there will be a buoyant force on the hot gas, which will cause it to "float" upward to the surface. Thus, this convective process replaces the radiation process that dominated in the interior layers. As a result, we delineate a *convection zone*, representing the upper 20% of the Sun's interior, as opposed to the *radiative zone*, which occupies most of the interior.

At the top of the convective zone, the hot gases radiate the energy away for its journey into space. Some of these photons will arrive at Earth eight minutes later.

For discussions and activities related to Compton scattering, see J. V. Kinderman, "Investigating the Compton Effect with a Spreadsheet", *The Physics Teacher*, **30**, 426, 1992 and D. Wilkins, "A New Angle on Compton Scattering", *American Journal of Physics*, **60**, 221, 1992. For more information on the internal structure of the Sun, see R. W. Noyes, *The Sun, Our Star*, Harvard University Press, Cambridge, 1982 and K. J. H. Phillips, *Guide to the Sun*, Cambridge University Press, Cambridge, 1992.

4.) Why do clear winter nights seem colder than cloudy nights?

If the sky is clear of clouds, then a significant amount of radiation can transmit through the atmosphere into outer space. Thus, the ground can cool off by this emission of radiation. If there are clouds in the sky, these clouds can absorb radiation emitted by the ground and re-radiate it, both upward into space and downward, back into the ground. Thus, in this case, the ground has an energy input that it did not have in the clear-sky case. As a result, the ground does not cool off as quickly and the cloudy night seems to be warmer than the clear night.

Sometimes, farmers may use *smudgepots* to create artificial clouds to keep their orchards warm, as discussed in Myth #2 in Chapter 25 of *PBWM*.

5.) Why does velvet look so black?

The surface of velvet is covered with short threads, oriented perpendicularly to the surface. These threads are relatively reflective, as can be seen by bending the fabric and noticing the sheen when light reflects from the sides of the threads. As light strikes the threads on an unbent piece of cloth, however, it is reflected deeper and deeper into the thickness of the velvet. There is no surface oriented so as to reflect the light back out. Thus, the velvet appears very black, since it tends to absorb almost all of the light incident upon it. For a Magic demonstration of this effect using razor blades, see The Razorblade Blackbody, in this chapter.

6.) When nuclear explosions take place high in the atmosphere, an *electromagnetic pulse* is generated, which can knock out communications and other electrical circuits on the surface. What is the origin of this pulse?

A nuclear explosion generates a <u>tremendous</u> number of gamma and X-ray photons. These photons undergo a large number of Compton scattering events with electrons in the atmosphere, resulting in many of the electrons being forced violently in a direction away from the explosion. This sudden, organized movement of charge establishes a large electromagnetic disturbance—the electromagnetic pulse. The strength of this pulse is such that unshielded electrical circuits can act as antennae and absorb enough energy from the pulse to disrupt the operation of the circuit or even "burn out" components in the circuit.

7.) Why are *pockets* of coals in the glowing embers from a fire so bright compared to the coals themselves?

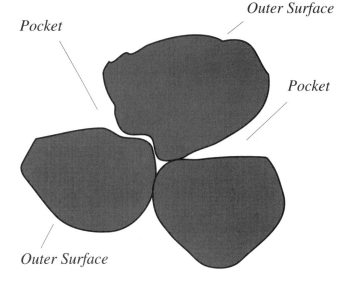

Pocket

Outer Surface

Pocket

Outer Surface

In a pile of burning material, there will be regions that are directed away from the other coals, which are indicated as *outer surfaces* in the diagram to the right. In addition, there will be regions "between" coals that we identify as *pockets*.

Radiation emitted from the outer surfaces will leave the burning pile and be absorbed in the environment. Some of the radiation emitted by surfaces in the pockets, however, will be incident on the neighboring coal *and be re-absorbed*. As a result, at a given time, there will be more energy in the pockets than in the outer surfaces. As a result, the pockets will stay warmer for a longer time and will glow more brightly than the outer surfaces.

𝕸agic:

The Razorblade Blackbody

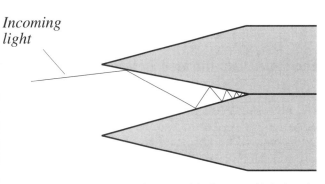

Incoming light

The diagram at the right shows an expanded view of the region between two blades. As light enters, it reflects off the edges, but there is no surface at an orientation that would reflect the light back out again. Thus, the light just keeps reflecting further into the pile of razor blades, until it is absorbed. Now, this absorption will raise the temperature of the blades, so that they will emit light, but the emitted light will be characteristic of an object at, or just slightly above, room temperature; it will be primarily in the infrared, to which our eyes are not sensitive. Thus, the pile of razor blades will provide no visible light and, it will appear extremely black. For a related effect with velvet cloth, see Mystery #5 in this Chapter.

The Filament Spectrum

This demonstration shows the behavior of thermal radiation as described by both the Stefan-Boltzmann Law and Wien's Law. At low voltages, at which the filament of the light bulb is barely visible, it is clear that very little power is being emitted, at least in the visible. In addition, the view through the diffraction grating will show little or no visible radiation at the violet end of the spectrum, but easily visible radiation from green to red.

When the voltage is increased to its highest value, two effects occur. First, the amount of radiation emitted in the visible increases dramatically, giving an indication of the increase in power described by the Stefan-Boltzmann Law, since the temperature of the filament is rising. Secondly, radiation at the blue-violet end of the spectrum becomes visible and challenges the other colors in its brightness, demonstrating the shift in peak wavelength described by Wien's Law. It is instructive to perform this rise in voltage again without looking through the diffraction grating and notice the shift in color of the filament from reddish-orange to yellowish-white, again a result of Wien's Law.

For information on the relationship between the color of a light bulb filament and its temperature, see W. S. Wagner, "Temperature and Color of Incandescent Lamps", *The Physics Teacher*, **29**, 176, 1991. For a technique to make the filament spectrum visible for large numbers of students, see R. Ebert, "Adapting Some Demonstrations for a Large Class", *The Physics Teacher*, **30**, 239, 1992.

Coffee Can Blackbody

Even though the top of the lid is painted black, and the inside of the can is very reflective, the hole will appear darker than the painted lid. The hole in the lid is acting as an approximation to the cavity model of a blackbody, as described in the discussion of Mystery #2. The light that leaves the hole is in thermal equilibrium with the inner surface of the can. Since that surface is at room temperature, the emitted light is in the far infrared and not visible to the human eye.

The Paper Cup Infrared Detector

The aluminum foil-lined cup will collect infrared radiation and reflect it around the inside of the cup, so that some will be absorbed by the thermometer. In addition, some radiation will be absorbed by the aluminum foil, slightly raising the temperature of the foil and, as a result, the air in the cup. The combination of both effects will result in a small, but measurable temperature rise on the thermometer. When the cup is aimed at the clear night sky, there is very little radiation to be collected, as discussed in Myth #5 in Chapter 14 in *PBWM*. Thus, the net flow of energy is *out of the cup* into the clear sky, the cup will cool off, and the temperature reading will drop. When the cup is aimed at the ground, it will collect infrared radiation leaving the ground toward space, and the temperature reading will rise.

𝕸𝖞𝖙𝖍:

1.) A blackbody is black.

The indication of blackness in the name *blackbody* refers to the blackbody's behavior as a perfect absorber. We think of an object which absorbs all incident light as appearing black. If the object is at room temperature, this is indeed true—the amount of emitted radiation is too little, and most of it is in the infrared, for us to perceive any visible radiation. At higher temperatures, however, a blackbody would not be black; it could appear in a variety of colors, depending on its temperature. It could even appear to be white, if the peak of the radiation occurs in the middle of the visible range of frequencies.

2.) Planck proposed the quantization of radiation (photons) to explain blackbody radiation.

Although both Einstein and Planck appealed to the same equation ($E = hf$) to explain two different phenomena (the photoelectric effect and blackbody radiation, respectively), there is a subtle difference in their interpretation. Planck proposed that the <u>oscillators</u> which were the source of the radiation were quantized so that they could only emit packets of energy given by multiples of $E = hf$. It was Einstein who initiated the concept that, regardless of the source of the radiation, the radiation <u>itself</u> is quantized. Thus, according to Einstein, the particle nature of radiation is an inherent property of electromagnetic radiation and is not imposed on the radiation by the source.

3a.) Light is a wave.
3b.) Light is a particle.

These statements need to be looked at in the spirit of Mystery #1 in Chapter 1. In the discussion of that Mystery, it was made clear that we do not know what mass, time, space and/or electric charge *are*. We only can make statements about how we perceive them to *behave*. Similarly, we cannot make a statement about what light *is*. We have a *model* of light as a combination of electric and magnetic fields which describes some of its behavior. We also have a model of light in terms of photons, which explains other facets of its behavior. Thus, the best statements we can make of this sort are as follows:

> Light *sometimes behaves as* a wave.
> Light *sometimes behaves as* a particle.

This dual behavior of light (and other entities) is referred to as the *wave-particle duality*, which will be discussed in Chapter 18.

4.) Blue is a cool color.

The statement in this Myth would appear appropriate when viewing a cool pool of water in a desert oasis or in a book on *art*. In painting, for example, blue often represents coolness—cool water in the ocean, for example. But what about a blue <u>star</u>? If a star appears blue, then the blackbody radiation curve must exhib-

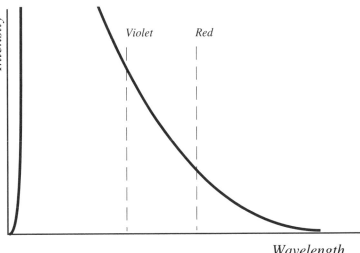

it much more radiation from the violet end of the spectrum than from the red end. In order to have this situation, the peak of the curve must be <u>below</u> the visible range, as shown in the diagram on the previous page (the peak is not shown as it is very far above the portion of the graph shown in the diagram).

According to Wien's Law, then, we must have a very high temperature for the peak to be in this region of the graph. Thus, a blue star represents a *very hot* star. In fact, blue stars are the hottest stars, with surface temperatures in the range of 30,000 K to 60,000 K, giving peak wavelengths of 48 nm to 97 nm, which lie in the extreme ultraviolet region of the electromagnetic spectrum.

5.) Einstein explained the experimentally-observed linear relationship between electron kinetic energy and illumination frequency for the photoelectric effect.

Although some textbooks imply that this is the case, the linear relationship between the kinetic energy (or, equivalently, the *stopping potential*—the retarding potential difference needed to turn back the most energetic electron) and the frequency *had not been observed in early photoelectric effect experiments*. Einstein's theoretical analysis was based on the experiments of Lenard (P. Lenard, *Annal der Physik*, **8**, 149, 1902). These experiments produced graphs of the photocurrent as a function of the voltage across the phototube. A typical graph from Lenard's results appears in the diagram to the right.

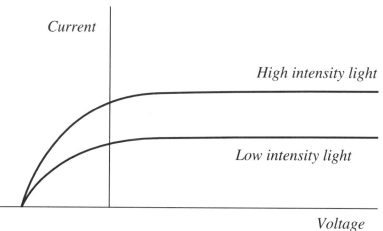

This graph shows that a higher intensity light shining on the metal results in more current, which is consistent with classical physics. The more intriguing result of Lenard's work is the indication that the negative voltage necessary to reduce the current to zero is independent of the intensity of the light. This is inconsistent with the classical physics point of view and requires the quantum approach for its explanation.

From his concept of the quantum of light, Einstein *predicted* that a graph of electron kinetic energy vs. frequency would have the shape of a straight line. Experimental verification of this prediction came later with the work of O. W. Richardson and K. T. Compton, "The Photoelectric Effect", *Phil. Mag. Series 6*, **24**, 575, 1912; A. L. Hughes, "On the Emission Velocities of Photo-electrons", *Phil. Trans. Roy. Soc. London, Series A*, **212**, 205, 1913; and R. A. Millikan, "A Direct Photoelectric Determination of Planck's Constant '*h*' ", *Phys. Rev.*, **7**, 355, 1916.

Chapter 18
Modern Quantum Theory

Mysteries:

$$\Delta x\, \Delta p_x \;\geq\; \left\{ \begin{array}{cc} h & ? \\[8pt] \hbar & ? \\[8pt] \dfrac{\hbar}{2} & ? \end{array} \right.$$

1.) The uncertainty principle appears in various texts with different right hand sides, as suggested in the accompanying diagram. Why is the right hand side of the uncertainty principle so *uncertain*?

2.) Why is it so difficult to locate the freezing point of helium in a table?

3.) What are the *units* of the wave function?

𝔐𝔞𝔤𝔦𝔠:

Nitrogen Bands

Compare the view through a diffraction grating of two spectrum tube sources—hydrogen in one and nitrogen in the second. Why is there a difference?

Hydrogen:

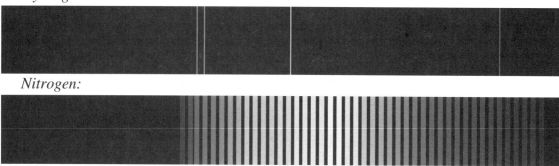

Nitrogen:

𝔐𝔶𝔱𝔥:

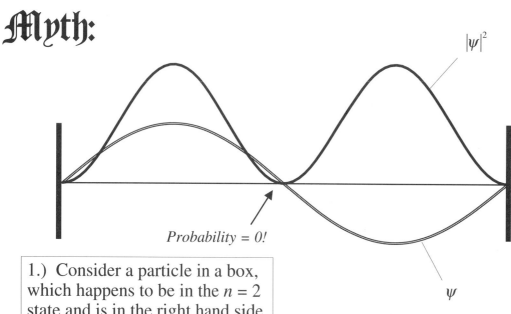

$|\psi|^2$

Probability = 0!

ψ

1.) Consider a particle in a box, which happens to be in the $n = 2$ state and is in the right hand side of the box. Since it has zero probability of being at the exact center of the box, it cannot pass through this point. Therefore, it can never be in the left side of the box.

𝔐𝔶𝔱𝔥:

What's going on here?
You can't be here!

Hey, You—outta here!

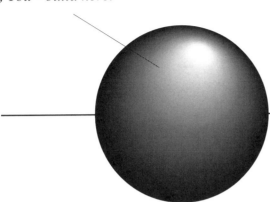

2.) The Pauli Exclusion Principle is:

"No two electrons in an atom can have the same four quantum numbers."

3.) The uncertainty principle has the following essence with regard to the two variables appearing in the expression (position-momentum; time-energy, etc.): The more accurately we determine the value of one variable, the more we *disturb* the other variable.

$$\Delta x \Delta p_x$$

$$\Delta x_{\Delta p_x}$$

4.) Quantization is only a microscopic phenomenon—we don't see it in everyday life.

𝔐𝔶𝔱𝔥:

5.) Conservation of energy is an absolute principle and cannot be violated.

E = constant

National Debt

6.) A quantum leap is a very large change.

7.) It is a fundamental principle that quantum systems tend toward lower energy.

Concepts of Modern Quantum Theory

In the previous chapter, we considered some of the phenomena that were investigated in the early years of the twentieth century. The models that seem to correctly describe these phenomena are based on the ideas that radiation has a particulate nature and, conversely, that particles have a wavelike character. This has been described as the *wave-particle duality*. The possession of two radically different types of properties for a given entity is a little disturbing. It is tempting to ask if

> *Wave-Particle Duality:*
>
> *Waves exhibit particle-like properties.*
>
> *Particles exhibit wave-like properties.*

one of the two descriptions, wave or particle, is more fundamental. As it turns out, we can develop a model in which the wave is the fundamental concept and the particle can then be built from waves. The essence of a particle is that it is a *localized entity*—its extent in space is very small. A pure wave, on the other hand, is infinitely long, assuming that "pure" means one single frequency. If we impose a beginning and an end to a wave, either in space or in time, we necessarily introduce an uncertainty in the frequency*.

Let us imagine that we begin with a single pure wave (*Wave 1*) as discussed above, that is infinitely long and, therefore, has *no sense of localization*. Now, we add to this wave another, of slightly different frequency (*Wave 2*). The result will be the familiar phenomenon we call *beats* when the waves are acoustical. The two waves and the result of their superposition are shown below:

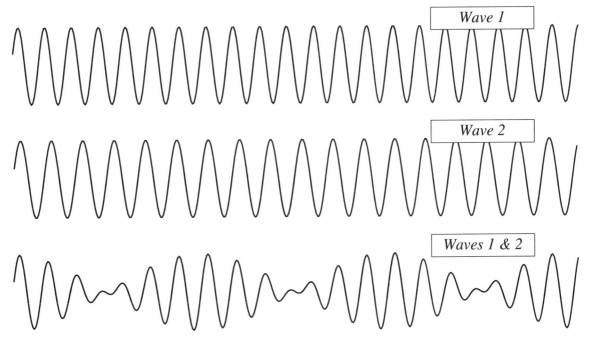

Wave 1

Wave 2

Waves 1 & 2

---

*This idea was explored in Mystery #3 of Chapter 17 in *PBWM*. In this Mystery, it was argued that modulating a pure wave at a certain frequency introduced discrete new frequencies. Restricting a pure wave to a limited region of space or time is a severe form of "modulation" that results in a continuous spread of frequencies.

Concepts of Modern Quantum Theory (continued)

Notice that there is now a *differentiation* among various points in space; in some places, the combined amplitude is large and, in other places, it is small. This is a first step toward *localization*—some regions of space are different than others. A pure wave has absolutely no localization—it is the same everywhere. A particle is an extreme example of localization—the region of space near the particle is very different (due to its electric charge, mass, spin, etc.) than regions very far away. Can we combine waves in a way that such extreme localization occurs? The answer turns out to be <u>yes</u>. Suppose we combine a *very large number* of waves, of *a wide range of frequencies*. We carefully choose their phases such that *one of each wave's crests occurs at a chosen point in space*. We can show mathematically that the waves then cancel everywhere in space except near the chosen point, where the wave crests add. Thus, we have combined waves of infinite extent and formed a localized entity—a *particle*! This model of a particle is called a *wave packet* and demonstrates to us how a localized entity such as a particle could have wave-like characteristics—it is *built* from waves! The result of this combination might appear as shown below (in one dimension):

> *One model of a particle is a <u>wave packet</u>.*

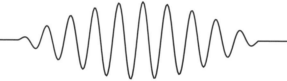

The model provides the localization necessary for our interpretation of a particle, but does not explain how the wave packet achieves such properties as mass, charge, spin, etc. This is still a subject of research.

This model leads us to a conceptual understanding of the Heisenberg Uncertainty Principle. Mathematically, this principle states the following:

$$\Delta x \Delta p_x \geq \frac{\hbar}{2}$$

where $\hbar$ is Planck's constant divided by 2π—a combination which occurs often in quantum physics. In words, this principle states that the product of the uncertainties in position and momentum of a particle is always larger than a certain minimum. As a result, this requires that, if we gain information about position* (and thereby reduce the uncertainty), we must have less information (implying larger uncertainty) about momentum, and

> *The Heisenberg Uncertainty Principle—if we insist on a particle model, we can't know everything about the particle.*

---

*In some sense, the uncertainty principle is a commentary on humankind's unwillingness to give up on such a comfortable notion as a *particle*. If we abandon the concept of a zero-size entity existing at a <u>single</u> point in space, then we no longer need to think of the concept of a single position (*x*) of the entity. Then, the uncertainty in position (Δ*x*) also loses its meaning. The "spread" in space is a natural consequence of the fact that we model the particle as a wave packet.

Concepts of Modern Quantum Theory (continued)

vice versa. The uncertainty in position is modeled as the spread in space of the wave packet. The uncertainty in momentum is modeled as the spread in wavelength of the waves making up the wave packet.

The notion of a wave packet *model* for particles, combined with the deBroglie hypothesis for the wavelike *character* of particles, encourages us to look for a fundamental wavelike *mathematical description* of particles. This is represented by the *wave function*, Ψ, which is also called the *probability amplitude*, as we shall see below. We can justify the existence of a wave function as follows. Let us imagine a familiar electromagnetic wave, with an electric field vector amplitude, E. We are aware that the square of the amplitude of the electromagnetic wave in a region of space is proportional to the intensity of the radiation:

$$E^2 \sim I$$

Now, we make a jump from the wave picture to the particle picture. The intensity of electromagnetic radiation is proportional to the number of photons arriving in the region of space per unit time:

$$E^2 \sim I \sim \text{\# of photons per unit time}$$

Now, the more photons arriving per unit time, the higher is the probability density (i.e., probability per unit volume) of finding a photon in the region of space:

$$E^2 \sim I \sim \text{\# of photons per unit time} \sim \text{probability density}$$

Thus, we have, looking at the extreme left and right of this proportionality,

$$E^2 \sim \text{probability density}$$

so that the probability density for finding photons is proportional to the square of the wave representing these particles.

Since we have seen a parallel between photons and massive particles, we adopt the same relationship for the massive particles—the probability density for finding the particle must be proportional to the square of the amplitude of the wave representing the particle. The problem we have is that there is not an easily identifiable, and physical, wave for massive particles like there is (the electromagnetic wave) for photons. Just the same, we want such a wave to be available to us, so we simply give the wave amplitude a symbol, Ψ, and a name which describes its function—the *probability amplitude* (or the *wave function*). The probability amplitude has no physical significance itself—it cannot be measured. This will allow *complex* functions to be valid as probability amplitudes. The measurable quantity is $|\Psi|^2$—the probability density.

Ψ—*The probability amplitude: a function which cannot be measured, but which represents the particle in its environment, and contains information about its motion*

Concepts of Modern Quantum Theory (continued)

Now, how do we find the probability amplitude for a given particle? The wave function will depend on the environment in which the particle finds itself and it will be a solution to a partial differential equation given to us by Schrödinger in the 1920's:

$$-\frac{\hbar^2}{2m}\frac{\partial^2\Psi(x,t)}{\partial x^2} + V(x)\Psi(x,t) = i\hbar\frac{\partial\Psi(x,t)}{\partial t}$$

In this one-dimensional equation, $V(x)$ is the potential energy function that represents the interaction of the particle with its local environment. It has been made explicit in the equation that the wave function Ψ depends on both position and time. We can also write a similar equation for more realistic three dimensional problems, but we will stick with one dimension to keep the treatment simple. Quantum mechanics textbooks can be consulted by the reader who wishes to study the three dimensional equation.

The equation above is the *time-dependent Schrödinger equation*. It can be shown that the wave function can be expressed as a product of a space function, which, in one dimension, we write as $\psi(x)$, and a time function, whose form is not important to our purposes here. The space function is a solution to the *time-independent Schrödinger equation*:

$$-\frac{\hbar^2}{2m}\frac{d^2\psi(x)}{dx^2} + V(x)\psi(x) = E\psi(x)$$

where E is the energy of the particle.

The Schrödinger equation (along with boundary conditions representative of the system) can be used to find, at least for simple systems, the *probability amplitudes* and *quantized energies* of bound systems. The Bohr theory for the hydrogen atom (Chapter 19) gave early recognition to the existence of quantized energies. The Schrödinger equation places these quantized energies on a firm mathematical and physical basis and allows us to calculate the energies for systems for which the equation is soluble. It is a warm sense of satisfaction that arises when the Schrödinger equation is applied to the hydrogen atom and predicts *exactly* the same quantized energies as the Bohr theory, which approached the atom from an entirely different starting point.

One physical phenomenon that the Schrödinger equation cannot predict is the existence of *spin*, or *intrinsic angular momentum*, which will be discussed in Chapter 19. This aspect of a particle is purely quantum mechanical, with no classical analog.

Discussions; Chapter 18—Modern Quantum Theory

𝔐𝔶𝔰𝔱𝔢𝔯𝔦𝔢𝔰:

1.) The uncertainty principle appears in various texts with different right hand sides, as suggested in the accompanying diagram. Why is the right hand side of the uncertainty principle so *uncertain*?

$$\Delta x \, \Delta p_x \; \geq \; \begin{cases} h & ? \\ \hbar & ? \\ \dfrac{\hbar}{2} & ? \end{cases}$$

If one consults a variety of treatments of the uncertainty principle in various textbooks, one will likely find all of the right hand sides indicated in the graphic accompanying this Mystery. Why can't authors agree on a standard right hand side? Actually, this is not the fault of the authors; it can be attributed to the nature of quantum mechanics. The uncertainties in position and momentum are defined explicitly in quantum mechanics. With respect to this definition, then, the product of the uncertainty in position and the uncertainty in momentum *depends on the particular choice of function to represent the wave packet for the particle*. The wave packet (as described in the Concepts section) can be approximated as a product of a trigonometric function (representing the oscillations) and a function defining the *envelope* for the packet.

For example, one choice of an envelope function might be,

$$f(x) \; = \; \begin{cases} 0 & x < -\pi/2 \\ A & -\pi/2 < x < \pi/2 \\ 0 & x > \pi/2 \end{cases}$$

where *A* is a constant. In this case, the wave packet has a shape such as the following:

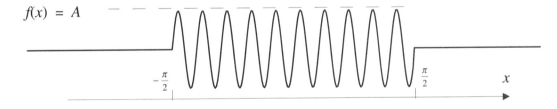

$f(x) = A$

$-\dfrac{\pi}{2}$ $\dfrac{\pi}{2}$ x

Another choice might be,

$$f(x) \; = \; \begin{cases} 0 & x < -\pi/2 \\ A\cos x & -\pi/2 < x < \pi/2 \\ 0 & x > \pi/2 \end{cases}$$

In this case, the wave packet might have the following shape:

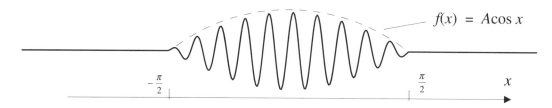

$$f(x) = A\cos x$$

Upon calculation, the two different wave packets shown above would have *different right hand sides* for the uncertainty principle.

The only "standard" right hand side that we can identify is the *minimum* value of the right hand side. This is associated with a *Gaussian* wave packet, which gives a minimum right hand side of $\hbar/2$. The Gaussian packet is described by,

$$f(x) = Ae^{-\sigma^2 x^2}$$

where σ defines the width of the packet. This function results in a wave packet having the general shape shown below:

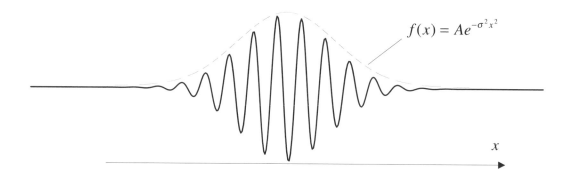

$$f(x) = Ae^{-\sigma^2 x^2}$$

2.) Why is it so difficult to locate the freezing point of helium in a table?

It is difficult to find the freezing point of helium because *it has no freezing point* (in an open container on the Earth). Helium is the only element which does not freeze; it will remain a liquid, even at a temperature of absolute zero. This is due to two factors. As an inert gas, helium atoms can only interact by means of the Van der Waals force, which is inherently weak, as discussed in Mystery #2 in Chapter 12. The strength of the Van der Waals force depends on the number of charges in the atom and, since helium is the lightest inert gas, it has the weakest bonding force of all the inert gases. As a result, it has the lowest boiling point (4.2 K) of the inert gases, and the boiling points of these gases rise as one moves down the column in the periodic table.

The second contribution is *zero point energy*. This is the energy that a system has in its lowest quantum state, and quantum physics tells us that this energy is not zero if the particle is restricted in some way. Atoms in a container are restricted to the container and thus have a zero-point energy. This energy generally rises as the mass of the particle decreases. Thus, helium, as a very light particle, has a high zero-point energy and a low bonding energy. The result is that the zero point energy is high enough to prevent the bonding from occurring, and helium does not solidify.

We can solidify helium with an additional consideration. If the *pressure* of the helium is increased to about 26 atmospheres, it can be solidified at temperatures very close to absolute zero.

3.) What are the *units* of the wave function?

The probability increment dP of finding a particle in a region of size dx near a point x in a one dimensional space is given by,

$$dP = |\psi(x)|^2 \, dx$$

The probability is a unitless number and the interval dx is measured in meters. Thus, the units of the wave function must be,

$$\psi(x) \sim m^{-\frac{1}{2}}$$

In three dimensions, the probability increment of finding a particle in a region of size dV near a point (x, y, z) is given by,

$$dP = |\psi(x, y, z)|^2 \, dV$$

The probability is a unitless number and the interval dV is measured in cubic meters. Thus, the units of the wave function *in three dimensions* must be,

$$\psi(x) \sim m^{-\frac{3}{2}}$$

𝔐𝔞𝔤𝔦𝔠:

Nitrogen Bands

The typical spectrum discussed with regard to atomic physics is a line spectrum, as seen in the upper portion of the diagram accompanying the Magic demonstration. The spectrum of hydrogen is a familiar example of this.

The spectrum of nitrogen shows a series of *bands*, as suggested in the lower half of the diagram. This is due to the fact that, in a typical classroom spectrum tube, nitrogen is in the molecular form, N_2, rather than the monatomic form—the form in which hydrogen exists in the tubes. Thus, the spectrum of nitrogen is a *molecular* spectrum while that of hydrogen is an *atomic* spectrum. In a molecular spectrum, the electronic quantum levels each have an associated set of *vibrational* energy levels, corresponding to various modes of vibrations of the molecule. In addition, each vibrational state has an associated set of *rotational* energy levels, corresponding to rotations of the molecule around two independent axes perpendicular to the bond direction. Thus, there are many more possible transitions that the molecules can make, resulting in many closely spaced spectral lines that take on the appearance of bands.

𝕸𝖞𝖙𝖍:

1.) Consider a particle in a box, which happens to be in the $n = 2$ state and is in the right hand side of the box. Since it has zero probability of being at the exact center of the box, it cannot pass through this point. Therefore, it can never be in the left side of the box.

This argument makes a deterministic assumption that is not valid at the microscopic level. That assumption is that a moving particle must exist at every point, at some time, between its initial and final points. The source of this assumption is our human experience in watching moving macroscopic particles. At the microscopic level, however, we must consider the behavior of *waves*, not *particles*. The wave function provides us with some information about where we might find the particle, but doesn't say anything about how it moves from one point to another. Even the concept of moving from one point to another is of little value in the microscopic world.

If we imagine a guitar string vibrating in the second mode, with a node at the center point, we have no trouble seeing energy passing through the center point (in both directions), even though this point never suffers a displacement. This is similar to the situation with the particle in a box in the $n = 2$ state. The quantum mechanical waves can have non-zero amplitudes on either side of the center point even though the wave function has a zero amplitude at the center point. It is only when we try to apply our macroscopic concept of a particle *moving* in the box that we run into trouble.

2.) The Pauli Exclusion Principle is:
"No two electrons in an atom can have the same four quantum numbers."

This is a common statement of the Pauli Exclusion Principle, but it is a special case of a more general idea. The Pauli Exclusion Principle applies to any particle belonging to the family called *fermions*, which are particles with half-integral spin. Fermions include electrons, protons, neutrons, quarks, neutrinos, etc. Single particle fermions have spin $1/2$, but there are combinations of these single particles that can have spin $3/2$, $5/2$, etc. These combination particles also obey the Exclusion Principle.

The rules of quantum mechanics show that *the probability of two fermions being in exactly the same quantum state is exactly zero. This* is the Pauli Exclusion Principle.

The principle arises due to symmetry requirements for exchange of two indistinguishable fermions. Quantum mechanics texts can be consulted for more details on these arguments.

This is to be compared to the situation with *bosons*, which are particles with integral spin (photons, helium atoms, gravitons, etc.). The symmetry requirements for these particles is such that there is no restriction on the number of bosons in a given quantum state. Thus, there is no Exclusion Principle for these particles.

In the case of electrons in an atom, then, since electrons are fermions, the rule becomes that stated in the Myth, since the four quantum numbers (principal, azimuthal, magnetic and spin, as described in the Concepts section of Chapter 19) define the quantum state.

3.) The uncertainty principle has the following essence with regard to the two variables appearing in the expression (position-momentum; time-energy, etc.): The more accurately we determine the value of one variable, the more we *disturb* the other variable.

The concept stated in the Myth appears often in physics textbooks. For example, one argument proceeds as follows. In order to specify the position of an electron, we need to observe where it is, which we could, in principle, do by scattering a photon off it. But, in scattering the photon, we would impart a momentum to the electron, thus losing information about its momentum. While this type of argument is somewhat satisfying to the quantum novice and can be used to approximate the uncertainty principle, it does not reflect the fundamental nature of the principle. It is nothing more than the ubiquitous idea in science that *we always disturb a system when we make a measurement*. For example, measuring a potential difference with a voltmeter requires "borrowing" a bit of current from the circuit; thus, we have perturbed the original circuit. We only measure the perturbed system, not the original. As another example, consider measuring the temperature of a glass of water with a thermometer. In general, the temperature of the thermometer will be different than that of the water. When the thermometer is immersed in the water, the thermometer and the water come to equilibrium at some temperature between their original temperatures. Thus, we measure the perturbed system, not the original system. In general, we can correct for such perturbations mathematically.

The two examples above have nothing to do with quantum physics. They don't even depend on the physics of waves, which we know to be very important in quantum physics. In contrast, the nature of the uncertainty principle is deeply rooted in the quantum physics of waves.

The uncertainty principle can be generated from the concept of wave packets (as in, for example, Chapter 6 of S. T. Thornton and A. Rex, *Modern Physics for Scientists and Engineers*, Saunders College Publishing, Fort Worth, 1993), which was discussed in the Concepts section. This argument depends only on the wave packet model of a particle and has nowhere within it a scattering event (as is necessary for the electron-photon argument above), or an event of any kind. The uncertainty principle can also be generated from the commutation behavior of operators representing momentum and position (as in, for example, Chapter 8 of L. E. Ballentine, *Quantum Mechanics*, Prentice-Hall, Englewood Cliffs, 1990 or Chapter 5 of R. L. Liboff, *Introductory Quantum Mechan-*

ics, Holden-Day, Inc., Oakland, 1980), again without appealing to any type of event. These types of arguments are fundamental in nature and represent the basic nature of the uncertainty principle. Because a pure wave (one single frequency) must be infinite in extent, any localization of the wave necessarily introduces a spread in frequencies, as discussed in Mystery #3 of Chapter 17 in *PBWM*. The localization of the wave is related to the position of the associated particle and the frequency is related to the momentum of the particle. Thus, if we gain information about the position (the wave becomes more localized), we lose information about the momentum (there is a wider spread in frequencies). This is the fundamental essence of the uncertainty principle. *It expresses an inherent uncertainty imposed by nature and does not represent our inability to make an accurate measurement.*

Another point to consider here is that the uncertainty principle is simply an artifact of our stubborn desire to think in particle terms, due to our macroscopic experience. We try to demand exact values of position and momentum, which are particle ideas. If we can ignore our particle history and think only in terms of waves, there is no need for an uncertainty principle. Without a particle to think about, there is no such thing as a definite position or momentum.

4.) Quantization is only a microscopic phenomenon—we don't see it in everyday life.

There are many examples of quantization in our macroscopic world. Some of these have to do with the counting of indivisible entities. For example, counts of people are quantized in units of one person. For very large populations, such as that of countries, the "graininess" of individual persons is not apparent, just as the graininess of the atoms in a gas are not visible. But for small numbers of people, the quantization can make quite a difference. This is the reason that studies involving humans use as large a sample as possible.

Other examples of macroscopic quantization involve quantized states. Pregnancy is an example. A woman exists in one state of a two state quantum system—the state of not being pregnant or the state of being pregnant. There are no other possibilities. Another two state system is that of being alive or dead, assuming that a suitable clinical definition of death has been accepted.

The results of throwing a single die or number of dice, as suggested in the diagram accompanying the Myth, is another example of macroscopic quantization. The number of states depend on the number of dice. There are six states (numbers 1 through 6) for one die, eleven for two dice (2 through 12), sixteen for three dice (3 through 18), etc.

The modes of vibration of a guitar string represent another set of quantized states in the macroscopic world. There are infinitely many allowed frequencies of vibration. This, of course, is intimately related to the microscopic form of quantization, since quantized states for microscopic particles arise from the condition of establishing standing quantum waves.

For a discussion of the quantized energy levels associated with placing a classroom chair in various equilibrium positions, see Z. Golab-Meyer, "'Piekara's Chair': Mechanical Model for Atomic Energy Levels", *The Physics Teacher*, **29**, 215, 1991.

5.) Conservation of energy is an absolute principle and cannot be violated.

This is only true in the macroscopic world. In the microscopic world, we can seemingly violate this principle, but only for a very short time. This arises from the energy-time uncertainty principle:

$$\Delta E \Delta t \geq \frac{\hbar}{2}$$

Let us interpret this slightly differently—the product of the uncertainties is *on the order of* $\hbar/_2$. Thus, we can violate energy conservation by an amount ΔE, as long as the violation occurs in a time interval Δt such that the product of ΔE and Δt is approximately $\hbar/_2$. A common application of this idea is the "leaking" of the wave function into the forbidden regions of a finite square well. A typical wave function for a particle in a finite square well is shown below.

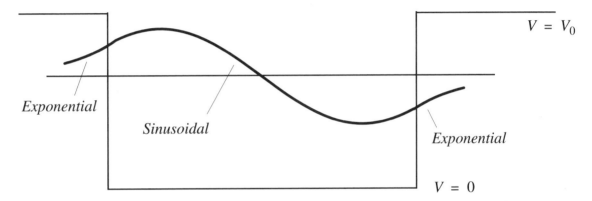

The portions of the wave function outside the vertical walls of the well are exponential in nature, as dictated by solutions to the Schrödinger equation. Thus, there is a finite probability that the particle is outside the walls of the well. But, in these regions, the potential energy is larger than the total energy, which is a clear violation of energy conservation. The uncertainty principle is often invoked here, saying that the particle can exist in these forbidden regions, as long as it is only there for a very short time, a time interval which will satisfy the uncertainty principle.

The energy-time uncertainty principle can also be used to estimate the mass of some particles. This was done in 1935 by Hideki Yukawa in estimating the mass of the *pion*, which he proposed as the exchange particle (see Chapter 23) for the nuclear strong force. In this application, we imagine that the mass energy of the exchange particle appears from nowhere, in violation of conservation of energy, but exists only for a short time, enough time to travel from one strongly interacting particle to another. The calculation proceeds as follows. It is assumed that the pion moves at approximately the speed of light over a distance of about 10^{-15} m, which is the range of the strong force. This gives a time interval of,

$$\Delta t = \frac{\Delta x}{v} = \frac{10^{-15}\,\text{m}}{3 \times 10^8\,\text{m} \cdot \text{s}^{-1}} = 3.3 \times 10^{-24}\,\text{s}$$

Now, from the uncertainty principle, we can estimate the minimum energy of the particle:

$$\Delta E \Delta t \approx \frac{\hbar}{2} \quad \rightarrow \quad \Delta E \approx \frac{\hbar}{2\Delta t} \approx \frac{6.6 \times 10^{-16} \text{eV} \cdot \text{s}}{2(3.3 \times 10^{-24} \text{s})} \approx 100 \text{MeV}$$

Thus, Yukawa predicted a particle of mass about 200 times that of an electron (0.511 MeV), which spurred an experimental search for this particle as described in the Concepts section of Chapter 23.

6.) A quantum leap is a very large change.

The phrase "quantum leap" has taken on a colloquial meaning of a very large change. The actual changes in quantum systems are *very small* on an energy scale. For example, transitions between states in the hydrogen atom are measured in electron volts, which are nineteen orders of magnitude smaller than joules. Even nuclear transition energies, in terms of MeV, are thirteen orders of magnitude smaller than a joule.

The more proper interpretation of the phrase "quantum leap" is a *discontinuous* change between discrete allowed energy states. Thus, it is a description of the *nature* of the change, not the *size*.

7.) It is a fundamental principle that quantum systems tend toward lower energy.

This is often stated as a general principle, explaining why excited atoms make transitions to the ground state, for example. The more general underlying principle, however, is the Second Law of Thermodynamics. Systems tend toward *maximum entropy*. Thus, in the excited state of the atom, the energy is localized within the atom, representing an ordered system. After the transition, the energy is distributed between the atom and the outgoing photon, so that the system is more disordered, and therefore, higher in entropy.

Chapter 19
Atomic Physics

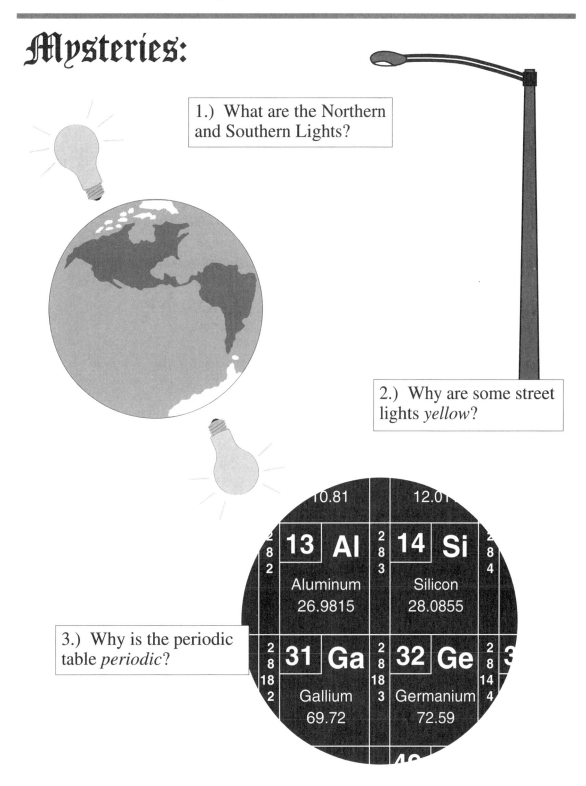

𝕸𝖞𝖘𝖙𝖊𝖗𝖎𝖊𝖘:

1.) What are the Northern and Southern Lights?

2.) Why are some street lights *yellow*?

3.) Why is the periodic table *periodic*?

10.81   12.01

2 8 2	**13 Al**	2 8 3	**14 Si**	2 8 4
	Aluminum 26.9815		Silicon 28.0855	
2 8 18 2	**31 Ga**	2 8 18 3	**32 Ge**	2 8 14 4
	Gallium 69.72		Germanium 72.59	

𝕸ysteries:

4.) What determines the color of a "neon" sign?

$NaCl...$

$Na_2CO_3...$

5.) Sodium does not occur in nature as a free element. Why not?

$NaHCO_3....$

$Na_2B_4O_7 \cdot 10H_2O...$

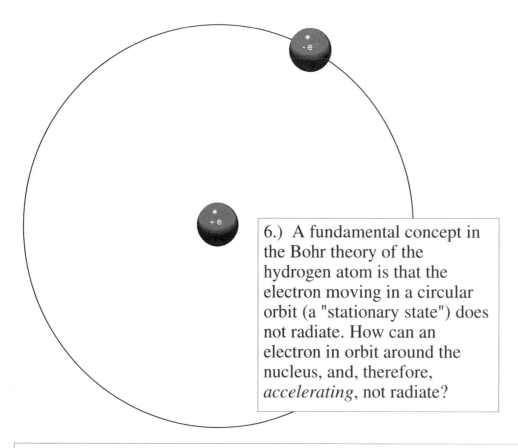

6.) A fundamental concept in the Bohr theory of the hydrogen atom is that the electron moving in a circular orbit (a "stationary state") does not radiate. How can an electron in orbit around the nucleus, and, therefore, *accelerating*, not radiate?

𝔐𝔶𝔰𝔱𝔢𝔯𝔦𝔢𝔰:

7.) Why do emission spectra have more lines than absorption spectra?

Emission:

Absorption:

8.) The Balmer series is the most well-known series of spectral lines in the hydrogen atom. Yet, in an absorption spectrum of hydrogen, the Balmer series does not appear. Why is this?

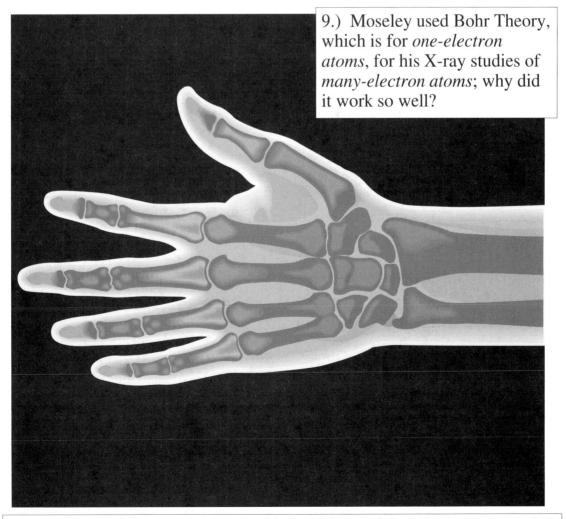

9.) Moseley used Bohr Theory, which is for *one-electron atoms*, for his X-ray studies of *many-electron atoms*; why did it work so well?

𝕸𝖞𝖘𝖙𝖊𝖗𝖎𝖊𝖘:

10.) A graph of ionization energy (the energy needed to remove one electron from the atom) of the elements is shown in the diagram. What causes the regular <u>peaks</u> in the data?

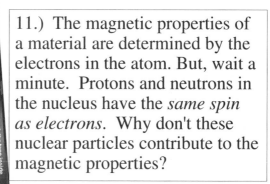

11.) The magnetic properties of a material are determined by the electrons in the atom. But, wait a minute. Protons and neutrons in the nucleus have the *same spin as electrons*. Why don't these nuclear particles contribute to the magnetic properties?

𝕸𝖆𝖌𝖎𝖈:

Atomic Physics in the Streets

Obtain a diffraction grating and mount it to a piece of cardboard with a narrow slit cut in it. Take this assembly out at night and use it to view overhead street lamps. From the result, determine the light source of the lamp.

𝔐𝔶𝔱𝔥:

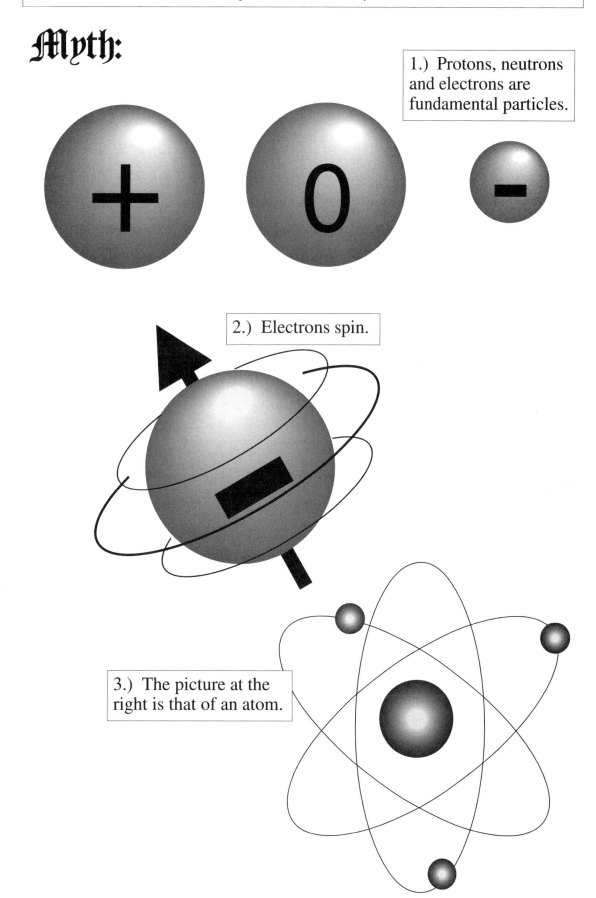

1.) Protons, neutrons and electrons are fundamental particles.

2.) Electrons spin.

3.) The picture at the right is that of an atom.

𝕸𝖞𝖙𝖍:

4.) The Balmer equation is shown to the right.

$$\frac{1}{\lambda} = R\left(\frac{1}{2^2} - \frac{1}{n^2}\right)$$

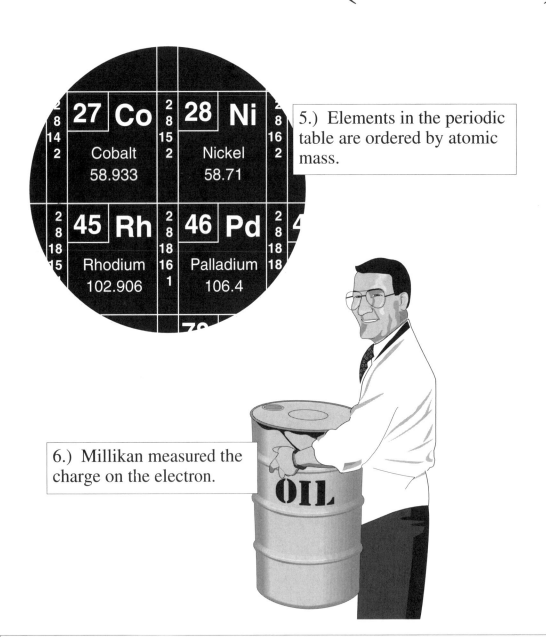

5.) Elements in the periodic table are ordered by atomic mass.

6.) Millikan measured the charge on the electron.

𝔐𝔶𝔱𝔥:

$E = -0.85\ eV$

$E = -1.5\ eV$

$E = -3.4\ eV$

7.) The energies shown in the accompanying diagram are *electron energy levels* in the hydrogen atom.

$E = -13.6\ eV$

8.) Bohr assumed angular momentum quantization as a fundamental postulate to arrive at his theory for the hydrogen atom.

$$L = n\hbar$$

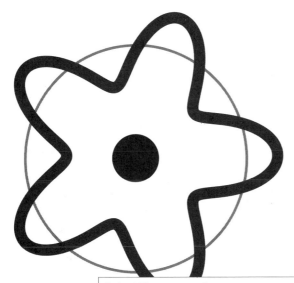

9.) The angular momentum quantization condition in the Bohr atom can be demonstrated by showing that an integral number of deBroglie wavelengths fit around the orbit of the electron.

𝔐𝔶𝔱𝔥:

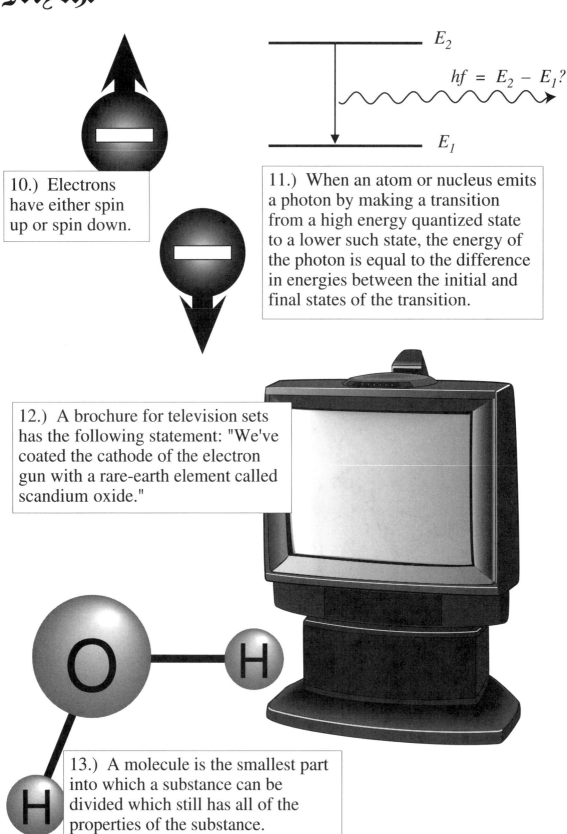

E_2

$hf = E_2 - E_1?$

E_1

10.) Electrons have either spin up or spin down.

11.) When an atom or nucleus emits a photon by making a transition from a high energy quantized state to a lower such state, the energy of the photon is equal to the difference in energies between the initial and final states of the transition.

12.) A brochure for television sets has the following statement: "We've coated the cathode of the electron gun with a rare-earth element called scandium oxide."

13.) A molecule is the smallest part into which a substance can be divided which still has all of the properties of the substance.

Concepts of Atomic Physics

In the latter half of the nineteenth century, the structure of the atom was not understood. Indeed, the discovery of the electron by J. J. Thomson did not occur until almost the turn of the century. There were clues to the structure, however, such as the discrete *spectra* from atoms. Hot objects, such as the filament in Thomas Edison's light bulbs emitted a continuous spectrum of colors, but atomic sources of light, such as hot gases, emitted *only certain colors*. Hydrogen was a well-studied gas in this regard. The *Balmer equation* was proposed (by J. J. Balmer, in a paper* published at age 60, and one of only three papers published by him in his lifetime) as an empirical description of the wavelengths of the spectral lines of hydrogen:

> *The Balmer Equation—an empirical fit to the data*

$$\lambda = 364.56 \, \frac{n^2}{n^2 - 4}$$

where *n* is an integer starting at 3 and the wavelength from this equation is expressed in nanometers.

This equation had no theoretical basis; at the time, it was simply a nice mathematical trick to allow a calculation of the wavelengths.

With the discovery of the electron, models of the atom, with the electron as a subunit, could be hypothesized. Thomson's own model came to be known as the *plum pudding model*, in which the electrons float about in a nebulous sea of positive charge. The death of the plum pudding model came about with Ernest Rutherford's experiments, in which he observed alpha particles undergoing large angle scattering when they interacted with atoms in a gold foil. This large angle scattering was inconsistent with Thomson's model. This experiment gave rise to the *nuclear model*, in which the positive charge of the atom is imagined to be concentrated in a very small region in the center of the atom.

> *The nuclear model of the atom is required to explain Rutherford's results.*

Once the nuclear model was proposed, the question turned to this—why don't the electron and the positive nucleus simply attract one another and cause a collapse of the atom? One strategy for avoiding this is to imagine that the electron is in orbit about the nucleus, just like the Earth is in orbit around the Sun. There is a problem with this approach, however, that is not present for the Earth orbit. The electron is an *electrically charged particle* undergoing a circular motion. It therefore has a centripetal acceleration, and accelerating electrically charged particles emit energy as electromagnetic radiation. Thus, the electron should continually transfer energy away and spiral into the nucleus—we have a collapsed atom again!

Bohr considered this problem and proposed that electrons simply do not radiate if they are in certain allowed orbits. These orbits are those whose angular

---

*J. J. Balmer, *Ann. Phys. und Chem.*, **25**, 80, 1885

Concepts of Atomic Physics (continued)

momentum is an integer (a *quantum number*) multiple of some constant ($\hbar$). Thus began the concept of *quantized states* for bound systems. The electron will radiate, according to Bohr, when it makes a *transition*, from one allowed orbit to one with a lower

> *Bohr—the electron moves in a circular orbit, but does not radiate.*

energy. The energy of the photon emitted by this process is approximated as (see Myth #11) the difference in energies between the two orbits. The success of the Bohr theory was based on its ability to provide a theoretical underpinning for the Balmer equation. The question as to why an accelerating charge does not radiate, however, remained unanswered. We will address this question in Mystery #6 in this chapter.

While the Bohr model provided some agreement with experiment for hydrogen atoms, it fails to provide a theoretical foundation as soon as we take one step higher in the periodic table, to helium. It is clear that more complicated processes are occurring in atoms above hydrogen. One of the fundamental principles that is necessary to understand the nature of higher atoms is the *Pauli Exclusion Principle* (see Myth #2 in Chapter 18 for discussion of this principle). When applied to atoms, this principle requires that only one electron occupy a given quantum state in the atom. The Pauli Exclusion Principle is the reason for the variations in chemical behavior for different elements and for their pattern of behaviors as described by the layout of the periodic table.

We can move from the simple theory of Bohr to a more sophisticated theory by assigning *three* quantum numbers to the electron rather than the one quantum number in the Bohr theory. The first steps were taken by A. Sommerfeld, who, in 1920, considered *elliptical* orbits rather than Bohr's circular orbits. In this approach, the shape and orientation of the elliptical orbits were quantized along with the energy, leading to two more quantum numbers. We will stick with the hydrogen atom, in order to keep things simple. The first quantum number, usually signified by n, is called the *principal quantum number* and is related to the quantized *energies* of the electron-nucleus system.

> *n—the quantum number related to the energy of the atom*

While Bohr used this same quantum number to quantize the angular momentum, the more sophisticated theory uses a second quantum number for this purpose. This number, signified by ℓ, is called the *azimuthal quantum number*, and is related to the quanti-

> *ℓ—the quantum number related to the magnitude of the orbital angular momentum*

zation of the *magnitude of the orbital angular momentum* of the electron-nucleus system. The orbital angular momentum changes with the shape of the elliptical orbit in the Sommerfeld model. The quantization condition is that the magnitude of the orbital angular momentum vector **L** is quantized

Concepts of Atomic Physics (continued)

and can only have values given by:

$$|\mathbf{L}| = \sqrt{\ell(\ell+1)}\,\hbar$$

where ℓ is an integer and can only have values ranging from 0 to $n - 1$. The values of ℓ are often described with an historic spectral notation: $\ell = 0$ is an s state, $\ell = 1$ is a p state, $\ell = 2$ is a d state, $\ell = 3$ is an f state, etc.

The third quantum number, m_ℓ, is called the *magnetic quantum number* and is related to the quantization of the *direction of the orbital angular momentum vector*. The condition is that the z-component of the orbital angular momentum vector, L_z, can only have values given by,

$$L_z = m_\ell \hbar$$

> m_ℓ—the quantum number related to the *direction* of the orbital angular momentum

The allowed values of m_ℓ are integers from $-\ell$ to $+\ell$. This quantum number is called *magnetic*, because a magnetic field applied to the atom can split the energies of states described by different values of m_ℓ.

These three quantum numbers (which arise from the mathematics of solving the Schrödinger equation) are not sufficient to describe the behaviors of atoms in the periodic table or the nature of some more complicated atomic spectra. We can adequately describe these behaviors only with the introduction of an additional angular momentum in the atom, provided by the electron itself. This angular momentum is independent of its orbital motion and appears to be an intrinsic property of the electron (and, actually, of most particles) itself. This extra angular momentum is properly called *intrinsic angular momentum*, but is more commonly (and, unfortunately!) simply called *spin*. Since it is an angular momentum, it must follow the same mathematical rules as orbital angular momentum. Thus, there is a quantum number related to the magnitude of the intrinsic angular momentum vector. This quantum number is called s and, for electrons, always has the value of $\frac{1}{2}$. Thus, the magnitude of the spin angular momentum vector $\mathbf{S}$ is always (for an electron),

$$|\mathbf{S}| = \sqrt{s(s+1)}\,\hbar = \sqrt{\frac{1}{2}\left(\frac{1}{2}+1\right)}\,\hbar = \frac{\sqrt{3}}{2}\hbar$$

Since this quantum number does not change for an electron, it is normally not given in lists of quantum numbers for electrons in atoms. What *is* given is the analog to m_ℓ—the quantum number m_s, which is related to the *direction* of the spin angular momentum vector. The allowed values of this quantum number follow the same rule as

> m_s—the quantum number related to the *direction* of the intrinsic angular momentum (spin) of the electron

Concepts of Atomic Physics (continued)

that for m_ℓ — m_s can range from $-s$ to $+s$ in steps of *one*, which, for an electron, gives only two possibilities: $m_s = -^1/_2$ or $m_s = +^1/_2$. Thus, the allowed z-components of the spin angular momentum vector, S_z, are,

$$S_z = m_s \hbar = \pm \frac{1}{2} \hbar$$

These are commonly called *spin up*, for the positive choice, and *spin down*, for the negative choice (but see Myth #10 in this Chapter).

Thus, the list of four quantum numbers *which can vary among electrons in an atom* is:

n	principal	$\rightarrow$	energy
ℓ	azimuthal	$\rightarrow$	magnitude of orbital angular momentum
m_ℓ	magnetic	$\rightarrow$	direction of orbital angular momentum
m_s	spin	$\rightarrow$	direction of intrinsic angular momentum (spin)

While a model based on these quantum numbers applied to orbits of electrons around the nucleus enjoys some success, there are still some shortcomings. For example, we still cannot understand why an accelerating electron does not radiate. Modern pictures of the electron in the atom reflect the *probabilistic* nature of microscopic particles discussed in Chapter 18. Imagining the electron to exist in a well-defined orbit

> *The electron cloud model of the atom is more sophisticated and applicable than the orbit model in many situations.*

about the nucleus is too deterministic—we are claiming too much knowledge about the motion of the electron. In order to satisfy the uncertainty principle, we replace this model with what is often called the *electron cloud model*. We realize that the position of the electron will be governed by probability and will be mathematically described by the square of the *wave function* of the electron. Imagine that each point in space around the nucleus is colored with a dot whose darkness is proportional to the probability of finding the electron in that region. Looking at the final result will give us a picture much like a cloud, with lighter areas and darker areas, light where the electron is not likely to be and dark where it is likely to be. This is the electron cloud model of the nucleus and we will see in Mystery #6 how this leads to an understanding of why Bohr's picture of an accelerating electron is inaccurate.

Discussions; Chapter 19—Atomic Physics

𝔐𝔶𝔰𝔱𝔢𝔯𝔦𝔢𝔰:

1.) What are the Northern and Southern Lights?

The light that comes from the sky during the Aurora Borealis, in the Northern Hemisphere, and the Aurora Australis, in the Southern Hemisphere, arises from emissions from atoms of oxygen and nitrogen in the atmosphere. These atoms are excited by collisions with energetic electrons. Much of the light from the aurora is greenish-white, from atomic oxygen in the ionosphere. Electrons penetrating more deeply into the atmosphere will excite neutral or ionized nitrogen, resulting in additional emissions in the red and violet regions of the visible spectrum.

While the origin of the light is relatively well understood, the origin of the energetic electrons that excite the atoms is a current area of research. Modern theories describe a complex interaction between the Earth's and Sun's magnetic fields and the Solar wind. The magnetic fields of the Earth and Sun cause charged particles in the Solar wind to separate, with positive particles being deflected by a magnetic force to one side of the Earth and negative particles to the other. This establishes a potential difference across the Earth. Since the Earth's magnetosphere contains a plasma of charged particles, the potential difference can drive a current. The electrons in this current are guided by the Earth's magnetic field lines from the negative charge distribution on one side of the Earth to the polar regions, through the ionosphere and back out along magnetic field lines to the positive charge distribution.

While the electrons are moving into the ionosphere, they collide with atoms, exciting them and producing the auroral glow.

The aurora process can be likened to an electromagnetic generator, resulting in a potential difference and a resulting current. The process is extremely powerful, with power ratings estimated at 1 to 10 million megawatts, which is equivalent to thousands of large power generating stations on Earth. For more information, see S. Akasofu, "The Aurora", pp. 866-870, in P. A. Tipler, *Physics for Scientists and Engineers*, 3rd. ed., Worth Publishers, New York, 1991.

2.) Why are some street lights *yellow*?

Many street lights use the emission of radiation from excited gases as a source of light. The light from these atomic sources is not continuous, but rather is discrete, as discussed in the Concepts section. Despite being discrete, if there are roughly equal contributions from several regions of the spectrum, the light could appear to be close to white. This is not the case with low pressure *sodium* lights. Sodium has very strong emission in the yellow region (at wavelengths 589.0 nm and 589.6 nm), which is the origin of the yellow color associated with these sources.

Mercury lights have a more even distribution of spectral lines, so that the color of the light from a mercury source is not nearly so evident. Upon close inspection of a mercury light source, however, one can detect a bluish tinge to the light, representing a very strong emission at 435.8 nm.

3.) Why is the periodic table *periodic*?

The periodicity of the periodic table is a reflection of the Pauli Exclusion Principle and the allowed values of the four quantum numbers used to describe states of the atom. If we imagine the first energy level, with primary quantum number $n = 1$, we must have $\ell = 0$, $m_\ell = 0$ and $m_s = \pm \,^1/_2$. Thus, two electrons can be in this first shell and no more, in order to satisfy the Exclusion Principle. Now, consider the next shell, for $n = 2$. In this case, we have the possibilities,

$$\ell = 0 \quad \rightarrow \quad m_\ell = 0 \;\; \text{and} \; m_s = \pm \,^1/_2 \qquad\qquad\qquad \rightarrow \quad 2 \text{ electrons}$$

$$\ell = 1 \quad \rightarrow \quad m_\ell = 1, 0, -1 \;\; \text{and (for each } m_\ell) \; m_s = \pm \,^1/_2 \quad \rightarrow \quad \underline{6 \text{ electrons}}$$

$$\textbf{Total} \qquad\qquad 8 \text{ electrons}$$

Thus, eight electrons can fill this shell, according to the Exclusion Principle. Now, let us compare helium, with $Z = 2$ and neon, with $Z = 10$. Helium has a filled $n = 1$ shell while neon has a filled $n = 2$ (*and* $n = 1$) shell. The chemical behavior of atoms is determined by the outer valence electrons and the degree of filling of the outer shells. Both helium and neon have filled shells, so that they have very similar chemical behavior. In fact, both of these elements are inert gases. Another inert gas occurs for the next shell closure, at $Z = 18$, for argon.

As another example, consider lithium, $Z = 3$ and sodium, $Z = 11$. Both of these atoms have one electron *outside* of a closed shell, so they are very active chemically, with a valence of +1. In general, the repeating character of the number of electrons outside of closed shells provides the periodic chemical behavior of the elements.

As we move to higher atomic numbers, however, we begin to see some complications due to a phenomenon called *nuclear shielding*. Starting with lithium at $Z = 3$ and continuing through the rest of the periodic table, we have electrons whose average physical positions are farther from the nucleus than other electrons in "inner" shells. This leads to the fact that the effective positive charge experienced by the outer electrons is the combination of the nuclear charge and the effect of the inner electrons. We describe this by saying that the nuclear charge is *shielded* by the inner electrons, so that the effective nuclear charge seen by the outer electrons is reduced. The result of this shielded nuclear charge is to reduce the binding energy of the outer electrons. The extent of this reduction in energy, however, depends on the ℓ-value of the electron. Those electrons with $\ell = 0$ (*s*-electrons) have a large probability of being close to the nucleus. As a result, *s*-electrons are only very mildly affected by nuclear shielding. Those electrons with $\ell = 1$ (*p*-electrons) spend more time far from the nucleus than do the *s*-electrons and are more affected by nuclear shielding. Thus, they are less tightly bound than they would be if the nuclear charge were not shielded, meaning that the energy of a *p*-electron moves *upward* on an energy level diagram when one includes the effect of nuclear shielding. For higher and higher values of ℓ, the effect of nuclear shielding becomes stronger and stronger.

This leads to the possibility that an energy level shifted upward by nuclear shielding could actually *cross over* and be higher in energy than a level which is affected to a lesser degree. We see this happening for the first time in the third row of the periodic table. The shifted 3*d* level has moved upward so that it is higher in energy than the 4*s* level. Thus, the 4*s* subshell fills with electrons *before* the 3*d* subshell, giving us potassium and calcium. Then, the 3*d* level fills with electrons, giving rise to the *transition elements* scandium (Z = 21) to zinc (Z = 30). For higher energies, the crossing of energy states becomes even more complicated, leading to additional transition elements as well as the lanthanide and actinide series of elements.

4.) What determines the color of a "neon" sign?

Neon-type signs use the emission of light from electrically excited gas atoms in glass tubing as the light source. The first neon sign was used for advertising a barber shop in Europe in 1909. The first use in the United States was in 1923, when a neon sign promoting the Packard automobile was imported from Paris. The origin of the light is similar to that from the street lamps in Mystery #2. The color of the light will depend on the particular atomic transitions occurring in the atoms (along with some secondary modification due to possible coloring in the glass tubing containing the gas). Neon has transitions resulting in very strong spectral lines in the red, so that true neon signs are red. Other gases can be used in the glass tubing to create other color effects.

5.) Sodium does not occur in nature as a free element. Why not?

Sodium, one of the most abundant elements on Earth, is an alkali metal, belonging to a family of *very* chemically active elements. The activity of the family arises due to the existence of one electron outside of a closed shell, as noted in Mystery #3. This electron is only weakly bound, due to the shielding effect of the nuclear charge by the inner electrons. Thus, only a small amount of energy will strip the atom of its electron, so that the alkali metals will react easily with other elements. Thus, sodium is not found as a free element, but rather reacts with other elements and is found in this form.

One must handle sodium and other alkali metals with great care, as they will react spontaneously and violently with water and other common materials. It is even possible for the reaction to set fire to the hydrogen which is liberated by the reaction of an alkali metal with water.

6.) A fundamental concept in the Bohr theory of the hydrogen atom is that the electron moving in a circular orbit (a "stationary state") does not radiate. How can an electron in orbit around the nucleus, and, therefore, *accelerating*, not radiate?

If we believe the Bohr model of the atom to be the correct picture, then it is very hard indeed to understand how orbiting electrons cannot emit energy by electromagnetic radiation. But keep in mind that the Bohr model is a very simplified model which can only explain a few features of hydrogenic atoms (see Myth #3).

The more fruitful model to consider is that of the *electron cloud*, in which the charge of the electron is imagined to be "smeared" out around the nucleus according to the probability of its being found in any region of space. For an electron in one of Bohr's "stationary states", this electron cloud, and, therefore, the charge distribution, is *constant in time*—therefore the atom does not radiate! When the atom makes a transition from one state to a lower state, it oscillates for a short time *between* the two states (a full understanding of this effect requires much deeper investigations into quantum electrodynamics than are appropriate for this book). The frequency of oscillation is given by the difference in energy between the states divided by Planck's constant (but see Myth #11). This oscillation between states results in an oscillation of the charge distribution which, as Bohr *and* Maxwell would both agree, results in radiation being emitted at the frequency of oscillation.

7.) Why do emission spectra have more lines than absorption spectra?

Let us consider hydrogen as a simple example. In an absorption spectrum of hydrogen at room temperature, only the lines representing transitions from $n = 1$ to higher levels will appear. The energy separation between the $n = 1$ and $n = 2$ states in hydrogen is 10.2 eV. The average thermal energy in the gas at room temperature is about $kT = 0.025$ eV. Thus, *almost all of the atoms in the gas are in the ground state*. In the emission spectrum, however, for which the atoms are excited by an external energy input, the atoms can make transitions from higher states to a lower, but still excited, state, say from $n = 4$ to $n = 2$. This will be followed by a subsequent transition from $n = 2$ to $n = 1$. Thus, the transition between $n = 2$ and $n = 1$ will appear in both spectra (2 to 1 in emission, 1 to 2 in absorption), while the transition between $n = 4$ and $n = 2$ will appear only in the emission spectrum. There are many such additional transitions available in the emission spectrum, so it is much richer in lines than the absorption spectrum.

8.) The Balmer series is the most well-known series of spectral lines in the hydrogen atom. Yet, in an absorption spectrum of hydrogen, the Balmer series does not appear. Why is this?

This is a closely related question to that in Mystery #7. The *Lyman* series in hydrogen is that set of spectral lines representing transitions between the $n = 1$ state and higher states. In an *emission* spectrum, the atoms are excited to higher states by some external energy source and will subsequently make transitions to the lower states. The final states will include $n = 1$, giving the Lyman series, as well as $n = 2$, giving the Balmer series, $n = 3$, giving the *Paschen* series, etc.

In an absorption spectrum, however, the sample is normally at room temperature and excited by the passage of continuous light. As a result, excitations that contribute to the absorption spectrum will be from $n = 1$, as discussed in Mystery #7, which dictates that the spectral lines will belong to the Lyman series.

9.) Moseley used Bohr Theory, which is for *one-electron atoms*, for his X-ray studies of *many-electron atoms*; why did it work so well?

Moseley was studying the *characteristic* X-rays from targets in 1913. These X-rays occur when an accelerated electron strikes a target atom and liberates an inner electron from the atom. The decay of a higher energy electron into the newly formed vacancy results in the emission of an X-ray photon. This is a separate mechanism from *bremsstrahlung*, which is X-radiation resulting from accelerations of the electrons as they scatter off atoms in the target material.

Let us imagine that an $n = 1$ electron has been ejected from the atom and an $n = 2$ electron is going to fill the vacancy. Moseley modeled the $n = 2$ electron as if it were in a Bohr orbit. Despite the fact that the target atom has many electrons, this model worked quite well, resulting in accurate results. Why could Moseley ignore the effects of the other electrons?

First, we can ignore the effects of the outer electrons by means of *Gauss' Law*. Since the $n = 2$ electrons have a large probability of being closer to the nucleus than the outer electrons, they will experience little electric field from these electrons.

The effective nuclear charge "seen" by the $n = 2$ electron is the nuclear charge less the negative charge of the one remaining $n = 1$ electron. Thus, we can model the $n = 2$ electron as being in a Bohr orbit around a nucleus of charge $Z - 1$. This is what Moseley did in his analysis, and the results were surprisingly good.

10.) A graph of ionization energy (the energy needed to remove one electron from the atom) of the elements is shown in the diagram. What causes the regular <u>peaks</u> in the data?

The peaks in the graph occur at the inert gases. Adding one more electron to form the alkali metals results in the lowest points in the graph. Between the alkali metal and the next inert gas, the ionization energy rises. The rise is due primarily to the increasing nuclear charge as one moves across a period in the periodic table. This increasing nuclear charge results in more tightly bound electrons and, therefore, an increasing value of the energy necessary to remove an electron.

Upon reaching an inert gas, the ionization energy reaches a local maximum. When the next electron is added (as well as a proton to the nucleus), it must go into a higher energy shell to obey the Pauli Exclusion Principle. As a result, it is less tightly bound than the previous electrons, and the ionization energy drops dramatically.

11.) The magnetic properties of a material are determined by the electrons in the atom. But, wait a minute. Protons and neutrons in the nucleus have the *same spin as electrons*. Why don't these nuclear particles contribute to the magnetic properties?

It is true that nucleons have the same spin as the electrons in an atom. But the magnetic properties are determined by the *magnetic moments* of the particles, not the spins. The magnitude of the magnetic moment of an electron (μ_e) is related to the spin by the following equation* involving the spin, the electric charge and the electron mass:

$$|\mu_e| = \frac{e}{m_e}|\mathbf{S}| = \frac{e}{m_e}\frac{\sqrt{3}}{2}\hbar = \sqrt{3}\left(\frac{e\hbar}{2m_e}\right) = \sqrt{3}\mu_B = 1.73\mu_B$$

where μ_B is defined as the *Bohr magneton*:

$$\mu_B \equiv \frac{e\hbar}{2m_e}$$

The direction of the magnetic moment is determined by the sign of the charge. For electrons, the negative charge results in a magnetic moment that is directed oppositely to the spin.

For protons, the magnetic moment is in the *same* direction as the spin. Its magnitude is measured experimentally to be,

$$|\mu_p| = 2.79\mu_N$$

where μ_N is the *nuclear magneton*:

$$\mu_N \equiv \frac{e\hbar}{2m_p}$$

Due to the difference in the masses of the electron and the proton, the nuclear magneton is much smaller than the Bohr magneton. This results in a *much smaller magnetic moment* for the proton than for the electron. As a result, it is the electrons which determine the magnetic behavior of atoms, not protons.

It is interesting to add at this point that the neutron, even though electrically neutral, has a *non-zero magnetic moment*:

$$|\mu_n| = 1.91\mu_N$$

This fact suggests that the neutron has an *internal charge structure*, which is consistent with the quark model, which will be discussed in Chapter 23.

𝕸𝖆𝖌𝖎𝖈:

Atomic Physics in the Streets

The spectra that you see will depend on the type of lamp. For an incandescent light, you will see a continuous spectrum of colors. From a low pressure sodium light, you should be able to see a very bright line in the yellow. A mercury lamp should exhibit strong lines in the blue and green. See Mystery #2 for more discussion.

---

* In practice, since the *x*- and *y*-components of **S** are not quantized, only the *z*-component of the magnetic moment is often considered: $\mu_{e,z} = \mu_B$. What's more, the magnetic moments given are *approximations*. Due to the interaction of the electron with the vacuum, more accurate expressions are, $\mu_e = 1.73406\mu_B$ and $\mu_{e,z} = 1.00116\mu_B$.

𝔐𝔶𝔱𝔥:

1.) Protons, neutrons and electrons are fundamental particles.

The current understanding of fundamental particles employs the *standard model*, more of which will be discussed in Chapter 23. In this model, the electron *is* a fundamental particle, in a family with five other particles (muon, tau, electron neutrino, muon neutrino and tau neutrino), collectively called *leptons*. In addition, there are six *antiparticles* corresponding to these six leptons. Protons and neutrons, however, along with many other particles, collectively called *hadrons*, can be shown to be combinations of *quarks* (some of the hadrons, those called *mesons*, are combinations of a quark and an antiquark). Thus, *the proton and neutron are not fundamental*.

2.) Electrons spin.

The spin of an electron, or any other particle, is an *intrinsic angular momentum*. We can not derive this angular momentum from classical physics. The electron is imagined to have no radius and, therefore, *the concept of a mechanical spin has no meaning*.

It is tempting to make an analogy to Earth—the motion around the Sun is analogous to the orbital motion of the electron and the Earth's rotation on its axis represents the electron spin. While this analogy has some merit in visualizing the two types of angular momentum, care must be taken to not adopt the spinning electron as the appropriate picture.

3.) The picture at the right is that of an atom.

The diagram accompanying this Myth, or a variation of it, is often seen in corporate logos and other everyday references to atomic physics. It is important to keep in mind, however, that this is a Bohr/Sommerfeld picture of the atom, with its well-defined circular or elliptical orbits. Thus, this picture has its origins in 1913 and has not kept up with the times. The current understanding of the atom, in terms of wave functions and probability distributions, has no well-defined orbits and would appear in picture form as a set of rather uninteresting smears of probability.

4.) The Balmer equation is shown to the right. $\frac{1}{\lambda} = R \left(\frac{1}{2^2} - \frac{1}{n^2} \right)$

J. J. Balmer did indeed develop, in 1885, an empirical equation to describe the spectral wavelengths of the hydrogen atom. The equation that he proposed, however, was of the following form, as discussed in the Concepts section:

$$\lambda = 364.56 \, \frac{n^2}{n^2 - 4}$$

where *n* is an integer starting at 3, and the wavelength will be in units of nanometers when applying this equation.

The equation was cast in a more useful form (in terms of its agreement with the results of the Bohr theory of the atom in 1913) by Johannes Rydberg and Walther Ritz:

$$\frac{1}{\lambda} = R\left(\frac{1}{2^2} - \frac{1}{n^2}\right)$$

where *R* is the *Rydberg constant*, $R = 1.097 \times 10^7$ m^{-1}. An even more useful form was proposed by Rydberg and Ritz in 1890, as follows,

$$\frac{1}{\lambda} = R\left(\frac{1}{n_f^{\,2}} - \frac{1}{n_i^{\,2}}\right)$$

where we have used symbols representing a more contemporary understanding of the significance of the integers than was had at the time of the first Rydberg-Ritz equation: n_f is the principal quantum number of the *final* state of the atomic transition, and n_i is the principal quantum number of the *initial* state.

5.) Elements in the periodic table are ordered by atomic mass.

Over the entire periodic table, this statement is generally true. But there are a couple of exceptions on a more local level. For example, let's look at cobalt ($Z = 27$) and nickel ($Z = 28$). Their atomic masses are, respectively, 58.933 and 58.71. Thus, even though nickel has more particles, it has less mass than cobalt (due to a difference in binding energy). Another example, with a much more dramatic difference in chemical behavior is argon ($Z = 18$, atomic mass = 39.948, inert gas) and potassium ($Z = 19$, atomic mass = 39.0983, alkali metal).

The periodic table was originally ordered by atomic mass and there appeared to be some problems with matching the chemical behavior, due to effects such as those described above. It was Moseley's X-ray work in the early part of the twentieth century which provided a method for determining the atomic number and allowed the correct ordering of the elements.

6.) Millikan measured the charge on the electron.

While this statement is common, it is not *strictly* true. Millikan, in his famous oil drop experiment, measured electrical charges on oil drops. These charges may have been due to excess electrons, but may also have been due to positive ions. In analyzing the common submultiple of the charges that were observed, Millikan was able to generate a value for the elementary charge. It was then a matter of reasoning to extend the value of this charge to the electron, as well as the proton.

There is danger in the statement given in the Myth that it will be interpreted to mean that Millikan worked directly with electrons, which is not the case.

7.) The energies shown in the accompanying diagram are *electron energy levels* in the hydrogen atom.

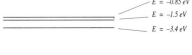

$E = -0.85\,eV$

$E = -1.5\,eV$

$E = -3.4\,eV$

$E = -13.6\,eV$

Electron energy levels is a very common phrase used to describe energy levels in atoms, but it should be remembered that the energy is not just that associated with the electron, but rather with the *entire system*—electron(s) and nucleus. An easy way to remind oneself of this is to remember that one contribution to the energy is the electric potential energy between the positively charged nucleus and the negatively charged electron. Electric potential energy (for that matter, *any* type of potential energy) requires two interacting entities. Thus, both the electrons and the nucleus must contribute to the system energy of the atom.

A similar erroneous phrase often occurs in describing gravitational potential energy systems. For example, one can ask, "What is the (gravitational) potential energy of the book on the table?" This question has no answer, since potential energy is only defined for a system of at least two interacting entities. Thus, the more proper question is, "What is the mutual (gravitational) potential energy of the *book-Earth system* when the book is on the table?". This is more cumbersome to say than the first question, so it will be difficult to persuade people to use the more correct wording!

8.) Bohr assumed angular momentum quantization as a fundamental postulate to arrive at his theory for the hydrogen atom.

The assumption of the quantization of angular momentum of the electron in a circular orbit,

$$L = n\hbar$$

is often given in textbook treatments of the Bohr theory as a fundamental postulate, from which the equations relating to the electron's motion are derived. It is true that Bohr used this quantization condition as a starting point in later papers, but *only after deriving it from a more fundamental concept in his first paper of 1913.*

For a particle of mass m moving in a circular orbit of radius r at speed v, the angular momentum is given by the simple expression,

$$L = mvr$$

It was recognized in the first decade of the twentieth century that Planck's constant has units of angular momentum, that is, the product of units for mass, speed and radius:

$$h \sim J \cdot s = \left(kg \cdot \frac{m^2}{s^2} \right) \cdot s = kg \cdot \frac{m}{s} \cdot m$$

This spawned a number of attempts to produce nuclear atom models that used this constant as a quantum of change in angular momentum in atomic processes. Bohr's successful theory ultimately included this quantum change, but it was generated from a more basic precept—the *Correspondence Principle*.

The Correspondence Principle in quantum mechanics states that quantum results must blend smoothly into classical results in the limit as the quantum systems become macroscopic. This is similar to the Correspondence Principle in relativity, in which relativistic results must blend smoothly into classical results as the speed of the particle becomes much smaller than the speed of light.

We can produce a macroscopic Bohr atom by letting the principal quantum number, n (the *only* quantum number in the Bohr theory), become very large. We will demonstrate a way of arriving at angular momentum quantization below from the Correspondence Principle. The process will be a bit long and mathematical, but straightforward. The particular result that we will consider is the *frequency of light* emitted from the atom. For a classical system, this frequency is simply the frequency of the circular motion of the electron:

$$f_{classical} = \frac{1}{T} = \frac{v}{2\pi r}$$

where T is the orbital period, r is the radius of the orbit and v is the electron's tangential velocity. Now, we can evaluate v from Newton's Second Law, the expression for the Coulomb force, and the expression for centripetal acceleration:

$$F = ma \quad \rightarrow \quad k\frac{e^2}{r^2} = m\frac{v^2}{r} \quad \rightarrow \quad v^2 = \frac{ke^2}{mr}$$

where m is the mass of the electron, e is the electric charge on the electron and proton, and k is the electrical constant ($k = 9 \times 10^9$ N·m²·C⁻²). Using this, we evaluate the square of the classical frequency:

$$f_{classical}^2 = \left(\frac{v}{2\pi r}\right)^2 = \frac{v^2}{4\pi^2 r^2} = \frac{\left(\frac{ke^2}{mr}\right)}{4\pi^2 r^2} = \frac{ke^2}{4\pi^2 mr^3} \tag{1}$$

Now, we calculate the Bohr model frequency. This will be the frequency of the photon emitted by the atom when it makes a quantum jump from an excited state to the next lower state. We start from the Rydberg-Ritz equation, as seen in the discussion of Myth #4:

$$\frac{1}{\lambda} = R\left(\frac{1}{n_f^2} - \frac{1}{n_i^2}\right) \quad \rightarrow \quad f_{Bohr} = \frac{c}{\lambda} = cR\left(\frac{1}{n_f^2} - \frac{1}{n_i^2}\right)$$

where c is the speed of light. We let $n_f = n$ and $n_i = n + 1$, whereby,

$$f_{Bohr} = cR\left(\frac{1}{n^2} - \frac{1}{(n+1)^2}\right) = cR\left(\frac{(n+1)^2 - n^2}{n^2(n+1)^2}\right) = cR\left(\frac{2n+1}{n^2(n+1)^2}\right)$$

Now, we let n become very large, and we can make the approximation (ignoring 1 compared to n in the previous expression),

$$f_{Bohr} \approx cR\left(\frac{2n}{n^2(n)^2}\right) = \frac{2cR}{n^3}$$

The Correspondence Principle demands that this frequency be the same as the classical frequency:

$$f_{Bohr} = \frac{2cR}{n^3} \quad \rightarrow \quad f_{classical} = \frac{2cR}{n^3} \tag{2}$$

We will need one more result before we can put this all together, and that relates to the *energy* of the electron in its orbit. We can express the total energy as the sum of kinetic and potential energies:

$$E = KE + PE = \frac{1}{2}mv^2 - k\frac{e^2}{r}$$

and we substitute for the square of the velocity the expression that we found above:

$$E = \frac{1}{2}m\left(\frac{ke^2}{mr}\right) - k\frac{e^2}{r} = \frac{1}{2}k\frac{e^2}{r} - k\frac{e^2}{r} = -\frac{1}{2}k\frac{e^2}{r}$$

If we multiply the Rydberg-Ritz equation by hc, then we can identify each of the two terms on the right hand side as an energy of a stationary state.

$$hc\frac{1}{\lambda} = hcR\left(\frac{1}{n_f^2} - \frac{1}{n_i^2}\right) \quad \rightarrow \quad hf_{Bohr} = hcR\left|\frac{1}{n_f^2} - \frac{1}{n_i^2}\right| = \left|E_f - E_i\right|$$

Thus, the energy of the atom can be expressed as,

$$E = -\frac{hcR}{n^2}$$

Setting the two expressions for the energy equal, we can solve for the radius of the orbit:

$$E = -\frac{hcR}{n^2} = -\frac{1}{2}k\frac{e^2}{r} \quad \rightarrow \quad r = n^2\frac{ke^2}{2hcR} \tag{3}$$

Now, if we set the two expressions for f^2 equal, from equations (1) and (2), and substitute the expression for r from equation (3), we can evaluate the Rydberg constant:

$$f_{classical}^2 = \frac{4c^2R^2}{n^6} = \frac{ke^2}{4\pi^2mr^3} = \frac{ke^2}{4\pi^2m}\frac{8h^3c^3R^3}{n^6k^3e^6} \quad \rightarrow \quad R = \frac{2\pi^2m(ke^2)^2}{ch^3}$$

The next step is to evaluate the velocity from the Correspondence Principle, by equating the two frequencies again, but leaving the classical frequency in terms of the velocity:

$$f_{classical} = f_{Bohr} \quad \rightarrow \quad \frac{v}{2\pi r} = \frac{2cR}{n^3} \quad \rightarrow \quad v = \frac{4\pi cRr}{n^3}$$

Now, we are ready to set up the angular momentum of the electron in its circular orbit:

$$L = mvr = m\left(\frac{4\pi cRr}{n^3}\right)r = m\left(\frac{4\pi c}{n^3}\right)Rr^2 = m\left(\frac{4\pi c}{n^3}\right)R\left(n^4 \frac{(ke^2)^2}{4h^2c^2R^2}\right) = mn\frac{\pi(ke^2)^2}{ch^2R}$$

and, finally, we substitute in this expression our value for R:

$$L = mn\frac{\pi(ke^2)^2}{ch^2\left(\dfrac{2\pi^2m(ke^2)^2}{ch^3}\right)} = n\frac{h}{2\pi} = n\hbar$$

Thus, the quantization of angular momentum is a result of the combination of classical physics, the Rydberg-Ritz equation, and the Correspondence Principle. From the length of this derivation, it is easy to see why it is tempting to adopt the quantization as a beginning postulate. In doing so, the generation of the allowed radii and energies of the hydrogen atom is relatively easy. On the other hand, beginning with the quantization condition is not historically accurate and hides from students a nice application of the Correspondence Principle.

9.) The angular momentum quantization condition in the Bohr atom can be demonstrated by showing that an integral number of deBroglie wavelengths fit around the orbit of the electron.

A common technique in modern physics textbooks is to "verify" the quantization of angular momentum in the hydrogen atom by showing that an integral number of deBroglie waves exactly fit around the circumference of the orbit. This is very tempting, as can be seen by the mathematical development. If the circumference is equal to an integral number of wavelengths, then,

$$n\lambda = 2\pi r$$

Now, we substitute the expression for the deBroglie wavelength for a non-relativistic particle:

$$n\frac{h}{mv} = 2\pi r$$

and we algebraically rearrange the factors in order to set up the product mvr:

$$mvr = n\frac{h}{2\pi} \quad \rightarrow \quad L = n\hbar$$

which is the Bohr quantization condition.

There are a number of conceptual difficulties with this approach, however. Some textbooks claim that there are *standing waves*, complete with nodes, around the orbit. If there are fixed nodes at various points along the orbit, what determines which points will be nodes and which points will not? The existence of special points (nodes) indicates that there is an *anisotropy* to the atom, which is not the case.

Other treatments do not discuss standing waves, but allow for the pattern of waves to move around the circumference. This approach suggests that *a one-dimensional wave travels around the orbit*. This is slightly more reasonable than the standing wave argument, but it must be kept in mind that this is a mixture of classical and quantum physics, just like the Bohr model. Thus, it does not represent a picture that is consistent. The full quantum treatment of the atom would require thinking of a *three dimensional* wave function in the region of the atom. While the integral wavelength idea may be mathematically tempting, it could lead to misconceptions in students' minds that there is a simple wave traveling around the orbit.

10.) Electrons have either spin up or spin down.

Although these are very common descriptions of the two spin states of an electron, they are not strictly true, at least if we interpret *up* as *straight up* and *down* as *straight down*. If a vector is straight up, with respect to a z-axis, say, then the length of the vector will be identical with the z-component of the vector. Let us check this in the case of the spin vector. Its length is,

$$|\mathbf{S}| = \sqrt{s(s+1)}\,\hbar = \sqrt{\frac{1}{2}\left(\frac{1}{2}+1\right)}\,\hbar = \frac{\sqrt{3}}{2}\hbar$$

Now, we calculate the z-component for the *spin up* case,

$$S_z = m_s\hbar = \frac{1}{2}\hbar$$

Thus, the length and the z-component *do not match*, so that the vector cannot be straight up.

We can use these two numbers to find the angle that the spin vector actually makes with the z-axis in this approach:

$$\theta = \cos^{-1}\left(\frac{S_z}{|\mathbf{S}|}\right) = \cos^{-1}\left(\frac{\frac{1}{2}\hbar}{\frac{\sqrt{3}}{2}\hbar}\right) = \left(\frac{1}{\sqrt{3}}\right) = 55°$$

Thus, the spin vector is *55° away* from the straight up orientation.

11.) When an atom or nucleus emits a photon by making a transition from a high energy quantized state to a lower such state, the energy of the photon is equal to the difference in energies between the initial and final states of the transition.

This is only true in the idealized case of an infinitely massive atom. Since the outgoing photon carries momentum, the atom must *recoil* to conserve momentum. Thus, a small amount of the decay energy is carried by the recoiling atom. We can determine this amount of energy by combining the conservation of momentum and energy equations. We assume that the recoil velocity of the atom will be very slow, so that we do not need to use relativistic equations.

We begin by setting up conservation of momentum and energy for the photon (subscript *ph*) and the atom (subscript *at*), of mass M, for a process in which the atom makes a transition between states separated in energy by ΔE:

Momentum : $\quad 0 = p_{ph} + p_{at} = -\dfrac{E_{ph}}{c} + \sqrt{2M\,KE_{at}} \qquad \rightarrow \qquad KE_{at} = \dfrac{E_{ph}^2}{2Mc^2}$

Energy : $\qquad 0 = E_{ph} + KE_{at} - \Delta E \qquad\qquad\qquad \rightarrow \qquad E_{ph} = \Delta E - KE_{at}$

Now, substituting KE_{at} from the first equation into the second equation, we obtain,

$$E_{ph} = \Delta E - \frac{(\Delta E)^2}{2Mc^2}$$

where we have used the approximation in the second term,

$$E_{ph} \approx \Delta E$$

since the kinetic energy of the atom is negligible compared to its rest energy. From this result, it is easy to see that the hypothetical infinitely massive atom would result in the photon energy being equal to the difference in energy between the states. For a real situation, however, the photon energy is slightly less than ΔE. Let us evaluate this difference. The biggest effect will be for the lightest atom, so let us imagine a transition from $n = 2$ ($E = -3.4$ eV) to $n = 1$ ($E = -13.6$ eV) in hydrogen:

$$\frac{(\Delta E)^2}{2Mc^2} = \frac{(13.6\,\text{eV} - 3.4\,\text{eV})^2}{2(938\,\text{MeV})} = 5.5 \times 10^{-8}\ \text{eV}$$

where the rest energy of the proton (938 MeV) has been substituted for the rest energy of the hydrogen atom, due to the relatively small rest energy of the electron. This shift, compared to the value of $\Delta E = 10.2$ eV, is essentially negligible. But what about *nuclear* transitions, resulting in the emission of gamma rays? Gamma ray energies are measured in MeV, so perhaps there may be a measurable shift here. As an example, let us consider the gamma ray decay of ^{11}Be, with a rest energy of 1.03×10^4 MeV. This isotope has a number of gamma ray energies; let us choose the highest, 7.97 MeV, and approximate this as ΔE. Then, the correction term is,

$$\frac{(\Delta E)^2}{2Mc^2} = \frac{(7.97\ \text{MeV})^2}{2(1.03 \times 10^4\,\text{MeV})} = 3.08 \times 10^{-3}\ \text{MeV}$$

This is still small, but not as small (relative to the photon energy) as in the case of atomic transitions. This correction is 0.04% of the energy of the photon.

If the atom emitting the photon is bound in a crystal, then the crystal as a whole can absorb the momentum. In many cases, the recoil of the atom causes a mechanical wave to move through the crystal, which we describe by saying that the atom emits a *phonon* at the same time as the *photon*. It is possible however, especially at low temperatures, for the photon to be emitted without an accompanying phonon, in which case the entire crystal takes up the recoil momentum. Since the mass of the crystal is so large, the photon energy is *extremely* close to the energy difference between the states. This type of recoil-less emission is called the *Mössbauer Effect*, which was first studied in the 1950's. It allows for very sharp measurements of photon energies. Mössbauer received the Nobel Prize in physics in 1961 for his discovery.

A number of applications of the Mössbauer Effect are discussed in Chapter 16 of R. Eisberg and R. Resnick, *Quantum Physics of Atoms, Molecules, Solids, Nuclei, and Particles*, 2nd ed., John Wiley & Sons, New York, 1985. The Mössbauer Effect was instrumental in the notable Pound-Rebka experiment in 1960, which demonstrated the gravitational red shift predicted by Einstein's General Theory of Relativity. This experiment is described in C. M. Will, *Was Einstein Right?*, Basic Books, Inc., New York, 1986.

There are a number of other contributions to variations from the simple energy relation $hf = \Delta E$. These include effects due to the uncertainty principle, the intensity of absorbed radiation, the Doppler effect for moving atoms, and collisions with neighboring atoms. Books on atomic physics can be consulted for information on these contributions.

12.) A brochure for television sets has the following statement: "We've coated the cathode of the electron gun with a rare-earth element called scandium oxide."

The phrase *scandium oxide* refers to a combination of atoms, making up a *compound*, not an *element*.

13.) A molecule is the smallest part into which a substance can be divided which still has all of the properties of the substance.

This erroneous statement appears in some books as the definition of a molecule. While a molecule may retain *some* of the characteristics of the substance, it does not exhibit those characteristics that depend on the *bulk behavior*. For example, a molecule of water will display similar light absorption to that exhibited by a collection of molecules, but does it make sense to discuss the *boiling point* of a water molecule? A "molecule" of salt, NaCl, is still identified as salt, yet it carries none of the *cubic structure* of a salt *crystal*. Thus, some properties are still present for a single molecule, such as absorption of electromagnetic radiation, intrinsic angular momentum, and others that depend only on the atomic structure of the molecule. Other properties depend on interactions *between* molecules, such as crystal structure, hardness, boiling and melting points, color, and the like. These properties are lost when we go to the single molecule stage.

Chapter 20
Solid State Physics

𝔐ysteries:

1.) Metals are *opaque* and they are good *electrical conductors*. Why?

2.) Many *electrical insulators* are *transparent*. Why?

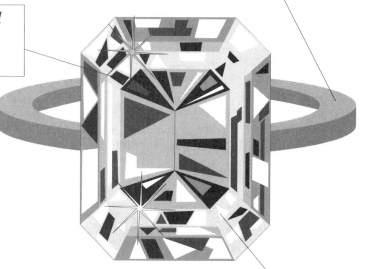

3.) Diamond is *very hard* and its room temperature *heat capacity is low*. Is there any relationship between these properties?

4.) Why is a red light safe in a darkroom?

Developer

Stop Bath

Fixer

𝕸𝖞𝖘𝖙𝖊𝖗𝖎𝖊𝖘:

5.) In an ionic crystal, the atoms attract because of the Coulomb force between opposite charges. Why don't these solids just *collapse* due to this force?

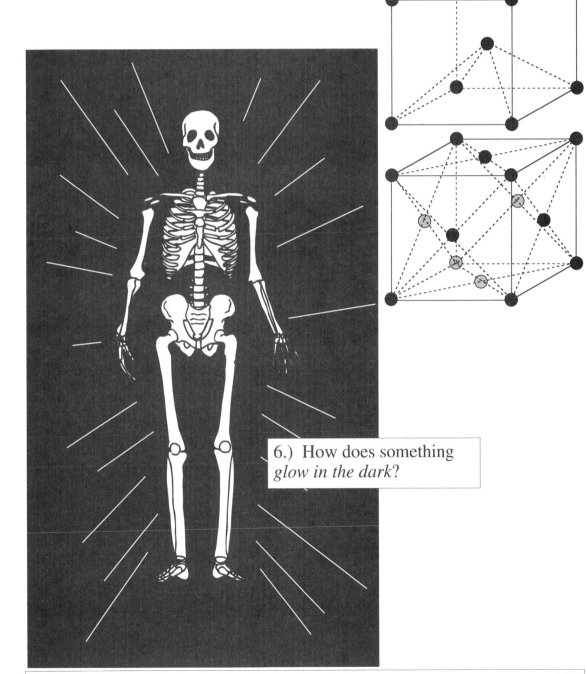

6.) How does something *glow in the dark*?

Mysteries:

7.) *Photochromic glasses* contain lenses which automatically darken when exposed to sunlight. How do these lenses work?

8.) Why is ice less dense than water?

9.) In old buildings, why is the glass in the windows thicker at the bottom than at the top?

Mysteries:

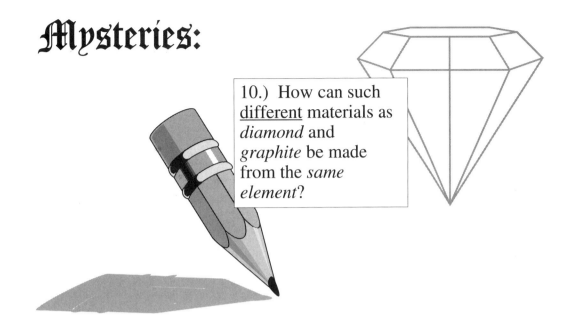

10.) How can such <u>different</u> materials as *diamond* and *graphite* be made from the *same element*?

Magic:

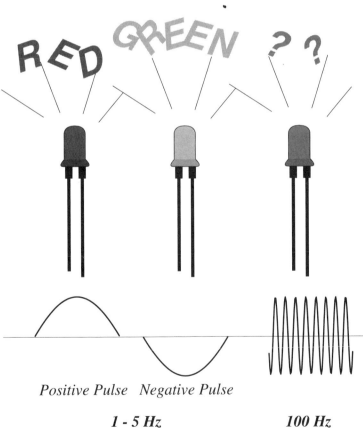

Positive Pulse   Negative Pulse

1 - 5 Hz

100 Hz

The Bicolor (Tricolor?) LED

Bicolor light emitting diodes are available. One such device has a red and a green LED in a single package, with the connections in reverse. Thus, if this LED is powered by an AC source at low frequency (say 1 - 5 Hz), it will alternately flash red and green as the voltage reverses. What color is it if the frequency is raised to, say, 100 Hz?

Magic:

Brightening Your Wash

Place some powdered laundry detergent under an ultraviolet light source. What do you see?

Myth:

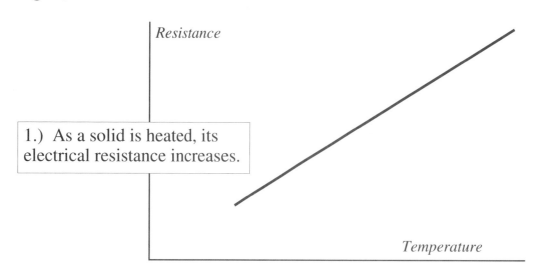

Resistance

1.) As a solid is heated, its electrical resistance increases.

Temperature

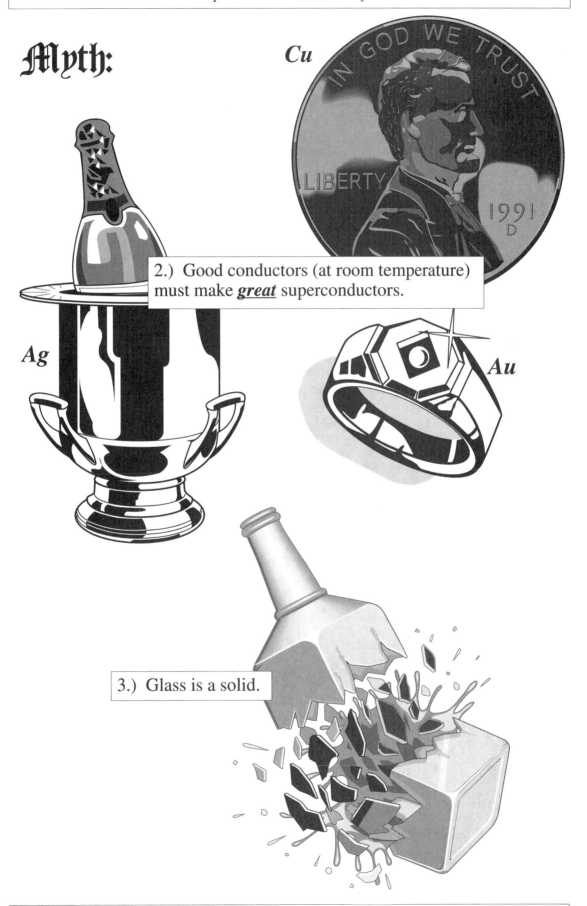

𝔐𝔶𝔱𝔥:

Cu

2.) Good conductors (at room temperature) must make ***great*** superconductors.

Ag

Au

3.) Glass is a solid.

Concepts of Solid State Physics

Gases are interesting because there are *very weak* interactions among the atoms, and the interatomic distances are large. This leads, for example, to the fact that the gas constant, R, is independent of the type of gas, and to the uniformity among molar heat capacities for gases. Solids are at the other extreme—there are *very strong* interactions among atoms. This is interesting, too, because it means that there will be a variety of behaviors among different solids, unlike the uniformity of behavior among gases. In addition, there will be new behaviors of solids that are meaningless for gases; for example, solids display varying degree of *brittleness*, but this property has no significance for a gas. We cannot hope to cover all of the theory of solids in this short Concepts section—entire books can be written on this subject (and have been!). We will provide a flavor of the study of solids and hope that the interested reader will pursue the topic further in other sources.

> *Solids have a wide range of properties, due to the strong interactions among atoms.*

The strong interatomic forces in a solid result in the atoms residing in permanent locations within the body of the solid, unlike in gases or liquids, in which atoms can move around within the bulk. There are two possibilities for the relationships of these permanent locations with each other. In an *amorphous* solid, there is no distinct pattern of locations. There are a variety of bond lengths and strengths. Thus, there is no sharp melting point for an amorphous solid. As the temperature rises, weaker bonds break first, followed in turn by stronger and stronger bonds as the temperature continues to increase. Thus, an amorphous solid simply *softens* as the temperature increases. Glass is a familiar example of an amorphous solid. These types of solids can even be interpreted as extremely viscous liquids, since they will *flow*, albeit very slowly.

The second possibility for the atomic positions is that there is a regular arrangement of atoms within the solid. For example, they may form an arrangement such that one can visualize cubic shapes, with an atom at each corner. A variety of other geometric shapes are also possible. These types of solids are called *crystalline*, and they will be the focus of our attention.

> *Amorphous solids have no regular arrangement of atoms. Crystalline solids have a regular arrangement of atoms.*

In understanding the properties of solids, we must start with an appropriate *model*. We will investigate two such models in this section.

The Spring Model

In this model, we imagine that the atoms are connected by springs, representing the interatomic forces. Even though each atom, in reality, interacts with all other atoms in the crystal, we build this model by imagining that an atom is connected by springs only to its nearest neighbors. A two-dimensional cross

Concepts of Solid State Physics (continued)

section through a cubic crystal in this model is shown in the diagram below.

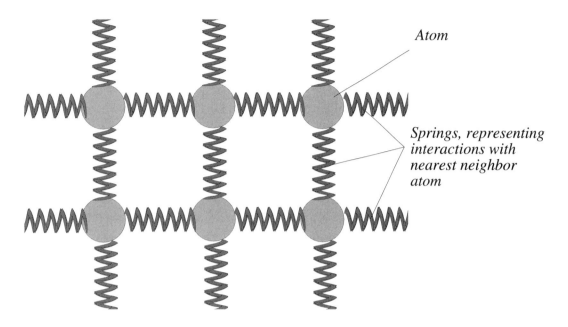

Atom

Springs, representing interactions with nearest neighbor atom

This model is useful for conceptually understanding some simple mechanical, thermal and acoustical properties. For example, a mechanical property which is successfully modeled here is *Young's Modulus*. By relating the macroscopic force on a piece of material to the compression of the microscopic interatomic springs, a prediction of Young's modulus for a solid can be made. In the realm of thermal properties, the specific heat for a solid can be modeled by considering the vibrations of the atoms about their equilibrium positions, combined with acoustic waves propagating through the material (see the section on *Debye Theory* in a modern physics or solid state physics book for further discussion of this). The speed of sound in a solid can be predicted by imagining a disturbance to pass along the line of springs.

While this model is useful and powerful for some applications, we will pay more attention to the second of our two models, which will allow us to predict *optical* and *electrical* properties of solids.

The Band Model

In our discussion of atomic physics (Chapter 19), we noted that there are *discrete* energy levels available to the atomic systems. Let us think about what happens to these levels when we bring two atoms together. We will state the result first and then consider an argument: *when two atoms are brought close enough together, such that their wave functions overlap, they can be considered to be a single system, and the discrete states of the single atoms split into two states (of different energy) of the two-atom system.*

We can argue this from the wave function. Since $|\psi|^2$ is physically significant, and ψ is not, a given atom can have either a positive-valued wave function,

Concepts of Solid State Physics (continued)

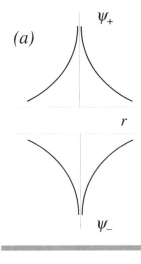

(a)

or a negative-valued wave function, and still have the same $|\psi|^2$. Thus, the sign of the wave function is immaterial for *single* atoms. The diagrams (*a*) to the left show simple wave functions for an atom, one positive, one negative, as a function of *r*, the distance of the electron from the nucleus. The diagrams (*b*) to the right show the result of *squaring* these wave functions. The squared wave function, which has the physical significance, is the same for both cases in (*a*), since squaring a negative number or function makes it positive. Thus, in making measurements on an atomic system, we cannot tell which of the two states in (*a*) the atom is in; they are equivalent.

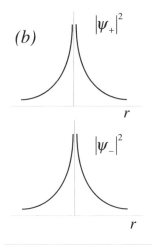

(b)

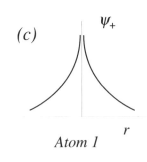

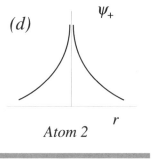

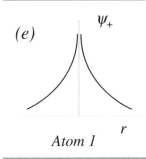

(c)

But now imagine *two atoms*. There are two possibilities for the *relative* signs of the wave functions—the wave functions of both atoms are positive (or both negative; this will give the same result when the composite is squared), or one is positive and one is negative. These possibilities are shown to the side. On the left (*c*) is the (positive) wave function of atom 1 and on the right (*d*) is the (positive) wave function of atom 2.

(d)

This is compared to the other possibility shown to the sides, of atom 1 in a positive wave function state (*e*) and atom 2 in a negative wave function state (*f*).

(e)

(f)

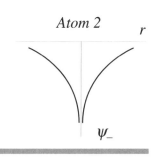

These diagrams represent the situation when the atoms are far apart. But suppose we bring them close together. Then, the wave functions will overlap and we should consider the *composite wave function* for the combined system, rather than two separate wave functions. When we bring the two positive wave function atoms (*c*, *d*) together, the positive values of the wave functions between the atoms will *add*. The result is shown to the right (*g*).

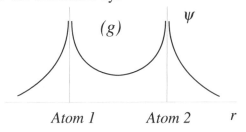

(g)

Concepts of Solid State Physics (continued)

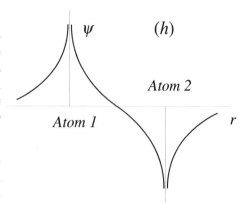

When we bring the positive-negative wave functions (*e*, *f*) together, the wave functions halfway between the atoms will *cancel*. The composite wave function in this case is shown to the right (*h*).

Thus, the composite probability amplitudes for the two possibilities are different. *These represent two possible states of the two-atom system.* Let us think in particular about these curves representing the probability amplitude of finding an electron. The positive-positive curve (*g*) shows some probability of finding the electron at the midpoint between the atoms. The positive-negative function (*h*) shows no such probability. If we think about these two states in terms of energy, they must have different energies. A state with an electron *between* two positive nuclei (resulting in a binding force from the Coulomb attraction of the electron on both nuclei) must have a different energy than that with the electron elsewhere! Thus, we see the *splitting* of the energy states into two levels due to the different ways of combining the wave functions. The energy difference is relatively small, so the two states are close together on an energy scale.

If we now extend this thought process to three atoms, we find three independent ways to combine the wave functions—positive-positive-positive, positive-negative-positive, positive-positive-negative. This will lead to three energy states. If we continue this process to Avogadro's number of atoms, we can argue that the single atom states will split into Avogadro's number of energy states. But, by combining this many atoms, we have built a macroscopic crystal! The crystal can be modeled on an energy scale by imagining a very large number of energy states separated by very small differences—we call such a collection of states a *band*. The forbidden energy regions between the *states* in single atoms will appear as forbidden gaps between the *bands* in the solid. Some of these forbidden regions will disappear in the solid, however, since the spreading in energy of the bands will cause overlaps between bands.

Bringing atoms into close proximity splits the energy states and forms <u>bands</u> of very closely-lying energy states.

Just as some states in an atom have electrons and others do not, some bands in the solid will have electrons and others will not. The highest energy band that is filled with electrons is called the *valence band*. The next highest band is called the *conduction band*. It is either empty or partially filled with electrons (if it were full, it would be the valence band, by definition!). It is these bands which will determine much of the optical and electrical behavior of the solid.

Concepts of Solid State Physics (continued)

Now that we have this new model, let us apply it to some additional properties of solids. For example, why are some solids transparent? If we imagine a photon of light entering a solid, it can give up its energy to an electron in the valence band and excite it into the conduction band. But what if the energy gap between the bands is larger than the energy of visible photons? Then, the photon cannot be absorbed and it passes right through the solid—the solid is transparent! If the energy gap is similar to the energy of visible photons, some of these photons may be absorbed while others are not, giving the solid a characteristic color, such as the green of an emerald.

The real value in this model is seen in its application to electrical properties. Consider a solid with an empty conduction band, as suggested in the energy diagram below:

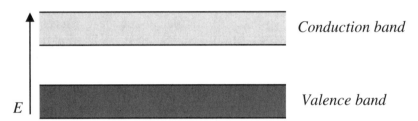

E Conduction band

                Valence band

If we apply a potential difference across a sample of this solid an electric field will be established within the interior. If we consider an electron as a system, it is generally possible for the electric force to transfer energy into the system (by work), which will be stored as kinetic energy—

> An insulator has a filled valence band and an empty conduction band.

the electron will move. If the electrons in the material were to move, we would have established an electric current. But in order to possess this additional energy, the electrons would have to move into higher energy states. The valence band is filled with electrons—there are no available empty states into which it can move. The conduction band has plenty of available states but no electrons! Thus, there will be no electric current in this material—we call such a material an *insulator*.

Now, consider a different situation—suppose that the conduction band is *partially* filled, as suggested below:

> A conductor has a filled valence band and a partially filled conduction band.

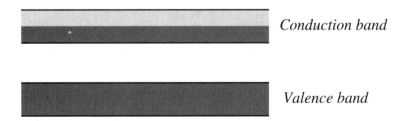

Conduction band

Valence band

In this case, the electrons in the conduction band can absorb energy from the

Concepts of Solid State Physics (continued)

electric field and move into the higher empty energy states. An electric current is established and we call the material that we have modeled in this way a *conductor*.

Finally, let us consider the same situation as that in the insulator, but suppose that the energy gap is relatively small, as suggested below.

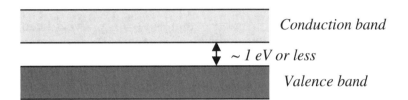

Conduction band

~ 1 eV or less

Valence band

It is possible that energy can be transferred to an electron by means of collisions with lattice atoms or other electrons. This is *thermal* excitation of the electron.

A semiconductor has a filled valence band and an empty conduction band, like an insulator, but also has a narrow forbidden energy gap.

For a small energy gap, there may be a significant number of electrons thermally excited from the valence band to the conduction band. Not only will this provide electrons in the conduction band that can carry a current, but it also leaves electron *vacancies*, called *holes*, in the valence band. These holes can act as effective *positive* charges, and can also participate in carrying current. Thus, an electric field applied to this type of solid will result in a weak current, and we call the material a *semiconductor*. The current is highly temperature dependent, since it depends on thermal excitations of the charge carriers.

This type of *intrinsic* semiconductor is of limited usefulness. More important is an *extrinsic* semiconductor, in which dopants are added, changing significantly the number of charge carriers. These types of doped semiconductors can be combined to form diodes and transistors. The discussion of these devices is beyond the scope of this book and the reader is referred to physics textbooks for further discussions.

Discussions; Chapter 20—Solid State Physics

𝕸𝖞𝖘𝖙𝖊𝖗𝖎𝖊𝖘:

1.) Metals are *opaque* and they are good *electrical conductors*. Why?

In a study of atomic energy levels, it is clear that the energy levels become closer together as the energy rises. In the Bohr theory (see Chapter 19), for example, the lowest two states of the hydrogen atom are separated by 13.6 eV – 3.4 eV = 10.2 eV, while the next two states are separated by 3.4 eV – 1.5 eV = 1.9 eV. It follows, then, that the *bands* which arise from these states, according to the band model of a solid, will also be closer together at higher energies. With states close together, and the states spreading out into bands, the probability of bands *overlapping* is very high. Thus, in many solids, the conduction band overlaps with higher bands to form a combination of bands which represents almost a continuum of states, with no gaps, up to the highest bound state.

According to the band model of a metal, we have electrons in the conduction band, which is why it is a good conductor, as discussed in the Concepts section. When a photon impinges on this structure, there are very many states in the continuum described above into which the electron can be excited. Since almost any energy transition is possible, essentially all photons are absorbed (except for those *reflected* from the surface). Thus, photons do not pass through the metal and it is *opaque*.

2.) Many *electrical insulators* are *transparent*. Why?

In an insulator, the highest energy electrons are at the top of the valence band, as discussed in the Concepts section. In many insulators, the band gap is larger than the energy of a visible photon. Thus, a visible photon entering the material cannot be absorbed, since there are no energy states in which to excite electrons. The photon passes through the material, leading to the concept of *transparency*.

3.) Diamond is *very hard* and its room temperature *heat capacity is low*. Is there any relationship between these properties?

The molar heat capacity of a solid depends on temperature, at least for low temperatures. But the phrase, "for low temperatures", has no meaning unless a *reference* temperature is given—low compared to *what*? This question is answered in the *Debye theory* for heat capacities. The essence of the theory is that energy absorbed by a solid is stored in standing waves of mechanical vibrations in the solid. The theory shows, in excellent agreement with experimental results, that the temperature behavior of the heat capacity is as shown in the diagram on the next page. For high temperatures, the heat capacity of all solids is 3 times the universal gas constant, *R*. For lower temperatures, the heat capacity drops to zero, in a similar way for all solids.

The references to high and low temperatures mentioned are relative to the *Debye temperature*, which is different for each solid and is indicated by the dashed line on the graph.

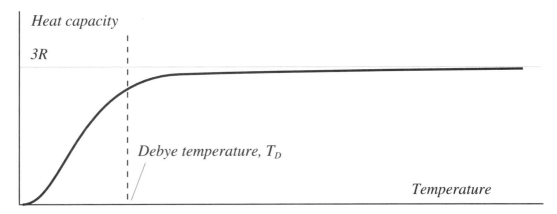

For a material with a very high Debye temperature, room temperature is to the left of the dashed line and the heat capacity at room temperature will be low. For a low-Debye temperature solid, room temperature is to the right of the dashed line and the heat capacity will be close to $3R$.

Debye showed that the Debye temperature, T_D, is given by,

$$T_D = \frac{h}{k} \left\{ \frac{9 N_A}{4 \pi V \left(\frac{1}{v_l^3} + \frac{2}{v_t^3} \right)} \right\}^{\frac{1}{3}}$$

where h is Planck's constant, k is Boltzmann's constant, N_A is Avogadro's number, V is the volume of the solid, and v_l and v_t are the longitudinal and transverse velocities of sound in the solid.

Now, diamond is very hard. This means, if we think about the spring model from the Concepts section, that the springs must have very large spring constants. Large spring constants mean that the interactions between atoms are very strong. Very strong interatomic interactions mean that the speed of sound will be very high. Considering the Debye temperature expression above, high speeds of sound lead to a large Debye temperature. And we have already argued that a large Debye temperature means a low room temperature heat capacity. So, although it is a somewhat complicated relationship, there *is* a relationship between the hardness of a material and its heat capacity!

4.) Why is a red light safe in a darkroom?

The safety of red lights in the darkroom is actually only true for black and white film processing. Since paper used in color processing must be sensitive to red light, in order to reproduce any reds in a picture, special safelights must be used for this type of processing. A number of such lights are available.

The paper used in black and white film processing is very insensitive to red light. The insensitivity depends on two factors associated with the silver halide crystals that are often used in film emulsions. The absorption of light in the crystals results in the promotion of electrons from the valence band of the crystal to the conduction band, and subsequent movement and trapping of the electrons, as well as similar processes which occur for the holes in the valence band. The excitation of electrons from the valence to the conduction band depends on the energy carried by the photon.

The forbidden gap energy between the valence and conduction bands in the crystals is on the same order as the energy of red photons. Thus, there will be a cutoff energy (and associated electromagnetic wavelength), below which the photon cannot excite the electron to the conduction band. Graphs showing this cutoff at about 660 nm (in the *red* region of the spectrum) are available in Chapter 17 of T. H. James, ed., *The Theory of the Photographic Process*, 4th ed., Macmillan Publishing Co., Inc., New York, 1977.

The second contribution to the insensitivity of the emulsion to red light is based on the absorption characteristics of the silver halide crystals. Experimentation shows that, even when the photon energy is sufficient to excite the electron to the conduction band, the absorption varies by several orders of magnitude over the visible range, with very little absorption at the red end of the spectrum. This behavior is related to the density of quantum states available to the electron in the conduction band. There are very few states at the low end of the conduction band and more as the energy increases, resulting in a low probability of absorption of lower energy (*red*) photons.

5.) In an ionic crystal, the atoms attract because of the Coulomb force between opposite charges. Why don't these solids just *collapse* due to this force?

The ions are attracted by the Coulomb force, as mentioned in the Mystery. As two ions become very close, however, the electron wave functions begin to overlap, and we change from two isolated systems to a *composite* system of two ions. But the quantum states of the composite system will have two electrons in the filled states. According to the Pauli Exclusion Principle (see Myth #2, Chapter 18), this is not allowed. Thus, electrons will move to higher energy states to avoid this violation. This represents an effective repulsive force, since pushing the atoms together requires an energy input, and is purely a quantum mechanical effect, with no classical analog. It is this repulsive force which balances the Coulomb attraction. See Myth #7 in Chapter 9 for the result of these forces on the thermal expansion of a solid.

6.) How does something *glow in the dark*?

Glowing in the dark is a phenomenon called *phosphorescence*. This phenomenon and *fluorescence* make up the class of behaviors known as *luminescence*. In general, luminescence refers to the excitation of a material, with the subsequent emission of photons that are lower in energy than the excitation. The original excitation is often optical, although it could also be biological (*bioluminescence*—a firefly!), mechanical (*tribolu-minescence*—chewed wintergreen candies), acoustical (*sonoluminescence*—radiation from sound-driven bubbles in a liquid) or chemical (*chemiluminescence*—light sticks).

If the photon emission occurs immediately after the excitation, the phenomenon is called fluorescence, as in fluorescent light bulbs. If there is a time delay, the process is called phosphorescence. In a phosphorescent material, the excited atomic systems make radiationless transitions to a *metastable state*. This is an excited state in which the probability of transition back to the ground state is relatively low. As a result, the system remains in the state for a relatively long amount of time. For a collection of a large number of such systems, as in a glow in the dark object, photons will be emitted for several minutes to hours after the original excitation. The intensity of the radiation will decrease, as the number of metastable states remaining excited decreases with time.

7.) *Photochromic glasses* contain lenses which automatically darken when exposed to sunlight. How do these lenses work?

This darkening of the photochromic lenses is performed by crystals of *silver chloride* in the glass. This is the same kind of molecule as in photographic film and the process is almost the same. When the crystals are exposed to the ultraviolet light from the Sun, the ionic compound AgCl is dissociated, forming silver and chlorine atoms. The collection of silver atoms formed is very dark and is what provides the darkness of the glasses. In photographic film, a second reaction causes the chlorine atoms to move away from the reaction zone, so that the process is permanent. This does not happen in the photochromic glasses and, upon removal of the ultraviolet light, the silver and chlorine atoms recombine to form the ionic compound AgCl again and the lenses lighten.

8.) Why is ice less dense than water?

When water molecules are in the liquid phase, the molecules can be relatively close together, since the hydrogen arm of one molecule can project into the space between the two hydrogen arms of a neighboring molecule, as suggested in the diagram to the right.

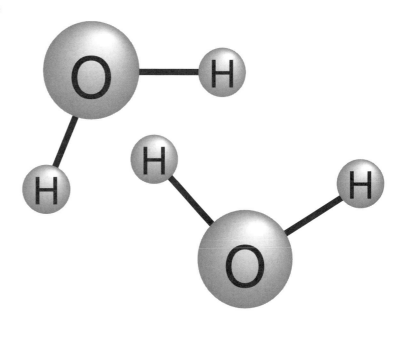

When the water freezes into ice, a crystalline structure is formed. There are a variety of structures into which water can freeze into ice, but the most common form has a crystalline structure with a hexagonal symmetry, as shown in the diagram below.

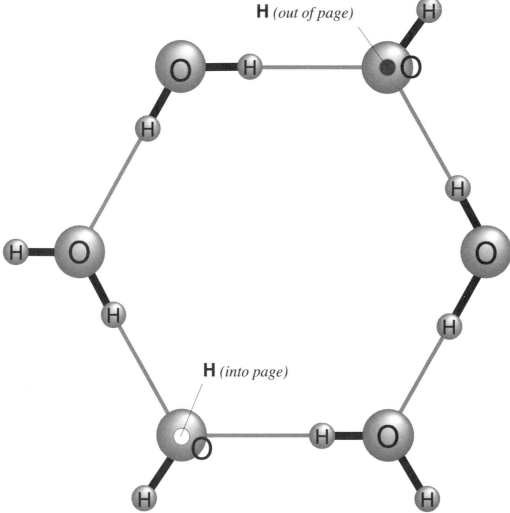

In this diagram, the six oxygen atoms are not all in the same plane. The upper left, lower left and far right atoms are in one plane and the other three are in a slightly lower plane, so that the structure is formed from "crinkled sheets" of oxygen atoms, using the language of N. H. Fletcher, *The Chemical Physics of Ice*, Cambridge University Press, Cambridge, 1970. In addition, the hydrogen atom positions shown represent only one possibility among many. While the *positions* of the hydrogen atoms are such that there are two in the vicinity of each oxygen, the *orientations* of the hydrogen-oxygen bonds are essentially random. The reader is referred to page 31 of the Fletcher text mentioned above for a more detailed discussion of atomic positions in ice.

For our purposes in responding to this Mystery, notice the large amount of *open space* in the structure pictured above. In order to form this very open structure, the molecules must move *apart* from their intermingled positions in the liquid state. By moving apart, the water expands and the density decreases. Thus, the density of the ice is less than that of water, so the ice floats, according to Archimedes' Principle.

9.) In old buildings, why is the glass in the windows thicker at the bottom than at the top?

Glass is an example of an *amorphous* solid, as opposed to a *crystalline* solid. In a crystalline solid, the atoms are arranged in a regular array. In an amorphous solid, there is no such regular array and the locations of the atoms are relatively random. As a result, an amorphous solid is more like a very viscous liquid, rather than a solid. As a liquid, an amorphous solid can flow. This is what happens in windows. Over many, many years, the constant pull of gravity causes the glass to flow toward the bottom of the pane, so that it is thicker at the bottom than at the top.

10.) How can such <u>different</u> materials as *diamond* and *graphite* be made from the *same element*?

Even though both materials mentioned are made from carbon, they have very different *crystal structures*, which leads to their different properties. Graphite consists of carbon atoms in long flat sheets that have very little attraction for each other. As a result, the sheets can move relative to each other easily and graphite tends to be soft and crumbly. On the other hand, diamond is formed from two interlocking face centered cubic structures (see a solid state physics textbook for more information on this and other crystal structures). This is a very strong structure, leading to the hardness of an object made from diamond.

𝕸agic:

The Bicolor (Tricolor?) LED

As mentioned in the description of the demonstration, the bicolor LED will flash red and green at the low frequency. At the 100 Hz frequency, the flashes will occur too rapidly to follow and the red and green will combine in the eye to form *yellow-orange*.

Brightening Your Wash

You should see a fluorescent glow in the detergent. Many powdered detergents contain a fluorescent material that helps make clothes bright, especially white shirts. If you have seen a group of people in a room lit with ultraviolet light, you may have seen very bright white shirts on some individuals!

𝕸yth:

1.) As a solid is heated, its electrical resistance increases.

This is true for most materials, but not *semiconductors*. As a semiconductor is raised in temperature, more electrons are thermally excited into the conduction band and the material becomes a better conductor. Thus, the resistance *decreases* as the semiconductor is heated.

2.) Good conductors (at room temperature) must make *great* superconductors.

Well, let's see. Below is a table of resistivity at room temperature (in order of increasing resistivity) and superconducting critical temperature for a number of metals.

Element	Resistivity ($\mu\Omega \cdot$cm)	Critical Temperature (K)
Silver	1.586	None
Copper	1.678	None
Gold	2.24	None
Aluminum	2.655	1.18
Tungsten	5.65	0.02
Zinc	5.92	0.85
Nickel	6.84	None
Tantalum	12.45	4.47
Niobium	12.5	9.25
Lead	20.65	7.20
Mercury	98.4	4.15

We see that the three best room temperature conductors (at the top of the table) do not even become superconductors and the next best conductors only become superconducting at very low critical temperatures. On the other hand, the poorer room temperature conductors at the bottom of the table become superconductors at relatively high critical temperatures—it is relatively easy to cause them to become superconductors.

Superconductivity in metals occurs when electrons bond in *Cooper pairs*. It may be hard to understand why two *like* charges would feel an *attractive* force and bond together. The bonding comes from an interaction with the positive lattice ions. If the ions are relatively free to move from their equilibrium positions, they can be drawn into the region *between* two electrons by the attractive Coulomb force. Then, there is an increased positive charge density in this region between the electrons. This positive charge density can exert an attractive Coulomb force on the negative electrons, providing the bonding. As the Cooper pair moves through the crystal, the displacement of ions moves along with it, maintaining the bonding of the electrons.

Now, let us address the apparent inverse behavior between room temperature conductivity and superconductivity. At room temperature, deviations (vibrations) of ions from their equilibrium positions due to thermal agitation leads to a larger effective cross sectional area for the lattice ions and higher resistance. Thus, the best room temperature conductors are those whose lattice ions are held the most rigidly in position by the strongest "springs". But this is exactly what we *don't* want in order to experience superconductivity. In this case, we want the lattice ions to move from their equilibrium positions relatively easily, so that we can form the positive charge density increase that we need to bond the Cooper pairs. Thus, the *best* conductors are the *worst* superconductors!

3.) Glass is a solid.

As mentioned in the Concepts section, glass is an *amorphous solid*, which can be considered to be a very viscous *liquid*. This was also explored in Mystery #9.

Chapter 21
Nuclear Physics

𝕸ysteries:

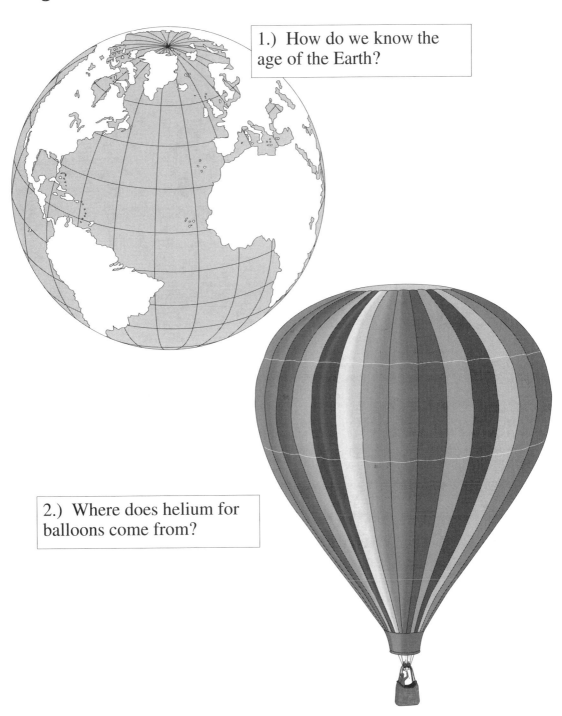

1.) How do we know the age of the Earth?

2.) Where does helium for balloons come from?

Mysteries:

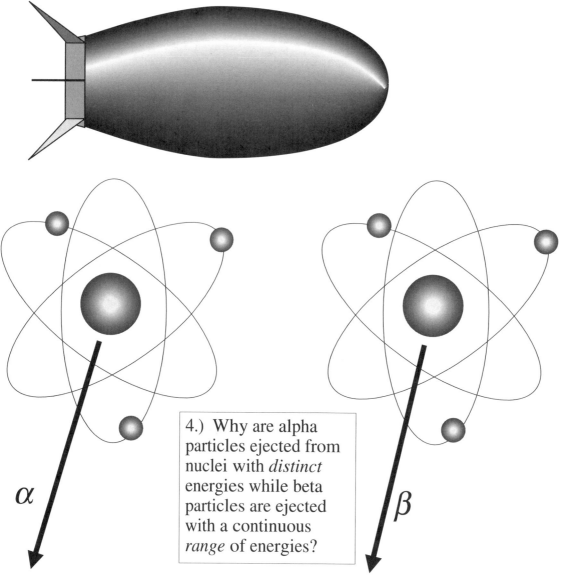

3.) The two nuclear bombs used in World War II had different shapes. Why?

4.) Why are alpha particles ejected from nuclei with *distinct* energies while beta particles are ejected with a continuous *range* of energies?

$$E_\alpha = 5.346 \text{ MeV} \qquad 0 < E_\beta < 3.895 \text{ MeV}$$

Mysteries:

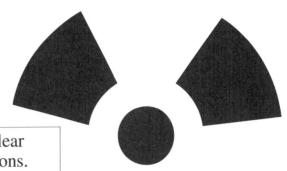

5.) A *moderator* is used in nuclear reactors to slow down the neutrons. Now, wait a minute. If you are trying to extract energy as efficiently as possible from nuclear fuel, why would you want to waste the neutron kinetic energy by *slowing them down*?

Carbon   12.011
Aluminum 26.981
Chlorine 35.453
Rubidium 85.468

6.) Why are the atomic masses of the elements not equal to integers?

7.) From an atomic spectrum, it is extremely difficult to determine the *isotope* of the source. A molecular spectrum allows the isotope to be determined rather easily. Why is there this difference?

Mysteries:

8.) A powerful non-invasive tool in medicine is *Magnetic Resonance Imaging* (MRI), which uses nuclear magnetic resonance to form images of interior portions of the body. If it uses nuclear magnetic resonance, why isn't the word *nuclear* in its name?

Magic:

Magic Numbers

The following numbers are referred to as "Magic numbers" in nuclear physics:

2...8...20...28...50...82...126...

What's so magic about them?

2   28   126

82   20   8   50

𝔐𝔶𝔱𝔥:

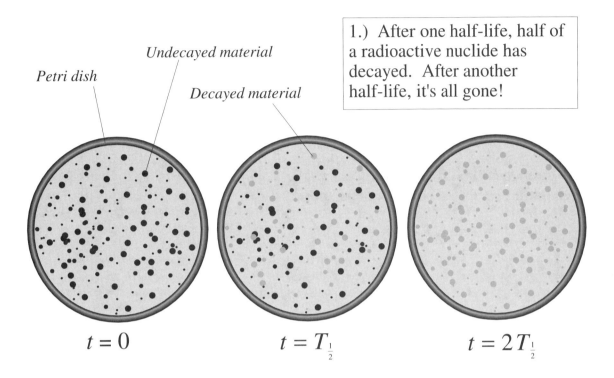

Petri dish

Undecayed material

Decayed material

1.) After one half-life, half of a radioactive nuclide has decayed. After another half-life, it's all gone!

$t = 0$ $t = T_{\frac{1}{2}}$ $t = 2T_{\frac{1}{2}}$

2.) In order to reduce heating losses, a house should be made as airtight *as possible*.

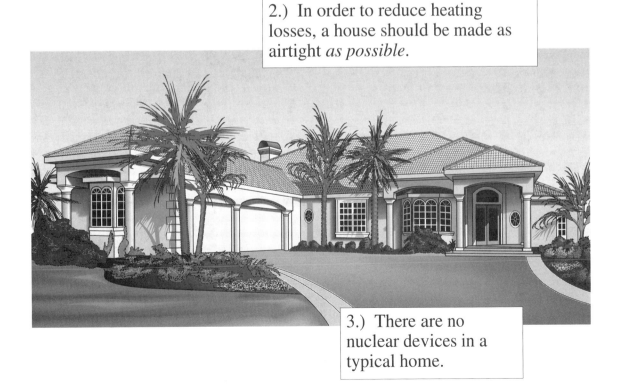

3.) There are no nuclear devices in a typical home.

$\mathfrak{Myth}$:

4.) A material left undisturbed in a room will eventually reach room temperature.

5.) Using $E = mc^2$, we can show that an endothermic nuclear reaction will occur when the kinetic energy of the incident particle just equals the mass difference (final products minus initial reactants) times the square of the speed of light.

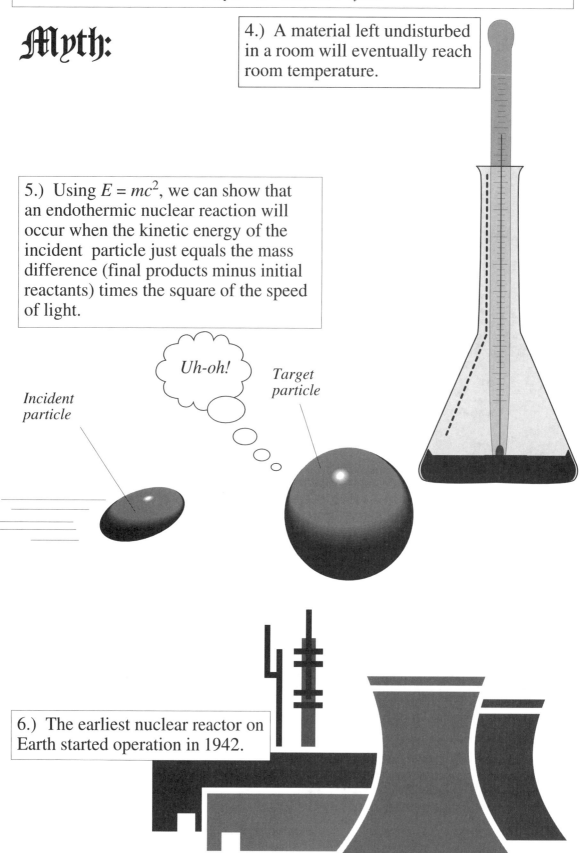

Uh-oh!

Target particle

Incident particle

6.) The earliest nuclear reactor on Earth started operation in 1942.

Myth:

7.) In the movie *Tarantula* (Universal Pictures, 1955), the lead actor looks at a vial in a scientific laboratory and says to the scientist, "That's an isotope, isn't it?"

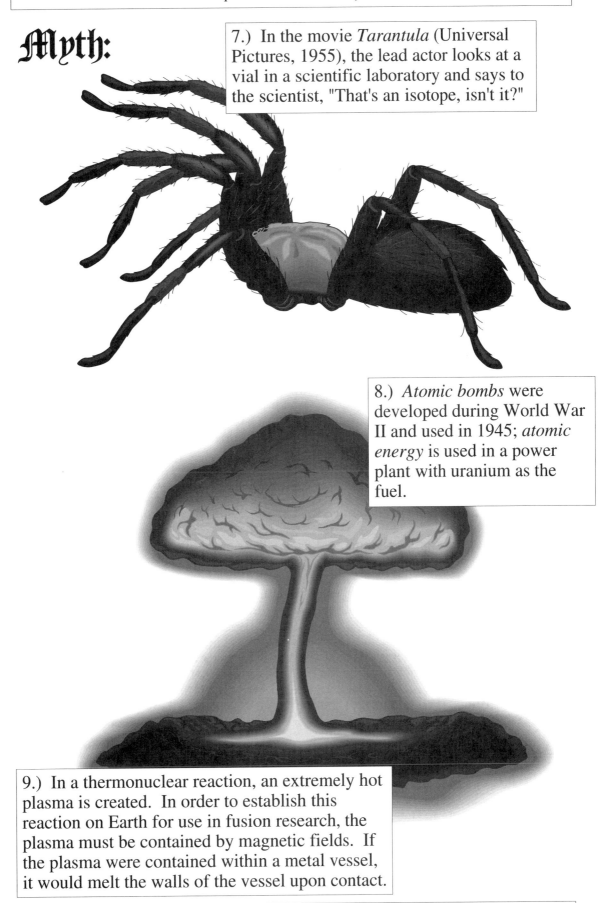

8.) *Atomic bombs* were developed during World War II and used in 1945; *atomic energy* is used in a power plant with uranium as the fuel.

9.) In a thermonuclear reaction, an extremely hot plasma is created. In order to establish this reaction on Earth for use in fusion research, the plasma must be contained by magnetic fields. If the plasma were contained within a metal vessel, it would melt the walls of the vessel upon contact.

Concepts of Nuclear Physics

The concept of the nuclear atom was initiated by the experiments of Ernest Rutherford in the early part of the twentieth century. Rutherford fired alpha particles at gold foil and found a significant number of the alpha particles were scattered through large angles. This was consistent only with a model in which the positive charge of the nucleus was concentrated in a very small region of space—the *nucleus*. The discovery of the neutron in 1932 provided us with two possible residents in the nucleus—the *proton* and the *neutron*.

The number of protons in the nucleus defines the element which the nucleus represents. This number is often represented as *Z*, and is called the *atomic number*. For given *Z*, varying numbers of neutrons may exist in the nucleus along with the protons, defining various *isotopes* of a given element. For example, hydrogen may exist as an atom with just a proton in the nucleus, a proton and one neutron (deuterium) or a proton and two neutrons (tritium). Some isotopes of an element are stable, while others will decay, through processes which we will investigate shortly. The *atomic mass number*, *A*, which is the sum of the numbers of protons and neutrons, is used to designate the isotope. Nuclei are often designated with a letter for the chemical symbol, with a pre-superscript representing *A* and a pre-subscript representing *Z*. For example,

$$Z - \textit{Atomic Number}$$
$$A - \textit{Atomic Mass Number}$$

$$^{4}_{2}He \quad \rightarrow \quad \textit{"helium 4", 2 protons, 2 neutrons}$$

$$^{137}_{55}Cs \quad \rightarrow \quad \textit{"cesium 137", 55 protons, 82 neutrons}$$

The pre-subscript is often omitted, since the use of both this and the chemical symbol is redundant.

One of the fundamental precepts of quantum physics is that restricting a particle in any way results in quantization of its energy. Protons and neutrons are highly restricted to a very small region of space in the nucleus and we do indeed find them in quantized states. Typical energy differences between these states (and, therefore, typical photon energies for transitions between these states) are measured in MeV. This means that photons representing absorption or emission between nuclear states are in the *gamma ray* range. Indeed, this is the source of gamma rays—transitions between quantized states in the nucleus.

Many nuclei are unstable, in the sense that they will maximize entropy by transferring energy out of the nucleus, leaving the nucleus in a lower energy state. One possibility for this instability is that the nucleus is *neutron-rich*. In this case, there is a disproportionate number of neutrons, so they must fill higher quantum states (because of the Pauli Exclusion Principle), while there are available proton states available at lower energies. By transform-

Concepts of Nuclear Physics (continued)

ing a high energy neutron into a lower energy proton, entropy is increased by emitting the energy difference in some form. These types of processes occur in radioactive isotopes of otherwise stable atoms.

Another possibility for nuclear instability is that the nucleus is so large that the short range of the nuclear strong force reduces its effectiveness in binding the nuclear particles together. This is the case for the heaviest elements, which have no stable isotopes.

A variety of radioactive decay mechanisms are observed. The primary mechanisms are described briefly below:

Beta (negative) **decay**; In a neutron-rich nucleus, a lower energy of the nucleus is achieved by the decay of a neutron into a proton, an electron and an antineutrino. The electron and antineutrino leave the nucleus. In the process, the atomic number of the nucleus increases by one and the atomic mass number remains constant.

Beta (positive) **decay**; In some nuclei, protons are in energy states with neutron states of lower energy available. Thus, a lower energy of the nucleus is achieved by the decay of a proton into a neutron, a positron and a neutrino. The positron and neutrino leave the nucleus. In the process, the atomic number of the nucleus decreases by one and the atomic mass number remains constant.

Alpha decay; The unit consisting of two protons and two neutrons (i.e., a helium nucleus, also called an *alpha particle*) is a particularly tightly bound combination which can be ejected from the nucleus as an entity. In the process, the atomic number of the nucleus decreases by two and the atomic mass number decreases by four.

Gamma decay; A nucleus can exist in an excited state. The energy of the nucleus can be reduced by emitting the energy difference as a photon. In the process, neither the atomic number nor the atomic mass number of the nucleus changes.

Electron capture; A nucleus with protons in higher energy states than available neutron states (as in beta positive decay above) can undergo another process besides beta positive decay. An electron can be captured, usually from the K shell, and combined with a proton to form a neutron. In the process, a neutrino is emitted from the nucleus and X-rays are often emitted as a higher shell electron falls to fill the vacancy in the K shell. In the process, the atomic number of the nucleus decreases by one and the atomic mass number remains constant.

These decay processes are statistical in nature. The rate at which we see the

Concepts of Nuclear Physics (continued)

nuclei decaying is proportional to the number of nuclei present. This leads to an exponential decrease in the number of undecayed nuclei remaining. One popular measure of the rate of decay is the *half-life*. This is the time for one half of the nuclei to decay. After another half life, half of what was left (one fourth of the initial number) is still undecayed. Nuclear half-lives range from fractions of a second to millions of years.

> *After each interval of one half-life, half of the material at the beginning of the interval remains.*

Another type of "decay" that is exhibited by very heavy nuclei is the random or stimulated splitting into two smaller nuclei. This process is called *fission*, and represents the transformation of nuclear potential energy into kinetic energy of the nuclear fragments and ejected neutrons. Uranium is often used in fission reactions on Earth, and the uranium nucleus can be stimulated to undergo fission by absorption of neutrons. The smaller nuclei that result from the splitting are neutron rich and will generally shed neutrons quickly during the process. This allows for the possibility of a sustained chain reaction if enough of the nuclei are present. The spontaneous fission decay of one nucleus releases neutrons which will stimulate other nuclei to undergo fission, releasing even more neutrons and so on. If this process is uncontrolled, a nuclear explosion occurs. A controlled chain reaction of this sort is the process occurring in nuclear power plants.

> *Fission: Transforming nuclear potential energy by <u>splitting</u> nuclei*
> *Fusion: Transforming nuclear potential energy by <u>combining</u> nuclei*

The fission process results in nuclei which have a lower total energy than the original nucleus. Thus, if we adopt the "tendency toward lower energy" point of view (which is really the maximization of entropy principle, as in Myth #7 in Chapter 18), we can argue that fission occurs because of a lowering of the energy of the remaining nuclei. Another process is available for lighter nuclei in which the energy of the remaining system is lower. If two light nuclei are combined, nuclear potential energy is transformed through the *fusion* process. This is the process that occurs in the cores of stars, in which hydrogen undergoes fusion to form helium (fusion of some nuclei higher in atomic number than hydrogen also occurs in some stars). There are technological problems associated with reproducing these reactions on Earth, since very high temperatures are necessary to develop atomic velocities high enough to overcome the Coulomb repulsion of the nuclei. In the core of a star, these high temperatures are readily available.

Discussions; Chapter 21—Nuclear Physics

𝔐𝔶𝔰𝔱𝔢𝔯𝔦𝔢𝔰:

1.) How do we know the age of the Earth?

Various individuals have determined the age of the Earth by a variety of methods, ranging from tracings of biblical families to estimates of the time required for rivers to bring the oceans up to their present level of salinity. A relatively accurate measurement, based on nuclear physics, can be made from the ratio of ^{238}U to ^{206}Pb. The uranium isotope decays through a chain of reactions to the stable lead isotope. Thus, if we make the assumption that the Earth started off with no lead, the ratio of the amounts of the isotopes will give the age of the Earth, if we know the half-life of the uranium isotope (we do—it is 4.5 billion years). The oldest rocks found on Earth have a ratio that is consistent with an age of about 4 billion years for the Earth.

2.) Where does helium for balloons come from?

Helium is found in the Earth and is the result of alpha decay of the enormous number of radioactive nuclei in the interior of the Earth. *Helium wells* are in existence in Texas, Oklahoma and Kansas.

It is interesting to note that helium obtains its name from the fact that it was first observed *on the Sun* (*helio-* is a prefix, meaning "Sun"). This was performed in 1868 when a previously unknown spectral line was observed in the light from a solar eclipse.

3.) The two nuclear bombs used in World War II had different shapes. Why?

The two bombs had different fuels and different mechanisms. The long bomb ("Little Boy") used uranium (^{235}U) as the fuel. Two subcritical masses of uranium were maintained at a large separation, hence, the elongated shape. Upon detonation, a gun device used conventional explosives to propel one piece of uranium into the other. The resulting supercritical mass then exploded. In the more rounded bomb ("Fat Man"), the fuel was plutonium (^{239}Pu). A slightly subcritical spherical mass of plutonium was surrounded by a spherical shell of conventional explosives, hence the rounded shape. Upon detonation, the plutonium sphere was compressed to a supercritical density and the nuclear explosion ensued.

4.) Why are alpha particles ejected from nuclei with *distinct* energies while beta particles are ejected with a continuous *range* of energies?

A primary difference between alpha decay and beta decay is that alpha decay is a *two-particle decay* (alpha particle and daughter nucleus), while beta decay results in *three particles* (beta particle, daughter nucleus and neutrino). In the two-particle alpha decay, conservation of momentum requires that the alpha particle and the daughter nucleus leave the decay in opposite directions. This is a *one dimensional* problem. Thus, we have four unknowns: the alpha particle energy and momentum and the daughter nucleus energy and momentum. We also have four equations: conservation of energy, conservation of momentum and the relation between momentum and energy (applied twice—once for each particle). With four equations and four unknowns, we can mathematically determine <u>exact</u> values for the unknowns, one of which is the alpha particle energy. Thus, the alpha particle energy has a *distinct* value. There is more than one possible value, since the daughter nucleus may be left in an excited state, leaving less energy available for the alpha particle. Thus, there will be a *set* of discrete energies for the alpha particle.

In the case of the beta decay, we have three particles leaving the decay, making it a *two-dimensional problem*. The number of unknowns is *eight*: six corresponding to the energy and momentum of the beta particle, the daughter nucleus and the neutrino, as well as the daughter nucleus angle (relative to the beta particle direction) and the neutrino angle (relative to the beta particle direction). Now, how many equations do we have? We have *six*: two for conservation of momentum in the *x*- and *y*-directions, conservation of energy, and the relation between momentum and energy (applied three times—once for each particle). With fewer equations than unknowns, there are a *range* of values of the beta particle energy (as well as all the other unknowns) that will mathematically satisfy the equations. Thus, *beta particles are not emitted with distinct energies*, but rather exhibit a range of energies from zero up to a maximum value.

5.) A *moderator* is used in nuclear reactors to slow down the neutrons. Now, wait a minute. If you are trying to extract energy as efficiently as possible from nuclear fuel, why would you want to waste the neutron kinetic energy by *slowing them down*?

Nuclear fuel is an enriched mixture of a few percent of fissionable ^{235}U and about 90% non-fissionable ^{238}U. The fast neutrons liberated during a fission reaction have a probability of being captured by ^{238}U that is comparable to the probability of being captured by ^{235}U (for a number of reasons—see a nuclear physics textbook for more information). Thus, without moderators, many of the neutrons are absorbed by the wrong isotope! The moderators *slow* the neutrons (by providing relatively light nuclei for scattering in which a significant fraction of the neutron kinetic energy is transferred to the light nucleus), increasing the chance that they will stimulate another fission reaction in the ^{235}U and keep the process going. Without the moderators, the fission reaction does not continue, so *no energy* can be extracted. Water is typically used as a moderator in modern reactors.

6.) Why are the atomic masses of the elements not equal to integers?

There are three contributions to the non-integer character of atomic masses. The first involves the binding energy. If we are packing an integral number of identical marbles in a bag, then the total mass will be an integral multiple of a single marble mass. But marbles do not bind to each other. If we pack an integral number of nucleons into a nucleus, there will be binding, which will reduce the overall energy remaining in the system of particles (some energy will be carried away by photons upon binding). Since mass is proportional to energy ($E = mc^2$), the mass will be reduced below the integral multiple of a single mass value.

Secondly, protons and neutrons have slightly different masses. Thus, we are not actually combining a group of particles with the same mass, as in the marble example above.

Finally, atomic masses given in the periodic table are averages for all of the stable isotopes of the element, weighted by the natural abundance. In general, this removes any resemblance to an integral multiple.

7.) From an atomic spectrum, it is extremely difficult to determine the *isotope* of the source. A molecular spectrum allows the isotope to be determined rather easily. Why is there this difference?

The variation among isotopes for a given element would be in the *nuclear mass*. Atomic spectra are determined by a complicated combination of electron-nucleus interactions, electron-electron interactions, spin-orbit coupling, nuclear shielding, spin-spin interactions, etc. The effect of a change in the nuclear mass would be very difficult to detect, since the majority of the contributions to the spectrum are *electromagnetic* in nature.

On the other hand, a major contribution to a molecular spectrum is *mechanical*. The molecular spectrum can be analyzed to obtain information about the *vibration* and *rotation* of the molecule. The energy of vibration depends on the frequency of vibration which, in turn, depends on the mass of the nucleus. For the simple mass and spring model of Chapter 10, the frequency is given by,

$$f = \frac{1}{2\pi}\sqrt{\frac{k}{m}}$$

where m is the vibrating mass and k is the spring constant of the spring. While the period of vibration for the molecule is a little more complicated than this, the dependence on the mass is still there. Thus, the differing masses of different isotopes can be detected.

Another useful isotope effect in molecular spectra comes from the rotation of the molecule. The dependence on mass here arises from the fact that the energy of rotation depends on the *moment of inertia* of the molecule, which is mass dependent.

8.) A powerful non-invasive tool in medicine is *Magnetic Resonance Imaging* (MRI), which uses nuclear magnetic resonance to form images of interior portions of the body. If it uses nuclear magnetic resonance, why isn't the word *nuclear* in its name?

The general public is very nervous about the word *nuclear*, so it is not used in the phrase to describe the technique.

𝕸𝖆𝖌𝖎𝖈:

Magic Numbers

As mentioned, the numbers indicated are the *magic numbers* of nuclear physics. They are "magic" in the sense that there are *discontinuities* in the stability, sphericity, and other nuclear properties, for nuclei with the following atomic mass numbers:

$$2, 8, 20, 28, 50, 82, 126$$

The discontinuities in properties of these nuclei are reminiscent of the changes in properties of atoms in the periodic table, as atomic shells fill. Indeed, if we appeal to a *shell model* of the nucleus, we find that there is a special significance to these numbers.

We assume that the nucleons are in orbit around some central point in a force field. Immediately, we have a possible conceptual problem—how can particles, packed into such a tiny volume, move in any kind of an orbit, when they would be continuously *colliding* with each other? If we do have a conceptual problem with this, then we are applying our deterministic ideas from our own world to the quantum world. We imagine these nucleons to be colliding because they are packed so tightly together. Remember, however, that on the quantum level, the energies are quantized. In order to make a collision, the energy of a particle must change. If there are no available energy levels into which the particle can move (remember that nucleons are fermions and must obey the Pauli Exclusion Principle), the collisions cannot occur, and therefore, *do* not occur. The result is that the nucleons move freely through the nucleus.

Given this model of nucleons in orbit around some central point, the Schrödinger equation for the nucleus can be solved, and we find that we can identify *the same quantum numbers for nuclei that we have for atomic electrons*:

$n \rightarrow$ principal
$\ell \rightarrow$ magnitude of orbital angular momentum
$m_\ell \rightarrow$ direction of orbital angular momentum
$m_s \rightarrow$ direction of intrinsic angular momentum (spin)

Using this model, and accounting for an interaction between the spin and orbital motions of the nucleons (called the *spin-orbit interaction*), a shell model of the nucleus can be generated. This model demonstrates a sense of *shell closure* at the magic numbers, with energy gaps between the shells. It is this shell closure which gives the discontinuities in the nuclear properties, similar to the discontinuities in atomic properties discussed in Mystery #10 of Chapter 19.

𝕸𝖞𝖙𝖍:

1.) After one half-life, half of a radioactive nuclide has decayed. After another half-life, it's all gone!

This would suggest a *linear* behavior in the amount of nuclear material remaining. The decay is actually *exponential* in character. After one half life, half of the material is gone and after another half-life, half of *that* material is remaining, or one fourth of the original. Thus, the amount of material remaining follows the behavior shown in the graph to the right. In principle, then, the material is never "all gone"!

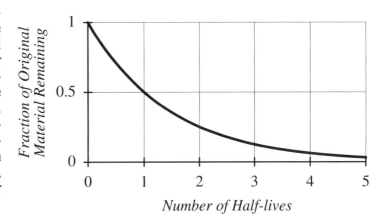

2.) In order to reduce heating losses, a house should be made as airtight *as possible*.

A major source of "heat loss" in a home is *infiltration*—leaks around doors and windows and many other cracks and openings in the structure of a house. These allow the exchange of warm interior air and cold exterior air. It would seem to be desirable to cut off as much as possible of this leakage. Some houses actually have plastic barriers built into the structure to stop this flow.

The problem with the excessive application of this plastic technique, and the source of the inaccuracy of the statement in the Myth, is the existence of *radon* gas in the air of a typical home. Radon (^{222}Rn) is one of the isotopes created in the decay chain of ^{238}U, which occurs naturally in the interior of the Earth. Radon is the only member of this decay chain which is a gas, and it is an *inert gas* to boot. Thus, as radon is formed, it can seep through the Earth (since it's a *gas*), interacting chemically with nothing along the way (since it's an *inert* gas), and eventually enter houses through basements and foundations. Once in the house, if the home is very tightly sealed against air leaks, the radon will spend a large amount of time in the air of the home and experience a relatively large probability of being inhaled by an inhabitant of the home. Once inhaled, the decay of the radon through the rest of the decay chain will expose the lungs of the inhabitant to possible radiation damage.

Thus, while tightly sealing a home will cut down on energy losses, it will increase the health risk of the inhabitants (as well as causing cooking odors to linger, etc.). Exchange of air with the outside is important in reducing this health risk. One possible solution is to tightly seal the house as described above, but to add *air exchangers* (fans) which will pass the air moving out of the house over *heat exchangers*, so that the air circulation is maintained while at least some of the internal energy in the air of the house is returned to the interior.

For more information on radon gas in homes, see C. Bettis and C. Throckmorton, "What Teachers Should Know About Radon", *The Physics Teacher*, **29**, 338, 1991.

3.) There are no nuclear devices in a typical home.

If you believe this, pull down the battery-operated *smoke detector* that you likely have hanging on a wall or ceiling and look inside. Many smoke detectors have an americium source (^{241}Am) of activity about 1 microcurie (about 37,000 decays per second). This source emits alpha radiation that ionizes the air between two parallel plates. This ionized air maintains a low current between the plates. When smoke enters the region between the plates, the ions in the smoke neutralize the ions in the air between the plates, and the current drops. The drop in current is detected and the alarm is activated.

4.) A material left undisturbed in a room will eventually reach room temperature.

This statement is true for most materials. But it may not be true for *radioactive* materials. For example, Pierre and Marie Curie found that a sample of *radium* maintained a temperature above that of room temperature. This can be accounted for by the continuous transformation of energy by the radioactive decay of the radium nuclei. Some of the decay energy is absorbed by the material and appears as internal energy. Thus, since the radium sample has a continuous "source" of energy from the nuclei, its temperature remains above that of the environment.

5.) Using $E = mc^2$, we can show that an endothermic nuclear reaction will occur when the kinetic energy of the incident particle just equals the mass difference (final products minus initial reactants) times the square of the speed of light.

In general, a nuclear reaction involves an *incident* particle, which strikes a *target* nucleus. These two particles are the *initial reactants*. As a result, an *outgoing* particle (or particles) leaves the reaction, leaving behind a *daughter* nucleus. These are the *final products*. We will restrict our attention in what follows to the case in which there are only two particles making up the final products—an outgoing particle and a daughter nucleus.

We can define a *Q-value* for a nuclear reaction, based on the mass difference between the initial and final nuclei and incident and outgoing particles. This represents *the negative of the change in rest energy of the system during the reaction* and is defined as follows (see Chapter 22 for discussions of rest energy):

$$Q = (m_{target} + m_{incident} - m_{daughter} - m_{outgoing})c^2$$

where c is the speed of light. In an endothermic nuclear reaction, energy must be provided for the reaction to occur. This is the case if the final products have a larger mass than the initial products. This energy is provided by the kinetic energy of the incident particle. The question that is addressed in this Myth is the *threshold* kinetic energy required. A first guess might be that the kinetic energy of the incident particle must be equal to the negative of the Q-value, since that is the energy that is required for the formation of the rest mass energy. We must be careful, however, to conserve *momentum* as well as energy, since the energy coming into the reaction is energy of *motion*. If the incident particle provided energy corresponding to the increase in rest energy, but the final particles were at rest, we would have a violation of conservation of momentum.

Let us calculate the threshold energy, including the requirement for conservation of momentum in the calculation. We assume that the target is at rest before the collision, and both daughter and outgoing particle are moving after the collision. Then, conservation of energy requires,

$$KE_{incident} = KE_{daughter} + KE_{outgoing} - Q$$

The kinetic energies will be small compared to the rest energies, so we use non-relativistic mechanics to make an approximation. We will consider conservation of momentum in the *center of mass frame*. We can calculate the velocity of the center of mass, assuming that the target is at rest and the incident particle moves with velocity v_{inc}:

$$v_{cm} = \frac{m_{inc}v_{inc} + m_{target}v_{target}}{m_{inc} + m_{target}} = \frac{m_{inc}}{m_{inc} + m_{target}}v_{inc}$$

In the center of mass frame, the incident particle moves at velocity $v_{inc} - v_{cm}$ while the target moves in the opposite direction at velocity v_{cm}. Now, we express conservation of energy, including rest energies, as,

$$E_{initial} = E_{final} \quad \rightarrow$$

$$\left[\frac{1}{2}m_{inc}\left(v_{inc} - \frac{m_{inc}}{m_{inc} + m_{target}}v_{inc}\right)^2 + m_{inc}c^2\right] + \left[\frac{1}{2}m_{target}\left(\frac{m_{inc}}{m_{inc} + m_{target}}v_{inc}\right)^2 + m_{target}c^2\right]$$

$$= m_{daughter}c^2 + m_{outgoing}c^2$$

where we have introduced the condition of threshold velocity of the incident particle by assuming that the kinetic energies (in the center of mass frame) of the final particles are zero. Notice that this does *not* say that the final particles are not moving in the laboratory frame. They simply are not moving relative to each other after the reaction. We can rearrange the above equation as follows:

$$\frac{1}{2}m_{inc}\left(v_{inc} - \frac{m_{inc}}{m_{inc} + m_{target}}v_{inc}\right)^2 + \frac{1}{2}m_{target}\left(\frac{m_{inc}}{m_{inc} + m_{target}}v_{inc}\right)^2$$

$$= m_{daughter}c^2 + m_{outgoing}c^2 - m_{inc}c^2 - m_{target}c^2 = -Q$$

where we have employed the definition of the *Q*-value. Now, if we carry out the squaring process on the terms in the previous expression, we have,

$$\frac{1}{2} m_{inc} v_{inc}^2 \left(1 - 2 \frac{m_{inc}}{m_{inc} + m_{target}} + \frac{m_{inc}^2}{\left(m_{inc} + m_{target} \right)^2} \right) + \frac{1}{2} m_{target} v_{inc}^2 \frac{m_{inc}^2}{\left(m_{inc} + m_{target} \right)^2} = -Q$$

$$\frac{1}{2} v_{inc}^2 \left\{ \left(m_{inc} - 2 \frac{m_{inc}^2}{m_{inc} + m_{target}} + \frac{m_{inc}^3}{\left(m_{inc} + m_{target} \right)^2} \right) + \frac{m_{inc}^2 m_{target}}{\left(m_{inc} + m_{target} \right)^2} \right\} = -Q$$

$$\frac{1}{2} v_{inc}^2 \left\{ \left(\frac{m_{inc} \left(m_{inc} + m_{target} \right)^2}{\left(m_{inc} + m_{target} \right)^2} - 2 \frac{m_{inc}^2 \left(m_{inc} + m_{target} \right)}{\left(m_{inc} + m_{target} \right)^2} + \frac{m_{inc}^3}{\left(m_{inc} + m_{target} \right)^2} \right) + \frac{m_{inc}^2 m_{target}}{\left(m_{inc} + m_{target} \right)^2} \right\} = -Q$$

$$\frac{1}{2} v_{inc}^2 \left(\frac{m_{inc} m_{target}}{m_{inc} + m_{target}} \right) = -Q$$

We write this final result as,

$$\frac{1}{2} m_{inc} v_{inc}^2 \left(\frac{m_{target}}{m_{inc} + m_{target}} \right) = -Q$$

Then, the combination below can be recognized as the threshold kinetic energy:

$$\frac{1}{2} m_{inc} v_{inc}^2 = KE_{threshold}$$

Thus, combining this with the previous expression and solving for the threshold kinetic energy,

$$KE_{threshold} = -Q \left(\frac{m_{inc} + m_{target}}{m_{target}} \right)$$

Thus, the threshold energy is *larger* than the negative of the Q-value. The degree by which it is larger depends on the masses of the incident and target nuclei. The origin of the larger value, as mentioned previously, is the requirement to conserve momentum as well as energy.

If we had used relativistic calculations through the procedure above, we would have arrived at the following expression:

$$KE_{threshold} = -Q \left(\frac{m_{inc} + m_{target}}{m_{target}} \right) + \frac{Q^2}{2 m_{target} c^2}$$

The first term is the one we derived non-relativistically, and the second is very small, since typical values of Q are on the order of a few MeV, while typical values of the target mass are measured in GeV.

6.) The earliest nuclear reactor on Earth started operation in 1942.

The date given in the Myth is that of the world's first nuclear reactor *built by humans*, developed by Enrico Fermi and his associates at the University of Chicago. There is strong evidence that a *natural* fission reactor existed and was operating about *two billion years ago* in the present-day country of Gabon in Africa. This evidence consists of a very large deposit of uranium, enough for a reactor to operate, as well as a distribution of fission products that bears a much closer resemblance to the isotopic distribution found in the spent fuel of a nuclear reactor than that expected in a natural deposit. For more information, see G. A. Cowan, "A Natural Fission Reactor", *Scientific American*, **235(5)**, 36, 1976.

7.) In the movie *Tarantula* (Universal Pictures, 1955), the lead actor looks at a vial in a scientific laboratory and says to the scientist, "That's an isotope, isn't it?"

The word *isotope* refers to nuclei with the same number of protons but differing numbers of neutrons. Thus, it is meaningless to look at a material and identify it as being an isotope, since all materials are, in principle, isotopes of a related material with a different number of neutrons in the nucleus. On the other hand, of course, the statement cannot be false, since, no matter what material it is, it is theoretically an isotope!

8.) *Atomic bombs* were developed during World War II and used in 1945; *atomic energy* is used in a power plant with uranium as the fuel.

In so-called *atomic* bombs and *atomic* energy, the transformation of energy is from *nuclear potential energy* to other forms, primarily internal energy. Thus, the more proper phrases should be *nuclear* bombs and *nuclear* energy.

In an explosion of dynamite, the energy that is transformed to other forms in the process is *chemical potential energy*, which, as identified in the Concepts section of Chapter 7 in *PBWM*, is *electrical potential energy* associated with the *atoms* of the dynamite. Thus, a stick of dynamite is an *atomic* bomb!

Similarly, the process of burning wood in a fireplace transforms electrical potential energy in the atoms of the wood into other forms of energy. As a result, a stick of wood is a source of *atomic* energy!

9.) In a thermonuclear reaction, an extremely hot plasma is created. In order to establish this reaction on Earth for use in fusion research, the plasma must be contained by magnetic fields. If the plasma were contained within a metal vessel, it would melt the walls of the vessel upon contact.

The heat capacity (see Myth #1 in Chapter 9) of the plasma is much smaller than that of the walls of a metal containment vessel. Thus, if contact were made between the metal and the plasma, the problem is not that the energy flow from the plasma to the walls would raise the temperature of the wall. Rather, *the temperature of the plasma would drop* by a large amount, causing the fusion reaction to cease.

Chapter 22
Relativity

Mysteries:

1.) Light cannot leave a black hole. So *what happens* to a photon as it tries to leave a region just outside the black hole? Does it *slow down*, like a baseball thrown up from the surface of the Earth?

2.) Suppose you weigh an object on a bathroom scale in an accelerating elevator. The reading is different from the actual weight. Now, "weigh" the same object on an equal arm balance in the accelerating elevator. How does this reading compare to that of the stationary balance?

Mysteries:

3.) Can you drive fast enough to cause a red traffic light to look green?

4.) Suppose that you take a job that requires you to travel to other planets at speeds close to the speed of light. Who would you like to punch your time card—*you*, or *your boss*, who stays on Earth?

𝔐agic:

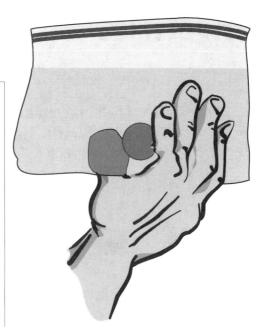

Do Ping Pong Balls Float in Water?

Fill a sealable plastic bag about two-thirds full with water. Drop a ping pong ball in and seal the bag. Now, work the ping pong ball to the bottom of the bag (the side opposite the sealed end) and hold the ball there with the sealed end of the bag at the top. The ball will tend to float because of its low density compared to water, but your hand will keep it at the bottom of the water. Now, drop the bag and watch the ball carefully. Does the ping pong ball float?

Vertical (?) Plants

Mount some growing vessels (pots, styrofoam cups, etc.) firmly on a powered turntable. Plant some seeds in the vessels. The particular choice of plant should be one that is fast growing and has a fairly linear stalk. Let the plants grow while the turntable is *rotating* continuously. Do the plants grow vertically?

𝕸𝖞𝖙𝖍:

1.) The Twin Paradox is a paradox.

2.) One of the basic principles of relativity is that an object's *mass increases* as it moves at speeds approaching that of light.

$$m = \frac{m_0}{\sqrt{1 - \dfrac{v^2}{c^2}}} = \gamma\, m_0$$

𝕸𝖞𝖙𝖍:

3.) Mass is a form of energy.

$$E = mc^2$$

4.) Two travelers, laterally separated by 2 m, move in the *same direction*. Their paths never cross.

5.) Plumb bobs hang straight down.

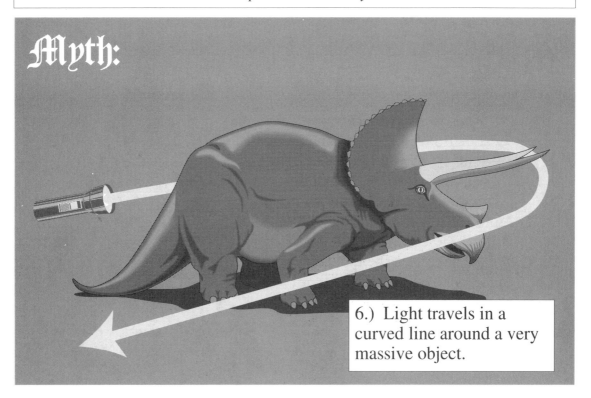

6.) Light travels in a curved line around a very massive object.

7.) An observer riding a train is located exactly midway between the engine and the last car. He passes a station, with a second observer standing on the platform. Just as the observers pass each other, lightning strikes both the engine and the last car. The observer on the platform claims that the lightning strikes were simultaneous. The observer on the train agrees.

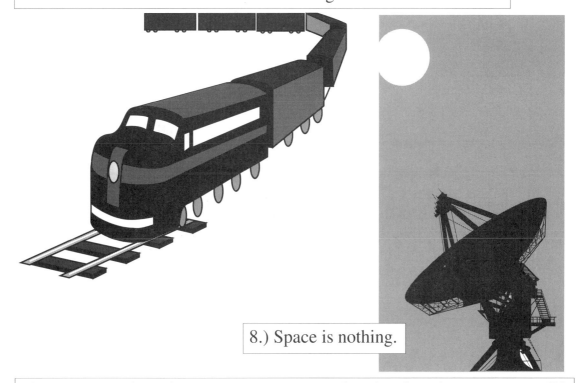

8.) Space is nothing.

Myth:

9.) In *Project 2061: Science for All Americans* (American Association for the Advancement of Science, Washington, D.C., 1989), the following is stated (paraphrased): If you run away from a clock such as Big Ben at 3:00 at the speed of light, you would never see the hands move, since the light from 3:01 would never reach you.

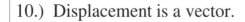

10.) Displacement is a vector.

11.) The Michelson-Morley experiment was an important impetus to Einstein in his work on special relativity.

Concepts of Relativity

The central theme in problems involving relativity is that *there is no absolute truth*, in terms of "correct" measurements made by an observer. The only "truth" we have available to us is that information that is obtained by making *observations* of the universe, but *different observers may make different observations.*

An example of the existence of different truths for different observers was explored in Myth #5 in Chapter 2 of *PBWM*. In this case, observers at different locations in a stadium will disagree on whether singers across the stadium from a loudspeaker are singing in unison with the music from the speaker or not.

As another example more closely related to the type we will explore in this Chapter, an observer riding on a train can throw a ball directly upward and see the ball move vertically up and then down, back into the hand. An observer watching the ball from the side of the tracks will see the ball follow a parabolic trajectory. Which observer is correct? This is a meaningless question. It asks for an absolute truth, in the form of a "correct" trajectory. In reality, both observers are correct—they have both made their observations carefully and have simply arrived at different results. The different results arise because the observers are in different *inertial reference frames*. An inertial reference frame is a system in which an observer is at rest, and which moves at a constant velocity with respect to other inertial reference frames. Thus, both the observer on the train and the one on the ground are in inertial frames. Since they are in *different* inertial reference frames, however, they make different, but correct, observations of the trajectory of the ball.

The predictions of the Special Theory of Relativity come from two postulates, suggested by Albert Einstein and based on his work as well as others preceding him. These postulates are:

The laws of physics have the same mathematical form in all inertial reference frames.

The speed of light is the same for all observers traveling in inertial reference frames.

These postulates lead to a number of startling, but verifiable, results. Some of these include:

Length contraction: The dimension of an object parallel to its direction of motion is measured to be shorter by an observer watching the object pass by at velocity v. The mathematical expression is:

$$L = L_0 \sqrt{1 - \frac{v^2}{c^2}} = \frac{L_0}{\gamma}$$

Concepts of Relativity (continued)

where L_0 is the *proper length*, measured by an observer at rest with respect to the object. The parameter γ appears often in relativity and is defined as,

$$\gamma = \frac{1}{\sqrt{1 - \dfrac{v^2}{c^2}}}$$

Time Dilation: the length of a time interval between two events is measured to be longer for an observer moving in an inertial reference frame at velocity v with respect to a second inertial reference frame, *in which the events occur at a fixed position*, than for an observer at rest in the second frame. The mathematical expression is:

> *Time Dilation: Moving clocks are measured to run slow.*

$$\Delta T = \frac{\Delta T_0}{\sqrt{1 - \dfrac{v^2}{c^2}}} = \gamma \, \Delta T_0$$

where ΔT_0 is the *proper time interval*, measured by an observer at rest with respect to the events. If the events are represented by the arrival of a clock at two particular instants of time, the clock appears to run more slowly to the observer in motion with respect to the clock than to the observer at rest with respect to the clock.

In *some treatments* of Special Relativity, it is considered that mass is measured to be larger to an observer with respect to whom the mass is in motion at velocity v. The mathematical expression is:

> *Relativistic Mass: Moving objects are measured to offer more resistance to changes in motion (this is <u>one interpretation</u>).*

$$m = \frac{m_0}{\sqrt{1 - \dfrac{v^2}{c^2}}} = \gamma \, m_0$$

where m_0 is the *rest mass*, measured by an observer at rest with respect to the object.

The postulates also lead to a new relationship between momentum and energy. *If we choose to adopt the relativistic mass interpretation* (see Myth #2), we can still write that the momentum is,

$$\mathbf{p} = m\mathbf{v}$$

as long as we use the relativistic mass m rather than the rest mass m_0 as the mass in the equation.

Concepts of Relativity (continued)

If we choose *not* to adopt the relativistic mass interpretation, the expression for the momentum is,

$$\mathbf{p} = \frac{m\mathbf{v}}{\sqrt{1 - \dfrac{v^2}{c^2}}}$$

where *m* is the rest mass of the particle. Notice that, in the interpretation of relativity that does not include the concept of relativistic mass, the rest mass (which is simply called *mass*, since it is invariant) is simply *m*, while, the relativistic mass interpretation requires two symbols, m_0 for the *rest mass*, and *m* for the relativistic mass. In this book, *we will not adopt the relativistic mass interpretation*, so that the symbol *m* will represent the invariant mass, and the symbol m_0 will not be used.

If the velocity of the particle is more than about 1% of the speed of light, the classical relationship between momentum and kinetic energy,

$$KE = \frac{1}{2}mv^2 = \frac{p^2}{2m}$$

leads to a noticeably incorrect result and must be replaced by the relativistic relationship,

$$E = \sqrt{E_0^2 + p^2c^2}$$

Rest energy is related to mass:

$$E_0 = mc^2$$

where the total energy E is the sum of the rest energy ($E_0 = mc^2$) and the kinetic energy: $E = E_0 + KE$. What's more, we can express the total energy in terms of the mass in a way parallel to the relationship between rest energy and mass:

$$E = \gamma mc^2$$

The *Special* Theory of Relativity describes events seen by observers in inertial reference frames. The *General* Theory of Relativity describes the effects of *gravity* on the universe. An underlying precept of the general theory is the *Principle of Equivalence*. In Newtonian mechanics, the Principle of Equivalence manifests itself in the equality of inertial and gravitational masses, as discussed in Mystery #9 in Chapter 3. In the mechanics of general relativity, the gravitational force is replaced by a distortion of spacetime by objects with masses. Then, the movement of another object through this distorted spacetime appears to deviate from the inertial straight line described by Newton's First Law. The deviation appears to the observer as if a force acted, but in the distorted spacetime, the object is simply following a

Concepts of Relativity (continued)

geodesic—the shortest distance between the initial and final points.

In the distorted spacetime of general relativity, the Principle of Equivalence carries a slightly different flavor: *it is impossible to perform an experiment which will differentiate between a gravitational field and an acceleration.* Thus, if a rocket ship pilot is accelerating forward in empty space, he or she will feel pressed into the back of the seat. If the rocket is sitting at rest vertically on the Earth before takeoff, the pilot will also feel pressed into the back of the seat by the gravitational field. In the accelerating case, if the forward acceleration were $a = g$, the pilot would feel pressed into the seat *with the same force as when the rocket is sitting at rest on the Earth.* If we imagine other experiments, we can argue that we cannot find an experiment which will tell us whether we are accelerating in one direction or in a gravitational field in the other direction with the same magnitude.

> *Principle of Equivalence: No experiment can be performed which will differentiate between an acceleration and a gravitational field.*

The Principle of Equivalence leads to the common statement that "light curves around massive objects". Suppose a rocket ship is accelerating forward, and a light beam enters a side window, in a direction perpendicular to the direction of acceleration. Since the light beam will travel an inertial straight line relative to space, it will appear to follow a *curved* path, toward the back of the accelerating rocket, to an observer in the rocket. If acceleration is indistinguishable from a gravitational field, however, the light must follow the same curved path if the rocket is at rest on a planet with a gravitational field value with the same magnitude as the acceleration. Thus, the light will appear to follow a curved path due to the gravitational field (but see Myth #6).

Discussions; Chapter 22—Relativity

𝔐𝔶𝔰𝔱𝔢𝔯𝔦𝔢𝔰:

1.) Light cannot leave a black hole. So *what happens* to a photon as it tries to leave a region just outside the black hole? Does it *slow down*, like a baseball thrown up from the surface of the Earth?

The photon does not slow down, as photons must always move at the speed of light. Thus, its behavior is very different from that of the thrown baseball.

As a photon moves upward in a gravitational field, especially a strong one such as that which exists around a black hole, there is a transformation of energy from the photon into gravitational potential energy for the photon-black hole system. But recall, as discussed in Chapter 17, that the energy of a photon is related to its *frequency*:

$$E = hf$$

Thus, as the photon energy decreases, its frequency drops. As a result, there is a shift toward longer wavelengths, which is why this effect is called the *gravitational red shift*. This was the basis of the Pound-Rebka experiment mentioned in Myth #11 in Chapter 19.

2.) Suppose you weigh an object on a bathroom scale in an accelerating elevator. The reading is different from the actual weight. Now, "weigh" the same object on an equal arm balance in the accelerating elevator. How does this reading compare to that of the stationary balance?

As stated in the Mystery, the reading on a bathroom scale will be incorrect in an accelerating elevator. The reading on the equal arm balance will be correct, however. This is an example of the *Principle of Equivalence*—in a closed system, it is impossible to perform an experiment that can determine whether the system is in a gravitational field or is accelerating. If an astronaut is standing in a vertical rocket at rest on the Earth, he or she will feel pressed into the floor, due to gravity. If the rocket is in outer space, far from any planets and accelerating forward, the astronaut will also be pressed into the floor. No experiment can be performed by the astronaut to determine which is the case (ignoring looking out the window—it's a closed system, remember!). This principle is the starting point for the general theory of relativity.

In the accelerating elevator, the acceleration will combine with the Earth's gravitational field to produce an *effective* gravitational field which is different from that of the Earth's. Thus, on the bathroom scale, the force of the scale on the object will be different from that in the rest situation, so the reading will be different. For the equal arm balance, however, even though the effective gravitational field has changed, it is still the same *on both sides of the balance*. Thus, the balance will remain in equilibrium and provide a correct reading.

3.) Can you drive fast enough to cause a red traffic light to look green?

This question relates to the Doppler Effect for light. This is significantly different than the Doppler Effect for sound, since there is no medium for light, as discussed in Myth #7 in Chapter 11. As a result, only a *relative* velocity between source and observer can be identified. On the other hand, for sound waves, the air acts as a medium and *separate* velocities for the source and the observer relative to the air can be identified.

The equation for the Doppler Effect for light is as follows:

$$f = \sqrt{\frac{c+v}{c-v}}\ f_0$$

where c is the speed of light, v is the relative velocity between source and observer, f is the apparent frequency of the light according to the observer, and f_0 is the actual frequency as measured by someone at rest with respect to the source.

Let us calculate the required speed for a red light to appear green. For the red light, we let λ_{red} = 650 nm $\rightarrow$ $f_0 = f_{red}$ = 4.6 x 10^{14} Hz. Now, for the green light, we let λ_{green} = 500 nm $\rightarrow$ $f = f_{green}$ = 6.0 x 10^{14} Hz. Then, we have,

$$f = \sqrt{\frac{c+v}{c-v}}\ f_0 \quad \rightarrow \quad v = c\frac{f^2-f_0^2}{f^2+f_0^2} = c\frac{\left(6.0 \times 10^{14}\,\mathrm{Hz}\right)^2 - \left(4.6 \times 10^{14}\,\mathrm{Hz}\right)^2}{\left(6.0 \times 10^{14}\,\mathrm{Hz}\right)^2 + \left(4.6 \times 10^{14}\,\mathrm{Hz}\right)^2} = 0.26c$$

This is clearly much faster than an automobile can travel, so it is not possible to drive fast enough to cause a red light to look green, at least not in a car!

4.) Suppose that you take a job that requires you to travel to other planets at speeds close to the speed of light. Who would you like to punch your time card—*you*, or *your boss*, who stays on Earth?

It would be better to have your boss punch your time cards, since your time, as the traveling individual, will move more slowly, due to time dilation. This is intimately related to the Twin "Paradox", discussed in Myth #1.

Magic:

Do Ping Pong Balls Float in Water?

This is a demonstration of the equivalence between acceleration and gravity, which is the essence of the *Principle of Equivalence*, discussed in Mystery #2. When the bag falls at the same acceleration as the value of the gravitational field, the *downward* acceleration is equivalent to an *upward* gravitational field. The net effect is that there is no *apparent* gravity. Thus, there is *no pressure gradient* in the water in the bag. According to Archimedes' Principle, without a pressure gradient, there is *no buoyant force*. Thus, the ball stays at the same position in the water as it falls, rather than floating to the top.

Vertical (?) Plants

You should find that the plants will be tilted in toward the center of the platform, with the plants toward the edge of the platform leaning the most. This is another example of the Principle of Equivalence. The centripetal acceleration of the plants results in an effective *outward* gravity, which adds to the Earth's gravitational field. The vector diagram below shows the actual gravitational field vector, the apparent gravity due to the centripetal acceleration, and their combination, which is the combined apparent gravity.

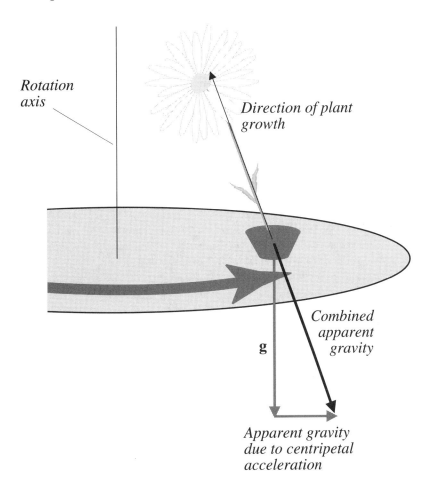

Rotation axis

Direction of plant growth

Combined apparent gravity

g

Apparent gravity due to centripetal acceleration

It is the behavior of plants that they grow in a direction opposite to that of the gravitational field. Thus, the plants on the rotating turntable grow in a direction opposite to that of the combined apparent gravity in the diagram above, resulting in their leaning inward.

𝕸𝖞𝖙𝖍:

1.) The Twin Paradox is a paradox.

The twin "paradox" is a popular conundrum related to relativistic kinematics. We imagine a pair of twins, with one taking a trip in a rocket ship to a far away planet and returning, traveling at relativistic speeds. The other twin stays at home on the Earth.

According to the twin on Earth, the rocketbound twin is traveling at a high speed and his or her clock will run slow. Thus, the twin on Earth will be older upon the return of the rocketbound twin. But, according to the rocketbound twin, he or she is stationary and the Earthbound twin moves off into space and returns. Thus, the rocketbound twin will be older upon return. The "paradox" lies in the fact that it appears that there is a symmetry in the situation, so that each twin thinks that the other ages more slowly.

In reality, the situation is not symmetric. *The twin on the rocket is not in a single inertial frame during the entire trip.* The velocity of the rocketbound twin, with respect to the Earth, changes when the rocket slows down and turns around. The velocity of the Earthbound twin, relative to the Earth, stays the same throughout the entire process. Thus, the rocketbound twin cannot make a single prediction for the entire trip based on special relativity, since he or she changes reference frames during the process. The Earthbound twin, however, remains in a single inertial reference frame during the entire process and can make a prediction, based on special relativity, that the moving biological clock of the rocketbound twin runs slowly. Thus, the Earthbound twin will be older when the twins meet again.

Suppose that the universe is *closed*, so that the rocketbound twin can return home without stopping and turning around? This is similar to traveling eastward on the Earth, going all the way around and returning to the starting point from the west. This question, and its resolution, is addressed in T. Dray, "The Twin Paradox Revisited", *American Journal of Physics*, **58**, 822, 1990.

2.) One of the basic principles of relativity is that an object's *mass increases* as it moves at speeds approaching that of light.

The increase in mass with speed is not a basic principle in relativity—*it is only one way of interpreting a particular equation.*

One of the results of analyzing conservation of momentum in relativistic collisions is that the equation for the momentum of a particle is,

$$\mathbf{p} = \frac{m_0 \mathbf{v}}{\sqrt{1 - \dfrac{v^2}{c^2}}}$$

where m_0 is the classical mass of the particle. (I know, we said in the Concepts section that we would not use m_0 in this book, but we must break that rule temporarily, so that we can discuss this issue of relativistic mass!)

There are two interpretations of this equation. One popular interpretation is to maintain the equation for momentum, **p** = *m***v**, by defining a *relativistic mass* as follows:

$$m = \frac{m_0}{\sqrt{1 - \dfrac{v^2}{c^2}}}$$

where *m* is the relativistic mass and m_0 is now called the *rest mass*. Under this interpretation, mass is a function of velocity. The faster a particle moves, the more massive it appears to become.

This interpretation was popular during much of the teaching of relativity theory, but fell into disfavor in the latter part of the twentieth century. One objection to this approach is related to applying forces in different directions, relative to a particle's motion, while trying to retain the form of Newton's Second Law as **F** = *m***a**. For example, imagine a particle moving in a circular path with a high speed, so that we are dealing with a relativistic situation, and a centripetal acceleration *a*. In this case, the velocity of the particle changes, but the speed remains constant. If we analyze this situation, we find that the expression above for relativistic mass is consistent with both **F** = *m***a** and **p** = *m***v**.

But suppose we apply a force *in the direction of travel* of a particle, such that the particle experiences an acceleration *a*. Now, the velocity and speed are *both* changing. The analysis of this situation shows that the expression for relativistic mass is not the same in the two equations, **F** = *m***a** and **p** = *m***v**. Thus, we have two different "relativistic masses", depending on the direction of the force. If the force **F** is at some angle to the velocity **v** other than 0° or 90°, the situation is even worse—then the mass depends on the *angle* between the force and velocity vectors.

This discrepancy in the masses in Newton's Second Law is indicated as "longitudinal and transverse relativistic masses" and represents one of the complaints about the relativistic mass concept.

The second interpretation of the momentum equation is that this is simply the way momentum is defined in relativity. The only mass to be considered is the rest mass, given the symbol *m*, and the mass is considered to be *invariant*. Thus, the symbol m_0 does not appear in this interpretation. In this interpretation, as a particle increases in speed, there is no change in the mass.

This interpretation is becoming more popular, but it also suffers from some conceptual difficulties. For example, if a glass of water is heated, so that the molecules move more rapidly, the mass of the molecules *does* increase, so that the rest mass of the glass of water increases because of the increased stored energy. But if the glass of water is moved through space, its mass does not increase. Thus, there is a mass increase for molecular velocity, but not for collective velocity.

For more discussions of these interpretations, see C. G. Adler, "Does Mass Really Depend on Velocity, Dad?", *American Journal of Physics*, **55**, 739, 1987; L. B. Okun, "The Concept of Mass", *Physics Today*, **42(6)**, 31, 1989; T. R. Sandin, "In Defense of Relativistic Mass", *American Journal of Physics*, **59**, 1032, 1991; and R. Baierlein, "Teaching $E = mc^2$: An Exploration of Some Issues", *The Physics Teacher*, **29**, 170, 1991.

3.) Mass is a form of energy.

This is a statement that often appears in treatments of relativistic dynamics, as the interpretation of Einstein's equation,

$$E = mc^2$$

The correctness of this interpretation depends on whether the concept of relativistic mass is used elsewhere in the treatment of dynamics. See Myth #2 for discussion of relativistic mass. If the relativistic mass interpretation is adopted, then *energy and mass changes occur in parallel.* Thus, if some process on an isolated system occurs, the total energy must be conserved, *as must the total mass.* If energy enters or leaves a system, there will be a corresponding increase or decrease of the mass of the system. Thus, the statement that "mass is a form of energy" is not appropriate in this model. It would be more appropriate to say that mass is a *measure* of energy, since energy in any form will be represented by an accompanying mass. Similarly, the idea of "converting mass to energy", which would suggest the possibility that as the mass of a system decreases, the energy could increase, is incorrect in this model—mass and energy vary in the same way.

On the other hand, if the relativistic mass interpretation is *not* adopted, then the rest mass is the only mass to be considered and the rest mass of an isolated system undergoing a process does exhibit a change. For example, the rest mass of a radioactive nucleus is different from the sum of the rest masses of the decay products. It is more appropriate in this case to claim that mass has been converted to energy (although it is even more appropriate to say that *rest energy* has been converted to other forms of energy). In the absence of a relativistic mass, it is also more appropriate to claim that mass is a form of energy, in terms of its role in defining the rest energy of a massive object.

For more points of view and further discussion of these ideas, see R. Baierlein, "Teaching $E = mc^2$", *American Journal of Physics*, **57**, 391, 1989; F. Rohrlich, "An Elementary Derivation of $E = mc^2$", *American Journal of Physics*, **58**, 348, 1990; L. Ruby and R. E. Reynolds, "Comment on 'An Elementary Derivation of $E = mc^2$, by F. Rohrlich", *American Journal of Physics*, **59**, 756, 1991; F. Rohrlich, "Response to 'Comment on 'An Elementary Derivation of $E = mc^2$, by F. Rohrlich', by L. Ruby and R. E. Reynolds", *American Journal of Physics*, **59**, 757, 1991; and M. M. Payne, "Does = Mean Equal?", *The Physics Teacher*, **29**, 548, 1991.

4.) Two travelers, laterally separated by 2 m, move in the *same direction*. Their paths never cross.

This is true in normal Euclidean flat space. General relativity analyzes motion in terms of *curved spacetime.* Such simple statements as that given in the Myth that are true in Euclidean space are not necessarily true in curved spacetime. As an example, consider two travelers on the Earth starting at the equator and separated by an east-west distance of 2 meters. Imagine that they both begin traveling exactly north. Thus, they will be traveling in the same direction—north—as prescribed by the statement in the Myth. But, when they both reach the North Pole, *their paths will cross.* The crossing of the paths is due to the *curved* nature of the surface of the Earth.

5.) Plumb bobs hang straight down.

Plumb bobs are used to define a vertical line for construction and decorating projects, since the assumption is made that the hanging plumb bob points toward the center of the Earth. This would only be strictly true, however, *if there were no rotation of the Earth.* Due to the Principle of Equivalence, the centripetal acceleration of the Earth at the location of the plumb bob is equivalent to a gravitational field directed away from the Earth's axis. This same idea was explored in the Magic demonstration Vertical (?) Plants in this Chapter.

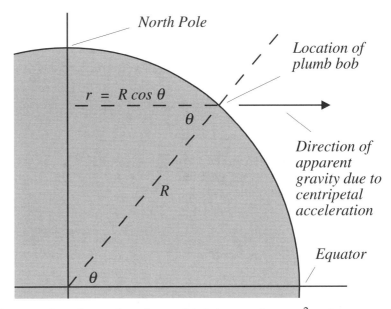

We can evaluate the deviation angle from the vertical for a plumb bob. Imagine a plumb bob hanging at a location with latitude angle θ, as in the diagram to the right.

We can now set up a vector addition, adding the actual gravitational field vector to the apparent gravity due to the centripetal acceleration, which is equal to $r\omega^2$, where r is indicated in the diagram above and ω is the angular velocity of the Earth. We exaggerate the effect of the centripetal acceleration to make it evident in the diagram below.

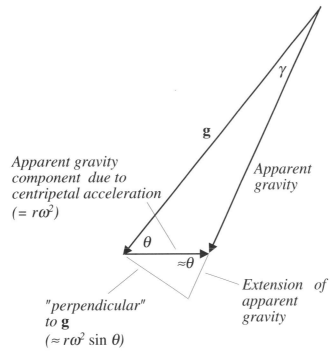

At the bottom of the diagram, we have drawn a line "perpendicular" to the vector **g**. It is not quite perpendicular, since it makes the same angle with **g** and the line consisting of the apparent gravity and its extension, but the angle γ is so small that the new line is *almost* perpendicular—the deviation from perpendicularity can be ignored. Notice also the angle marked "$\approx \theta$"—this angle is clearly not equal to θ *in the diagram above*. But recall that the centripetal acceleration has been *exaggerated* in the diagram. If the centripetal acceleration were shrunk to its actual value in the diagram, angle γ would become very small, and the angle marked "$\approx \theta$" would be very close to θ. The length of the line "perpendicular" to the vector **g**, from trigonometry, is approximately $r\omega^2 \sin\theta$. Since the angle γ is so small, we can approximate the line as the arc length of a sector of a circle of radius g. Thus, using the definition of an angle in radians, and the relationship between r and R, seen in the diagram on the previous page,

$$\gamma = \frac{arc\,length}{radius} = \frac{r\omega^2 \sin\theta}{g} = \frac{R\omega^2 \cos\theta \sin\theta}{g}$$

This is the angle from the vertical by which a plumb bob deviates. Let's evaluate this to see if this is a serious problem. Choosing the maximum deviation, which will occur at $\theta = 45°$, we have, in radians,

$$\gamma = \frac{R\omega^2 \cos\theta \sin\theta}{g} = \frac{6.4 \times 10^6\,\text{m} \left(\dfrac{2\pi}{24\,\text{h}} \dfrac{1\text{h}}{3600\,\text{s}} \right)^2 \cos 45° \sin 45°}{9.8\,\text{m} \cdot \text{s}^{-2}} = 1.7 \times 10^{-3}$$

This is about a tenth of a degree, so is negligible unless very high accuracy is needed.

We can compare this to the deviation on Saturn (of course, construction could not take place on the gaseous surface of Saturn!), which is larger ($R = 6.0 \times 10^7$ m), and rotates faster ($T = 10.2$ h) than the Earth:

$$\gamma = \frac{R\omega^2 \cos\theta \sin\theta}{g} = \frac{6.0 \times 10^7\,\text{m} \left(\dfrac{2\pi}{10.2\,\text{h}} \dfrac{1\text{h}}{3600\,\text{s}} \right)^2 \cos 45° \sin 45°}{9.05\,\text{m} \cdot \text{s}^{-2}} = 9.7 \times 10^{-2}$$

This is a larger deviation, equivalent to over 5°.

6.) Light travels in a curved line around a very massive object.

The response to this statement is similar to that in Myth #4. According to the General Theory of Relativity, light travels in a spacetime which is distorted by the gravity of massive objects. While it may appear to a distant observer that the direction of the light changes due to a large gravitational field, the light is actually traveling a *geodesic* in the distorted spacetime, which represents the minimum time of travel between the initial and final points. In Euclidean flat space, a geodesic is a straight line. Thus, in essence, light is traveling a "straight line" in a curved spacetime!

7.) An observer riding a train is located exactly midway between the engine and the last car. He passes a station, with a second observer standing on the platform. Just as the observers pass each other, lightning strikes both the engine and the last car. The observer on the platform claims that the lightning strikes were simultaneous. The observer on the train agrees.

This was an early thought ("*gedanken*") experiment of Einstein. The problem with the final statement in the Myth is due to the fact that the observer on the train is in motion with respect to the points at which the lightning strikes. To the observer standing still on the platform at the midway point between the ends of the train, the lightning strikes appear to be simultaneous. But let's concentrate on the observer on the train, midway between the endpoints, who passes by the observer on the platform just as the lightning bolts strike. The situation at the time the lightning strikes is shown in the first diagram (*a*) below.

(a) As the lightning strikes:

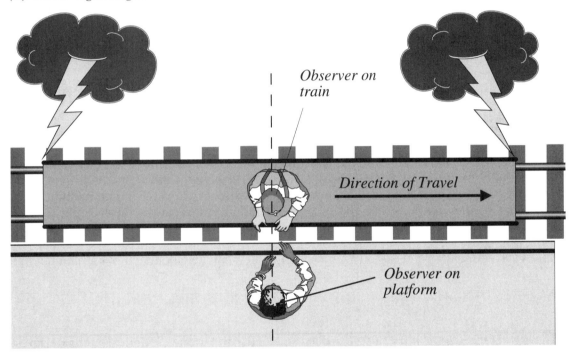

During the time that the light from the lightning takes to reach the observers, the observer on the train will move to the right. The second diagram (*b*) on the next page shows this situation at some time before the light reaches either observer.

Since the observer on the train has moved during this time, the light coming from the right hand lightning strike does not have as far to travel to reach this observer as the light from the left hand strike. Thus, even though the observer on the platform will see the strikes as occurring simultaneously, *the observer on the train will see the right hand strike first and then the strike from the left.*

(b) A short time later:

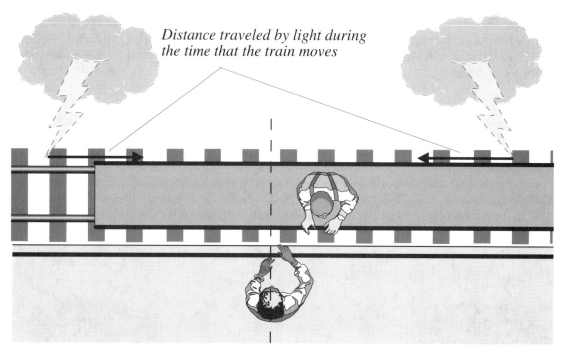

Distance traveled by light during the time that the train moves

8.) Space is nothing.

Early attempts to understand the passage of light through space proposed that space was filled with a *luminiferous ether*, which served as the medium through which light travels. The null result of the Michelson-Morley experiment was interpreted as indicating that no such ether exists. Thus, space is considered as empty, and light does not require a medium.

But, wait a minute. Light has a certain speed, which can be calculated from parameters:

$$c = \frac{1}{\sqrt{\varepsilon_0 \mu_0}}$$

where ε_0 is the permittivity of free space, an electrical parameter, and μ_0 is the permeability of free space, a magnetic parameter. These are parameters of *space*, which we have claimed is *nothing*. But how can *nothing* have *parameters*? There must be some properties of the "nothing" that determine the values of the parameters! So can it really be *nothing*?

Another approach to the statement stems from the *Dirac theory* of the electron, described in Mystery #4 of Chapter 23. In this model, space is filled with a sea of electrons in negative energy states. Since every state is filled, there is no electrical effect, so we can move through this sea without detecting it. Thus, in this model, space is not nothing—space is filled with electrons!

9.) In *Project 2061: Science for All Americans* (American Association for the Advancement of Science, Washington, D.C., 1989), the following is stated (paraphrased): **If you run away from a clock such as Big Ben at 3:00 at the speed of light, you would never see the hands move, since the light from 3:01 would never reach you.**

One problem with this argument is that it assumes that an observer could move at the speed of light, which is impossible. Let us ignore this problem, however, and consider another problem with the argument.

This argument is based on a false conceptual understanding which assumes that the speed of light changes as the speed of the observer changes—it assumes an ether! The problem is in the last phrase—"the light...would never reach you". According to the argument given, by running faster, the relative speed of light supposedly decreases, until, when the runner is moving at the speed of light, he or she is running "right along with the waves", so that there is no net motion. The speed of the light relative to the observer is supposedly *zero*. This is inconsistent with one of the fundamental postulates of relativity—the constancy of the speed of light for all observers.

10.) Displacement is a vector.

As discussed in Arm Rotations in Chapter 7, quantities which act as vectors must obey certain mathematical rules. One of the rules which vectors must obey is that the square of their "length", as measured by the sum of the squares of the components, must be invariant under a transformation of the coordinate system. Thus, a vector representing a displacement in a walk across the ground must have the same magnitude if north and south were rotated to be what used to be east and west.

Let us consider a displacement vector as viewed by someone in motion along the *x*-axis with respect to the vector. The observer's observations can be considered a transformation of coordinate system, using the *Lorentz transformations* (see a modern physics textbook for discussions of these transformation equations):

$$x' = \gamma(x - vt)$$
$$y' = y$$
$$z' = z$$
$$t' = \gamma\left(t - \frac{xv}{c^2}\right)$$

where the unprimed coordinates are those claimed by an observer at rest with respect to the vector, the primed coordinates are measured by a second observer moving with respect to the first observer at velocity *v*, and γ was defined in the Concepts section:

$$\gamma = \frac{1}{\sqrt{1 - \dfrac{v^2}{c^2}}}$$

Let us calculate the square of the "length" of the displacement vector in the primed frame, using the Pythagorean theorem:

$$(x')^2 + (y')^2 + (z')^2 = \gamma^2(x-vt)^2 + y^2 + z^2 = \gamma^2 x^2 + 2\gamma^2 xvt + \gamma^2 v^2 t^2 + y^2 + z^2$$

Thus, the square of the length of the vector in this frame is not the same as it is in the unprimed frame, which is just $x^2 + y^2 + z^2$.

The intimate relation between space and time that is inherent in the Lorentz transformations results in a change in our approach to vectors. We no longer have valid vectors in three dimensional space, but must extend our focus to *four dimensional* vectors in *spacetime*. The appropriate spacetime vector for our purposes combines length and time with components x, y, z, and ict, where,

$$i = \sqrt{-1}$$

Thus, the square of the length of this *four-vector*, according to a four dimensional Pythagorean theorem is,

$$(x)^2 + (y)^2 + (z)^2 + (ict)^2 = x^2 + y^2 + z^2 - c^2 t^2$$

Let us evaluate this for our observer in motion with respect to the vector:

$$(x')^2 + (y')^2 + (z')^2 - c^2(t')^2 = \gamma^2(x-vt)^2 + y^2 + z^2 - c^2\gamma^2\left(t - \frac{xv}{c^2}\right)^2$$

$$= \gamma^2 x^2 + 2\gamma^2 xvt + \gamma^2 v^2 t^2 + y^2 + z^2 - c^2\gamma^2 t^2 + 2c^2\gamma^2\frac{xvt}{c^2} - c^2\gamma^2\frac{x^2 v^2}{c^4}$$

$$= \gamma^2\left(1 - \frac{v^2}{c^2}\right)x^2 + y^2 + z^2 - c^2\gamma^2\left(1 - \frac{v^2}{c^2}\right)t^2$$

$$= \gamma^2\left(\frac{1}{\gamma^2}\right)x^2 + y^2 + z^2 - c^2\gamma^2\left(\frac{1}{\gamma^2}\right)t^2$$

$$= x^2 + y^2 + z^2 - c^2 t^2$$

Thus, the "length" of the four-vector is invariant under a Lorentz transformation and satisfies this rule for a vector.

Many other four-vectors can be set up in relativistic analyses. For example, the energy-momentum four-vector has three momentum components and the energy appears in the fourth.

11.) The Michelson-Morley experiment was an important impetus to Einstein in his work on special relativity.

The Michelson-Morley experiment is often used as the beginning of a study of relativity, followed by the development of relativity theory according to Einstein. While this may make pedagogical sense, it should not be inferred that Einstein was influenced by the experiment. There is strong evidence that Einstein was influenced far more by earlier experiments on stellar aberration and ether drag and that the Michelson-Morley paper was not even studied by Einstein until after he published his seminal 1905 paper. His response to the experimental result was that it fit well with his theoretical predictions. For further discussion, see R. Resnick, "Misconceptions About Einstein", *Journal of Chemical Education*, **57**, 854, 1980.

Chapter 23
Particle Physics and Cosmology

𝔐ysteries:

1.) Why did it take so long to detect the neutrino?

2.) If a change in the interior of the Sun occurred, we would know about it by means of neutrino data long before we would actually *see* any visual change. Why?

𝔐𝔶𝔰𝔱𝔢𝔯𝔦𝔢𝔰:

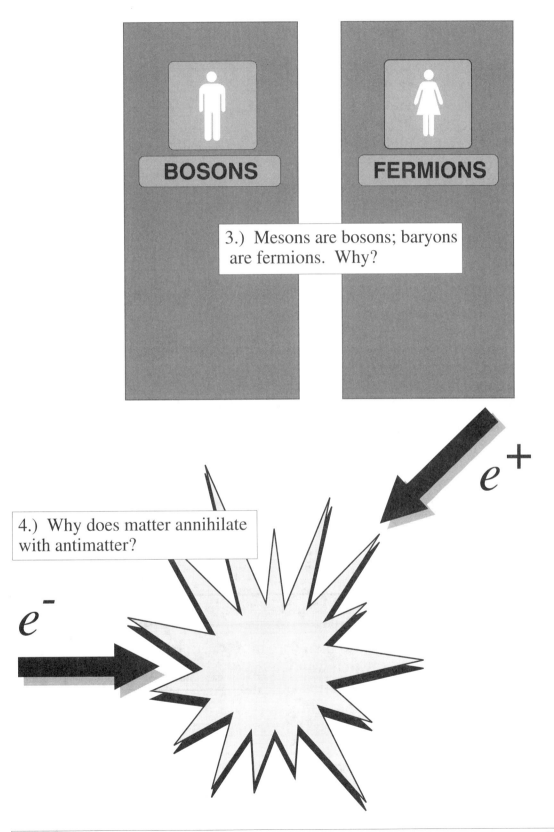

3.) Mesons are bosons; baryons are fermions. Why?

e^+

4.) Why does matter annihilate with antimatter?

e^-

𝔐𝔶𝔰𝔱𝔢𝔯𝔦𝔢𝔰:

5.) Particle accelerators use a *collision* process in which counter-rotating beams of particles smash into each other. Why is this more desirable than having a single beam of particles strike a stationary target?

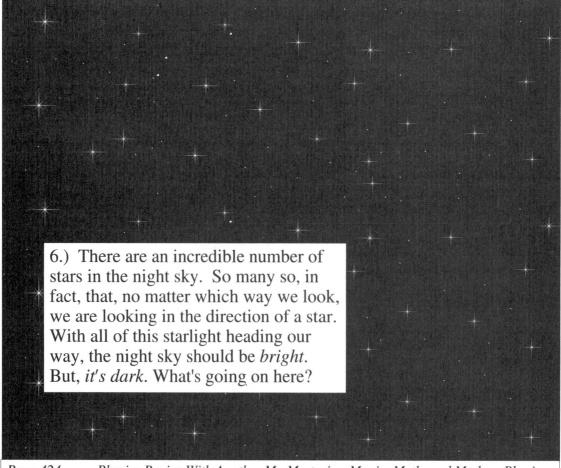

6.) There are an incredible number of stars in the night sky. So many so, in fact, that, no matter which way we look, we are looking in the direction of a star. With all of this starlight heading our way, the night sky should be *bright*. But, *it's dark*. What's going on here?

Magic:

The Expanding Universe

A simulation of the expansion of the universe can be made on paper. Using a drawing program on a computer, prepare a page full of dots of random sizes and locations as shown below. If you do not have access to such a capability, photocopy the dots from the page below. Print out a sheet of these dots. Now, enlarge the size of your whole collection of dots by 5% and print this new version on a transparency (if you photocopy the dots below, make another copy onto a transparency, using an enlarging photocopier set on 105%). Lay the transparency over the first sheet and line up a corresponding pair of dots, one on the paper and one on the transparency. You will see the rest of the dots expanding away from your choice of center. Now, line up another pair of dots. No matter which pair you choose as the center, the Universe expands from that point!

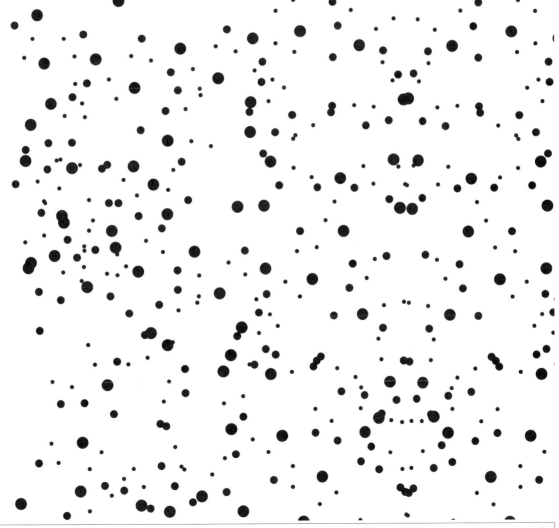

Magic:

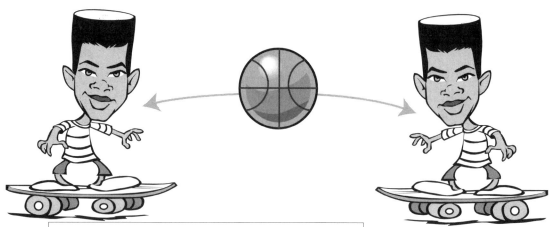

The Skateboard Exchange Force

Place two volunteers on skateboards and have them throw a basketball back and forth. They will move apart as if there is a repulsive force between them.

Myth:

Quark!

1.) Quarks are colored.

Myth:

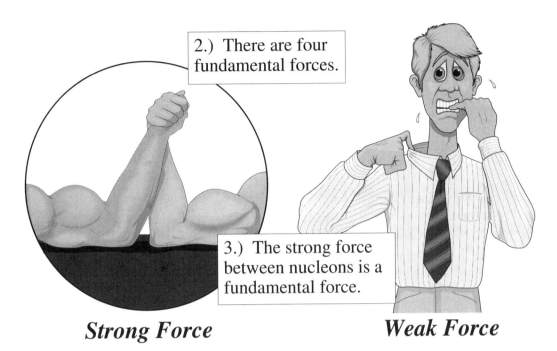

2.) There are four fundamental forces.

3.) The strong force between nucleons is a fundamental force.

Strong Force

Weak Force

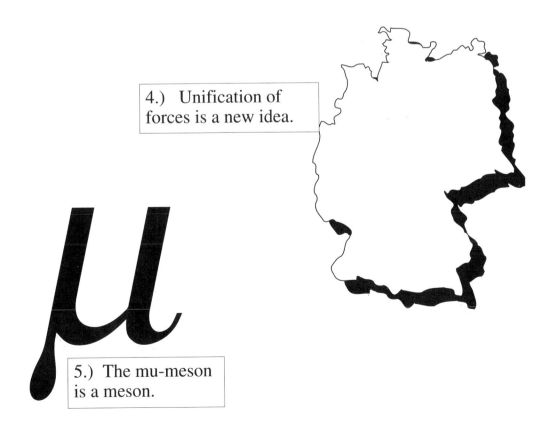

4.) Unification of forces is a new idea.

5.) The mu-meson is a meson.

6.) In the movie *This Island Earth* (Universal, 1954), some scientists walk into a laboratory and are startled by a cat. One of the scientists says, "Oh, that's only Neutron. We call him that because he is so positive."

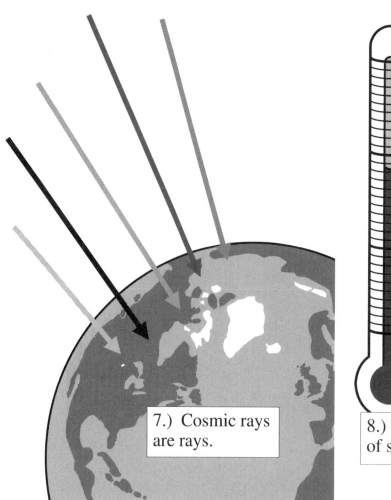

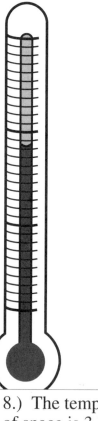

7.) Cosmic rays are rays.

8.) The temperature of space is 3 K.

Concepts of Particle Physics and Cosmology

Before 1897, there was no subfield of physics called *particle physics*. Although the existence of the atom was well on its way to general acceptance, there was no knowledge of the internal structure of the atom. In 1897, J. J. Thomson identified the properties of the electron and the beginning of a steady stream of "elementary" particles was begun. Until well into the twentieth century, it seemed that there were only three such particles—electrons, protons and neutrons. But additional experimentation and theoretical calculations indicated other, more exotic particles. The *positron*, the first piece of *antimatter* observed, was predicted by Dirac's theory of the electron, and detected in cosmic ray showers by Carl Anderson in 1932. In 1935, Hideki Yukawa predicted that a particle of mass about 200 times that of the electron would represent the exchange particle for the nuclear strong force, as discussed in Myth # 5 in Chapter 18. It was believed that this particle was found in 1938 by Carl Anderson with the discovery of the *muon*, with a mass of 207 electron masses. It turned out that this was not the correct particle, since the muon does not interact with other particles by means of the strong force. The particle that Yukawa predicted was discovered in 1947

> *The number of "elementary" particles proliferated during the twentieth century.*

with the detection by C. P. Powell of the *pion*. This particle exists in charged forms, both positive and negative, each with a mass of 274 electron masses, and an uncharged form of mass 264 electron masses. The apparent violation of conservation of energy in beta decay led to the prediction by W. Pauli, in 1930, of the *neutrino*. This particle interacts only by means of the weak force and thus is very hard to detect. The neutrino was finally observed with a sophisticated experiment in 1956 by C. Cowan and F. Reines.

The number of "elementary" particles grew into the hundreds during the middle part of the twentieth century. It did not seem reasonable that there would be so many fundamental particles; there must be an underlying structure to the particles themselves. In the 1960's, the *quark model* was proposed. In this model, *some* of the collection of elementary particles are still considered elementary. These include the electron, the muon and the tau particle, along with a neutrino associated with each. These elementary particles are collectively called *leptons*, meaning "light particles". The properties of the leptons are summarized in the table below.

> *Leptons are the lightest particles and are believed to be truly elementary.*

Lepton	Symbol	Elec Charge	Approximate Mass (MeV)
Electron	e	-1	0.511
Muon	μ	-1	106
Tau	τ	-1	1777
Electron neutrino	ν_e	0	$< 7 \times 10^{-6}$
Muon neutrino	ν_μ	0	< 0.27
Tau neutrino	ν_τ	0	< 33

Concepts of Particle Physics and Cosmology (continued)

The rest of the particles, in the category of *hadrons*, which interact via the strong force, are considered to be built from another set of elementary particles called *quarks*. Just as there are six leptons, there are six quarks—*up*, *down*, *strange*, *charmed*, *bottom* and *top*, all of which have spin $1/2$. The properties of these quarks are shown in the table below.

> *Hadrons can be developed as combinations of quarks.*

Quark	Symbol	Elec Charge	Strangeness	Approximate Mass (MeV)
Up	*u*	$+ 2/3$	0	340*
Down	*d*	$- 1/3$	0	340
Strange	*s*	$- 1/3$	-1	1.5×10^2
Charmed	*c*	$+ 2/3$	0	1.5×10^3
Bottom	*b*	$- 1/3$	0	5×10^3
Top	*t*	$+ 2/3$	0	$\sim 10^5$

One of the properties listed is *strangeness*, which is a quantum number introduced to account for the unusual decay behavior of some particles. This quantum number arose from observations beginning in the 1950's of the decays of particles such as the kaon (see the table of mesons on the next page). The reader is referred to modern physics textbooks for more information on strangeness.

The subset of hadrons that are called *baryons* are formed from three quarks. As a result, all baryons have half-integral spin. The familiar atomic particles, the neutron and the proton, are in this category. They belong to a subset of the baryons, all having spin $1/2$, as in the following table.

> *Baryons consist of three quarks.*

Particle	Symbol	Elec Charge	Strangeness	Mass (MeV)	Antiparticle
Proton	p	1	0	938.3	$\bar{p}$
Neutron	n	0	0	939.6	$\bar{n}$
Lambda	Λ^0	0	-1	1115.6	$\bar{\Lambda}^0$
Sigma	Σ^+	1	-1	1189.4	$\bar{\Sigma}^+$
Sigma	Σ^0	0	-1	1192.5	$\bar{\Sigma}^0$
Sigma	Σ^-	-1	-1	1197.3	$\bar{\Sigma}^-$
Xi	Ξ^0	0	-2	1314.9	$\bar{\Xi}^0$
Xi	Ξ^-	-1	-2	1321.3	$\bar{\Xi}^-$

---

*Some books will give the mass of the up quark as 5 MeV and that of the down quark as 10 MeV. Others will give the masses in the range of 340 MeV. The lower values are estimates of the quark masses *as if the quarks were not confined to a hadron*. Confining the quarks to a hadron (which is the usual case—they cannot be liberated, as far as we know) raises the rest energy, according to the uncertainty principle, and, therefore, the mass. For further discussion, see B. R. Holstein, "Answer to Question #2 ["Quark Masses and Binding Energy in a Proton"], *American Journal of Physics*, **63**, 14, 1995.

Concepts of Particle Physics and Cosmology (continued)

The neutron and proton can be built from three quarks as follows:

Neutron: *udd*
Proton: *uud*

Other, more exotic particles in this category can be built from quarks, also. For example, we can build a Σ^- particle as,

Σ^- particle *dds*

or the Λ^0 particle as,

Λ^0 particle *uds*

There are other, even more exotic, baryons with half-integral spins other than $^1/_2$ that can also be built from quarks (for example, the Ω^- particle has three strange quarks, and a spin of $^3/_2$). Chapters on elementary particles in physics textbooks can be consulted for more detail about these particles.

Mesons consist of a quark and an antiquark.

Another category of hadrons is the set of particles called *mesons*. These are integral spin particles and can be constructed from a quark and an antiquark. We can identify nine types of mesons with spin 0 (including antiparticles) as in the following table.

Particle	Symbol	Elec Charge	Strangeness	Mass (MeV)	Antiparticle
Pion	π^0	0	0	135.3	itself
Pion	π^+	+1	0	139.6	π^-
Kaon	K^+	+1	+1	493.7	K^-
Kaon	K^0	0	+1	497.7	$\overline{K}^0$
Eta	η	0	0	548.8	itself
Eta Prime	η'	0	0	957.6	itself

As an example of the quark construction of a meson, the positive pion can be built from quarks as follows:

Pion (π^+) $u\overline{d}$

The *Standard Model* incorporates these quark constructions along with *exchange particles*, which are the mediators, or carriers, of the fundamental forces. The identification of the exchange

Forces are considered to be mediated by exchange particles.

Concepts of Particle Physics and Cosmology (continued)

particles with the forces is as follows:

Force	Exchange Particle
Electromagnetic	*photons*
Gravitational	*gravitons*
Strong	*gluons*
Weak	*W* and *Z*

In this model, forces between particles are imagined to be the result of the passing back and forth of exchange particles.

The fields of cosmology and particle physics have been joined by the increase in theoretical understanding of the first few moments of the Universe. In the first 10^{-43} s after the Big Bang, the fundamental forces were unified into a single force. After this time, but before 10^{-35} s, the gravitational force separated out and became distinguishable from the other forces. Between 10^{-35} s and 10^{-13} s, the strong force separated out. This is the earliest era about which physicists feel that there is reasonable theoretical understanding. During this time, quarks, leptons and their antiparticles formed. By 10^{-3} s, protons and neutrons formed, and the electroweak force separated into the electromagnetic and weak forces. After this time, as the Universe continues to expand, nuclei formed, followed by the formation of atoms, and atoms began to combine into planets and stars.

> *Advances in particle physics help us to understand the earliest moments of the Universe.*

Discussions; Chapter 23—Particle Physics and Cosmology

𝔐𝔶𝔰𝔱𝔢𝔯𝔦𝔢𝔰:

1.) Why did it take so long to detect the neutrino?

The detection of particles depends on the interaction of the particle with matter. For example, your television screen detects the arrival of electrons by the resulting fluorescence of the material on the screen. Your eyes detect the arrival of photons by their interaction with the light sensitive structures on the retina—the rods and cones. The detection in both of these cases is due to the fact that the electrons and photons interact by means of the electromagnetic force with the matter which they encounter.

The neutrino is uncharged, so that it cannot interact by means of the electromagnetic force. It has little or no mass, so that there is virtually no gravitational interaction. It is not made from quarks, so there is no nuclear strong (color) force. This leaves only the weak interaction as the means by which a neutrino can interact with matter. And, as it says, this a *weak* interaction. Neutrinos can easily pass through the Earth without being absorbed.

Since the probability of interaction between a neutrino and matter is so small, a very careful experiment must be devised to detect the neutrino. This did not take place successfully until 1956, with the work of Cowan and Reines, who detected neutrinos from a nuclear reactor by means of an inverse beta process.

2.) If a change in the interior of the Sun occurred, we would know about it by means of neutrino data long before we would actually *see* any visual change. Why?

As discussed in Mystery #3 in Chapter 17, energy carried by photons from the core of the Sun takes 10 million years to reach the surface. Thus, any change in the interior would take a very long time to make a *visible* change. Neutrinos, however, interact only weakly with matter, as discussed in Mystery #1, and will pass almost freely from the core to the surface of the Sun. Thus, a change in the interior of the Sun would cause a change in the neutrino flux which would be detected at the Earth only minutes after it happened, assuming that a suitable neutrino detector is in operation.

3.) Mesons are bosons; baryons are fermions. Why?

We can understand this from the quark theory. Baryons (such as neutrons and protons) are formed by combinations of three quarks. For example, a proton is an up-up-down (*uud*) combination, while the neutron is an up-down-down (*udd*) combination. More baryons can be built from a combination of three quarks selecting from up and down and more exotic quarks such as *charmed*, *strange*, *top* and *bottom*, as discussed in the Concepts section. For example, the Ξ⁻ (Xi-minus) particle has a quark structure of down-strange-strange (*dss*). The common feature of all baryons is that they are formed from a combination of *three* quarks. Since quarks are fermions, with half-integral spin, any combination of an *odd number* of quarks, such as three, will also be a fermion, since only half integral spins will result from adding three half integral spins.

Now, what about mesons? These can be formed in the quark model from a combination of *two* particles—a quark and an antiquark. For example, the π^+ meson is a combination of up and antidown ($u\bar{d}$). A combination of two half-integral spins must result in an integral spin. Thus, all mesons are bosons.

4.) Why does matter annihilate with antimatter?

We can respond to this question in one way by considering Dirac's model of the electron, published in 1928. Dirac attempted to combine the successes of quantum mechanics and relativity into a relativistic quantum theory of the electron. Consistent with our understanding of relativity, the energy of the electron can be given by, as seen in the Concepts section of Chapter 22,

$$E = \pm\sqrt{E_0^2 + p^2 c^2}$$

At first, Dirac ignored the negative root, which is required by the mathematics, but was difficult to analyze physically. Eventually, he accepted the negative root, and imagined electrons with negative energy. The implication changed the view of the vacuum. Rather than being nothing, the vacuum is a sea of electrons with negative energies, as discussed in Myth #8 in Chapter 22. This is not inconsistent with our intuitive experience with a vacuum. Indeed, since the negative charge of these electrons fills all space homogeneously and isotropically, we would not be able to detect such a charge.

According to the Pauli Exclusion Principle, all of the negative energy states are filled, each with one electron. Additional electrons in the universe must reside in the available positive energy states—these are the electrons that we detect. Now, suppose an electron in a negative energy state absorbs energy and is excited to a positive energy state. The result is an additional electron with which we can interact, along with a vacancy in the negative sea, which acts just like a positive charge. This vacancy is defined as the *antiparticle* of the electron—a *positron*. The process just described is that of *pair production*, in which energy from a gamma ray is transformed into the rest energy of an electron and a positron.

Given this introduction, we can now answer the Mystery. The annihilation of matter and antimatter, say, of an electron and a positron, is simply the dropping of an electron from a positive energy state into an available negative energy state, with the emission of two photons of total energy equal to the difference in energy between the states.

5.) Particle accelerators use a *collision* process in which counter-rotating beams of particles smash into each other. Why is this more desirable than having a single beam of particles strike a stationary target?

The colliding beam technique is more efficient at transforming the kinetic energy of the particles into rest energy of the particles created in the collision. The reason is based on conservation of *momentum*. We look first at a collision between a moving particle and a stationary target. Let us consider the center of mass of the incoming and target particles. Before the collision, this center of mass is moving, in the same direction as that of the accelerated particle. If the accelerated particle collides with a stationary particle, conservation of momentum requires that the center of mass continue to move with the same velocity. Thus, the fragments of the resulting reaction must have a momentum component in the original direction. As a result, the energy of the collision is split between the rest energy of the resulting particles and the kinetic energy of the particles, which must include a component of momentum in the original direction.

On the other hand, in a counter-rotating collision between identical particles, the center of mass is at rest, with no momentum. When the particles collide, the energy of collision goes into rest energy of the created particles and their kinetic energy. There is no requirement to have a component of momentum, since the total momentum is zero, and more energy is available to create new particles of higher rest energy.

As a classical example, consider driving a car into another identical but stationary car at rest. Compare the damage to your car to the case of driving your car head-on into the car if it is moving at the same speed toward you. More energy is available to damage the cars in the latter case.

6.) There are an incredible number of stars in the night sky. So many so, in fact, that, no matter which way we look, we are looking in the direction of a star. With all of this starlight heading our way, the night sky should be *bright*. But, *it's dark*. What's going on here?

This is a problem which plagued some famous scientists, such as Johannes Kepler, Edmund Halley and Lord Kelvin, as well as some famous people who were not scientists, such as Edgar Allan Poe.

Let us first consider some details associated with arguments that the sky *should* be *bright*. Assume that the Universe is filled with a relatively uniform distribution of stars. Then, if we imagine a spherical shell at a distance r from the Earth, let us assign the number of stars contained in this shell to be N. Now, imagine a larger shell, of radius $2r$. Since the surface area of the spherical shell increases as the square of the radius, this shell will have four times the area of the original shell. As a result, it will contain four times as many stars.

Now, consider the intensity of light from stars. The intensity will fall off according to an inverse square law. Thus, although there are four times as many stars in the larger shell in the above discussion, the intensity from each star (on the average) is only one fourth as great. As a result, *the total intensity of light from stars in a shell of any arbitrary radius is the same as that from any other shell.*

If we imagine the Universe to be infinite in extent, then there are an infinite number of shells of varying radii. Thus, if we add the identical intensities of starlight from each shell, we will arrive at an *infinite total intensity*! Thus, the night sky should be blindingly bright.

Another argument is based on the finite size of a star—it is *not* a point source—and the assumed endless extent of the Universe. A line-of-sight drawn from the Earth to any point in the sky will ultimately encounter the disk of a star, based on these assumptions. Thus, wherever you look, you should be looking at a star and the night sky should be bright.

This clearly is not the case; we find that the night sky is *dark*, with relatively little light from stars. There are a couple of ways to attack this conundrum. One argument that has been made is to invoke the *Doppler Effect* for light. According to Hubble's Law, the farther a galaxy is from Earth, the faster it is moving. Thus, light from stars that are very far away from Earth would be severely redshifted, so much that the region of highest power would be shifted out of the visible. Detailed calculations show that the redshift may be sufficient to *dim* the sky somewhat, but not to *darken* it.

The second argument, and the one widely accepted, is based on the *finite life of stars*, which is shorter than the age of the Universe. Some stars have already lived out their life and the light from these stars has passed by the Earth. Other stars may be somewhere in the early stages of their life, but they are so far away that the light from their birth has not yet reached the Earth. The intensity and line-of-sight arguments given above assume that light from all stars reaches the Earth at the same time. This is not the case. We know that the lifetime of stars is less than the age of the Universe. Thus, even though the light from all stars will *eventually* encounter the Earth at some time during the life of the Universe, at any given time, the light from only *some* of the stars is arriving at Earth. Thus, the night sky is dark, with points of light from those stars whose light is arriving at the time.

For more information on a number of arguments made throughout history, see E. Harrison, *Darkness at Night*, Harvard University Press, Cambridge, 1987.

𝔐𝔞𝔤𝔦𝔠:

The Expanding Universe

(*a*)

This is a two-dimensional demonstration of a feature of an expanding universe. If a collection of objects is ejected from a single origin (as in the Big Bang), all objects move apart from each other. Thus, everyone who looks at other galaxies, regardless of where they are, *sees themselves at the center of the expansion*. This is demonstrated in the diagram to the right (*a*), using a miniaturized version of the dots accompanying the Magic description. The original dots are in the frame in the diagram with the thin border. The thick bordered frame contains the same dots, but is 5% larger. The

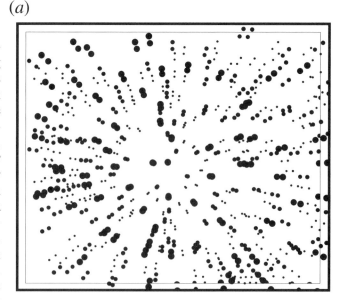

(*b*)

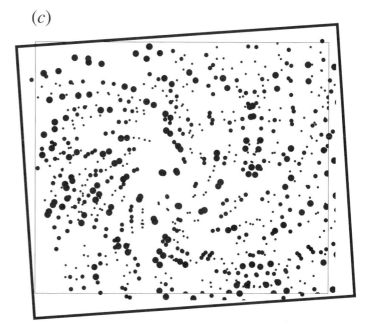

(*c*)

centers of the frames are aligned, and it appears that the dots are expanding from the center of this "Universe". Compare this with the second diagram (*b*), which shows the same pair of frames, but with the alignment of dots occurring in the lower right of the frames. Once again, the expansion is seen, but now it appears that the center of the expansion is in the lower right! The transparency can be moved around with respect to the paper and the center of the expansion can be made to appear to be anywhere in this "Universe".

One point of caution—make sure that the sides of the transparency and the sheet of paper are <u>parallel</u>. If there is a small angle between the sides, there will appear a "swirling" or "spiraling" effect in the combination, which will detract from the intended result. This is shown in diagram (*c*) to the right, in which the dots in the thick bordered frame have been rotated with respect to those in the thin bordered frame by 4°.

One final point—for presenting this demonstration to a large group, *both* sets of dots can be printed on transparencies and presented with an overhead projector.

For a larger sheet of dots that will fill an entire transparency, see D. Chandler, "An Expanding Universe in the Classroom", *The Physics Teacher*, **29**, 103, 1991. This article contains both the original and "expanded" universe, so that an enlarging photocopier will not be needed.

The Skateboard Exchange Force

This demonstration simulates the force that exists between particles by means of exchanging particles back and forth. The two volunteers on the skateboards will move apart as they throw the basketball back and forth, as if there is a repulsive force between them.

𝔐𝔶𝔱𝔥:

1.) Quarks are colored.

The word *color* is used as a quantum characteristic for quarks, but it is not to be confused with the physiological sensation of color related to the frequency of light waves. The need for this quantum "number" can be seen by considering, for example, a proton, with two up quarks and a down quark. Since quarks have half integral spin, they must obey the Pauli Exclusion Principle. Yet we have *two up quarks together in the proton*. It would seem that this violates the Exclusion Principle, since both quarks have the same value of the quantum "number"—*up*. Another, more dramatic, example is the Ω^- particle, with *three* strange quarks. In order to satisfy the Exclusion Principle, a new quantum number, called *color*, was introduced. The allowed values of color are red, blue and green. In this way, the Exclusion Principle is satisfied by requiring that a particle made from quarks be *colorless*, meaning that *one of each color* must be present in a baryon. In a meson, a color quark will combine with a quark with the *anti*-color. For example, a red quark will combine with an *antired* quark to create a colorless combination.

In some ways, the property of color is very similar to electric charge, except that three colors are necessary for neutrality, compared to two for electrical situations. In fact, color is often called *color charge* and the attractive force between quarks is the *color force*. These concepts are fundamental to the theory of *quantum chromodynamics*. Modern physics textbooks can be consulted for more information on quantum chromodynamics.

2.) There are four fundamental forces.

Four fundamental forces are often identified—gravitation, electromagnetism and the nuclear strong and weak forces. The number of fundamental forces, however, depends on the current state of efforts to *unify* the forces. In the early part of the nineteenth century, scientists did not recognize an *electromagnetic* force. Since the connection between electricity and magnetism was not well understood at the time, electricity and magnetism were treated as two *separate* forces. Thus, at that time, *three* fundamental forces would be claimed—electricity, magnetism and gravity (the nuclear strong and weak forces were not understood nor theorized at that time). The electric and magnetic forces were unified by means of the work of Oersted, Faraday and Maxwell. Some scientists of the time might have claimed even more than three forces, since the nature of friction, contact forces, etc., were not completely understood.

For much of the twentieth century, the concept of four fundamental forces was in vogue. By the last decades of the twentieth century, it was clear that the electromagnetic and weak forces could be unified into the *electroweak* force above about 100 GeV, leaving only three fundamental forces. It is the goal of theoretical physicists to continue this process of unification, with the lofty objective of showing that all forces are manifestations of a *single* universal force.

3.) The strong force between nucleons is a fundamental force.

The interaction between particles exhibiting the strong force, such as neutrons and protons is actually *a secondary manifestation of a more fundamental force*. The fundamental force is that between quarks. It is often called the *color force*, because of the quantum characteristic of quarks called color (see Myth #1), and the mediator of the color force is called a *gluon* (since the color force is the "glue" which keeps the quarks together in a hadron). The strong force between hadrons is then in reality a combination of color forces between the quarks making up the hadrons.

Perhaps an electrical analogy might clear this up further. We have no problem imagining the electrical force between two charged particles. But what about the electrical force between two *electric dipoles*? Each dipole is electrically neutral, so does that mean that there is no electric force between the dipoles? There certainly *is* a force between the dipoles, but it is not a new kind of force. It is simply the combination of electrical forces between the charges that make up the dipoles.

4.) Unification of forces is a new idea.

As addressed in the discussion of Myth #2, the unification of forces has been occurring for some time, with a major example being the unification of electricity and magnetism in the nineteenth century.

As an additional and earlier example, we consider the work of *Newton*, who performed his research in the seventeenth century. Newton's contribution to unification was to recognize that the force holding the Moon in its orbit around the Earth was the same force causing an apple to fall to the ground on the surface of the Earth. Today, we almost take it for granted that these are the same force, but this was a major advance in understanding at the time of Newton.

By the way, if you did not recognize the shape of the country accompanying this Myth related to *unification*, it is *Germany—*get it?

5.) The mu-meson is a meson.

In the early part of the twentieth century, physicists were developing the exchange particle model for forces. In this model, the force between particles is a result of an exchange of particles. For example, the mediator of the electromagnetic force is the photon. This is a special kind of photon, however, called a *virtual photon*. It is called this because it only exists for a finite time, the time for the photon to move from one of the charged particles to the other. This photon cannot be long-lived, because while it is moving between the particles, there is a temporary violation of conservation of energy (see Myth #5 in Chapter 18). The photon energy has seemed to appear from nowhere, but that's acceptable as long as the time interval during which it exists is short.

The exchange particle model was so appealing to physicists that they began to theorize about exchange particles for the other forces. In the case of the nuclear strong force, the hypothesized exchange particle was called a *meson*, which comes from the Greek word *meso*, meaning "middle". As discussed in the Concepts section, Hideki Yukawa predicted in 1935, based on relativistic calculations involving the observed range of the force, that the exchange particle should have a mass about 200 times as large as the electron. In 1938, Carl Anderson observed a particle in cosmic radiation with a mass of just this size. The particle was later called the *mu-meson*, or *muon*, due to its early identification as the exchange particle for the nuclear strong force. But this turned out to be the wrong particle! The muon did not exhibit a strong interaction with the nucleus. Yukawa predicted the exchange particle to be a boson, but the muon was a fermion!

Later, in 1947, C. P. Powell observed the *pi-meson*, or *pion*, which turned out to be the particle which Yukawa had predicted. The name *meson* for the muon was too well entrenched in the language of physicists to be corrected. Thus, we find that the muon, even though it is a lepton and is not built from quarks, still carries the incorrect *meson* label.

6.) In the movie *This Island Earth* (Universal, 1954), some scientists walk into a laboratory and are startled by a cat. One of the scientists says, "Oh, that's only Neutron. We call him that because he is so positive."

This must simply be a mistake which no one caught, since neutrons are *uncharged*, not *positive*!

7.) Cosmic rays are rays.

The phrase *cosmic rays* is in common use, but these are not *rays*. Cosmic rays are *particles* entering the Earth's atmosphere from space. Typical energies are in the 1000 MeV range, although energies as high as 10^{15} MeV have been observed.

For a discussion of taking cosmic ray readings while on a ski trip, see B. Jones, "Cosmic Ray Studies on Skis and on Campus", *The Physics Teacher*, **31**, 458, 1993.

8.) The temperature of space is 3 K.

As explored in Mystery #1 in Chapter 14 of *PBWM*, the temperature of *empty space* has no definition, since temperature is often defined as a property of a collection of particles. Another definition of temperature is related to *thermal radiation*, explored in Chapter 17. This is the context in which the temperature of about 3 K arises, but it is not to be interpreted as the temperature of *space*, but rather the temperature of the *Universe*. While the initial temperature of the Universe, just after the Big Bang, was very high, the expansion of the Universe results in a theoretical temperature of about 3 K today. The microwave radiation representing this temperature was detected by A. Penzias and R. Wilson in 1965.

Illustration Credits

While some illustrations were drawn by the author, most of the artwork in this book was obtained from computer clip art collections published by the following software distributors and used with permission. Some of the clip art illustrations were modified by the author. The names of the software packages appear under the manufacturer in the list below.

3G Graphics, Inc. (114 Second Ave. S., Suite 104, Edmonds, Washington 98020)

> *Images with Impact—Business 1*
> *Images with Impact—Graphics & Symbols 1*
> *Images with Impact—People 1*
> *Images with Impact—Places & Faces 1*

AB PRODUKTUM 88 (Egnahemsvägen 26c, S413-21, Göteborg, Sweden)

> *Provektor II*
> *Provektor Pro 3000*

Cartesia Software (5 South Main Street, P. O. Box 757, Lambertville, N. J. 08530)

> *MapArt Vol 4: Metro Area Maps—USA*

EDUCORP Computer Services (7434 Trade St., San Diego, California 92121)

> *Color Space Photos*

Gazelle Technologies, Inc. (7434 Trade St., San Diego, California 92121)

> *Desktop Publishing CD-ROM 3.0*

Multi-Ad Services, Inc. (1720 West Detweiller Drive, Peoria, Illinois 61615)

> *Kwikee InHouse PAL—Professional Art Library Potpourri*

Metro ImageBase, Inc. (18623 Ventura Blvd., Suite 210, Tarzana, California 91356)

> *Metro ImageBase CD—Volume 1*

OLDUVAI Corporation (7520 Red Road, Suite A, South Miami, Florida 33143)

> *Art Clips*

Oswego Co. (610 SW Alder Street, Portland, Oregon 97205)

> *Oswego Illustrated Archives CD-ROM*

TechPool Studios (1463 Warrensville Center Rd., Cleveland, OH 44121)

> *LifeArt™ Collections*

T/Maker Company (1390 Villa Street, Mountain View, California 94041)

> *ClickArt EPS Animals & Nature*
> *ClickArt EPS Business*
> *ClickArt EPS Illustrations*
> *ClickArt EPS Sports & Games*
> *ClickArt EPS Symbols & Industry Vol. 1*
> *ClickArt Incredible Image Pak*

Totem Graphics, Inc. (6200-F Capitol Blvd., Tumwater, Washington 98501)

Birds	*Borders & Accents*
Deluxe Business Images #1	*Deluxe Business Images #2*
Deluxe Travel	*Domestic Animals*
Education	*Fish*
Flowers	*Food*
Health Care	*Holidays*
Insects	*Nautical*
Sports	*Tools*
Wild Animals	*Women*

Wayzata Technology (2515 East Highway 2, Grand Rapids, Minnesota 55744)

> *epsPRO Volume 1: Design Elements* (combines the work of Christopher
> Marshall Designs (CMD) and LasArt)

Bibliography

Books

Anikouche, W. A. and Sternberg, R. W., *The World Ocean: An Introduction to Oceanography*, 2nd ed., Prentice Hall, Inc., Englewood Cliffs, 1981

Arons, A. B., *A Guide to Introductory Physics Teaching*, John Wiley & Sons, New York, 1990

Ashford, N. and Wright, P. H., *Airport Engineering*, 3rd ed., John Wiley & Sons, New York, 1992

Backus, J., *The Acoustical Foundations of Music*, 2nd ed., W. W. Norton & Company, New York, 1977

Ballentine, L. E., *Quantum Mechanics*, Prentice-Hall, Englewood Cliffs, 1990

Beal, J. D., *Adventurous Film Making*, Focal Press, London, 1980

Benade, A. H., *Fundamentals of Musical Acoustics*, Oxford University Press, New York, 1976

Blades, J., *Percussion Instruments and Their History*, Frederick A. Praeger, Publishers, New York, 1970

Böhm-Vitense, E., *Introduction to Stellar Astrophysics; Volume 1—Basic Stellar Observations and Data*, Cambridge University Press, Cambridge, 1989

Bolemon, *Physics: An Introduction*, Prentice Hall, Englewood Cliffs, N. J., 1989

Bolt, B. A., *Inside the Earth*, W. H. Freeman and Company, San Francisco, 1982

Brancazio, P. J., *SportScience; Physical Laws and Optimum Performance*, Simon and Schuster, New York, 1983

Bullen, K. E. and Bolt, B. A., *An Introduction to the Theory of Seismology*, 4th ed., Cambridge University Press, Cambridge, 1985

Clancy, E. P., *The Tides: Pulse of the Earth*, Doubleday & Co., Garden City, New York, 1968

Curtis, A. R., *Monitoring NASA Communications*, Tiare Publications, Lake Geneva, Wisconsin, 1992

Davies, P. C. W. (ed.), *The New Physics*, Cambridge University Press, Cambridge, 1989

Eaton, G. T., *Photographic Chemistry*, Morgan & Morgan, Inc., Dobbs Ferry, New York, 1965

Eisberg, R. and Resnick, R., *Quantum Physics of Atoms, Molecules, Solids, Nuclei, and Particles*, 2nd ed., John Wiley & Sons, New York, 1985

Faraday, M., *The Chemical History of a Candle*, The Viking Press, New York, 1960 (reproduction of the original book, published in 1861)

Feynman, R. P., Leighton, R. B. and Sands, M. L., *The Feynman Lectures on Physics*, Addison-Wesley Publishing Co., Inc., Reading, Massachusetts, 1963

Finch, C., *Special Effects: Creating Movie Magic*, Abbeville Press, New York, 1984

Fletcher, N. H., *The Chemical Physics of Ice*, Cambridge University Press, Cambridge, 1970

Foyer, C. H., *Photosynthesis*, John Wiley & Sons, New York, 1984

Gibb, T. C., *Principles of Mössbauer Spectroscopy*, Chapman and Hall, London, 1976

Greenler, R., *Rainbows, Halos, and Glories*, Cambridge University Press, Cambridge, 1980

Halliday, D., Resnick, R. and Walker, J., *Fundamentals of Physics*, 4th ed., John Wiley & Sons, New York, 1993

Happé, L. B., *Basic Motion Picture Technology*, Hastings House, Publishers, New York, 1975

Harrison, E., *Darkness at Night*, Harvard University Press, Cambridge, 1987

Hewitt, P. G., *Conceptual Physics*, 2nd ed., Addison-Wesley Publishing Co., Menlo Park, California, 1992

Horonjeff, R. and McKelvey, F. X., *Planning and Design of Airports*, 4th ed., McGraw-Hill, Inc., New York, 1994

James, T. H., ed., *The Theory of the Photographic Process*, 4th ed., Macmillan Publishing Co., Inc., New York, 1977

Jelley, J. V., *Cerenkov Radiation, and its Applications*, Pergamon Press, New York, 1958

Jewett, J. W., *Physics Begins with an M...Mysteries, Magic, and Myth*, Allyn and Bacon, Boston, 1994

Jordan, E. C., ed., *Reference Data for Engineers: Radio, Electronics, Computer and Communications*, 7th ed., Howard W. Sams & Co., Inc., Indianapolis, 1985

Jorgensen, O. H., *Tuning*, Michigan State University Press, East Lansing, 1991

Kimball, D., *Recycling in America: A Reference Handbook*, ABC-CLIO, Inc., Santa Barbara, 1992

Kleppner, D. and Kolenkow, R. J., *An Introduction to Mechanics*, McGraw-Hill Book Co., New York, 1973

Langford, J. J., *Galileo, Science and the Church*, The University of Michigan Press, Ann Arbor, Michigan, 1992

Lawlor, D. W., *Photosynthesis: Molecular, Physiological and Environmental Processes*, 2nd ed., Longman Scientific & Technical, London, 1993

Laws, K., *The Physics of Dance*, Schirmer Books, New York, 1984

Lay, M. G., *Ways of the World*, Rutgers University Press, New Brunswick, 1992

Lee, O., *The Skin Diver's Bible*, Doubleday, New York, 1986

Levy, M. and Salvadori, M., *Why Buildings Fall Down*, W. W. Norton & Company, New York, 1992

Liboff, R. L., *Introductory Quantum Mechanics*, Holden-Day, Inc., Oakland, 1980

Long, D. D., *The Physics Around You*, 2nd ed., Wadsworth Publishing Co., Belmont, California, 1988

Middleton, W. E. K., *A History of the Thermometer and its Use in Meteorology*, The Johns Hopkins Press, Baltimore, 1966

Moye, F. J. and Wicander, R., *Great Ideas for Teaching Geology*, West Publishing Company, St. Paul, 1992

Noyes, R. W., *The Sun, Our Star*, Harvard University Press, Cambridge, 1982

Ohanian, H. C., *Principles of Physics*, W. W. Norton & Company, New York, 1994

Ott, H. W., *Noise Reduction Techniques in Electronic Systems*, 2nd ed., John Wiley & Sons, New York, 1988

Phillips, K. J. H., *Guide to the Sun*, Cambridge University Press, Cambridge, 1992

Pierce, A. D., *Acoustics: An Introduction to its Physical Principles and Applications*, McGraw-Hill Book Company, New York, 1981

Piper, J. D. A., *Paleomagnetism and the Continental Crust*, Halsted Press, New York, 1987

Price, W. C. and Chissick, S. S., eds., *The Uncertainty Principle and Foundations of Quantum Mechanics*, John Wiley & Sons, London, 1977

Rao, V. V. L., *The Decibel Notation*, Asia Publishing House, London, 1966

Reseck, J., *Scuba Safe and Simple*, Prentice-Hall, Inc., Englewood Cliffs, New Jersey, 1975

Rohlf, J. W., *Modern Physics from α to Z^0*, John Wiley & Sons, New York, 1994

Rossing, T. D., *The Science of Sound*, 2nd ed., Addison-Wesley Publishing Company, Reading, 1990.

Smith, J. W., *Vibration of Structures*, Chapman & Hall, London, 1985

Tarling, D. H., *Paleomagnetism*: *Principles and Applications in Geology, Geophysics and Archaeology*, Chapman and Hall, London, 1983

Thornton, S. T. and Rex, A., *Modern Physics for Scientists and Engineers*, Saunders College Publishing, Fort Worth, 1993

Thurman, H. V., *Introduction to Oceanography*, 7th ed., Macmillan Publishing Company, New York, 1994

Tipler, P. A., *Physics for Scientists and Engineers*, 3rd ed., Worth Publishers, New York, 1991

Walker, J., *The Flying Circus of Physics with Answers*, John Wiley & Sons, New York, 1977

Wertheim, G. K., *Mössbauer Effect: Principles and Applications*, Academic Press, New York, 1964

Whitt, F. R. and Wilson, D. G., *Bicycling Science*, The MIT Press, Cambridge, Massachusetts, 1974

Will, C. M., *Was Einstein Right?*, Basic Books, Inc., New York, 1986

Williams, L. P., *Michael Faraday*, Basic Books, Inc., New York, 1964

Wood, E. A., *Science From Your Airplane Window*, 2nd rev. ed., Dover Publications, Inc., New York, 1975

Wright, J. L., *Space Sailing*, Gordon and Breach Science Publishers, Philadelphia, 1992

Yeomans, D. K., *Comets: A Chronological History of Observation, Science, Myth, and Folklore*, John Wiley & Sons, New York, 1991

Journal Articles

AAPT Metric Education and SI Practices Committee, "The Radian—That Troublesome Unit", *The Physics Teacher*, **31**, 84, 1993

Abendschan, J. and Speakman, D., "Laser-Enhanced Vibrating String", *The Physics Teacher*, **29**, 114, 1991

Abramowicz, M. A. and Lasota, J. P., "On Traveling Round without Feeling it and Uncurving Curves", *American Journal of Physics*, **54**, 936, 1986

Adney, K. J., "If the Sun Were a Light Bulb", *The Physics Teacher*, **29**, 96, 1991

Allen, R., "Another Complication", *The Physics Teacher*, **29**, 71, 1991

Alonso, M, "Fields, Waves and Mysteries", *The Physics Teacher*, **31**, 328, 1993

Ansbacher, T. H., "Left-Right Semantics?", *The Physics Teacher*, **30**, 70, 1992

Arons, A. B., "Basic Physics of the Semidiurnal Lunar Tide", *American Journal of Physics*, **47**, 934, 1979

Bachman, C. H., "The Equinox Displaced", *The Physics Teacher*, **28** 536, 1990

Baierlein, R., "Teaching $E = mc^2$", *American Journal of Physics*, **57**, 391, 1989

Baierlein, R., "Teaching $E = mc^2$: An Exploration of Some Issues", *The Physics Teacher*, **29**, 170, 1991

Baierlein, R., "Entropy and the Second Law: A Pedagogical Alternative", *American Journal of Physics*, **62**, 15, 1994

Bartlett, A. A., "How to Cool an Elephant", *The Physics Teacher*, **29**, 196, 1991

Bartlett, A. A., "Warmth and Temperature: A Comedy of Errors", *The Physics Teacher*, **22**, 517, 1984

Bauman, R. P., "Physics the Textbook Writers Usually Get Wrong—I; Work", *The Physics Teacher*, **30**, 264, 1992

Bauman, R. P., "Physics the Textbook Writers Usually Get Wrong—II; Heat and Energy", *The Physics Teacher*, **30**, 353, 1992

Bauman, R. P., "Physics the Textbook Writers Usually Get Wrong—III; Forces and Vectors", *The Physics Teacher*, **30**, 402, 1992

Berg, R. E., "Rotating Liquid Mirror", *American Journal of Physics*, **58**, 280, 1990

Bernard, W. H., "Internal Work: A Misrepresentation", *American Journal of Physics*, **52**, 253, 1984

Bettis, C. and Throckmorton, C. "What Teachers Should Know About Radon", *The Physics Teacher*, **29**, 338, 1991

Bohren, C. F. and Fraser, A. B., "Newton's Zero-Order Rainbow: Unobservable or Nonexistent?", *American Journal of Physics*, **59**, 325, 1991

Bohren, C. F. and Fraser, A. B., "Fall Streaks: Parabolic Trajectories with a Twist", *American Journal of Physics*, **60**, 1030, 1992

Borgwald, J. M. and Schreiner, S., "Classroom Analysis of Rotating Space Vehicles in *2001: A Space Odyssey*", *The Physics Teacher*, **31**, 406, 1993

Brancazio, P. J., "Trajectory of a Fly Ball", *The Physics Teacher*, **23**, 20, 1985

Brecher, K. and Brecher, K., "The 'Videostrobe' Water Drop Gravimeter", *The Physics Teacher*, **28**, 108, 1990

Briggs, L. J., "Effect of Spin and Speed on the Lateral Deflection (Curve) of a Baseball; and the Magnus Effect for Smooth Spheres", *American Journal of Physics*, **27**, 589, 1959

Brody, H., "Physics of the Tennis Racket", *American Journal of Physics*, **47**, 482, 1979

Brody, H., "Physics of the Tennis Racket II: The 'Sweet Spot'", *American Journal of Physics*, **49**, 816, 1981

Brody, H., "Models of Baseball Bats", *American Journal of Physics*, **58**, 756, 1990

Brody, H., "How Would a Physicist Design a Tennis Racket?", *Physics Today*, **48(3)**, 26, 1995

Brown, R. A., "Maximizing the Range of a Projectile", *The Physics Teacher*, **30**, 344, 1992

Bruning, D. H., "Determining the Earth-Moon Distance", *American Journal of Physics*, **59**, 850, 1991

Bucheit, F. , "A Momentum Transfer Demonstration with 'Happy/Unhappy' Balls", *The Physics Teacher*, **32**, 28, 1994

Calkin, M. G., "The Motion of an Accelerating Automobile", *American Journal of Physics*, **58**, 573, 1990

Calkin, M. G., "Motion of a Falling Spring", *American Journal of Physics*, **61**, 261, 1993

Case, W. B. and Swanson, M. A., "The Pumping of a Swing from a Seated Position", *American Journal of Physics*, **58**, 463, 1990

Chandler, D., "An Expanding Universe in the Classroom", *The Physics Teacher*, **29**, 103, 1991

Clemmons, J. H. and Evans, R. H., "Auroral Measurements from Space Brought into the Classroom", *The Physics Teacher*, **33**, 34, 1995

Cowan, G. A., "A Natural Fission Reactor", *Scientific American*, **235(5)**, 36, 1976

Crane, H. R., "Digital Electronic Balances: Mass or Weight?", *The Physics Teacher*, **29**, 142, 1991

Crawford, F. S., "Running Crooke's Radiometer Backwards", *American Journal of Physics*, **53**, 1105, 1985

Crawford, F. S., "Cube Corner Retroreflectors for Sound Waves", *American Journal of Physics*, **59**, 176, 1991

Crawford, F. S., "Speed of Gravity Waves in Deep Water: Another Elementary Derivation", *American Journal of Physics*, **60**, 751, 1992

Davis, J. F. and Greenslade, T. B., "Computer Modeling of Mirage Formation", *The Physics Teacher*, **29**, 47, 1991

Day, M. A. and Walker, M. H., "Experimenting with the National Guard: Field Artillery Gunnery", *The Physics Teacher*, **31**, 136, 1993

Díaz-Jiménez, A. "The Standing High Jump", *The Physics Teacher*, **31**, 534, 1993

Dietz, E. R., "Vector Analysis and the Hydrostatic Paradox", *American Journal of Physics*, **59**, 89, 1991

Domann, F. E., "Damaging Reflections", *The Physics Teacher*, **31**, 190, 1993

Dray, T., "The Twin Paradox Revisited", *American Journal of Physics*, **58**, 822, 1990

Ebert, R., "Adapting Some Demonstrations for a Large Class", *The Physics Teacher*, **30**, 239, 1992

Edge, R. D., "Murphy's Law or Jelly-Side Down", *The Physics Teacher*, **26**, 392, 1988

Edge, R. D., "Why is the String Colored?", *The Physics Teacher*, **18**, 518, 1980

Edmiston, M. D., "Agitation Solution", *The Physics Teacher*, **30**, 325, 1992

Ehrlich, R., "'Ruler Physics': Thirty-four Demonstrations Using a Plastic Ruler", *American Journal of Physics*, **62**, 111, 1994

Emery, C., "Refractive Puzzle", *The Physics Teacher*, **31**, 413, 1993

Eng, J. and Lietman, T., "Measuring the Velocity of a Tennis Serve", *The Physics Teacher*, **32**, 168, 1994

Evans, H. E., "Raindrops Keep Falling on My Head", *The Physics Teacher*, **29**, 120, 1991

Fletcher, H., and Munson, W. A., "Loudness, Definition, Measurement and Calculation", *Journal of the Acoustical Society of America*, **6**, 59, 1933

Frank, M. T. and Kluk, E., "Velocity of Sound in Solids", *The Physics Teacher*, **29**, 246, 1991

French, A. P., "Isaac Newton's Thermometry", *The Physics Teacher*, **31**, 208, 1993

French, A. P., "Newton's Thermometry: The Role of Radiation", *The Physics Teacher*, **31**, 310, 1993

Gabuzda, D. C., "The Charge Densities in a Current-Carrying Wire", *American Journal of Physics*, **61**, 360, 1993

Galili, I., Goldberg, F. and Bendall, S., "Some Reflections on Plane Mirrors and Images", *The Physics Teacher*, **29**, 471, 1991

Galili, I., Bendall, S. and Goldberg, F., "Author's Response to 'Left-Right Semantics?'", *The Physics Teacher*, **30**, 70, 1992

Galili, I. and Goldberg, F., "Left-Right Conversions in a Plane Mirror", *The Physics Teacher*, **31**, 463, 1993

Gardner, M., "Stabbing an Eggshell", *The Physics Teacher*, **29**, 149, 1991

Gardner, M., "Fields, Waves and Mysteries", *The Physics Teacher*, **31**, 330, 1993

Godwin, R. P., "The Hydraulic Jump ("Shocks" and Viscous Flow in the Kitchen Sink)", *American Journal of Physics*, **61**, 829, 1993

Golab-Meyer, Z., "'Piekara's Chair': Mechanical Model for Atomic Energy Levels", *The Physics Teacher*, **29**, 215, 1991

Goodman, F. O., "Measuring the Earth's Radius While Boating on One of its Lakes", *American Journal of Physics*, **61**, 378, 1993

Grindlay, J., "Bruised Apples", *American Journal of Physics*, **61**, 469, 1993

Gupta, P. D., "Coloration on a String Vibrating in a Standing Wave Pattern", *The Physics Teacher*, **26**, 371, 1988

Haaland, C. M., "Minimum Engine Size for Optimum Automobile Acceleration", *American Journal of Physics*, **60**, 415, 1992

Halada, R. S., "Parachutes in the Classroom", *The Physics Teacher*, **31**, 50, 1993

Hall, J., (picture of light bulb package), *The Physics Teacher*, **30**, 367, 1992

Hatze, H., "Objective Biomechanical Determination of Tennis Racket Properties", *International Journal of Sport Biomechanics*, **8**, 275, 1992

Hatze, H., "Impact Probability Distribution, Sweet Spot, and the Concept of an Effective Power Region in Tennis Rackets", *Journal of Applied Biomechanics*, **10**, 43, 1994

Haugland, O. A., "Hot Air Ballooning in Physics Teaching", *The Physics Teacher*, **29**, 202, 1991

Henry, D. C. and Danielson, S. A., "Experiments and Demonstrations with Soldering Guns", *The Physics Teacher*, **31**, 42, 1993

Hesketh, R. V., "How to Make a Swing Go", *Physics Education*, **10**, 367, 1975

Hobson, A., "Fields, Waves and Mysteries", *The Physics Teacher*, **31**, 330, 1993

Holstein, B. R., "Answer to Question #2 ["Quark Masses and Binding Energy in a Proton"], *American Journal of Physics*, **63**, 14, 1995

Honig, E., "New Wine into Old Bottles: A Nuptial Arch", *American Journal of Physics*, **59**, 472, 1991

Hood, C. G., "Teaching About Quantum Theory", *The Physics Teacher*, **31**, 290, 1993

Hough, S. E., Friberg, P. A., Busby, R., Field, E. F., Jacob, K. H., and Borcherdt, R. D., "Sediment Induced Amplification and the Collapse of the Nimitz Freeway", *Nature*, **344**, 853, 1990

Hughes, A. L., "On the Emission Velocities of Photo-electrons", *Phil. Trans. Roy. Soc. London*, Series A, **212**, 205, 1913

Inouye, C. S. and Chong, E. W. T., "Maximum Range of a Projectile", *The Physics Teacher*, **30**, 168, 1992

Jewett, J. W. and Johnson, D. C., "Demonstrating Induced Voltages with an LED", *Journal of College Science Teaching*, **20**, 196, 1992

Jewett, J. W., "Computer Monitor as Stroboscope for Tuning Forks", *The Physics Teacher*, **32**, 489, 1994

Jones, B., "Cosmic Ray Studies on Skis and on Campus", *The Physics Teacher*, **31**, 458, 1993

Jones, D. E. H., "The Stability of the Bicycle", *Physics Today*, **23(4)**, 34, 1970

Jones, G. E. and Ferguson, J. L., "Easy Displacement versus Time Graphs for a Vibrating String: Tuning a Guitar by Television", *American Journal of Physics*, **48**, 362, 1980

Jones, G. T., "The Physical Principles of Particle Detectors", *The Physics Teacher*, **29**, 578, 1991

Jones, G. T., "A Simple Estimate of the Mass of the Positron", *The Physics Teacher*, **31**, 95, 1993

Kagan, D. T., "The Effects of Coefficient of Restitution Variations on Long Fly Balls", *American Journal of Physics*, **58**, 151, 1990

Kagan, D. T., "The Ultimate 'Pith Balls'", *The Physics Teacher*, **29**, 197, 1991

Kasting, R., "Airplane Dynamics: Engine Thrust, Engine Braking, and Wing Lift", *The Physics Teacher*, **26**, 122, 1988

Kettler, J. E., "Listening for Young's Modulus", *The Physics Teacher*, **29**, 538, 1991

Kinderman, J. V., "Investigating the Compton Effect with a Spreadsheet", *The Physics Teacher*, **30**, 426, 1992

Klein, N. H., "Square Wheel", *American Journal of Physics*, **61**, 893, 1993

Kowalski, L., "On Field Lenses", *The Physics Teacher*, **30**, 366, 1992

Krane, K. S., "The Falling Raindrop: Variations on a Theme of Newton", *American Journal of Physics*, **49**, 113, 1981

Kruglak, H., "An Exercise on the Altitude of the Noon Sun", *The Physics Teacher*, **30**, 236, 1992

Kruglak, H., "Diffraction Demonstration with a Compact Disc", *The Physics Teacher*, **31**, 104, 1993

Lange, D., Sher, M., Sivillo, J. and Welsh, R., "A Hand-Held Demonstration of Cosmological Phase Transitions", *American Journal of Physics*, **61**, 1049, 1993

Lapp, D. R., "Determining Plane Mirror Image Distance from Eye Charts", *The Physics Teacher*, **31**, 59, 1993

Laws, K., "The Physics of Dance", *Physics Today*, **38(2)**, 24, 1985

Leff, H. S., "Illuminating Physics with Light Bulbs", *The Physics Teacher*, **28**, 30, 1990

Leff, H. S. and Mallinckrodt, A. J., "Stopping Objects with Zero External Work: Mechanics Meets Thermodynamics", *American Journal of Physics*, **61**, 121, 1993

Lehrman, R. L., "Energy is Not the Ability to Do Work", *The Physics Teacher*, **11**, 15, 1973

Lehrman, R. L., "Confused Physics: A Tutorial Critique", *The Physics Teacher*, **20**, 519, 1982

Levine, Z. H., "How to Measure the Radius of the Earth on Your Beach Vacation", *The Physics Teacher*, **31**, 440, 1993

Lonc, W., "A Simple Demonstration of the Barkhausen Effect", *American Journal of Physics*, **60**, 860, 1992

Lopez, C. and Gonzalo, P., "Using LED's to Demonstrate Induced Current", *The Physics Teacher*, **27**, 218, 1989

Mallinckrodt, A. J. and Leff, H. S., "All About Work", *American Journal of Physics*, **60**, 356, 1992

Maor, E., "A Repertoire of S.H.M.", *The Physics Teacher*, **10**, 377, 1972

Martin, D. P., "String Waves in Slow Motion", *The Science Teacher*, **59(3)**, 31, 1992

Matteucci, G., "Electron Wavelike Behavior: A Historical and Experimental Introduction", *American Journal of Physics*, **58**, 1143, 1990

May, J. C., "Myths I Have Taught", *The Science Teacher*, **48(4)**, 23, 1981

McGervey, J. D., "Why $\ell(\ell + 1)$ instead of ℓ^2?", *American Journal of Physics*, **59**, 295, 1991

Mellen, W. R., "Spring String Swing Thing", *The Physics Teacher*, **32**, 122, 1994

Memory, J. D., "Appropriate Usage of the Term 'Quantum Leap'", *The Physics Teacher*, **31**, 391, 1993

Menz, P. G., "The Physics of Bungee Jumping", *The Physics Teacher*, **31**, 483, 1993

Millikan, R. A., "A Direct Photoelectric Determination of Planck's Constant 'h' ", *Phys. Rev.*, **7**, 355, 1916

Milonni, P. W., "Why $\ell(\ell + 1)$ instead of ℓ^2?", *American Journal of Physics*, **58**, 1012, 1990

Minstrell, J. , "Explaining the 'At Rest' Condition of an Object", *The Physics Teacher*, **20**, 10, 1982

Mires, R. W. and Peters, R. D., "Motion of a Leaky Pendulum", *American Journal of Physics*, **62**, 137, 1994

Mitschele, J., "Nonlinear Springs", *American Journal of Physics*, **59**, 584, 1991

Montalbano, W. D., "Earth Moves for Vatican in Galileo Case", *Los Angeles Times*, November 1, 1992

Ninio, F., "Acceleration in Uniform Circular Motion", *American Journal of Physics*, **61**, 1052, 1993

Oberhofer, E. S., "Different Magnitude Differences", *The Physics Teacher*, **29**, 273, 1991

O'Keefe, R. and Ghavimi-Alagha, B., "The World Trade Center and the Distance to the World's Center", *American Journal of Physics*, **60**, 183, 1992

Okun, L., "The Concept of Mass", *Physics Today*, **42(6)**, 31, 1989

Pasachoff, J. M., "Daylight Savings", *The Physics Teacher*, **29**, 71, 1991

Payne, M. M., "Does = Mean Equal?", *The Physics Teacher*, **29**, 548, 1991

Petroski, H., "Predicting Disaster", *American Scientist*, **81(2)**, 110, 1993

Porter, W. S., "Potential Energy of a Vertical Oscillator", *The Physics Teacher*, **31**, 175, 1993

Price, R. H., "Negative Mass Can be Positively Amusing", *American Journal of Physics*, **61**, 216, 1993

Reid, B., "Bad Physics for Geographers", *The Physics Teacher*, **29**, 154, 1991

Resnick, R., "Misconceptions About Einstein", *Journal of Chemical Education*, **57**, 854, 1980

Richardson, O. W. and Compton, K. T., "The Photoelectric Effect", *Phil. Mag. Series 6*, **24**, 575, 1912

Rial, J. A., Saltzman, N. G. and Ling, H., "Earthquake-Induced Resonance in Sedimentary Basins", *American Scientist*, **80**, 566, 1992

Rohrlich, F., "An Elementary Derivation of $E = mc^2$", *American Journal of Physics*, **58**, 348, 1990

Rohrlich, F., "Response to 'Comment on ' An Elementary Derivation of $E = mc^2$ ', by L. Ruby and R. E. Reynolds", *American Journal of Physics*, **59**, 757, 1991

Romer, R. H., "What Do 'Voltmeters' Measure?: Faraday's Law in a Multiply Connected Region", *American Journal of Physics*, **50**, 1089, 1982

Rossing, T. D., Russell, D. A. and Brown, D. E., "On the Acoustics of Tuning Forks", *American Journal of Physics*, **60**, 620, 1992

Ruby, L. and Reynolds, R. E., "Comment on ' An Elementary Derivation of $E = mc^2$ ', by F. Rohrlich", *American Journal of Physics*, **59**, 756, 1991

Rueckner, W., Goodale, D., Rosenberg, D., Steel, S. and Tavilla, D., "Lecture Demonstration of Wineglass Resonance", *American Journal of Physics*, **61**, 184, 1993

Sae, A. S. W., "Dynamic Demos", *The Science Teacher*, **58(7)**, 22, 1991

Salow, R., Thornton, J. and Siegel, P., "Is the Yellow Light Long Enough?", *The Physics Teacher*, **31**, 80, 1993

Sandin, T. R., "In Defense of Relativistic Mass", *American Journal of Physics*, **59**, 1032, 1991

Savarino, G. and Fisch, M. R., "A General Physics Laboratory Investigation of the Thermodynamics of a Rubber Band", *American Journal of Physics*, **59**, 141, 1991

Schroeder, M. C. and Smith, C. W., "Estimating the Speed of Light with a TV Set", *The Physics Teacher*, **23**, 360, 1985

Shapiro, A. E., "Comment on 'Newton's Zero-Order Rainbow: Unobservable or Nonexistent?'" by C. F. Bohren and A. B. Fraser, *American Journal of Physics*, **60**, 749, 1992

Sherwood, B. A., "Pseudowork and Real Work", *American Journal of Physics*, **51**, 597, 1983

Shkolnik, A., Taylor, C. R., Finch, V. and Borut, A., "Why Do Bedouins Wear Black Robes in Hot Deserts?", *Nature*, **283**, 373, 1980

Sconza, A., Torzo, G. and Viola, G., "Experiment on the Physics of the PN Junction", *American Journal of Physics*, **62**, 66, 1994

Smith, N. F., "Bernoulli and Newton in Fluid Mechanics", *The Physics Teacher*, **10**, 451, 1972

Stern, S. A., "An Optimal Speed for Traversing a Constant Rain", *American Journal of Physics*, **51**, 815, 1983

Subagyo and van den Berg, E., "Momentum, Waves and Money", *The Physics Teacher*, **30**, 509, 1992

Sullivan, P. W., "Inertia Demo with a Flair Pen", *The Physics Teacher*, **31**, 427, 1993

Tan, A., Frick, C. H. and Castillo, O., "The Fly Ball Trajectory: An Older Approach Revisited", *American Journal of Physics*, **55**, 37, 1987

Taylor, E. F., "Why Does Nothing Move Faster than Light? Because Ahead is Ahead!", *American Journal of Physics*, **58**, 889, 1990

Taylor, J. R., "Firewalking: A Lesson in Physics", *The Physics Teacher*, **27**, 166, 1989

Tian, R., Li, Z., "The Speed and Apparent Rest Mass of Photons in a Gravitational Field", *American Journal of Physics*, **58**, 890, 1990

Tilly, G. P., Cullington, D. W. and Eyre, R., "Dynamic Behavior of Footbridges", *International Association for Bridge & Structural Engineering, IABSE Periodica*, **S-26/84**, 13, 1984

The Times (London), April 15, 1831, April 18, 1850, April 19, 1850, April 20, 1850, April 22, 1850, April 23, 1850

Touger, J. S., "When Words Fail Us", *The Physics Teacher*, **29**, 90, 1991

Van Zandt, L. L., "The Dynamical Theory of the Baseball Bat", *American Journal of Physics*, **60**, 172, 1992

Wagner, W. S., "Temperature and Color of Incandescent Lamps", *The Physics Teacher*, **29**, 176, 1991

Walker, J. D., "The Amateur Scientist—The Physics and Chemistry Underlying the Infinite Charm of a Candle Flame", *Scientific American*, **238(4)**, 154, 1978

Walker, J. D., "The Amateur Scientist—How to Get the Playground Swing Going: A First Lesson in the Mechanics of Rotation", *Scientific American*, **260(3)**, 106, 1989

Wallingford., J., "More on Mirage Formation", *The Physics Teacher*, **29**, 485, 1991

Walters, J., "Football Physics", *Sports Illustrated*, **79(19)**, 143, 1993

Walton, A. J., "Archimedes' Principle in Gases", *Contemporary Physics*, **10**, 181, 1969

Watts, R. G. and Ferrer, R., "The Lateral Force on a Spinning Sphere: Aerodynamics of a Curve Ball", *American Journal of Physics*, **55**, 40, 1987

Weltner, K., "A Comparison of Explanations of the Aerodynamic Lifting Force", *American Journal of Physics*, **55**, 50, 1987

Wheeler, J. E., "Prediction and Control of Pedestrian Induced Vibration in Footbridges", *Journal of the Structural Division, Proceedings of the American Society of Civil Engineers*, **108(ST9)**, 2045, 1982

Wilkins, D., "A New Angle on Compton Scattering", *American Journal of Physics*, **60**, 221, 1992

Wilson, A. E., "Jogging in a Centrifuge", *The Physics Teacher*, **32**, 5, 1994

Withers, M. M., "Why do Tides Exist?", *The Physics Teacher*, **31**, 394, 1993

Young, R. A., "Longitudinal Standing Waves on a Vertically Suspended Slinky", *American Journal of Physics*, **61**, 353, 1993

Zandy, H. F., "Galileo, Einstein, and the Church", *American Journal of Physics*, **61**, 202, 1993

Zemansky, M. W., "The Use and Misuse of the Word 'Heat' in Physics Teaching", *The Physics Teacher*, **8**, 295, 1970

Zollman, D., "The Latent Heat of Fusion of a Witch", *The Physics Teacher*, **30**, 448, 1992

Zwicker, "The Smart Table", *The Physics Teacher*, **19**, 633, 1981

Zwicker, E., Lietz, G., Behof, A., and Ellenstein, M., "Illuminating Standing Waves", *The Physics Teacher*, **24**, 449, 1986

Index